STRATEGIC INTELLIGENCE

STRATEGIC INTELLIGENCE

5

INTELLIGENCE AND ACCOUNTABILITY: SAFEGUARDS AGAINST THE ABUSE OF SECRET POWER

Edited by
Loch K. Johnson

Intelligence and the Quest for Security

PRAEGER SECURITY INTERNATIONAL
Westport, Connecticut • London

Library of Congress Cataloging-in-Publication Data

Strategic intelligence / edited by Loch K. Johnson.
    p. cm.—(Intelligence and the quest for security, ISSN 1932-3492)
  Includes bibliographical references and index.
    ISBN 0-275-98942-9 (set : alk. paper)—ISBN 0-275-98943-7 (vol. 1 : alk. paper)—
ISBN 0-275-98944-5 (vol. 2 : alk. paper)—ISBN 0-275-98945-3 (vol. 3 : alk. paper)—
ISBN 0-275-98946-1 (vol. 4 : alk. paper)—ISBN 0-275-98947-X (vol. 5 : alk. paper)
1. Military intelligence.   2. Intelligence service—Government policy.   I. Johnson,
Loch K., 1942–

UB250.S6385 2007
327.12—dc22   2006031165

British Library Cataloguing in Publication Data is available.

Library of Congress Catalog Card Number: 2006031165
ISBN: 0-275-98942-9 (set)
        0-275-98943-7 (vol. 1)
        0-275-98944-5 (vol. 2)
        0-275-98945-3 (vol. 3)
        0-275-98946-1 (vol. 4)
        0-275-98947-X (vol. 5)
ISSN: 1932-3492

First published in 2007

Praeger Security International, 88 Post Road West, Westport, CT 06881
An imprint of Greenwood Publishing Group, Inc.
www.praeger.com

Printed in the Untied States of America

The paper used in this book complies with the
Permanent Paper Standard issued by the National
Information Standards Organization (Z39.48-1984).

10 9 8 7 6 5 4 3 2 1

CONTENTS

Appendixes

PREFACE

THIS FIVE-VOLUME SERIES IN INTELLIGENCE IS SOMETHING of a landmark in the study of intelligence. Thirty years ago, one would have been hard-pressed to find enough good articles on the subject to fill two volumes, let alone five. In those three decades since 1975, however, the study of intelligence has grown considerably. Today there are several solid professional journals in the field, including the premier publications *Intelligence and National Security* (published in the United Kingdom), *International Journal of Intelligence and Counterintelligence* (the United States), and *Studies in Intelligence* (from the Central Intelligence Agency, in both classified and unclassified form). In just the past two years, bulging anthologies on the general topic "strategic intelligence," as well as a "handbook" on intelligence and a collection of chapters within the more specialized niche of "intelligence and ethics" have appeared, along with a tidal wave of books and articles on one aspect or another of this subject (see the bibliographic essay in volume 1).

Except in times of scandal (Watergate in 1973, CIA domestic spying in 1974, the Iran-*contra* affair in 1987), one could find in this earlier era little newspaper coverage of intelligence activities, so tightly held were these operations by the government. Now, fueled by the events of the September 11, 2001, terrorist attacks and the erroneous prediction in 2002 that weapons of mass destruction (WMDs) were being developed and stockpiled by Iraq, hardly a week goes by without reports on intelligence in the *New York Times* and other leading newspapers. These days, the *Atlantic Monthly* and the *New Yorker*, America's top literary magazines, visit the subject with some regularity, too. The latter has hired Seymour M. Hersh, the nation's most well-known investigative reporter with an intelligence beat.

Intelligence studies has come of age.

Certainly the chapters in these volumes display a breadth of inquiry that suggests an admirable vibrancy in this relatively new field of study. Presented here are empirical inquiries, historical treatments, theoretical frameworks, memoirs, case studies, interviews, legal analyses, comparative essays, and ethical assessments. The authors come from the ranks of academe (twenty-five); the intelligence agencies (thirteen); think tanks (seven); Congress, the State Department, and the National Security Council (three); and the legal world (three).[1] Over a quarter of the contributors are from other nations, including Canada, England, Germany, Israel, Scotland, Switzerland, and Wales. The American writers come from every region of the United States. As a collective, the authors represent a wide range of scholarly disciplines, including computer science, history, international affairs, law, sociology, political science, public administration, public policy studies, and strategic studies. Many of the contributors are from the ranks of the top intelligence scholars in the world; a few young ones stand at the gateway to their academic careers.

Notable, too, is the number of women who have entered this field of study. Thirty years ago, it would have been rare to find one or two women writing on this subject. Seven have contributed chapters to these pages, and another two wrote documents that appear in the appendixes. This is still fewer than one would like, especially in light of the major contribution women have made as intelligence officers. One thinks of the heroic efforts of British women in code breaking and in the Special Operations Executive during World War II, and the American women who contributed so much to the analytic efforts of the Office of Strategic Studies (OSS) during that same war. At least, though, the number attracted to the scholar study of intelligence appears to be rapidly expanding.

The end result of this mix is a landscape illuminated by a variety of methods and appreciations—a rich research trove that examines all the key aspects of intelligence. In addition, each of the volumes contains backup materials in the appendixes. These documents provide the reader with access to significant primary and secondary sources referred to in the chapters.

The volumes are organized according to the major topics of studies in the field. The first volume, titled *Understanding the Hidden Side of Government*, introduces the reader to methods commonly used in the study of intelligence. It imparts, as well, a sense of the "state of the discipline," beginning with a bibliographic essay (by the editor) and continuing with an examination of specific approaches scholars have adopted in their inquiries into this especially difficult discipline, where doors are often shut against outsiders.

In the bibliographic essay that opens the volume, I argue that the literature on intelligence has mushroomed over the past thirty years. Some of this literature is unreliable, but much of it is of high quality. Amy B. Zegart follows my chapter with an important caveat: the literature may be more voluminous these days, but intelligence studies as an academic field has yet to be accepted as a vital part of national security scholarship. The mainstream journals of history, international affairs, and political science have still regarded the study of intelligence as a marginal pursuit. In this regard, Zegart points out, there is a major disconnect between academic scholarship and those who make decisions in Washington, London, and other capitals around the world.

Following this introduction, Len Scott and Timothy Gibbs look at methods that have been used to study intelligence in the United Kingdom; Stuart Farson and Reg Whitaker in Canada; and Michael Warner in the United States. The volume then turns to a more specific inquiry into the central question of how intelligence is interpreted by professionals—the issue of analysis—explored by John Hollister Hedley. An overview of the sometimes turbulent relationship between intelligence officers and the policy makers they serve is explored by James J. Wirtz; and British scholar Peter Gill recalls the failures associated with the 9/11 attacks and the poor judgments about Iraqi WMDs, in hopes of extracting lessons from these intelligence disasters. In the next chapter, the youngest scholar represented in this collection, Harold M. Greenberg, takes us back in time with a remembrance of the legendary CIA officer and Yale history professor Sherman Kent, often known as the dean of CIA analysts. Kristin Lord rounds out the first volume with a look forward into future prospects for a more transparent world—the ultimate goal of intelligence.

As with each of the books, Volume 1 has a set of appendixes designed to supplement the original chapters with supportive materials from government documents and other sources. Appendix A contains the relevant intelligence excerpts from the National Security Act of 1947—the founding charter for the modern American intelligence establishment. Appendix B provides a history of U.S. intelligence since 1947, prepared for the Aspin-Brown Commission in 1995–96 by staff member Phyllis Provost McNeil. These two documents present a contextual backdrop for the Volume 1 chapters. Appendix C provides "wiring diagrams" of the intelligence community, that is, organizational blueprints for the sixteen agencies and related entities. One chart displays the community as it is today, and another displays how it looked in 1985. As the contrast between the two illustrates, the events of September 11, 2001, have led to a larger and more complex intelligence apparatus in the United States. Appendix D shows a photograph of the CIA Headquarters Building, as an example of what one of the secret agencies actually looks like from an aerial perspective. The white dome in the foreground is an assembly hall seating around 600 people and to its left is the main entrance to the original CIA headquarters, built during the Eisenhower years. Behind this older wing is the new green-glass structure erected during the Reagan administration, often known as the Casey addition because William J. Casey was the Director of Central Intelligence (DCI) at the time of its construction during the 1980s.

Appendix E lists the top leadership in the America's intelligence community: the DCIs from 1947–2005 and today's DNI. Included here as well are the leaders in Congress who have been responsible for intelligence accountability in the past, along with the current members of the two congressional Intelligence

Committees: the Senate Select Committee on Intelligence (SSCI, or "sissy" in the unflattering and sometimes true homophone of Capitol Hill vernacular) and the House Permanent Select Committee on Intelligence (HPSCI or "hipsee"). Appendix F presents a 1955 statement from historian and CIA analyst Sherman Kent about the need for a more robust intelligence literature. He would probably be amazed by how much is being written on this subject now. Appendix G offers an overview on the purpose and challenges of intelligence, drawn from the introductory chapters of the Aspin-Brown Commission Report. Finally, Appendix H provides an opening glimpse into the subject of counterintelligence, a world of counterspies and betrayal taken up more fully in Volume 4.

With the second volume, titled *The Intelligence Cycle: The Flow of Secret Information From Overseas to the Highest Councils of Government*, the focus shifts from a broad overview of intelligence to a more detailed examination of its core mission: the collection, analysis, and dissemination of information from around the world. The National Security Act of 1947, which created America's modern intelligence establishment, made it clear that the collection, analysis, and dissemination of information would be the primary duty of the intelligence agencies. As Allen Dulles—the most famous DCI (America's top intelligence official, until this title changed to director of National Intelligence or DNI in 2005)—put it, the intelligence agencies were expected "to weigh facts, and to draw conclusions from those facts, without having either the facts or the conclusions warped by the inevitable and even proper prejudices of the men whose duty it is to determine policy."[2] The collection and interpretation of information, through espionage and from the public record, would be the primary responsibility of America's secret agencies.

At the heart of this mission lies the so-called intelligence cycle. Professional intelligence officers define the cycle as "the process by which information is acquired, converted into intelligence, and made available to policymakers."[3] The cycle has five phases: planning and direction, collection, processing, production and analysis, and dissemination (see Appendix A in Volume 2 for a depiction). As former CIA officer Arthur S. Hulnick notes, however, in the opening chapter, the idea of a "cycle" fails to capture the complexity of how intelligence is collected, assessed, and distributed by intelligence officers.

The next five chapters in Volume 2 take us into the world of the "ints," that is, the specialized "intelligences" (methods) used by intelligence officers to collect information. Patrick Radden Keefe and Matthew M. Aid probe the method of signals intelligence or SIGINT, a generic term used to describe the interception and analysis of communications intelligence and other electronic emissions, from wiretapping telephones to studying the particles emitted by missiles in test flights. Both authors are sensitive to the possible abuse of these techniques, which can be and have been used to spy on Americans without a proper judicial warrant. Jeffrey T. Richelson explores the IMINT domain, that is, imagery intelligence or, in simple terms, photographs taken by surveillance satellites and reconnaissance airplanes (piloted and unpiloted). Telephone conversations can be revealing, but in the old saying, a picture can be worth a thousand words. (Appendix B provides photographic examples of these spy platforms, and Appendix C offers illustrations of the IMINT data they can collect.)

Important, too, is information that can be acquired by human agents ("assets") guided by case officers inside the CIA or the Defense Department, the topic of human intelligence or HUMINT, examined by Frederick P. Hitz. Not all the information needed by policy makers is acquired through SIGINT, IMINT, or HUMINT; indeed, the overwhelming majority—upward of 95 percent—is already in the public domain. This open-source intelligence (OSINT) must be sorted through, organized, and integrated with the secretly gained information. Robert David Steele's chapter looks at OSINT and its ties to the other ints.

In the next chapter, Daniel S. Gressang IV dissects some of the technological challenges faced by intelligence agencies in sorting through the avalanche of data that pours into their headquarters from various intelligence collectors around the world. Here is the Herculean task of sorting out the wheat from the chaff (or the signal from the noise, in another widely used metaphor) in the search for information that may warn the nation of impending peril. Here is the vital task of providing "indicators and warnings" (I&W) to a nation's leaders.

One of the most difficult relationships in the complex process of collection, analysis, and dissemination of information comes at the intersection between intelligence professionals and policy makers—groups of individuals that often have very different training, aspirations, and cultures. Jack Davis sheds light on this often turbulent relationship in the United States, and Michael Herman tackles the same topic in the United Kingdom. Minh A. Luong offers a case study on economic intelligence that underscores some of the difficulties encountered as information travels from the collectors and analysts (the "producers" of intelligence) to the policy makers (the "consumers"). Finally, Max M. Holland takes a look at how intelligence agencies examine their own mistakes ("postmortems") and attempt to make corrections—and how political consideration enter into the process.

By way of supporting documentation, in addition to the appendixes already mentioned, Appendix D outlines the general types of reports prepared by the producers of intelligence, along with a listing of specific examples. Appendixes E and F provide samples of key intelligence products: National Intelligence Estimates (NIEs)—the most important long-range and in-depth forecasting carried out by the U.S. secret agencies ("research intelligence," in contrast to shorter intelligence reports that tend to focus on near-term events, or "current intelligence"); Special National Intelligence Estimates (SNIEs), which concentrate on a narrow, high-priority information requirement (say, the capabilities of the Chinese military); and the *President's Daily Brief* (PDB), the most exclusive current intelligence report prepared by the intelligence agencies for the consumption of the president and a few other high-ranking officials.

In light of the fact that every study of the 9/11 and Iraqi WMD intelligence failures find fault, in part, with America's capacity for human intelligence—

especially in the Middle East and Southwest Asia—Appendix G presents one of the most searing critiques of this int. The critique, by the House Permanent Select Committee on Intelligence, has become all the more significant because the panel's chairman, Representative Porter Goss (R-FL), soon after the completion of the report rose to the position of the DCI. Last, Appendix H provides an excerpt from a key report on the Iraqi WMD mistakes, prepared by the "Roberts Committee": the Senate Select Committee on Intelligence, led by Pat Roberts (R-KS).

The third volume, titled *Covert Action: Behind the Veils of Secret Foreign Policy*, enters an especially controversial compartment of intelligence: the means by which the United States attempts to not just gather and analyze information about the world—hard enough—but to manipulate global events through secret activities in the advancement of America's best interests. An ambiguous passage of the National Security Act of 1947 charged the National Security Council (NSC), the boss over the sixteen U.S. secret agencies, to "perform such other functions and duties related to intelligence [over and beyond collection-and-analysis] affecting the national security as the National Security Council may from time to time direct."[4] The phrase "other functions and duties" left the door open for launching the CIA (and more recently the Pentagon) on a wide range of covert actions around the world.

Covert action (CA), sometimes referred to as the "quiet option," is based on the supposition that this secret approach to foreign affairs is likely to be less noisy and obtrusive than sending in the Marines. Sometimes professional practitioners also refer to covert action as the "third option," between diplomacy and open warfare. As former Secretary of State and National Security Adviser Henry Kissinger once put it: "We need an intelligence community that, in certain complicated situations, can defend the American national interest in the gray areas where military operations are not suitable and diplomacy cannot operation."[5] Still others prefer the euphemism "special activities" to describe covert action. Whatever the variation in terminology, the goal of covert action remains constant: to influence events overseas secretly and in support of American foreign policy.

Covert action operations are often grouped according to four broad categories: propaganda, political, economic, and paramilitary (PM) activities. An example of a propaganda operation was the CIA's use of Radio Free Europe during the Cold War to transmit anti-communist themes into nations behind the Iron Curtain. A political CA during the Cold War was the CIA's clandestine funneling of funds to the anti-communist Christian Democratic Party in Italy. An economic example: the CIA attempted to destroy electric power stations in Nicaragua during the 1980s, as a means of undermining the Marxist-oriented *Sandinista* regime. PM operations can including everything from assassination plots against foreign heads of state to arming and guiding pro-American insurgent armies in one country or another. Little wonder this has been a controversial subject.

Gregory F. Treverton introduces the reader to covert action in the first chapter of Volume 3. He is followed by Kevin A. O'Brien and Ephraim Kahana, who discuss the use of covert action by other nations. The next four chapters illuminate certain aspects of CA, with James M. Scott and Jerel A. Rosati providing an overview of CA tradecraft (that is, the tools used to implement such operations); Michael A. Turner evaluating the merits of CIA covert propaganda operations; William J. Daugherty looking at political and economic examples of covert action; Jennifer D. Kibbe exploring the entry of the Defense Department into this domain; and former diplomat John D. Stempel contrasting the uses of covert action to diplomatic initiatives. Winding up the volume is Judge James E. Baker's legal analysis of covert action.

Supporting documents include excerpts from the Church Committee Report on the evolution of covert action as carried out by the CIA (Appendix A). The supervision of covert action went from an informal to a highly formal process, as a result of a law known as the Hughes-Ryan Act, passed on December 31, 1974. The language of this statute is presented in Appendix B, and the covert action procedures that resulted from the law are outlined in Appendix C. At the center of the covert action decision process since the Hughes-Ryan Act is the *finding*, a term of art that stems from the passage in the law that requires the president to "find" that a particular covert action proposal is important and has the president's approval. Appendix D contains two findings from the Iran-*contra* era in the mid-1980s. Covert actions must have an organizational apparatus to carry them out, and Appendix E displays what that apparatus looked like during the Cold War (and in basic form remains the organizational chart today, with a few name changes in the boxes).

One of the most controversial forms of covert action has been the assassination of foreign leaders. Appendix F presents a case study from the Church Committee on the CIA assassination plot hatched against the leader of the Republic of Congo, Patrice Lumumba, in 1960. The Committee's exposé of this and other plots led President Gerald R. Ford to sign an executive order prohibiting assassination as an instrument of American foreign policy (see Appendix G). The executive order has been waived in times of authorized warfare against other nations, however, leading to failed attempts to assassinate Saddam Hussein in the first and second Persian Gulf Wars (he was eventually captured alive in 2004, hidden away in a hole near his hometown in Iraq) and Al Qaeda leader Osama bin Laden during the Clinton administration. Considerable ambiguity exists regarding the current status of the executive order and under what conditions it might be waived by administrations. Finally, Appendix H—drawing on a presidential commission study and congressional hearings—examines covert action at its lowest state: the Iran-*contra* affair of the 1980s, when this approach to foreign policy subverted the U.S. Constitution and several laws (including the Hughes-Ryan Act).

A third intelligence mission, after collection-and-analysis and covert action, is counterintelligence (CI) and its associated activity, counterterrorism (CT).

Here is the concentration in Volume 4, titled *Counterintelligence and Counter-terrorism: Defending the Nation Against Hostile Forces*. Like covert action, CI went without specific mention in the National Security Act of 1947. By the early 1950s, however, it had similarly achieved a status of considerable importance as an intelligence mission. CI specialists soon waged nothing less than a secret war against antagonistic intelligence services (especially the Soviet KGB); and, after the Cold War, CT specialists would focus on efforts to block terrorists who targeted the United States and its allies. Explaining why the mission of coun-terintelligence/counterterrorism evolved, a CI expert has pointed out that "in the absence of an effective U.S. counterintelligence program, [adversaries of de-mocracy] function in what is largely a benign environment."[6]

The practice of counterintelligence consists of two matching halves: security and counterespionage. Security is the passive or defensive side of CI, involv-ing such devices as background investigations, fences, sentries, alarms, badges, watchdogs, and polygraphs (lie detection machines). Counterespionage (CE) is the offensive or aggressive side of CI. The most effective CE operation is the infiltration of an American agent or "mole" into the enemy camp, whether a hostile intelligence service or a terrorist cell—a ploy called a penetration. Thus, the practice of security is, according to one of America's top counterintelligence experts, "All that concerns perimeter defense, badges, knowing everything you have to know about your own people," whereas the CE side "involves knowing all about intelligence services—hostile intelligence services: their people, their installations, their methods, and their operations."[7]

Stan A. Taylor and Nigel West clarify these issues in the first two chapters of this volume, then in the next two chapters Katherine A. S. Sibley and Athan Theoharis examine the challenges of keeping the United States spy-free. Rhodri Jeffreys-Jones looks at the efforts in Europe to create a counterintelligence capa-bility similar to that practiced by America's Federal Bureau of Investigation (FBI). Glenn Hastedt takes the reader into the counterterrorism thicket in Wash-ington, DC, explaining how politics influences CI and CT operations. Richard L. Russell and Jennifer Sims discuss the ups and downs of trying to establish an effective counterterrorism response in the United States, complicated by the fragmentation of authority and widely differing cultures among the sixteen U.S. intelligence agencies. Finally, Katharina von Knop looks at the rising role of women in terrorist organizations.

The back-of-the-book documents in Volume 4 begin with a look at the Church Committee findings regarding counterintelligence in 1975 (Appendix A), followed by the notorious Huston Plan—a master counterintelligence spy plan drafted by White House aide Tom Charles Huston in 1970, in response to a nation at unrest over the war in Vietnam (Appendix B). The Huston Plan is a classic illustration of overreaction in a time of domestic strife. In Appendix C, the Senate Select Committee on Intelligence summarizes its findings about the Aldrich H. Ames counterintelligence disaster. Next the appendixes include a series of U.S. commission conclusions about how to improve intelligence in the struggle against global terrorism, whether locating and penetrating their cells in advance of a terrorist attack or thwarting the ability of terrorists to acquire WMDs. The panel reports include: the Hart-Rudman Commission of 2001 (Appendix D); the 9/11 or Kean Commission of 2004 (Appendix E); and the Silberman-Robb Commission of 2005 (Appendix F). For purposes of comparison, the final appendix (G) examines the conclusions reached by a British commission that also probed the Iraqi WMD failure: the Butler Report of 2004.

The fifth volume in the series, titled *Intelligence and Accountability: Safeguards Against the Abuse of Secret Power*, stems from a concern that secret power might be misused by those in high office. This danger was underscored in 1975 when Congress found the U.S. intelligence agencies guilty of spying against law-abiding American citizens, and again in 1987 during the Iran-*contra* affair when some elements of the intelligence community violated the public trust by ignoring intelligence laws. The United States has been one of the few nations in the world to conduct an ongoing experiment in bringing democratic accountability to secret government activities. Democracy and spying don't mix well. Secrecy runs counter to democratic openness, while at the same time openness possesses a threat to the success of espionage operations. Democracies need intelligence agencies to acquire information that may protect them, but thoughtful citizens worry about having secret agencies in an open society.

Until 1975, the nation's remedy for the tension between intelligence gathering and democracy was to trust the intelligence agencies and hope for the best. Elected officials treated the secret services as exceptional organizations, immune from the checks and balances envisioned by the framers of the Constitution. Lawmakers were satisfied with this arrangement, because if an operation went awry they could duck responsibility. When James R. Schlesinger, DCI in 1973, attempted to inform John Stennis (D-MS), a key member of the Senate Armed Services Committee, about an approaching operation, the Senator stopped him short: "No, no, my boy, don't tell me. Just go ahead and do it, but I don't want to know."[8]

This attitude on Capitol Hill—overlook rather than oversight—underwent a dramatic turnabout in December 1974, however, when the *New York Times* reported on allegations of CIA spying at home and questionable covert actions in Chile. Congress might have waved aside the revelations about Chile as just another Cold War necessity in the struggle against regimes leaning toward Moscow, but spying on American citizens—voters—was another matter altogether. In January 1975, President Ford created the Commission on CIA Activities Within the United States (the Rockefeller Commission, led by his vice president, Nelson Rockefeller). Later that month the Senate established a select committee to investigate intelligence activities. The committee was headed by Frank Church, D-ID, and became known as the Church Committee (the editor served as Church's assistant). A counterpart House committee, led by Representative Otis Pike (D-NY), began investigations the following month.

These various panels, especially the Church Committee, found many more improprieties than they had expected. Not only had the CIA engaged in domestic spying in violation of its charter, so had the FBI and several military intelligence units. Furthermore, the FBI had carried out secret operations, known collectively as COINTELPRO, against thousands of civil rights activists, members of the Ku Klux Klan, and Vietnam War dissenters. The objective was to make their lives miserable by disrupting their marriages and employment. The Bureau even attempted to blackmail Dr. Martin Luther King Jr. into committing suicide. Church Committee investigators also discovered CIA assassination plots against foreign leaders and efforts to topple President Salvador Allende of Chile, even though he had been democratically elected.

These revelations convinced lawmakers that the time had come to bring accountability into the dark recesses of government. Congress established intelligence oversight committees in both chambers—the Senate in 1976 and the House a year later—and, by 1980, required by law timely reports on all secret intelligence operations. The new Committees pored over intelligence budgets, held regular hearings (mostly in closed session to protect spy sources and methods) and seriously examined the performance of America's intelligence agencies. No other nation has ever so thoroughly applied democratic principles to its secret services, although a number are now beginning to follow the leadership of the United States toward greater intelligence supervision.[9]

Since 1975, this effort has evolved in fits and starts. Sometimes lawmakers have insisted on close accountability, as when they enacted the Intelligence Oversight Act of 1980 with its stringent reporting requirements for covert operations, or when a series of laws in the 1980s sought to end covert actions in Nicaragua. At other times, members of Congress have loosened the reins—for example, repealing in 1985 a prohibition against covert action in Angola. On still other occasions, Congress has concentrated on helping the intelligence agencies improve their security and performance, as with a law in 1982 that prohibited exposing the names of undercover officers. The Iran-*contra* scandal of 1987 was a major setback to this new oversight, as the Reagan administration bypassed most of these rules and statutes in its conduct of a covert war in Nicaragua against the will of Congress. The scandal was an alert to lawmakers. The Intelligence Oversight Act of 1991 further tightened intelligence supervision by clarifying reporting requirements. Lawmakers also set up an Office of Inspector General in the CIA, confirmed by and accountable to Congress.

The pulling and tugging has continued, most recently over whether President George W. Bush violated the Foreign Intelligence Surveillance Act (FISA) of 1978 by conducting warrantless wiretaps as part of the war against terrorism in the aftermath of the 9/11 attacks. The FISA required warrants, but the White House claimed (when the secret operation leaked to the media) the law had become to cumbersome and, besides, the president had inherit authority to conduct the war against terrorism as he saw fit. This debate aside for the moment (several authors address the issue in these volumes), one thing is certain: the intelligence agencies in the United States are now very much a part of the nation's system of checks and balances. Americans want and deserve both civil liberties and a secure defense against threats; so the search continues for an appropriate balance between liberty and security, democracy and effectiveness—precisely the topic of Volume 5.

The set of chapters on intelligence accountability are introduced with a chapter by David M. Barrett, the foremost authority on the history of accountability in the early years of modern U.S. intelligence (1947 to 1963). The chief counsel of the Church Committee, Frederick A. O. Schwarz Jr., then reflects back on the effects of that watershed inquiry. Next, the editor offers a previously unpublished interview with DCI William E. Colby, who stood at the helm of the intelligence community as it weathered the storm of the investigations into domestic spying during 1975. Mark Phythian presents a chapter on the British experience with intelligence accountability; and, comparing British and American oversight, Lawrence J. Lamanna contrasts the responses on both sides of the Atlantic to the faulty Iraqi WMD assessments in 2002.

The next chapter, written by Cynthia M. Nolan, looks at contemporary issues of intelligence oversight in the United States. Hans Born and Ian Leigh follow with a comparative dimension by contrasting intelligence accountability practices in a variety other nations. Finally, A. Denis Clift and Harry Howe Ransom, who have witnessed the unfolding of intelligence accountability over the past four decades, offer their appraisals of where the experiment stands today.

The first supporting document in this volume is a succinct legislative history of intelligence accountability from 1947 to 1993, prepared by the Senate Select Committee on Intelligence (Appendix A). Then come a series of important oversight laws, beginning with FISA in 1978. With this law, members of Congress sought to rein in the open-ended authority of the executive branch to wiretap and otherwise spy on individuals considered risks to the national security—a privilege abused by a number of administrations from the 1930s forward. Henceforth, FISA required a warrant from a special court (the FISA Court, whose members are appointed by the Chief Justice of the Supreme Court) before such intrusive measures could be carried out. This law, a hot topic in 2005–6 when critics charged the second Bush administration with violation of the warrant requirement, can be found in Appendix B.

The Intelligence Oversight Act of 1980 is presented in Appendix C. This is a brief but nonetheless far-reaching law, enacted by Congress as an attempt to become an equal partner with the executive branch when it came to intelligence. The 1991 Intelligence Oversight Act (Appendix D) emerged after the Iran-*contra* scandal and provided a tightening and clarification of the language in its 1980 precursor, especially with respect to the approval and reporting rules for covert action. The political tug-of-war over the drafting of this currently prevailing oversight statute was intense, leading to the first and only presidential veto of an intelligence act. President George H. W. Bush found the proposal's insistence on prior reporting of covert action objectionable in times of emergency. Lawmakers entered into a compromise with the chief executive, settling on a two-day reporting delay in emergencies. The bill passed Congress again, this time without a presidential veto.

In 1995, the House Permanent Select Committee on Intelligence launched an inquiry into a wide assortment of intelligence issues, stimulated initially by counterintelligence concerns (Aldrich Ames's treasonous activities at the CIA had recently been discovered) but turning into an opportunity for a broad review of new challenges that faced the secret agencies now that the Cold War had ended. In Appendix E, an excerpt from the Committee's final report examines the state of intelligence accountability in the mid-1990s. The next document, in Appendix F, carries the examination into the twenty-first century, with the appraisal of the 9/11 Commission on the same subject. The commissioners were unimpressed, referring to intelligence accountability as "dysfunctional."

At the center of any efforts to maintain accountability for the secret agencies lies the question of funding—the mighty power of the pursue, held in the hands of lawmakers. Appendix G draws on the findings of the Aspin-Brown Commission to provide official documentation about how the United States spends money for spying. Finally, in Appendix H, DCI Robert M. Gates (1991–93) offers observations about oversight from the perspective of the intelligence community management team, located at that time on the Seventh Floor of the CIA.

Here, then, is what the reader will find in these five volumes. The editor and the contributors hope the chapters and documents will help educate the public about the importance of intelligence agencies, as well as stimulate scholars around the world to further the blossoming of this vital field of study. I am pleased to acknowledge my gratitude to Praeger's Heather Staines, senior project editor, and Anne Rehill, development editor, each a pleasure to work with and most helpful in their guidance; Julie Maynard at the University of Georgia for her administrative assistance; Lawrence J. Lamanna, my graduate research assistant, for his good counsel and logistical help; Leena S. Johnson for her indispensable encouragement and support; and the contributors to these volumes for their outstanding scholarship and their much appreciated cooperation in keeping the publishing train running on time.

These volumes are enthusiastically dedicated to Harry Howe Ransom, who has done so much in the United States to lead the way toward a serious discipline of intelligence studies.

Loch K. Johnson

NOTES

1. Some of the authors have had multiple careers, so in categorizing them I have counted the place where they have spent most of their professional lives.

2. Quoted by Senator Frank Church (D-ID), in *Congressional Record* (January 27, 1976), p. 1165.

3. *Fact Book on Intelligence* (Washington DC: CIA Office of Public Affairs, April 1983), p. 17.

4. National Security Act of 1947, signed on July 26, 1947 (P.L. 97-222; 50 U.S.C. 403, Sec. 102).

5. Comment, "Evening News," NBC (January 13, 1978).

6. Editor's interview with a FBI counterintelligence specialist, Washington, DC (May 16, 1975).

7. Editor's interview with Raymond Rocca, CIA/CI specialist, Washington, DC (November 23, 1975).

8. Editor's interview with James R. Schlesinger, Washington, DC (June 16, 1994).

9. See Hans Born, Loch K. Johnson, and Ian Leigh, *Who's Watching the Spies? Establishing Intelligence Service Accountability* (Washington, DC: Potomac Books, 2005).

CONGRESSIONAL OVERSIGHT OF THE CIA IN THE EARLY COLD WAR, 1947–63

DAVID M. BARRETT

INTRODUCTION

A DEMOCRATIC NATION-STATE IN A DANGEROUS WORLD faces two obvious dilemmas that might be labeled "openness versus secrecy" and "fair play versus dirty tricks." *Openness* is at the heart of democratic theory and practice. If a nation's government is not substantially open about what it is doing and how it is doing it, then that nation's citizens can hardly pass effective judgment about the government in periodic elections. However, in a world full of perils, any government must employ much secrecy about its military and intelligence capabilities and plans.

Meanwhile, many citizens and leaders of democratic nation-states—certainly the United States—consider themselves to believe in fair play. President George Washington's famous farewell address set a standard along these lines by calling for the U.S. government to follow "exalted virtue" in its dealings with other nations. This, he predicted, would ultimately lead other nations to become habituated toward doing the right thing in their foreign affairs.

This is not to say that U.S. foreign policy was consistently virtuous across the ensuing decades. A century and a half later, a secretive commission advising President Dwight Eisenhower explicitly parted company with Washington. The world had become uniquely dangerous, due to the expansionist, communist, and nuclear-armed Soviet Union, "an implacable enemy whose avowed objective is world domination by whatever means and whatever cost. . . . If the United States is to survive, longstanding concepts of 'fair play' must be reconsidered." The United States would have "to learn to subvert, sabotage, and destroy our enemies by more clever, more sophisticated, and more effective methods than those used against us." Dirty tricks were necessary.[1]

Solutions to these two dilemmas were and are imperfect, to say the least. Still, they are at least mitigated for the United States by having some constitutionally elected leaders know of and give direction to covert action, espionage, and other morally unsavory policies. Most obviously, the President—having the executive power and commander-in-chief roles—should carry out such duties. The U.S. Constitution, though, gives the Congress the law-making power (shared with a veto-endowed President), which includes the right the pass spending laws. In light of this, during Washington's presidency, Congress first asserted a constitutionally implied right to monitor and investigate executive branch agencies.

THE LITERATURE ON CONGRESS AND THE CIA
IN EARLY COLD WAR YEARS

Writings on Congress and the Central Intelligence Agency (CIA) in the Truman-Eisenhower-Kennedy era have been very few in number. Harry Howe Ransom provided rare early and thoughtful scholarly treatments of legislative oversight in books and articles on CIA, finding in 1958 that the agency operated "with only nominal legislative surveillance."[2] Despite his best efforts to learn details of CIA-Congress relations, Ransom was handicapped by the secrecy surrounding the agency. A later and more extensive (retrospective) treatment of the topic came from the Church Committee of the mid-1970s, named for its chairman, Senator Frank Church (D-ID). That committee came into being as a result of various published allegations in the *New York Times* and certain books concerning certain questionable actions of the CIA in previous decades. Though the committee's main focus was not on legislative oversight of CIA, it did give substantially more attention to the topic than had occurred before. It found that "from the beginning," the House and Senate subcommittees charged with monitoring the CIA "were relatively inactive."[3] Newspapers and magazines in the United States sporadically paid attention to congressional oversight of CIA in the early Cold War years. An early example was the Richmond *News-Leader,* which charged Congress in the early 1950s with ignoring the CIA's "free-wheeling" status.[4]

Working from much fuller evidence that has become available in the past decade, it is fair to say that the two adjectives that best describe congressional oversight of the CIA during the Truman, Eisenhower, and Kennedy eras are *limited* and *informal*. This is especially so when that oversight is compared to the oversight that Congress instituted and has carried out from the mid-1970s through the early 21st century. In the modern era, there are many hundreds of interactions between Capitol Hill and the CIA per year; the House and Senate Intelligence Committees are large and have substantial staffs. By contrast, from 1947—when the CIA was created by President Truman and Congress—through the early 1960s, there were anywhere from eight to thirty hearings held each year.

There were scores of other interactions between individual legislators and CIA personnel annually. But the hearings and the smaller, more informal sessions were almost all carried out under conditions of extreme secrecy. The legislators who conducted them were mostly on four tiny House and Senate Appropriations and Armed Services subcommittees that were mandated to monitor the CIA. Those legislators were assisted in these tasks by a small number of staff assistants, none of whose jobs were exclusively devoted to intelligence affairs.

Still, most of the literature on Congress and the CIA has been erroneous in asserting that there was virtually no intelligence oversight in the early Cold War era, especially by the late Eisenhower era. Claims are common that Director of Central Intelligence (DCI) Allen Dulles (1953–61) only had jocular but shallow meetings with legislators. Dulles's own experience of legislative oversight is instructive: In 1958, he spent parts of at least twenty-five days on Capitol Hill. There, he met with ten or more different committees or subcommittees. During his long tenure and afterward, he periodically clamed that legislative oversight of the CIA had been reasonably substantive, though few have taken his claim seriously.[5]

The political atmosphere was challenging for Dulles in a year like 1958. For example, many Congress members had publicly expressed doubts that CIA had alerted President Eisenhower and others that (1) the Soviet Union was likely to launch an earth satellite in the autumn of 1957, that (2) Venezuelans were likely to riot and almost kill Vice President Richard Nixon on a "good will" visit to that country, or that (3) the pro-American government of Iraq would be overthrown by a coup, thus provoking American intervention in nearby Lebanon. Dulles was relatively honest with legislators in that year's secret hearings, responding that CIA had alerted President Eisenhower and at least one congressional subcommittee that the USSR might launch an earth satellite in 1957, that CIA had relied too much on Venezuelan security services for its intelligence on the dangers Nixon might face, and that the Agency had simply failed to anticipate the Iraqi coup. In the next few years, following the U-2 and Bay of Pigs incidents, CIA's challenges on Capitol Hill would be greater.[6]

One element missing from most of the literature on Congress and the CIA is treatment of a particular kind of accountability that existed: DCIs Roscoe Hillenkoetter (1947–50), Walter B. Smith (1950–53), Dulles, and John McCone (1962–65) literally feared what congressional barons heading the CIA subcommittees might do to the Agency if its leader were discovered to have lied or refused directives received on Capitol Hill. (The intelligence directors met those powerful legislators privately more often than they did in subcommittee sessions. Such meetings were poorly documented, unfortunately.) When Vice President Lyndon Johnson warned McCone in 1962 that Armed Services Committee chair Richard Russell (D-GA)—who was the most knowledgeable senator about CIA affairs—could "destroy" the Agency and McCone if he were not responsive on a current controversy, the DCI was being told something that he already knew. By virtually all accounts of those who worked for the four directors, keeping the members (especially chairs and ranking minority members) of the CIA sub-committees satisfied was of prime importance.[7]

This is not to say that the Agency faced anything like systematic scrutiny by Congress over its first decade and a half. As CIA legislative liaison John Warner occasionally pointed out to colleagues, the leaders of the CIA sub-committee were often too busy to pay as much attention to the Agency as they should have.

ESSENTIAL FEATURES OF CIA OVERSIGHT
BY CONGRESS, 1947–63

Within a year of the CIA's creation in 1947, the House and Senate Armed Services and Appropriations Subcommittees began emerging and holding in-formal hearings with Agency leaders present. The frequency of those sessions in the late 1940s was low, and they have never been well documented. It was inevitable that the Appropriations Subcommittees (not formally named, but oc-casionally referred to by members simply as the "CIA Subcommittees") would come into being, because the CIA needed funds, but no one at the Agency, on Capitol Hill, or at the White House wanted the full Appropriations Committees to have access to information on the new Agency. CIA was already doing analysis and coordination of the writing of estimates; also, some of its personnel were doing espionage and covert action. Thus, during the Agency's first few years, no more than five Appropriations members at the House and fewer than three at the Senate knew any details about CIA's budgets, which were moving upward to-ward the $100 million mark.[8]

The Armed Services Committees successfully asserted their claims as the relevant law-making bodies to deal with CIA-related issues. But their chairs had no more interest than the Appropriations leaders in having all Committee members interact with CIA. The commonly expressed view—both in public and in private—was that CIA's work was too important for it to be endangered by leaks to the press, which would, in turn, inform the Soviet Union of such infor-mation. The resulting subcommittees were also small and met as infrequently as one to four times per year in the late 1940s.

Though the frequency of hearings and other meetings of the CIA sub-committees grew substantially in the 1950s and 1960s, certain features remained constant across the Truman, Eisenhower, and Kennedy eras. One was the dom-inance of their chairmen and ranking minority members. In the Senate, the chairs of the committees also headed the CIA subcommittees. In the House, this was also the case until the late 1950s, when the Armed Services and Appropriations Com-mittee chairs—Democrats Carl Vinson (GA) and Clarence Cannon (MO)—turned over their CIA subcommittee chairmanships to Paul Kilday and George Mahon, both Texas Democrats. Nonetheless, Vinson and Cannon usually attended sub-committee meetings.

There seems to have been greater knowledge on the part of chairs and ranking minority members than there was among the other subcommittee members. In the Appropriations Subcommittees, for example, a few years passed before leaders informed other members of the existence of the U-2 program, which sent spy flights across the Soviet Union. This conforms to what Stephen Horn later wrote: the chairs and ranking minority members of Senate Appropriations were "lord and masters" of the Committee.[9]

Another feature of the subcommittees' dynamics was the lack of partisanship. Relations between the majority and minority party leaders and members were trusting and respectful most of the time. This made it "a joy to work there," said Bill Darden, a leading staffer at the Senate Armed Services Committee. Also, on those occasions in the 1940s and 1950s when party control of Congress changed, most staffers who interacted with CIA frequently (like Darden) stayed on in their jobs. There were not many such staff members, though. In any given year, fewer than ten of them—from the four subcommittees and the occasional other committee that looked into CIA matters—were designated by their bosses to do such work. With few exceptions (especially Senator Styles Bridges [R-NH], who was an ally of powerful columnist Drew Pearson), neither staffers nor members of the CIA subcommittees leaked to the press.

DID SUBCOMMITTEE MEMBERS KNOW THE CIA'S INTIMATE SECRETS?

Covert Action

Contrary to what is commonly found in the literature, it is clear that subcommittee leaders and/or members knew a fair amount about covert action. This should not be surprising: Congress members, whether they were on CIA subcommittees or not, mostly favored aggressive action. Records that have been uncovered in recent years show that many legislators went to executive branch leaders and suggested covert action in various parts of the world. "Why don't we instigate a large program of stirring up guerrilla activity on the Chinese mainland?" asked one out-of-the-loop legislator in 1950. Indeed, such Congress members who were not knowledgeable about the CIA managed to pass an amendment in 1951 that handed $100 million to the Truman administration to try to "roll back" Soviet influence in Eastern Europe. The money was not used because it was not needed by CIA, which was then funded by the House and Senate Appropriations CIA subcommittees at a level of almost half a billion dollars, much of it for covert action.[10]

Two of the best remembered covert actions of the early Cold War era were the removal of the left-leaning government of Guatemala in 1954 (during the Eisenhower presidency) and the wildly unsuccessful attempt to overturn Fidel Castro's government of Cuba in 1961's Bay of Pigs incident (during the Kennedy presidency). Did the CIA subcommittee members and/or other legislators have advance knowledge of those planned covert actions? The evidence regarding Guatemala is extremely fragmentary, but it is likely that at least the heads of the subcommittees and some other legislators knew of those plans in advance. Furthermore, leaders at the CIA and elsewhere in the executive branch felt heat from Congress, who feared a Latin American outpost of the Soviet Union enough to insist that the executive branch "do something" about Guatemala.

As for the Bay of Pigs invasion, two different documents made available at the end of the 20th century show that DCI Dulles and associates went before the full CIA Subcommittees of the House Armed Services and Appropriations Committees to tell them what the Agency was prepared to do in the coming weeks. Although the documents show only a little of what transpired in the secret hearings, it is clear that some questions of the feasibility of the planned operation were raised; but there is no evidence that any legislator advised the Agency's leaders not to intervene in Cuba. The more significant point, however, is that the Subcommittees' members were told in advance of the Cuba plans. Russell and some other members on the Senate side were almost certainly told in advance, but no documentation seems to have been declassified regarding this.[11]

It is also clear that the practice of giving details about past and future covert actions did not begin in the Eisenhower or Kennedy era. Documents from the Truman era are less plentiful, but some of them support memories of former Agency personnel that, for example, DCI Walter "Beetle" Smith occasionally gave detailed operational briefings to members of CIA subcommittees. On one occasion, when a legislator asked a vague question about operations around the world, Smith pulled out a list of all ongoing covert action programs and reviewed them with subcommittee members.[12]

In summary, in the sensitive area of covert action, CIA subcommittees had a fair amount of knowledge, resulting from some of the few hearings each subcommittee held each year. It is likely, however, that many (especially smaller) operations occurred without being highlighted to legislators.

Intelligence Estimates

The sharing of information with the subcommittees (and occasionally other congressional bodies) was considerable. More than anything else, what legislators of the early Cold War era wanted from CIA leaders was their estimates of political and other conditions in nations around the world, especially the Soviet Union. DCIs Hillenkoetter, Smith, Dulles, and McCone routinely gave spoken summaries of analyses that CIA and other agencies had created. On the one hand, with the exception of the Joint Committee on Atomic Energy (JCAE)—which had a legal right to intelligence estimates on nuclear topics—the CIA rarely, if ever, gave copies of National Intelligence Estimates to committees, subcommittees, or their members to keep beyond the time of hearings. On the other hand, the CIA routinely prepared special estimates for legislators to keep.

One of the most sensitive topics treated by intelligence estimates came in the late summer and early autumn of 1962, when news media outlets and certain legislators (especially Senator Kenneth Keating [R-NY]) claimed that the Soviet Union was placing medium- or intermediate-range nuclear-armed missiles in Cuba. These claims contradicted U.S. intelligence estimates that called such a Soviet move unlikely. On such a topic, CIA subcommittee heads—who could be quite trusting and deferential toward the Agency during quiet times—became all business. As Deputy Director of Central Intelligence (DDCI) Marshall Carter noted on September 26, 1962, he had talked to Leverett Saltonstall, the ranking Republican on the Senate Armed Services CIA subcommittee, about the growing Soviet militarization of Cuba. "He said that he and Senator Russell considered this a very important matter and would like to be kept currently advised of whatever developed in the way of hard intelligence."

Over the ensuing weeks, during what became the Cuban missile crisis, Agency heads bent over backward to keep subcommittee leaders informed about the CIA's knowledge. Indeed, within twenty-four hours of President Kennedy being informed that the Soviets had missiles in Cuba, Russell summoned a nervous Carter and legislative liaison John Warner to his office to hear the full story. The CIA men knew that Kennedy had directed that the intelligence on missile sites be kept absolutely secret. Just after Carter and Warner greeted the Senator, Russell was called to a telephone and informed by the President that the CIA had important news for him. The briefers' task had been made immeasurably easier by the President's phone call, which apparently resulted from an alert to the White House by McCone concerning Russell's request for the latest intelligence.[13]

Counterintelligence

At certain points in the early Cold War, some legislative bodies pushed the CIA to share information about counterintelligence problems and controversies. Besides the CIA subcommittees, in the early 1950s, Republican Senator Joseph McCarthy's Permanent Subcommittee on Investigations harassed DCIs Hillenkoetter and Dulles about various (and sometimes nonexistent) problems. Also the House Un-American Activities Committee (HUAC) had interactions with the Agency on alleged infiltration of Soviet spies and sympathizers into the U.S. government. Few records of CIA-HUAC encounters seem to exist, though a tense encounter at a 1952 public hearing between DCI Smith and members of HUAC can be seen (in retrospect) to show the Director choosing his words carefully to avoid any mention of the harm done to U.S. intelligence by British traitor Kim Philby (who, in reality worked for the Soviet Union). However, Smith offered to be much more forthcoming with the Committee in a private hearing.[14]

A decade later, HUAC was more aggressive than the House Armed Services CIA Subcommittee in investigating the defection of two employees of the National Security Agency (NSA) in 1960. While the latter Subcommittee conducted a brief investigation accompanied by hearings, HUAC (under chairman Francis Walter [D-PA]) pursued the topic for two years and forced certain reforms in personnel hiring, training, and clearance procedures at the NSA.[15]

Domestic Involvements of the CIA

The sensitive topic that the Agency may have withheld from the CIA subcommittees and other congressional bodies was that of periodic involvement in matters at home in the United States. The Church Committee and other mid-1970s investigations showed that the CIA sometimes spied on American citizens (such as peace activists), tested drugs on unwitting citizens, and illegally opened letters being handled by the U.S. Post Office. There are virtually no records even hinting that the CIA ever informed any congressional bodies or members of these activities in the 1950s or early 1960s. However, because only a handful of (usually partial) transcripts of CIA subcommittee hearings survive or have been declassified, and even detailed notes of such meetings are not plentiful, it is possible that the Agency did inform certain legislators about such legally questionable activities.

THE "OTHER" COMMITTEES AND THE CIA

Nothing is clearer in the papers of President Dwight D. Eisenhower than his hostility toward congressional "meddling" in the affairs of the CIA. Eisenhower directed his anger not toward the little subcommittees on CIA, though; despite occasional differences with them, he trusted men like Russell, Saltonstall, and Vinson to be discreet and responsible in their interactions with the Agency. Eisenhower's fury—there is no better word to describe it—was over the actions of other legislative bodies, whose leaders sometimes successfully insisted on having CIA leaders testify at hearings. Besides the Permanent Investigations Subcommittee and the HUAC, those bodies included the following.

The Senate Foreign Relations Committee

A few years before J. William Fulbright (D-AR) famously assumed the chairmanship of the committee in 1959, Foreign Relations had begun requesting testimony by Dulles on the CIA's analyses of worldwide political conditions and on its occasional intelligence failures. The frequency of such events is not well documented for all years, but—despite the unhappiness of Eisenhower over such Agency appearances on Capitol Hill—Dulles testified four or five times before the Committee or one of its subcommittees in 1958 and three times in 1959. Among the topics that the committee had Dulles analyze in their presence were Soviet military capabilities, the chances for Tibet to resist occupation by

China, and the odds that Cuban leader Fidel Castro would turn out to be a communist.

Among the real or alleged intelligence failures committed by CIA that DCI Dulles had to discuss with the Foreign Relations Committee in 1956–60 were the Hungarian and Suez crises in 1956, the launch of *Sputnik* in 1957, the 1958 attacks on Vice President Nixon in Venezuela, the Iraqi coup that same year, and the U-2 incident in 1960. Although Dulles generally received high marks from Committee members, the Agency received many criticisms and warnings in those sessions.[16]

The Air Force and Preparedness Subcommittees of the Senate Armed Services Committee

In 1956–57 hearings, the Air Force Subcommittee, headed by Stuart Symington (D-MO), was permitted by Committee chair Richard Russell to examine charges and supposed "intelligence" showing that the Soviet Union was far ahead of the United States in bomber aircraft capabilities. Later, Russell designated the Preparedness Subcommittee, headed by Senator Lyndon Johnson (D-TX), to examine charges that the Soviets excelled in long-range missile capabilities in 1958–60. But Symington, a member of Johnson's Subcommittee, often outdid the Texan in publicizing and identifying himself with the missile "gap."

The discreet Russell had mixed feelings about Symington, but the gap controversies were too fierce to be ignored. While Russell's own CIA Subcommittee could and did discuss the issues with Dulles and other Agency leaders, the Georgia Senator insisted that such hearings be kept secret. Thus, Symington's and Johnson's hearings, though held in "executive" (that is, secret) sessions, were much discussed in the press. Both senators readily discussed the hearings with journalists.

In testimony before the Air Force and Preparedness Subcommittees, Dulles denied Symington's charges that the Eisenhower administration had somehow misused intelligence or that the CIA itself had seriously underestimated Soviet military capabilities. The President himself responded in a 1960 press conference to Symington's charges that the administration had distorted intelligence as a means to reduce the size of the U.S. defense budget. In the words of a *New York Times* reporter, Eisenhower "appeared to control himself with effort." Such charges were "despicable," said the President, who added, "If anybody— anybody!—believes that I have deliberately misled the American people, I'd like to tell him to his face what I think about him." There was little doubt in anyone's mind about the identity of "him." Eisenhower was almost as angry, in private, against Dulles for "giving such detailed figures to the Congress."[17]

The Joint Committee on Atomic Energy

No committee of Congress angered Eisenhower more for its insistence on obtaining CIA estimates and testimony (on nuclear weapons topics) than the

JCAE. President Harry S Truman had been no fan of the Joint Committee either. On a good day, Truman might merely complain that "those fellows . . . think they are the board of directors" on atomic energy matters. When really angry (according to Atomic Energy Commission Chair David Lilienthal's diary), Truman "glared through his thickish glasses" and erupted over "those bastards on the Hill." Indeed, the JCAE was mandated by law to have full knowledge and substantial control over nuclear policies. In 1949, after the CIA failed to predict that the Soviet Union would conduct a successful test explosion of its first atomic bomb, the Joint Committee virtually skinned alive DCI Hillenkoetter in a secret hearing. In the 1950s, Dulles's usual responsiveness to JCAE requests for information and testimony was a chronic irritant in the DCI's relationship with the White House.[18]

THE WAXING AND WANING OF OVERSIGHT

Records that have been declassified or otherwise made available in recent years show clearly that congressional oversight of the CIA varied from one year to the next. Why did the Agency appear before no more than a dozen hearings in 1955, but testify twice as often in 1958? There are two fairly obvious answers.

The Political Environment

In an influential 1984 article, political scientists Matthew McCubbins and Thomas Schwartz suggested that conditions in the American political environment largely determined whether Congress would aggressively investigate failures and wrongdoing by executive branch agencies or remain relatively passive and deferential toward them. As they point out, with the Legislative Reorganization Act of 1946, Congress mandated itself to engage in continuous, assertive oversight (what McCubbins and Schwartz called "police patrol" oversight). But the reality of the ensuing decades was that Capitol Hill became assertive only when "fire alarms" were set off by interest groups, the news media, the public, or others complaining that one or more agencies had somehow failed.[19]

On the whole, the fire alarms analysis fits well with the surviving evidence about Congress and the CIA in the early Cold War decades. An examination of the news in 1955 and 1958, for example, shows that there were many more alarms ringing in the latter year: a firestorm over *Sputnik*'s launch late in the previous year, Nixon's encounter with South American rioters, and the coup in Iraq. There was enormous critical news coverage of the CIA that year—more than in any previous year—as well as letters from citizens to newspapers, Congress, and the White House. After the year ended, an aide to Dulles reflected in a work diary on the "ground swell developing for more frequent briefings of these committees on some systematic basis."[20]

Attributes of Legislators

Much as the level of controversy in the American political environment affected the amount of congressional oversight of CIA, there can be no doubt that attributes of the legislators charged with carrying out such duties mattered, too. Consider the different approaches to CIA used by Representative John Taber (R-NY) and Senator Carl Hayden (D-AZ).

Taber chaired the House Appropriations Committee and its CIA Sub-committee during the two first years of the Eisenhower presidency, when the Republican Party held a majority of seats in Congress. By all accounts, he was not a likable man and had no real friends in the House, but he was tough and capable. As chair, Taber hired new staff to examine the budgets of the CIA and many other bureaucracies. The Subcommittee held more hearings annually with the CIA than had ever been the case. He obtained more detailed descriptions of CIA successes and failures in covert action than apparently had been given by Agency heads before. He placed limitations on both spending and new hires at the Agency, provoking widespread complaints there. A new verb joined the Washington lexicon—to *taberize* was to cut budgets. After Democrats regained control of Congress, Taber continued to show an active interest in CIA affairs.[21]

Hayden was genuinely popular and respected in the Senate, but by the time he assumed the chair of its Appropriations Committee in 1955, he was seventy-seven years old. Though bright and hard-working, Hayden was overly busy. He had high regard for Richard Russell, the most senior of his colleagues on Appropriations. Since Russell chaired Armed Services and its CIA Subcommittee, Hayden and he agreed some time around 1956 that they would combine their subcommittees' oversight of CIA, under Russell's leadership. Although this could have led to reasonably effective monitoring of the Agency, it did not, at least concerning budgetary matters. Hayden was the least effective of any heads of CIA subcommittees in the 1950s.

Scrutiny of proposed CIA budgets was far greater in the House, where Clarence Cannon (D-MO) chaired Appropriations from 1955 through his death in 1964. Cannon has been criticized in histories of the CIA as essentially an old fool who did no more oversight than to trade stories with Dulles and McCone and ask them if the CIA had "enough" money. The reality was different. For example, before anyone else in Washington, Cannon insisted in 1958 that Dulles answer a simple question: "How much does the United States government spend annually on intelligence activities?" Theoretically, a Director of Central Intelligence managed the entire American intelligence establishment, but the reality was that agencies other than the CIA received almost no direction from Dulles or other early DCIs. It took months of work by the CIA and other agencies before Dulles could give Cannon a reasonably accurate response in 1958. They would have to give a fuller report the following year.[22]

Among the other legislators who interacted with the Agency, there were many who—even if respectful toward CIA—were reasonably assertive, especially when alarms were going off. These included in the Senate: Symington, Bridges, John Stennis (D-MS), and Kenneth McKellar (D-TN). In the House, Francis Walter, chair of HUAC, was a periodic thorn in the side of Dulles. The two men actually argued in one telephone conversation, with the chairman hanging up on the DCI.[23] Also in the House, starting around 1957, Clarence Cannon appointed the widely respected George Mahon (D-TX) to head the Appropriations CIA Subcommittee. Cannon remained periodically active in relation to CIA, but Mahon took more of the burden and stepped up the frequency and substance of hearings.

Similarly, Carl Vinson appointed the well-regarded Paul Kilday (D-TX) to head the Armed Services CIA Subcommittee and improve its work. Among other things, Kilday oversaw very secretive investigations of the CIA in 1959 and the NSA in 1960. Kilday attempted to increase examinations of the CIA's budget by the General Accounting Office (GAO), an arm of Congress. Vinson had long relied on Kilday for assistance on crucial work, but on the GAO issue, Vinson withdrew his support of Kilday and the idea died.

Kilday believed that the appropriate subcommittees of Congress should monitor intelligence agencies, but Vinson wavered on this point. After Kilday retired in 1961, Vinson resumed chairing the Armed Services Subcommittee and actually told DCI McCone at the beginning of 1962 that "it was not necessary that the Subcommittee know everything concerning Agency affairs." (In fairness to Vinson, records show that when Congress was in session, his Subcommittee held hearings with CIA witnesses almost monthly in 1962 and 1963, and discussed topics that Agency censors were still "sanitizing" from documents released early in the 21st century.)[24]

Others in the House and Senate displayed the sort of deference that Vinson voiced. Saltonstall, the ranking Republican on Senate Armed Services, had such faith in Dulles and McCone—both actual friends of the Senator—that he seems to have only rarely pushed hard for information about the CIA.

In summary, although it is fair to say that congressional oversight of the CIA generally increased across the years from 1947 through 1963, the trend was not steady. In years when events seemed less threatening to U.S. national security, oversight was likely to decrease. Still, the rise and fall of oversight depended, too, on the attributes of those legislators on the CIA subcommittees or elsewhere in Congress.

TWO DEBATES ABOUT CIA'S ACCOUNTABILITY

On the floors of the House and Senate, members only occasionally discussed the CIA. When they did, it was usually because of some surprise in world politics. Occasionally, though, the Agency's place in the U.S. political system was the topic. Two of the most substantive debates about whether or not it was subject to direction from constitutionally elected leaders occurred in 1956, when Senator

Mike Mansfield (D-MT) offered a resolution to create a joint congressional committee on intelligence, and in 1962, when the Senate debated President Kennedy's nomination of John McCone to become DCI.

The Mansfield Resolution

Mike Mansfield was an atypical politician—not a back-slapper, not long-winded, and not especially egotistical. He cared and thought about democratic governance. Though an early supporter in the House of the CIA, after entering the Senate in 1953, Mansfield came to believe that the Agency was free from reasonable controls by the White House and Congress. He could do little to make Presidents give more attention to the Agency, but Congress (he thought) should become far more active in monitoring the CIA and other intelligence agencies.

The Montanan had been promoting his resolution since 1953. By early 1956, he had won many supporters, including a bipartisan majority of the members on the Armed Services Committee. In April debates, Mansfield said that everything about the Agency was "clothed in secrecy," and that this invited "abuse." Furthermore, it seemed likely that "all is not well with CIA," in light of reports that Congress suffered from "a woeful shortage of information about the CIA."

On the first day of debate, the main defender of the existing oversight system was Leverett Saltonstall. The Massachusetts Senator stumbled badly in that role, though, speaking of the "difficulty in connection with asking questions and obtaining information . . . which I personally would rather not have, unless it was essential for me, as a Member of Congress, to have it." He had not said that he did not obtain sensitive information, but that was the impression he left.

Two days later, Richard Russell tried to make up for Saltonstall's weak defense. His CIA Subcommittee had asked Dulles "very searching questions about some activities which it almost chills the marrow of a man to hear about." Russell even claimed that the CIA faced more congressional oversight than most other government agencies. In light of that assertion, his pledge about the future may not have signified much: "I shall undertake to exercise as close supervision over this Agency as is ordinarily exercised by parent committees of the Congress in dealing with agencies which are responsible to them."

Mansfield was not helped by allies. Wayne Morse (D-OR) charged Saltonstall with supporting an "American police state system." Joseph McCarthy spoke of incompetence and communist infiltration at CIA and complimented "the able senator from Montana," but the once fearsome McCarthy was in the late stages of alcoholism—"a piteous specter with a bloated face" that day, noted a Senate observer.[25]

Some senators who implied that the CIA needed more oversight were not willing to vote for it. One defended his surprising vote with the claim that to establish an intelligence committee with a significant staff, would "dry up sources of information."

Though the debate over CIA's functioning in a democratic system was notable, it probably had nothing to do with the outcome. Russell and his ally, Majority Leader Lyndon Johnson, marshaled votes, with an assist from the White House and Allen Dulles, and fifty-nine senators voted "no." The CIA subcommittees, with periodic assists from other congressional bodies would—for better or worse—continue to be the system by which Congress monitored the Agency's performance.[26]

The McCone Confirmation Debate

When prior DCIs were nominated by Presidents Truman and Eisenhower, Senate debates were perfunctory and the voice votes unanimously favorable. When President Kennedy nominated Republican John McCone, a businessman who had served the two most recent Presidents (among other things, heading the Atomic Energy Commission), it provoked serious debate and actual opposition. Part of this was a result of McCone's longtime substantial holdings in corporations that had major contracts with the United States or foreign governments, and part derived from his lack of direct experience in intelligence. But the nomination was also hostage to a serious conviction in the Senate that as Eugene McCarthy (D-MN) said, "There is no regular or normal procedure ... by which committees of the Congress are consulted or informed of CIA activities." Sooner or later, the question of proper congressional oversight of the Agency and its questionable operations "will have to be the basis for a great debate. I think this is the proper time to start that debate."

Most disappointing to the Kennedy administration was the decision of Senator Fulbright to join McCarthy's fight against McCone. Fulbright said he could have voted for McCone as Secretary of State, for that position was subject to "constant review and exposure to criticism." A DCI clearly influenced policy making, Fulbright claimed, but McCone had not been required to state his policy views when he had testified before the Armed Services Committee days before. In the face of assertions by CIA/McCone supporters that the Agency did not have a major influence over U.S. foreign policy, the Foreign Relations chair stated bluntly that this was "not in accord with the facts as I know them."

Senator Russell was horrified "that we air on the floor of the Senate all the things that CIA is reputed to have done or not to have done in foreign countries." He avoided saying that CIA Subcommittee members often had specific knowledge of such things, but claimed, "No Director of Central Intelligence would think of undertaking any activities anywhere on the face of the earth without the approval and consent of the President." Furthermore, there had been "six or seven hearings" before the Senate Armed Services and Appropriations Subcommittees in 1961, so Fulbright's charge that the CIA was not accountable to Congress was inaccurate. Fulbright's real complaint (Russell charged) must be that "it is not all under his Committee."[27]

The fierceness of the opponents to the confirmation before and during the debates actually unnerved the usually tough McCone. While traveling abroad as director-designate, he wondered (in a wire to his associates at the CIA) if it would be best if his nomination were withdrawn. John Warner and a colleague cabled back, "The President retains fullest confidence in you.... We believe it unnecessary and undesirable to even consider withdrawal." An "overwhelming affirmative" vote was likely, they said, and they were correct. The vote was seventy-one to twelve. As the *New York Times* noted, though, that numerical tally obscured the considerable "uneasiness about the agency's freedom from congressional supervision." Many of McCone's supporters were like Mike Mansfield, by then the Majority Leader in the Senate: they voted for the new DCI mostly out of loyalty to the President.[28]

CIA AND DEMOCRATIC ACCOUNTABILITY, 1947–63

Was the CIA responsive to constitutionally elected leaders in the Truman-to-Kennedy era? While CIA–White House relations are not the focus of this chapter, it is worth pointing out that the weight of scholarship in recent decades has suggested that rather than being a "rogue elephant," the CIA was substantially a tool of the White House.[29] What about Congress? Numerous documents from the CIA and Capitol Hill have only become available recently, after many decades with very little publicly available evidence to go on. In those years, there was no possibility of a large body of literature on CIA's accountability to Congress. Even now, so much remains classified—or was destroyed or never committed to paper—that it is entirely possible we will never have a truly detailed documentary record of CIA-Congress interactions in the early Cold War decades.

Based on what has become available, however, a better debate can take place over who was right: Senators Mike Mansfield and Eugene McCarthy or Senators Richard Russell and Leverett Saltonstall? Was CIA mostly free from accountability to anyone in Congress, as Mansfield and McCarthy charged, or did a select number of legislators usually know of bone-chilling Agency activities?

I argue that neither of those two stances was quite right. There were far more Agency appearances on Capitol Hill and many more descriptions of sensitive activities to the CIA subcommittees than Mansfield or McCarthy knew. Any future scholarly treatment of the CIA's democratic accountability in the early Cold War must take into account, especially, the documentary record of Allen Dulles's and John McCone's substantial time on Capitol Hill.

Regarding covert action, perhaps the most controversial realm in which the CIA was active, there is now substantial evidence to negate Mansfield's suggestions that such operations were done without knowledge or support on Capitol Hill.

There were even a few congressional investigations of the CIA: by Taber in 1953, Joseph McCarthy in the early 1950s, Kilday in 1959, and Stennis in 1963.

There may have been others. Also, investigations headed by Johnson, Symington, and some others touched partly on the CIA.

To the extent that the subcommittees did not know of certain morally or legally questionable activities, though, it appears that the legislators were as much to blame as Agency leaders. Clearly, sometimes people like Vinson or Saltonstall did not want the subcommittees to know the CIA's darkest secrets, and they may have chosen not to hear them either in hearings or in private.

However, the available records hardly suggest support for Richard Russell's claim that the CIA was more extensively monitored that most other bureaucracies of the executive branch. In a typical year, each subcommittee on the CIA met with Agency leaders a few times. The leaders of those subcommittees were busy heading other important congressional bodies; and the staffers who assisted those subcommittee leaders always had to divide their time between work on CIA matters and that of other agencies such as the Department of Defense. It may be revisionist to suggest that oversight of some real substance occurred in the early Cold War years, but it would be bizarre to claim that such oversight was systematic or comprehensive.

NOTES

1. William Leary, ed., *The Central Intelligence Agency: History and Documents* (Tuscaloosa: University of Alabama Press, 1984), pp. 143–45.

2. Harry Howe Ransom, *Central Intelligence and National Security* (Cambridge, MA: Harvard University Press, 1958), p. 145.

3. Select Committee to Study Governmental Operations with Respect to Intelligence Activities, *Book 1: Foreign and Military Intelligence,* p. 150.

4. David M. Barrett, *The CIA and Congress: The Untold Story from Truman to Kennedy* (Lawrence: University Press of Kansas, 2005), p. 174. Papers of over two dozen legislators who interacted with CIA from 1947 to 1960—used in writing this chapter—are available in the David M. Barrett Research Files at the Richard Russell Library, University of Georgia.

5. Barrett, *CIA and Congress,* p. 321, has brief treatment of numbers for autumn 1957 through autumn 1958. Specific documents on 1958 can be found in that year's folders of the Barrett Research Files at the Russell Library.

6. Barrett, *CIA and Congress,* chaps. 27–29.

7. McCone, "Meeting Attended by the President…," October 9, 1962, *Foreign Relations of the United States: Cuba, 1961–63,* vols. 10–12, microfiche. The memo closes with a description of the private LBJ-McCone meeting. A good example of a DCI's adherence to directives is in McCone, Memo for File, August 21, 1962, in Mary McAuliffe, *CIA Documents on the Cuban Missile Crisis* (Washington: CIA, 1992), p. 21.

8. Barrett, *CIA and Congress,* chap. 3. In one or two of those earliest years, it may have been only the chair of House Appropriations who knew budget details.

9. Stephen Horn, *Unused Power: The Work of the Senate Committee on Appropriations* (Washington, DC: Brookings, 1970). Horn's book features rare, early treatment of a CIA subcommittee; see pp. 38–40, 76, 97–100, 127, 135, 178, 186.

10. Barrett, *CIA and Congress*, pp. 96, 103–12.

11. Barrett, *CIA and Congress,* pp. 438–46; Jack Pfeiffer, *Official History of the Bay of Pigs Operation,* vol. 3, pp. 194–95, CIA Miscellaneous Records, Box 1, JFK Assassination Records Collection, National Archives.

12. Interview with Walter Pforzheimer (CIA's first legislative liaison), September 30, 1994, Washington, DC.

13. Interview with John Warner, October 19, 1999, Washington, DC; Carter, memo for the record, September 26, 1962, CREST (CIA Records Search Tool), National Archives, College Park, MD; M. Bundy to President Kennedy (re: Russell request), October 17, 1962, document no. 654, Cuban Missile Crisis collection, National Security Archive, Washington, DC.

14. Barrett, *CIA and Congress,* pp. 127–34.

15. Ibid., p. 421; James Bamford, *The Puzzle Palace: A Report on America's Most Secret Agency* (Boston: Houghton Mifflin, 1982), pp. 81–85, 147–50.

16. Barrett, *CIA and Congress,* chaps. 25–29, 34, 39.

17. Ibid., pp. 367, 369–70.

18. Ibid., pp. 51, 56–62, 142, 209, 322.

19. Matthew McCubbins and Thomas Schwartz, "Congressional Oversight Overlooked: Police Patrols Versus Fire Alarms," *American Journal of Political Science* 28 (1984), pp. 165–79.

20. L. K. White, diary, February 4, 1959, quoted in Barrett, *CIA and Congress,* p. 322.

21. Barrett, *CIA and Congress,* chap. 15.

22. Ibid., pp. 317–18.

23. Ibid., p. 421.

24. Warner, memo for the record (Vinson), January 16, 1962, CREST. On Kilday, see Barrett, *CIA and Congress,* pp. 334–39, 391–92, 440–46; on Mahon, Barrett, *CIA and Congress,* pp. 121–22, 296–97, 341–46, 453–55.

25. Richard Riedel, *Halls of the Mighty: My 47 Years at the Senate* (Washington: Robert B. Luce, 1969), p. 229.

26. Barrett, *CIA and Congress,* pp. 223–33; *Congressional Record,* April 9 and April 11, 1956, pp. 5891–939, 6048–68.

27. *Congressional Record,* January 29, January 30, and January 31, 1962. Quotations are from lengthy memoranda prepared by CIA personnel for McCone, obtained from CREST.

28. [Name censored] and Warner to McCone, undated (from late January 1962), CREST; *New York Times,* February 1, 1962, p. 9.

29. See, for example, Christopher Andrew, *For the President's Eyes Only: Secret Intelligence and the American Presidency from Washington to Bush* (New York: Harper Collins, 1995); Thomas Powers, *The Man Who Kept the Secrets: Richard Helms and the CIA* (New York: Knopf, 1979); and Don Bohning, *The Castro Obsession: U.S. Covert Operations Against Cuba, 1959–1965* (Washington: Potomac Books, 2005). Despite the Church Committee's view that congressional oversight of CIA was severely lacking, it did not endorse the "rogue elephant" analogy.

2

INTELLIGENCE OVERSIGHT

The Church Committee

FREDERICK A. O. SCHWARZ JR.

THIRTY YEARS AGO, THE CHURCH COMMITTEE COMPLETED what was and still is the most exhaustive look at our government's (or any government's) secret intelligence agencies. The Committee's hearings and reports to the U.S. Senate and to the American public revealed much that broke America's laws and did not honor America's values.[1]

Not knowing a single senator, I was honored to be asked, and privileged to serve, as the Committee's chief counsel. Now, thirty years later, when America again faces and fears a ruthless enemy, I am frequently asked about the Church Committee and whether its lessons are important in a time of terror. They are. Most important, in its extensive review of excess and abuse over the course of approximately thirty years during the Cold War, the Church Committee showed that in times of crisis, even constitutional democracies are likely to violate their laws and forget their values. This was a lesson as old as the Alien and Sedition Acts and as recent as the internment of Japanese Americans during World War II. But the Church Committee analyzed the toxic elements of secrecy and the extensions of a climate of fear for decades instead of the shorter periods involved in the earlier periods of excess. The danger signals raised by an indefinite war on terror are obvious. Whether an oversight committee can make a difference is affected to a considerable extent by whether it and the country it serves is overly partisan or not. In 1975–76, the climate was far less partisan than today. Although there were some differences among Church Committee members, these were not major, focusing mainly on details of recommendations and whether some material should be made public (e.g., the Assassinations Report, or the names of companies that turned over all their cables to the National Security Agency [NSA]). These differences were not partisan, and the Committee never divided on partisan lines.

The less toxic atmosphere of the day helped. And so did the Committee's willingness to expose facts concerning—and criticize icons of—both parties.

Today, public comment looking back tends to identify Cold War abuses with the Nixon years, or even just Watergate. This hides more than it explains. Richard M. Nixon makes a convenient larger-than-life villain. But as revealed by the Church Committee, no single man, no single administration, no single party caused the abuses and overreaching of the Cold War period. In fact, overly broad investigations, lawless conduct, and a departure from America's ideals haunted all administrations from Franklin D. Roosevelt through Nixon.[2]

Lack of congressional oversight was one of the causes of these failures. This lack, coupled with excessive secrecy and the use of fuzzy standards in administrative directives, and sometimes in the laws themselves, was the fertilizer for abuse and excess.

Today, compared with the era of the Church Committee, not only are we more partisan as a nation and in government, but the problem of oversight during the war on terror is that oversight must necessarily be of a sitting administration. This makes it much harder. Nonetheless, principles that the current administration has advocated—such as that presidents are above the law—raise concerns that our founders understood and guarded against and create precedents that are dangerous in the hands of a president of any party. So the question is whether those who are responsible for oversight have the wisdom and the courage to rise above the moment and together take a long term, nonpartisan view of what best serves our country.

CREATING THE COMMITTEE

On January 27, 1975, the U.S. Senate created a Select Committee to investigate the intelligence agencies of the United States, including the Federal Bureau of Investigation (FBI) and the Central Intelligence Agency (CIA). The Committee's mandate was to investigate the full range of government intelligence activities. The two most basic questions were (1) the extent to which the agencies' actions had been "illegal, improper or unethical," and (2) oversight: "the nature and extent of executive branch oversight" and the "need for improvement" of congressional oversight.[3] The Committee became known as the Church Committee for its chair, Idaho's Frank Church (D), elected nineteen years earlier at the age of thirty-two.

The Committee issued its final reports in April 1976. Here are just two examples of the disclosures. First, internal FBI documents used Orwellian language to label Martin Luther King Jr. the leader of a "Black Nationalist *Hate* Group." Then the Bureau set out secretly to destroy King, including sending an anonymous letter with an enclosed tape that appeared to be designed to induce him to commit suicide.[4] A second revelation was the years of CIA assassination plots, including the hiring of Mafia members to try to kill Fidel Castro.[5]

Other examples of intelligence agency misconduct are mentioned below. Beyond exposure of agency misconduct, the Committee highlighted grave deficiencies of presidents, attorneys general, and other high executive branch officials. The same went for Congress.

HOW DID THE INVESTIGATION HAPPEN?

Powerful, secretive intelligence agencies do not like their dirty laundry exposed. Presidents do not want executive branch responsibility examined. Congress traditionally had shied away from its intelligence oversight responsibilities. Why, then, in 1975 did the Senate—and later the House—launch major investigations of the intelligence agencies?

For the investigation to happen, pent-up interest in what America's hidden government had been doing was necessary. There had been rumors of assassination plots. A break-in to an FBI office in Pennsylvania had found documents suggesting secret harassment of dissidents. And finally, in December 1974, Seymour Hersh wrote a series of *New York Times* articles exposing "massive" CIA domestic spying and illegal intelligence operations directed against antiwar activists and other American dissidents.[6]

Coupled with interest in what our secret government had been doing was increased public mistrust of government. This stemmed from the Vietnam War and Watergate. Many senators and members of Congress also worried about their country and about the balance of power between the executive and legislative branches.

But while the interest and the increased mistrust were *necessary* for the investigation, neither would have been *sufficient* to unleash or allow the Church Committee investigation. Three factors helped.

First, Gerald R. Ford had recently become our first unelected president. He had pardoned Richard Nixon. Having taken over from a man discredited and disgraced for violating the law and abusing his power—including attempting to coopt the CIA and the FBI—President Ford had a problem. On the one hand, he wanted to appear open or, perhaps more important, did not want to appear to be hiding impropriety. On the other hand, powerful advisors like Henry Kissinger opposed any meaningful cooperation. Ford had to be pushed—repeatedly—to allow the Committee access to the crucial raw files and relevant witnesses. Nonetheless, ultimately he chose not to face a public fight with the Senate committee over access.[7]

Second, after directing the FBI for almost fifty years, J. Edgar Hoover was dead. With good reason, public officials feared Hoover, as well as the general public's reverence for the FBI. The Church Committee came across a striking example of Hoover's power. After understanding the colorful details of the Castro assassination plots (and others), the crucial question became whether Presidents Eisenhower, Kennedy, and Johnson had authorized the plans. In the case of

Kennedy, the Committee uncovered the fact that a mistress of the Mafia don hired by the CIA to kill Castro was at the same time one of JFK's mistresses. Was she a go between? We concluded no. But in the course of examining this case, we came upon a letter from Hoover to the White House and Attorney General Robert Kennedy that revealed that Hoover knew about the joint mistress.[8] After this, it surely would have been difficult for President Kennedy or his brother to replace Hoover or even effectively control him. Similarly, it seems unlikely that with Hoover alive, Congress would have unleashed a major investigation of the FBI.

Third, in contrast to today's Congress—where partisan diatribes chill debate and make wise action more difficult—Congress was then more collegial. Evidence was the decision by Majority Leader Mike Mansfield (D-MT) that the Select Committee's membership be six Democrats to five Republicans, at a time when regular committees were divided more favorably to the Democrats. It is also possible that some senators assumed revelations of presidential misconduct would be limited to the already disgraced Nixon. As it turned out, however, one of the Committee's most important contributions was to show that all presidents, starting with FDR, had failed in their duty to supervise the secret government. Moreover, most had themselves been complicit in abuse.

AT HOME AND ABROAD: THE COMMITTEE'S DUAL FOCUS

The Church Committee covered domestic and foreign issues, as indicated by the titles of its main reports: *Alleged Assassination Plots Involving Foreign Leaders,* an Interim Report; *Foreign and Military Intelligence, Final Report Book I*; *Intelligence Activities and the Rights of Americans, Final Report Book II*; and *Detailed Staff Reports on Intelligence Activities and the Rights of Americans, Final Report Book III*. There were, of course, many common themes and questions. Had excessive secrecy facilitated abuse and caused mistakes harmful to the national interest? The same question was asked with respect to vague, ambiguous, or open-ended authorizing language voiced by presidents or contained in statutes. Had the executive branch exercised proper control? Did Congress have appropriate oversight? Had the programs and policies served the national interest? Finally, the most fundamental question: Should the United States, when faced with crisis, react by adopting "the tactics of the enemy?" In addition, the evidence, particularly as developed in questions by Senator Walter "Fritz" Mondale (D-MN), who led the work focused on the rights of Americans, showed that attitudes developed in foreign intelligence operations seeped through at home. Thus, disregard for the "niceties of law" was "brought home" from war by some of the FBI officials who were responsible for examples of despicable conduct at home, including the effort to destroy Dr. King.[9]

Despite the similarities, there were also fundamental differences between the Committee's approach to domestic and foreign issues. This is partially explained by the different standards applicable to intelligence activities affecting the rights of Americans, as opposed to intelligence activities overseas. To simplify, the former can be held to the U.S. Constitution, the Bill of Rights, and the majesty of the law. But the latter can best be held to the more general early words of the Declaration of Independence: "a decent respect to the opinions of mankind." In addition, reflecting a number of factors, the reports other than Book I were based on the supposition that detailed facts drive reform and thus were more fact-based and reflective of investigation. In contrast, Book I was more policy-oriented. Loch K. Johnson's book, *A Season of Inquiry* discusses the differences in approach in more detail.[10]

THE INGREDIENTS OF SUCCESSFUL OVERSIGHT

Frank Smist, in his book *Congress Oversees the United States Intelligence Community, 1947–1989,* divided *oversight* into two categories: "institutional" and "investigative." The institutional model sees oversight as a "cooperative relationship between the legislative and executive branches." The investigative model views oversight as involving an "adversarial relationship" between the two branches.[11] Of all the congressional committees responsible for intelligence oversight from 1947 through 1989 reviewed by Smist, the Church Committee was the only one characterized as "Investigative and Institutional Oversight Combined."[12] Oversight by the permanent Intelligence Committees created after the Church Committee are, generally speaking, examples of institutional oversight.

Recognizing the limits of my experience, I nonetheless tender five elements needed for successful oversight: a historical perspective; delving deeply and comprehensively into the facts; handling secrecy sensitively; having empathy for but also maintaining distance from the agencies; and being nonpartisan and sharing core values. (Discussion of the first four elements follows immediately; the last is discussed in the section on values.)

The Need to Understand History

One of the Church Committee's tasks was to assess how well our government had balanced liberty and national security during a time of crisis—the Cold War, roughly a 40-year period. What happened during earlier crises was also instructive. There was a pattern of overreaching, including the Alien and Sedition Acts at the dawn of our Constitution, the Palmer Raids after World War I, and the internment of Japanese Americans in World War II. The Cold War period was different from these in two respects: first, the crisis was much longer; and second, unlike the earlier periods, most of what the government did was secret. For the Church Committee to fulfill its mandate, it had to understand both the similarities to and the differences from the earlier eras.

In addition to remembering episodes from much earlier time, it was valuable to understand the historical origins of the programs reviewed by the Committee.

For example, consider how the FBI went from investigating possible criminal conduct to enormously broad spying on Americans who had done nothing to threaten their country. This, too, required a look at history.[13]

Harlan Fiske Stone was appointed attorney general by President Calvin Coolidge in 1924. Later he described the conduct of the Justice Department and the Bureau of Investigation (the original name of the FBI) before he took office, as "lawless, maintaining many activities which were without any authority in federal statutes and engaging in many practices which were brutal and tyrannical in the extreme." Shortly after taking office, Stone set a new standard for the Bureau. He warned that "a secret police may become a menace to free government and free institutions, because it carries with it the possibility of abuses of power that are not always quickly appreciated or understood." He then announced that the Bureau "is not concerned with political or other opinions of individuals. It is concerned only with their conduct and then only such conduct as is forbidden by the laws of the United States."[14]

Stone cleaned house and—with the support of the American Civil Liberties Union (ACLU)—promoted J. Edgar Hoover to direct the Bureau. Eight years later, Hoover was still marching to Stone's drum, telling Congress that because the Bureau was subject to "the closest scrutiny," it should not investigate matters which "from a federal standpoint, have not been declared illegal."[15]

But then, leading up to World War II, President Franklin Roosevelt issued a series of conflicting and confusing directives to Hoover. Some were consistent with the Stone standard, referring to investigation of conduct "forbidden by the laws of the United States" such as espionage, sabotage, and violations of the neutrality regulations. Others added the loose term "subversion." The President, Attorney General Homer Cummings, and Hoover explicitly decided not to seek legislation about their plans for expanded domestic intelligence; "in order to avoid criticism or objections," the plans "should be held in the strictest confidence," not even revealed to Congress.[16]

What was actually done during the Roosevelt years usually was appropriate investigation of possible criminal conduct by Nazis or Nazi sympathizers. But the Bureau did, on occasion, investigate perfectly lawful conduct of entirely legal groups such as the League for Fair Play, formed, according to the Bureau, by "two ministers and a businessman for the purpose of furthering fair play, tolerance, adherence to the Constitution, democracy . . . and good will among all creeds, races and classes." The FBI also started a decades-long infiltration of the National Association for the Advancement of Colored People (NAACP), even though it was clear from the outset that its purposes were entirely lawful. And at the Roosevelt White House's request, the Bureau opened files on all who had sent telegrams to the White House expressing approval of a speech by Charles Lindbergh, one of the President's leading critics.[17] Still, what was most important about the Roosevelt era was that the vague word subversion, and the decision to keep secret the fundamental change in approach planted seeds for the abuses highlighted by the Church Committee.

The Importance of Facts

Without facts, oversight will be empty. Moreover, the facts must be detailed and cover a wide range. Only with that kind of record can one or be sure one understands patterns or be confident of conclusions.

An Emotional High Point: Senator Phillip Hart Shows
How Facts Can Change Minds

On November 18, 1975, the Committee began its public hearings on the FBI. Reflecting the Committee's bipartisan approach, Senator Church and Vice Chairman John Tower (R-TX) opened the hearings by stressing the importance of "periodic public scrutiny" (Church) and "establishing a complete and open record" (Tower).[18] Further demonstrating the bipartisan nature of the inquiry, the hearing started with Chief Counsel Schwarz and Minority Counsel Curtis Smothers jointly providing a lengthy opening presentation of evidence and what it showed about the Bureau, presidents, and attorneys general.[19]

After counsel provided a detailed and disturbing litany of lawlessness, Chairman Church turned to questions and comments from senators, first recognizing Michigan's Senator Phillip Hart (D). Church expressed pleasure at Hart's return after "some weeks of absence." What Church did not say—but everyone knew—was that Hart had been away being treated for the cancer that killed him the next year.

Noting that he did not "recommend that others pursue the course I took to get this advantage" of commenting first, Hart began by telling how he had for years rejected claims of FBI impropriety: "As I'm sure others have, I have been told for years by, among others, some of my own family, that this is exactly what the Bureau was doing all of the time, and in my great wisdom and high office, I assured them that they were—it just wasn't true. It couldn't happen. They wouldn't do it." Then Hart described how the facts recounted by counsel had changed his mind and set out the two broad challenges facing the Committee:

> What you have described is a series of illegal actions intended squarely to deny first amendment rights to some Americans. That is what my children have told me was going on.
>
> The trick now, as I see it, Mr. Chairman, is for this Committee to be able to figure out how to persuade the people of this country that indeed it did go on. And how shall we insure that it will never happen again? But it will happen repeatedly unless we can bring ourselves to understand and accept that it did go on.[20]

Johnson's book about the Committee describes this as an "emotional high point"—Hart's weakened voice, tears in the eyes of staffers, and "in the opinion of many observers, the Committee's finest moment."[21]

Access to Facts and Witnesses

But of course, there can be no mind changing unless one has the facts.

Reports about the facts by the government agency itself are often useful but seldom sufficient. A good example of where internal reports can be insufficient, indeed misleading, arose in the Committee's investigation of the FBI's Counterintelligence Program (COINTELPRO)—"an ugly little acronym which would have been at home in any police state."[22] After hints about COINTELPRO appeared, Attorney General William B. Saxbe asked for an internal report. Revealingly, even though the Bureau was part of the Justice Department, it resisted letting the Attorney General's office see the COINTELPRO files, claiming that to do so would jeopardize national security. Instead, the Bureau said it would summarize the facts of each COINTELPRO action. These summaries were often extremely misleading. For example, one described a letter, purporting to come from the Chicago Black Panthers, that was sent by the FBI to the leader of the Blackstone Rangers, a "black extremist organization in Chicago." The Bureau's summary described the letter's purpose as to "hopefully drive a wedge between" the two groups. The actual letter, however, said the Panthers had "a hit out" for the Rangers' leader. And the actual cover memo that supported sending the letter said that the Rangers were prone to "violent type activity, shooting and the like." The cover memo predicted the letter may lead to "reprisals" against the Panthers' leadership.[23]

Development of a serious factual record also requires access to the actual contemporaneous documents and to witnesses, at both high and low levels. On this, the CIA proposed that an agency monitor should accompany any current or former intelligence official called in for questioning, including preliminary questioning by staff. In addition to observing, the monitors could give the witness "advice." Again showing the Committee's bipartisan approach, Senator Richard Schweiker (R-PA) said if this were allowed, "we'd be the laughing stock of the Hill," and Vice Chair Tower made the motion leading to a unanimous vote to reject.[24] Witnesses thereafter always appeared untethered.

Handling Secrecy Sensitively

Investigating secret government programs requires access to secrets. It forces analysis of the overuse of secrecy stamps and of the harm caused by excessive secrecy. Ultimately, it may require describing and revealing secrets. Nonetheless, obviously there are legitimate secrets. Oversight or an investigation that is heedless of that is doomed, as well as irresponsible.

The Church Committee worked out reasonable arrangements with the agencies and the White House. There were two key agreements. First, when the agencies were producing documents, they could, in the first instance, redact—or black out—the names of informers (not agents). Thus, the Committee would learn about the fact of FBI infiltration of the NAACP or what the FBI called the

Women's Liberation Movement and see the reports of the informers, without getting the informer's name. Then, if the Committee felt it was important to have the name, it would press for it. Second, the Committee agreed that before it issued its reports, it would let agencies see them to be able to argue that more details were being released than necessary or appropriate.

The Committee's reports are enormously detailed. They reveal much information that had been secret. No improprieties were withheld. But sensible limits were placed on the details disclosed. For example, the actual names of lower-level undercover agents who had been tasked by bosses to do unseemly or illegal acts were not used in the reports; the bosses's names, however, were included. Another example is shown by the introduction to the Staff Report on Covert Action in Chile, 1963–75, which noted that: "With few exceptions, names of Chileans and of Chilean institutions have been omitted in order to avoid revealing intelligence sources and methods and to limit needless harm to individual Chileans who cooperated with the Central Intelligence Agency."[25] These sensible agreements did not get in the way of the Committee's mission. The Committee was also helped by its record of avoiding leaks.[26] In contrast to the Church Committee, the parallel House committee floundered at the outset and floundered at the end on issues of secrecy.[27]

Having Empathy for but Maintaining Distance from the Agencies Being Overseen

The Church Committee started with the premise that "properly controlled and lawful intelligence is vital to the nation's interest." It is used, for example, to "monitor potential military threats . . . to verify compliance with international agreements . . . and to combat espionage and international terrorism."[28] In addition, fairness also required understanding for the difficult problems of the men and women who worked for the intelligence agencies. The government gave them assignments that were in many ways impossible to fulfill. They were expected to predict or prevent every possible crisis, respond immediately with information on any question, act to meet all threats, and anticipate and respond to the demands of presidents. Under that kind of pressure, is it any wonder that some cut corners? An additional point of perspective is that the illegal, improper, indecent, and silly conduct of some should not and does not indict whole agencies like the FBI and CIA that in the past and today perform vital work for this country.

Nonetheless, while understanding and respect are both necessary and appropriate, distance is also required. Many oversight bodies stumble by becoming too close to or advocates for the agencies they are meant to oversee. Moreover, agencies may try to divert overseers from their job—as FBI headquarters did in their first meeting with the Committee's chief counsel by showing pictures of severed heads on a city street. Certainly, the world of intelligence deals with many dangers. But the issue for oversight remained whether the agencies had been "governed and controlled in accord with the fundamental principles of our constitutional system of government," and whether they had done things that were "illegal, improper and unethical."[29]

A SUMMARY OF THE FACTS CONCERNING THE RIGHTS OF AMERICANS

The Church Committee concluded that too much was collected from too many for too long. What was collected was distributed far too broadly. Excessively intrusive (and often knowingly illegal) techniques were used to gather intelligence. Covert action—secret punishment—was used to harass, disrupt, discredit, and destroy law-abiding citizens and domestic groups. Vague language in statutes and instructions by high officials facilitated abuses. There was waste and inefficiency. There was political abuse of intelligence information by presidents and by the intelligence agencies, who sometimes distorted the facts on important national issues like civil rights and the Vietnam War. Finally, the law and the U.S. Constitution were repeatedly violated and often simply ignored. Extensive documentation of all these findings is in the Committee's reports and hearings. Here are just a few illustrative examples.

Too Much Was Collected from Too Many for Too Long

The NAACP was infiltrated by government informers for twenty-six years, even though it was clear from the outset that its purposes were entirely lawful.[30] The FBI also conducted a broad-scale investigation of the Women's Liberation Movement. Meetings of women all over the country were infiltrated. Voluminous reports were filed on their beliefs. And once this spying started, it just kept going in blind disregard of its total irrelevance to any lawful government interest. Thus, one lengthy report concluded that the purpose of the infiltrated women's gathering had been to "free women from the humdrum existence of being only a wife and mother." Based on that, was the investigation stopped? No, the recommendation was to keep on investigating.[31] The CIA's Operation Chaos also investigated the Women's Liberation Movement, even though the CIA was barred by the act that created it from "internal security functions."[32]

The Socialist Workers Party was infiltrated by government informers for forty years—even though bureau officials conceded it had not committed any crimes and that its rhetoric fell far short of incitement to violence. When the man in charge of that investigation was asked what sort of information was passed back to the FBI, he replied that it included their political positions on the "Vietnam War," on "food prices," on "racial matters," on "U.S. involvement in Angola," and on any of the Party's efforts to support a non-Party candidate for office.[33] That's a pretty wide net.

The numbers of people affected are further proof of how pervasive the government's surveillance network became.

- The FBI opened over 500,000 domestic intelligence files, each of which typically contained names of several individuals.[34]
- The NSA obtained copies of millions of international cables. Indeed, from 1947 until 1975 it obtained copies of every single cable sent by individuals or businesses from this country to overseas locations.[35]
- The Army investigated some 100,000 Americans for political reasons between the mid-1960s and 1971. These included such vitally important matters as a Catholic priests' conference on birth control in Colorado, and a Halloween party of Washington schoolchildren which was investigated because the Army suspected a local "dissident" would be present.[36]
- The CIA's illegal mail opening program produced a computerized index of nearly 1.5 million names.[37]

Against these huge numbers, the FBI's secret list of 26,000 citizens to be rounded up in the event of a national emergency pales by comparison. But how broad the Bureau's version of the threat was perceived to be is illustrated by two names on that list—Dr. King and Norman Mailer. Mailer was on a list of persons who would have to be locked up because of "subversive associations and ideology." This list included: professors, teachers, and educators; labor union organizers and leaders; writers, lecturers, newsmen and others in the mass media field, scientists, doctors and lawyers. King was also characterized as subversive.[38]

Surveillance Techniques

In addition to infiltrating many lawful domestic groups like the NAACP, the Socialist Workers Party, and the Women's Liberation Movement, intelligence agencies used techniques like break-ins, mail opening, wiretaps, and bugs.[39] Break-ins and mail opening were both conceded as illegal. Nonetheless, they were justified internally by the vague words subversion and national security.[40] In each case, the illegal program followed the pattern of expanding enormously as time went on. Thus, for example, the CIA's watch list for opening letters started with fewer than twenty names, but by the late 1960s had grown to approximately 600, including many citizens and organizations engaged in purely lawful and constitutionally protected protest against government policies. Among the domestic organizations on the list were Clergy and Laymen Concerned About Vietnam, *Ramparts* magazine, the Student Non-Violent Coordinating Committee, and the American Friends Service Committee. But it was not just people on a watch list who had their mail opened. Many others had their letters unsealed and read, including Senator Frank Church and author John Steinbeck. During the

1968 presidential campaign, the CIA opened a letter passing between a speech writer and Richard Nixon.[41]

Warrantless wiretaps and bugs can be seen as a more complicated story. But the essence is simple. Every time Congress or the Supreme Court restrained use of these techniques, the executive branch secretly evaded the restrictions. For example, after the Supreme Court applied to federal agents a congressional limit on warrantless wiretaps, Attorney General Robert Jackson ordered the FBI to stop such wiretaps. But President Roosevelt overruled his attorney general, saying (in a "confidential memorandum") that he was sure the Court did not mean to require warrants for "persons suspected of subversive activities against the United States." As with his earlier order to FBI Director Hoover, however, Roosevelt did not explain what he thought "subversive" meant or why warrants could not be sought. A decade later, the Supreme Court reaffirmed that evidence obtained from a warrantless bug that had been placed in a house through a break-in could not be used in a criminal prosecution. The Court was particularly offended by the microphone being planted in a bedroom. But just after this ruling, Herbert Brownell, attorney general in the Eisenhower administration, sent a secret memo to Hoover authorizing the continued "unrestricted use" of bugs whenever the Bureau concluded it was in the "national interest." Brownell said the FBI did not even have to inform the attorney general. This secret order, using fuzzy phrases like "national interest," again manifested a clear disregard for the law and opened the door for many abuses, such as the bugs of Dr. King's hotel rooms.[42]

Congress, supposedly responsible for overseeing the FBI, failed to uncover any of this for decades. But as the Church Committee concluded after its exhaustive look at all important activities of the intelligence agencies over more than three decades: "The imprecision and manipulation of labels, such as 'national security,' 'domestic security,' 'subversive activities' and 'foreign intelligence' have led to unjustified use" of methods like wiretaps and bugs, and excessive surveillance of Americans.[43]

Domestic Covert Action

Echoing the COINTELPRO effort to cause "violent reprisals" against the leader of the Chicago Black Panthers, the San Diego FBI office boasted about how our most respected law-enforcement agency was fomenting violence: "Shootings, beatings, and a high degree of unrest continues to prevail in the ghetto area of southeast San Diego. Although no specific counter-intelligence action can be *credited* with contributing to this overall situation, it is felt that a substantial amount of the unrest is directly attributable to [COINTELPRO]."[44]

There was much more to the FBI's campaign to destroy Martin Luther King than a note intended to provoke a suicide. After King's "I Have a Dream" speech, the FBI's Domestic Intelligence Division concluded that this "demagogic speech" established Dr. King as the nation's "most dangerous Negro leader." The FBI decided to "take him off his pedestal." It decided to secretly select and promote its own candidate to "assume the role of the leadership of the Negro people." Later, Bureau headquarters explained to the field that King must be destroyed, because he was seen as a potential messiah who could "unify and electrify" the "black nationalist movement." King was then described as a threat because he might "abandon his supposed 'obedience' to white liberal doctrines (non-violence)."[45] In short, a nonviolent man was to be secretly attacked and destroyed as insurance against his abandoning nonviolence.

The effort to destroy King was part of COINTELPRO, which meant illegal investigations and secret punishment, administered not by a court but by the government's chief law enforcement agency. Its aim was not a public arrest or a judicial trial, but a secret program to "harass and disrupt" dissidents and others deemed to be unacceptable. COINTELPRO's tactics were designed, for example, to break up marriages of civil rights workers, get teachers fired, destroy reputations of lawyers, sabotage political campaigns, encourage violent retribution by falsely and anonymously labeling intended victims as government informers, and stop citizens from speaking, teaching, writing, or publishing.[46]

COINTELPRO "resulted in part from frustration with Supreme Court rulings limiting the government's power to proceed overtly against dissident groups."[47] The government had the right and duty to prosecute lawless acts done, for example, by the Black Panthers or the Ku Klux Klan. But it had no right to secretly usurp the functions of judge and jury by covertly taking the law into its own hands. It had no right to try to foment deadly gang warfare against the Black Panthers. And it had no right to send dirty anonymous letters to the wife of a Klan member seeking to break up her marriage.[48]

The targets of COINTELPRO were not limited to the famous like Dr. King or those on the fringes of law abiding society like members of the Klan or the Black Panthers. Thus, among hundreds of examples:

- The Unitarian Society of Cleveland was targeted because its minister and some members had circulated a petition calling for the abolition of the House Un-American Activities Committee.[49]
- "Disinformation" concerning housing was sent to demonstrators coming to Chicago for the 1968 Democratic National Convention to cause them "long and useless journeys."[50]
- Nonviolent citizens who were against the Vietnam War were targeted because they gave "aid and comfort" to violent demonstrators by lending respectability to their cause.[51]

Political Abuse

All administrations from Franklin Roosevelt to Richard Nixon asked for and got political information from the FBI.[52] But there was a marked increase during the Johnson and Nixon administrations. Much of the information obtained was derogatory and personal. Most of the information reflected the FBI's having collected and filed too much from too many for too long.

- Examples of information asked for by the Johnson White House: during the closing days of the 1964 campaign, on all persons employed in the Senate Office of Senator Barry Goldwater (R-AZ); in the 1968 campaign, on vice presidential candidate Spiro Agnew's long-distance telephone calls; on seven senators who criticized bombing of North Vietnam; on all people who signed letters to Senator Wayne Morse (D-OR), supporting his criticism of the Vietnam War; on many mainstream journalists, including NBC anchor David Brinkley and *Life Magazine*'s Washington Bureau chief; and on authors of books critical of the Warren Commission report on the assassination of President Kennedy. For the Democratic Convention in Atlantic City in 1964, President Johnson directed the assignment of an FBI "special squad." Perhaps the original purpose was to guard against civil disorders. But as so often was the case, what started modestly grew beyond the pale. For example, the FBI sent many memos to the White House from the convention reporting on the political plans of the Mississippi Freedom Democratic Party and of Dr. King.[53]
- Examples of information asked for by the Nixon White House: on CBS reporter Daniel Schorr; on the Chairman of Americans for Democratic Action; on Ralph Abernathy (Dr. King's successor as head of the Southern Christian Leadership Conference) for the purpose of "destroying his credibility." The administration also received the fruits of warrantless wiretaps, lasting from 1969 to 1971 in a leak investigation of three newsmen and fourteen executive branch employees. Again this shows a widening of surveillance far beyond the purported reason for seeking the taps. The information reported was not focused on leaks but included: a report on a plan of Senator Edward Kennedy (D-MA) to give a speech on Vietnam; the planned timing of Senator J. William Fulbright's (D-AK) hearings on Vietnam; Senator Mondale's "dilemma" about a trade bill; and, what former President Johnson had said about the candidacy of Senator Edmund Muskie (D-ME) for the Democratic presidential nomination. The wiretaps continued on two targets after they left government to work on Muskie's campaign. (Revealingly, the memos began to be sent to H. R. Haldeman, the President's political advisor, rather than Henry Kissinger, who had first demanded the warrantless wiretaps for "national security reasons.")[54]

The FBI also used intelligence information to influence social policy and political action on the most important national issues, including civil rights and Vietnam.

In 1956, the FBI sent memos to the White House about the NAACP (which it had secretly infiltrated). In general, it suggested that communist or communist-front organizations were causing "a marked deterioration in relationships between the races." Director Hoover briefed the Eisenhower Cabinet on alleged communist influence in the civil rights movement. According to one historical account, this briefing "reinforced the President's passivity" on civil rights legislation.[55]

In 1963, the Bureau's Domestic Intelligence Division submitted to Hoover a memo detailing the Communist Party's "efforts" to exploit black Americans. It concluded the efforts were an "obvious failure." Hoover was not pleased. He made clear "we had to change our ways or we would all be out on the street." A new memo was sent: "The Director is Correct." Dr. King was the "most dangerous Negro" from the "standpoint of communism . . . and national security." It was "unrealistic" to limit ourselves to "conclusive proofs." Communist Party influence over Negroes "one day *could* become decisive." When the Hoover subsequently testified to Congress, he said communist influence *was* "vitally important."[56]

On Vietnam, President Johnson told Hoover he had "no doubt" communists were behind the demonstrations against the Vietnam War. Hoover agreed. Back at the FBI, Hoover told his associates that he knew the Bureau might not be able to "technically state" what the President wanted. But he wanted and got a "good, strong memorandum" that made communist "efforts" sound like communist success.[57]

The Law: Breaking It, Ignoring It, and Fuzzy Words Replacing It

The Church Committee uncovered lots of illegal, improper, and immoral conduct, which can only be touched on here.[58] What did the actors think about what they were doing? Did the vague and fuzzy secret instructions and the pressure they got from presidents and other high officials open the door to misconduct?

Many never gave a thought to the law or the Constitution. As the man who headed the FBI's Domestic Intelligence Division for ten years testified: "Never once did I hear anybody, including myself, raise the question: 'Is this course of action which we have agreed upon lawful, is it legal, is it ethical or moral.' We never gave any thought to this line of reasoning, because we were just naturally pragmatic."[59] Similarly, the White House author of the Huston Plan (see Volume 4, Appendix B), where the heads of the major intelligence agencies proposed to President Nixon knowingly illegal mail opening and break-ins (not saying the proposed actions were already actually being done), testified that nobody at the meetings ever objected to undertaking illegal acts—indeed legality or constitutionality was never discussed.[60]

The first reaction of the National Security Agency's general counsel to learning that the Committee had found out that for decades the NSA had illegally obtained every single cable sent out of the United States by Americans was that the Constitution and the law did not apply to the NSA because it worked on "foreign" intelligence. Similarly, when asked if he was concerned about the legality of the NSA's warrantless interceptions of electronic communications, the agency's deputy director replied: "That particular aspect didn't enter into the discussions."[61]

And when the former head of the Bureau's Racial Intelligence Section was asked whether during COINTELPRO's history anybody at the FBI discussed its constitutionality or legality, he answered, "no, we never gave it a thought."[62]

Of course, there were many others who did think about legality and who clearly knew their actions were illegal. For example, at least four internal memoranda recognized that the CIA's mail opening program had "no legal basis," that "federal statutes preclude the concoction of any legal excuse," and that exposure could "give rise to grave charges of criminal misuse of the mails by government agencies."[63] Similarly, despite receiving advice from the Federal Communications Commission that its monitoring of the radio communications of amateur radio operators was illegal, the Army Security Agency plowed ahead with the monitoring.[64]

The CIA's experiments with the effect of drugs such as LSD started with volunteers but moved to unsuspecting victims—or in the Agency's sterile jargon, "unwitting subjects"—at "all social levels, high and low, native American and foreign." Recognizing that drugging unknowing subjects was illegal and potentially dangerous, Richard Helms, who later became Director of Central Intelligence, successfully sought approval: "While I share your uneasiness and distrust for any program which tends to intrude on an individual's private and legal prerogatives, I believe it is necessary that the agency maintain a central role in this activity." One of the subjects was Dr. Frank Olson, a scientist working with the U.S. Army Biological Center. At a conference of CIA and Army scientists, he was given a dose of Cointreau laced with LSD. He later died.

Knowledge of the CIA's illegal and unethical drug experiments was kept secret for decades, because, as the CIA's Inspector General wrote: "Precautions must be taken not only to protect operations from exposure to enemy forces, but also to conceal these activities from the American public in general. The knowledge that the Agency is engaging in unethical and illicit activities would have serious repercussions in political and diplomatic circles and would be detrimental to the accomplishment of its mission." After Olson's death had dramatized the dangers, the Agency continued to experiment with unwitting subjects for ten years. Those involved in Olson's doping were given a letter from CIA Director Allen Dulles that criticized them for not giving "proper consideration to the rights of the individual to whom it was being administered." But Helms was instructed to inform them that the letter was "not [a] reprimand," and that no personnel file notation was made.[65]

OBSERVATIONS REGARDING OVERSIGHT OF
AMERICA'S FOREIGN INTELLIGENCE AGENCIES

Given space limitations (and the fact that after completion of the Assassinations Report, I did not focus on foreign intelligence), I make only a few points about foreign intelligence here. To begin with, before the Church Committee, congressional oversight of the CIA and other foreign intelligence agencies was an embarrassment. The Senate and House intelligence oversight subcommittees lacked written records, and often they asked no questions; never did they ask tough questions. As Clark Clifford reflected later, "Congress chose not to be involved and preferred to be uniformed." A longtime CIA general counsel concluded that the lack of congressional oversight ultimately caused *problems* for the Agency because "we became a little cocky about what we could do."[66]

William Colby, CIA director during most of the Church Committee investigation, reached a similar conclusion. The congressional investigations were "necessary" and "effective." "This year's excitement," he wrote in a February 1976 *New York Times* op ed piece, "has made clear that the rule of law applies to all parts of the American Government, including intelligence . . . this will strengthen American intelligence."[67] In its *Final Report*, Book I, the Church Committee provided extensive analysis of the strengths and weaknesses of America's foreign intelligence agencies, calling, for example, for more attention to be given to human intelligence—that is, regular spying.

VALUES SUSTAIN INVESTIGATIONS

Having obtained and disclosed the facts, the Committee had to answer two big questions that depend on values.

- Should the United States, faced with a powerful, often unscrupulous, and sometimes vicious enemy adopt the enemy's tactics?
- Should Congress—and the American public—be trusted with the truth?

The Committee first publicly addressed these questions in its report on assassinations.

On November 20, 1975, the Senate convened in executive session to discuss the Committee's *Interim Report* on assassination plots. All eleven Committee members had signed the report. However, President Ford and CIA Director Colby opposed its public release. At this executive session, the first crack in the Committee's unity began to appear. Senator Barry Goldwater said he had signed the report only as "an act of gratitude for the hard work done by the Committee and the staff"; public release of the report would be a "spectacle of public self-flagellation" that would hurt our reputation abroad. On the Senate floor, Senator Tower who, along with Senators Church and Gary Hart (D-CO), had been the Committee members on a subcommittee that worked for weeks on the report before it was presented to the full Committee, said he was "distressed and sorry," but he wanted "to publicly disassociate [himself] from public release of the report" because a number of senators had decided they did not want to vote on the issue of public release.[68] After several hours of discussion, but without any vote against (or for) release, the report was issued when the Senate adjourned shortly after 1 P.M.[69]

Beyond the fascinating stories about plot details (see, e.g., Volume 3, Appendix F) and beyond the question of presidential authorizations lay key principles—key then and key today. Should the United States, when faced by unscrupulous enemies, adopt their tactics? Should the American people be allowed to know what their government had been doing? Would doing so harm our reputation in the rest of the world?

The Committee's work as a whole stands as answers to these questions. Those answers were first expressed publicly in the assassinations report whose last words, in an epilogue, were:

> The Committee does not believe that the acts which it has examined represent the real American character. They do not reflect the ideals which have given the people of this country and of the world hope for a better, fuller, fairer life. The United States must not adopt the tactics of the enemy. Means are as important as ends. Crisis makes it tempting to ignore the wise restraints that make men free. But each time we do so, each time the means we use are wrong, our inner strength, the strength which makes us free, is lessened. Despite our distaste for what we have seen, we have great faith in this country. The story is sad, but this country has the strength to hear the story and to learn from it. We must remain a people who confront our mistakes and resolve not to repeat them. If we do not, we will decline; but, if we do, our future will be worthy of the best of our past.[70]

There have been, of course, those who say the tactics of the enemy *should* be adopted. They claim necessity. Thus, for example, in 1954 the secret report of a special committee, formed to advise President Eisenhower on covert activities, said the United States may have to adopt tactics "more ruthless than those employed by the enemy." "Hitherto acceptable norms of human conduct do not apply." "Long standing American concepts of American fair play must be reconsidered."[71]

The Church Committee noted that "it may well be ourselves that we injure most if we adopt tactics more ruthless than the enemy's."[72] And the committee's *Foreign and Military Intelligence Report* concluded that those planning covert actions "rarely noted" the possible harm the actions could cause to "this nation's ability to exercise moral and political leadership throughout the world."[73]

Throughout, the Church Committee's view was that the United States must not adopt the tactics of the enemy. On this, the Ccommittee members never wavered, never split.

On the second big question—whether the American public could be trusted with the truth—the Committee also remained united that the embarrassing and unseemly revelations in the report on *Intelligence Activities and the Rights of Americans* should be made public. Indeed, Senators Robert Morgan (D-NC) and Howard Baker (R-TN) in their additional statements commented (in a bipartisan way) on the favorable impact of making the *Rights of Americans* Report public.

- Morgan: "Releasing this report is a great testament to the freedom for which America stands." He added, "It is my sincere hope that the Report . . . will rekindle in each of us the belief that perhaps our greatest strength lies in our ability to deal frankly, openly and honestly with the problems of our government."[74]
- Baker: While disagreeing (articulately as always) with a number of the Committee's recommendations for reform, Baker opined that the abuses being "fully aired to the American people" would have a "cathartic effect" on the FBI and CIA. (He supported this conclusion by quoting the article by former CIA Director Colby that said "this year's excitement" will "strengthen American intelligence.") Baker added: "It is important to disclose to the American public all of the instances of wrongdoing we discovered."[75]

Earlier, Senator Charles M. Mathias (R-MD) provided eloquent and concise views on both the two big values questions:

- "Painful political problems are seldom solved by silence. As crude as the story unfolded here may seem, it can be the source of important lessons for the future." And, quoting James Madison, he said, "Knowledge will forever govern ignorance and a people who mean to be their own Governors must arm themselves with the power which knowledge gives," adding, the Committee "sought to stop the erosion of society's values caused by excessive secrecy and unchecked Executive power by making the factual record as accurate and clear as possible."
- "History shows that men and governments have come to recognize the compelling force of ethical principles. The torturer who was once an adjunct of the courts themselves is today an international outlaw. By recognizing the sacredness of human life, mankind has sought to shed such barbarisms, barbarisms that have usually led to further violence and often to the destruction of the leaders and nations who resorted to them."[76]

WRESTLING WITH RESPONSIBILITY

On the question whether presidents, attorneys general, and other high-level officials in the executive branch were responsible for the many acts of agency misconduct recounted in the Committee's reports, the Committee's thinking evolved toward a "yes" answer.

Early in the assassinations investigation, Senator Church speculated to the press that the CIA may have acted as a "rogue elephant on a rampage," conceiving and carrying out the plots without authorization from outside the agency.

In contrast, other senators, also speculating, opined that the CIA "took orders from the top."[77]

When the assassinations report was issued several months later, the Committee rejected both theories, demonstrating that there was support for either conclusion but saying the conflicting evidence made it impossible to be sure whether Presidents Eisenhower and Kennedy (both dead for many years) had authorized the plots during their administrations. (The Committee found that President Johnson had not.[78])

Five months later, when it issued its final reports covering the gamut of its investigation, the Committee was ready to fix responsibility at the top. In the *Final Report on Foreign and Military Intelligence (Book I)*, the Committee concluded: "On occasion, intelligence agencies concealed their programs from those in higher authority; more frequently, it was the senior officials themselves who, though pressure for results created the climate within which the abuses occurred."[79]

The Final Report on Intelligence Activities and the Rights of Americans (Book II) reached the same ultimate conclusion with more details. Though intelligence agencies did, on occasion, fail to reveal their programs or acts to their superiors, "the most serious breaches of duty were those of senior officials who were responsible for controlling intelligence activities and generally failed to assure compliance with the law."[80] The Committee elaborated: fault at the top was shown by "demanding results" without paying attention to means, "failing to inquire further" after receiving indications that improper activities had been occurring, delegating broad authority using fuzzy phrases like "national security" or "subversion" and then failing to require adequate guidelines or procedural checks on what actually was done, and "exhibiting a reluctance to know about secret details of programs."[81]

The change in emphasis as the Committee's work progressed was the product of exposure to the whole record. Looking at specific agency acts individually sometimes did show the agencies acting on their own, or even misleading their superiors. But when the full record, over many years, was examined, ultimate responsibility was properly fixed with the presidents, attorneys general, and other high executive branch officials for the sorts of reasons already outlined. To the Committee's chief counsel looking backward thirty years later, it seems there were also at least three more reasons to fix that ultimate responsibility with higher authority. The power of the FBI was such that although it was wrong, it was not surprising that attorneys general exercised only weak oversight. But they knew that was what they were doing. The doctrine of plausible denial was originally designed to implement covert actions overseas in a way calculated to conceal American involvement if the actions were exposed. The doctrine was then extended to the internal decision-making processes of the government itself. As explained by Richard Bissell (the principal CIA architect of the assassination plots), the Director of the CIA (Allen Dulles, who was dead) was supposed to have informed the presidents of the plots (and other covert actions) by talking "circumlocutiously."[82] The Committee described the doctrine of plausible deniability as "a delusion and at times a snare."[83]

One consequence of plausible denial was that witnesses before the Committee constantly confronted it with a bureaucratic shell game. High-level officials, generally outside the agencies, repeatedly disclaimed knowledge of improper or illegal activities—and suggested that agency personnel were concealing their own nefarious acts. Officials within the agencies consistently said they had the *tacit* approval of their superiors, and suggested the superiors were dissembling about their knowledge and approval. The Committee found both accusations to be true at times. But it found in all cases that the authorization and responsibility facts were confused. It seems likely that both bosses and operatives found that useful. It is certain that ambiguity as to authorization increases the risk of abuse.

However one cuts through the fog of plausible deniability to decide who was responsible for any given action, what is crystal clear is that the presidents, national security advisors, and other high executive branch officials knew about the plausible deniability system. Therefore, if—and this is a big if—they did not know about a particular action, they were nonetheless culpable because they had knowingly turned a blind eye to what was going on.

Finally, presidents and other high-level executive branch officials also knew that all intelligence activities, domestic and foreign, were smothered in layers of excess secrecy. They knew that Congress and the courts played no meaningful role. And they knew (or should have known) that the combination of excessive secrecy, the absence of checks and balances, and the use of fuzzy, vague authorizations were (as they remain today) a recipe for excess and abuse.

SOME GENERAL LESSONS

First, prolongation of crisis is particularly hard for constitutional democracies. There were more than thirty years between Franklin Roosevelt's re-institution of an open-ended, secret (indeed concealed), and poorly controlled security regime and Nixon's fall. For all this time, America was at war, or in a Cold War. It felt beleaguered. To refer again to the language of the Church Committee report on assassinations, crisis "makes it tempting to ignore the wise restraints that make men free," and to use means that are wrong—means that lessen "our inner strength, the strength that makes us free," as well as undermining the reputation that helps make us strong.

Second, a perfect storm of institutional shortcomings stirred a brew of immoral or illegal acts that could not be squared with a "decent respect to the opinions of mankind." It was not evil that caused us to do what we ought not to have done. It was zeal, fostered by excessive secrecy; vague instructions and implicit nudges or winks joined to pressure for results without attention to means; and oversight that was either lacking altogether, empty, or knowingly chose to turn a blind eye.

Third, foolish secrecy fertilizes the soil from which abuse grows. Clearly, there is much about intelligence work that is properly kept secret. Examples such as the names of agents and technological details of collection methods are obvious. Nonetheless, unnecessary secrecy served to inhibit and often prevent any sober review of the basic programs and practices themselves. If a tactic cannot survive the light of day, it likely should not be born. A related point is that seldom, if ever, were the consequences of exposure weighed before a program was begun. Similarly, a foolish expectation of perpetual secrecy increased the likelihood that the harmful effect on America's reputation of adopting the tactics of the enemy would be ignored.

Fourth, secrecy was the handmaiden of blinded oversight—or sometimes intentionally blind oversight. Congress played no meaningful role. Congress is not perfect, but it can add wisdom and help avoid mistakes. Because of excessive secrecy, the good sense of the American public was also barred from any debate.

Fifth, whatever the explanation for the use of euphemisms or simple falsehoods to describe or justify dirty business, it seems certain that failure to call dirty business by its rightful name increases the chance of dirty business being done. Words about dirty business were often sterilized. For example, Bissell thought CIA directors should talk to presidents about killing using euphemisms or circumlocuitous language. (Even years later, during the Committee's investigation, those who had worked on killings could not bring themselves to use simple, honest, direct words to describe what they had done. Instead, just as in the contemporaneous documents, they used phrases such as "dispose of," or "get rid of," or "eliminate," or some such euphemistic circumlocution.) Similarly, when Richard Helms recommended that the CIA continue to experiment by giving drugs to unwitting subjects, he used sanitized, bleached, and lifeless words— "uneasiness," "distaste," "tends to intrude"—about stark realities of death and lawlessness. Finally, when Bureau officials used Orwellian language to describe Martin Luther King Jr. as the leader of a black nationalist "hate" group, perhaps deep down they hoped to feel better about the dirty business they set out to do.

Sixth, every intelligence program we looked at started with investigating, harassing, or attempting to destroy targets who were on the fringes of law-abiding society and then moved progressively further toward mainstream dissidents and finally began to cover ordinary citizens. Thus, as shown, the CIA's knowingly illegal mail opening program was initially advocated as a way to catch foreign spies and ended up checking up on organizations like the American Friends Service Committee. COINTELPRO started by harassing the U.S. Communist Party and ended by harassing hippies. The NSA started by decoding encrypted telegrams from foreign embassies and widened its net to include anti–Vietnam War and civil rights protestors.

In criticizing his own earlier efforts, Tom Charles Huston (White House coordinator of the Huston Plan in which the CIA, the NSA, and other intelligence agencies sought official sanction for lawlessness for things they had long been doing and which they continued to do after President Nixon rescinded his written approval) put well the tendency for the net to widen. There is, he testified to the Committee, the risk that governmental surveillance would: "Move from the kid with a bomb to the kid with a picket sign, and from the kid with the picket sign to the kid with the bumper sticker of the opposing candidate. And you just keep going down the line."[84]

Seventh, those who conclude that reform is needed need to make their case based on facts exposing wrongdoing. Nonetheless, a "Senate Committee is not a prosecutor, a grand jury or a court." It is far better suited to determine how things went wrong and what can be done to prevent their going wrong again, than to resolve disputed questions of individual "guilt" or "innocence."[85]

Congressional committees or citizen commissions that fail to recognize this distinction make splashes, but not waves. As the Church Committee said, they provoke a national debate on "who did it," not on "how did it happen and what can be done to keep it from happening again?"[86]

NOTES

1. The Church Committee reports cited most extensively are: *Final Report of the Select Committee to Study Governmental Operations with Respect to Intelligence Activities, United States Senate: Foreign and Military Intelligence* (Washington, DC: Government Printing Office, 1976), hereafter Bk. I; Book II: *Intelligence Activities and the Rights of Americans* (Washington, DC: Government Printing Office, 1976), hereafter Bk. II; Book III: *Supplementary Detailed Staff Reports on Intelligence Activities and the Rights of Americans* (Washington, DC: Government Printing Office, 1976), hereafter Bk. III; *Interim Report: Alleged Assassination Plots Involving Foreign Leaders* (Washington, DC: Government Printing Office, 1975), hereafter *Assassinations*. The seven volumes of Church Committee hearings are *Hearings Before the Select Committee to Study Government Operations with Respect to Intelligence Activities of the United States Senate, Volume 1: Unauthorized Storage of Toxic Agents; Volume 2: Huston Plan; Volume 3: Internal Revenue Service; Volume 4: Mail Opening; Volume 5: The National Security Agency and Fourth Amendment Rights; Volume 6: Federal Bureau of Investigation; and Volume 7: Covert Action* (Washington. DC: Government Printing Office, 1976). A full text archive of all reports and hearings of the Church Committee is available online at http://www.aarclibrary.org/publib/church/reports/contents.htm. Books on the Church Committee include Loch K. Johnson, *A Season of Inquiry: The Senate Intelligence Investigation* (Lexington: University Press of Kentucky, 1985); Frank J. Smist, *Congress Oversees the United States Intelligence Community, 1947–1994* (Knoxville: University of Tennessee Press, 1994), esp. chap. 2; LeRoy Ashby and Rod Gramer, *Fighting the Odds: The Life of Senator Frank Church* (Pullman: Washington State University Press, 1994), esp. chap. 16, pp. 453–92.

2. See Bk. II, p. viii.

3. Senate Resolution 21, January 27, 1975. The resolution is also an appendix to Johnson, *A Season of Inquiry*.

4. For the FBI's treatment of King generally, see Bk. II, pp. 11–12, 219–23, and Bk. III, "Dr. Martin Luther King, Jr., Case Study," pp. 79–184. For "hate group," see Bk. III,

pp. 179–80. For effort designed to get King to commit suicide, see Bk. II, pp. 11 and 220–21, and Bk. III, pp. 158–61.

5. For Castro plots, see *Assassinations*, pp. 17–180, 255, 257, 263–70, 270, 274–77.

6. See Johnson, *Season of Inquiry*, p. 9, for reference to various articles, including Hersh's.

7. For a summary of these disputes and their resolution, see Johnson, *Season of Inquiry*, pp. 27–44, 45–48.

8. This incident is described in *Assassinations*, pp. 129–30.

9. For "brought home," see Bk. II, p. 212n.7.

10. Johnson, *Season of Inquiry*, pp. 23–44, 86, 125–29, 273.

11. Smist, *Congress Oversees*, pp. 19–24.

12. Ibid., chap. 2, pp. 25–82.

13. For the Church Committee's history of the FBI, see Bk. II, "The Growth of Domestic Intelligence," pp. 21–136, and Bk. III, "The Development of FBI Domestic Intelligence Investigations," pp. 373–538. The FBI's antecedents and its early history are in Bk. II, pp. 23–28, and Bk. III, pp. 378–400. For the Committee's history of the CIA, see Bk. I, pp. 97–125.

14. For Stone's views on the Bureau and his policy announcement, see Bk. II, pp. 23–24; Bk. III, pp. 388–95.

15. See Bk. III, pp. 384, 391.

16. The Roosevelt memos and Hoover's records of conversations with Roosevelt are set out in Bk. III, pp. 391–406 and summarized in Bk. II, pp. 24–27.

17. For the League for Fair Play, see Bk. II, p. 32, and Bk. III, p. 415. For the NAACP, see Bk. III, p. 416. For Lindbergh, see Bk. II, p. 33.

18. For "periodic public scrutiny," see *Hearings Before the Selection Committee to Study Government Operations with Respect to Intelligence Activities of the United States Senate, Volume 6: Federal Bureau of Investigation* (Washington: Government Printing Office, 1975), p. 1. For "establishing a complete and open record," see ibid., p. 3.

19. Ibid., pp. 4–40.

20. Ibid., p. 41.

21. Johnson, *Season of Inquiry*, p. 129.

22. For "ugly little acronym," see Frederick A. O. Schwarz Jr., "Intelligence Activities and the Rights of Americans,"*The Record of the Association of the Bar of the City of New York* 32, no. 1/2 (January/February 1977), pp. 43, 46. For COINTELPRO generally, see Bk. II, pp. 10–12, 65–94, 211–23. See also Bk. III, "COINTELPRO: The FBI's Covert Action Programs Against American Citizens," pp. 1–79.

23. Bk. II, pp. 271–72n.20.

24. See Johnson, *Season of Inquiry*, p. 43.

25. See Staff Report on *Covert Action in Chile, 1963–75*, preface.

26. There were only two leaks stemming from the Church Committee. One included information about Kennedy's romantic relationship to the person whom the Committee's report described as a mutual "friend" of the President and the mafia boss hired to kill Castro. The other involved a staff member who was overheard in a restaurant discussing a position that had been taken by a Senator (not on the Committee) in connection with oversight. (The staffer was fired.) Neither leak affected national security. See Smist, *Congress Oversees*, 38, 48–49.

27. See Smist, *Congress Oversees*, chap. 4, pp. 134–213, particularly pp. 136–37, 143, 156–57, 169–71, 175–76, 183–87, 211–13.

28. Bk. II, p. v.

29. Bk. II; Senate Resolution 21.

30. For general discussion of too much information being collected, see Bk. II, pp. 6–10, 165–82. For NAACP, see Bk. II, pp. 8, 179–80.

31. Bk. II, p. 7.

32. Ibid., p.102.

33. Ibid., p.180.

34. Ibid., p. 6.

35. For the numbers, see Bk. II, pp. 6, 12; Bk. III, p. 740 ("the largest governmental interception program affecting Americans"). For the NSA generally, see Bk. II, pp. 6, 12, 104, 210–12; Bk. III, "National Security Agency Surveillance Affecting Americans," pp. 733–83.

36. For the numbers, see Bk. II, p. 6. For the birth control conference and Halloween party, see Bk. II, p. 8. For Army investigations generally, see Bk. II, pp. 77, 167, and Bk. III, "Improper Surveillance of Private Citizens by the Military," pp. 785–834.

37. See Bk. II, p. 6. For the CIA (and FBI) illegal mail opening programs, see Bk. III, "Domestic CIA and FBI Mail Opening," pp. 559–677.

38. For general discussion of the Bureau's detention lists, see Bk. II, pp. 54–56, and Bk. III, pp. 436–47, 510–16, 542–48. For the categories of detention and "subversive associations," see Bk. II, p. 55. For Mailer's inclusion on the list, see Bk. II, p. 56. For King's inclusion, see Bk. III, p. 87.

39. For break-ins generally, see Bk. II, pp. 61–62, 190–92, 204–5. See also Bk. III, "Warrantless Surreptitious Entries: FBI 'Black Bag' Break-Ins and Microphone Installations," pp. 353–71. For mail openings generally, see Bk. II, pp. 58–59, 190–92, 203. See also Bk. III, "Domestic CIA and FBI Mail Opening Programs,"pp. 559–677.

40. For illegal and combating subversion, see Bk. III, p. 358; for national security, see Bk. II, for example, pp. 141, 144, 145.

41. For growth in the CIA's watch list and the people and organizations covered, see Bk. II, pp. 208–9 and Bk. III, 573–74. For the letter to Nixon, see Bk. II, p. 8. For nearly 1.5 million names in a CIA database derived from mail-opening, see Bk. II, p. 6.

42. See Bk. III, pp. 278–79. Jackson reversed the Justice Department's policy concerning wiretapping in Order No. 3343, issued March 15, 1940, prohibiting all FBI wiretapping. Bk. III, p. 279, quoting memorandum from Roosevelt to Jackson, May 21, 1940; Bk. II, p. 190, quoting memorandum from Brownell to Hoover, May 20, 1954.

43. Bk. II, 205. See also Justice Robert H. Jackson's opinion in *Youngstown Sheet and Tube* referring to the "loose and irresponsible" use of "adjectives . . . without fixed or ascertainable meanings" like "inherent" or "war" powers. *Youngstown Sheet and Tube v. Sawyer*, 343 U.S. 579, 646–47 (1952).

44. Bk. II, p. 218 (emphasis added).

45. For "most dangerous and effective Negro leader," see Bk. II, p. 11, and Bk. III, pp. 107–9. For "take him off his pedestal" and "assume the role of the leadership," see Bk. II, p. 11, and Bk. III, pp. 136–37. For "hate group," see Bk. III, pp. 179–80. For "messiah," see Bk. II, pp. 11–12, and Bk. III, p. 180.

46. For examples of COINTELPRO methods, see Bk. II, pp. 216–19. See also Bk. III, pp. 7–8. For "embarrass the Bureau," see Bk. II, p. 156, quoting the FBI Manual.

47. See Bk. II, p. 211, and Bk. III, pp. 10–11. For the Smith Act, see 18 U.S.C. §2385 (which remains on the books); *Yates v. United States*, 354 U.S. 298 (1957); *Watkins v. United States*, 354 U.S. 178 (1957).

48. See Bk. II, pp. 216–17; Bk. III, COINTELPRO chapter, pp. 51–52.

49. Bk. II, p. 214n.14.

50. Ibid., p. 216n.34.

51. Ibid., p. 213. See also Bk. II, p. 214n.19.

52. For political uses generally, see Bk. II, pp. 225–52.

53. Bk. II, pp. 228–31, 235–36.

54. Ibid., pp. 230–31, 23–36.

55. See Bk. II, pp. 232–33. For "marked deterioration," see Bk. II, p. 233n.40. For Hoover's subsequent briefing, see Bk. II, pp. 250–51n.151a. For the historical account, see J. W. Anderson, *Eisenhower, Brownell, and the Congress: The Tangled Origins of the Civil Rights Bill of 1956–57* (Tuscaloosa: University of Alabama Press, 1964), p. 34.

56. Bk. II, p. 250, emphasis added.

57. Ibid., 251.

58. The Church Committee's first finding in *Intelligence Activities and the Rights of Americans* covered "Violating and Ignoring the Law," Bk. II, pp. 137–63.

59. Bk. II, pp. 14 and 141.

60. Ibid., 141.

61. Author's recollection of conversation with NSA general counsel. Testimony of NSA Deputy Director Benson Buffham, *Hearings Vol. 5: The National Security Agency and Fourth Amendment Rights*, p. 45.

62. Bk. II, p. 140.

63. Ibid., pp. 142–48.

64. Ibid., p. 144; and see generally Bk. III, "Improper Surveillance of Private Citizens by the Military," pp. 785–834.

65. For CIA drug experiments generally, see Bk. I, "CIA Drug Testing Programs," pp. 392–411. For "unwitting subjects," p. 391; Helms memo, p. 394; Olson story, pp. 394–99; I.G. memo, p. 394; continuation, p. 403; Dulles letter, pp. 398–99.

66. The Clifford and CIA general counsel quotes are in Smist, *Congress Oversees*, pp. 5 and 9.

67. William Colby, "After Investigating U.S. Intelligence," *New York Times*, (February 26, 1976), p. A30.

68. Johnson, *Season of Inquiry*, pp. 130–37.

69. Ibid.

70. *Assassinations*, epilogue, p. 285.

71. See James Doolittle, et al., *The Report on the Covert Activities of the Central Intelligence Agency*, September 30, 1954, quoted in Bk. I, p. 50, and *Assassinations*, p. 259n.1.

72. *Assassinations*, p. 259.

73. Bk. I, p. 156.

74. Bk. II, pp. 363–65.

75. Ibid., pp. 373–75.

76. *Assassinations*, pp. 345–46.

77. Johnson, *Season of Inquiry*, p. 57.

78. For authorization evidence and conclusions as seen in *Assassinations*, see pp. 6–7, 51–70 (Lumumba), 91–180 (Castro).

79. Bk. I, p. 137.

80. Bk. II, p. 137.

81. Ibid., pp. 139, 265.

82. *Assassinations*, pp. 111, 118.

83. For plausible deniability generally, see *Assassinations*, pp. 11–12, 277–78.

84. Bk. II, p. 4.

85. Ibid., viii.

86. Ibid. See also Aziz Huq and Frederick A. O. Schwarz Jr., *Unchecked and Unbalanced: Presidential Power in a Time of Terror* (New York: New Press, 2007).

3

A CONVERSATION WITH FORMER DCI WILLIAM E. COLBY, SPYMASTER DURING THE "YEAR OF THE INTELLIGENCE WARS"

LOCH K. JOHNSON

AS EXAMINED IN THE PRECEDING CHAPTER, the Church Committee carried out a sweeping inquiry in 1975 into charges that the Central Intelligence Agency (CIA) had violated its charter by spying on citizens within the United States. This year is remembered by historians as the most extensive probe into the CIA since its founding in 1947. Many intelligence professionals inside the Agency recall the investigation as a period of great trauma—the Year of the Intelligence Wars between the CIA and Congress.[1] At the helm of U.S. intelligence at the time was William Egan Colby, the Director of Central Intelligence (DCI). In that capacity, he was the titular leader of the entire intelligence community and directly in charge of the CIA, where the office of the DCI was located at the time (and until 2005) on the Seventh Floor of the Agency's headquarters building in Langley, VA, adjacent to McLean.

As DCI, Colby conceded to *New York Times* reporter Seymour M. Hersh that a laundry list of wrongdoing by CIA officers, dubbed the "family jewels" by Agency insiders, had been compiled by his predecessor, James R. Schlesinger, who during his few months as DCI in 1973 set out to clean house.[2] It was, to say the least, a turbulent time for Colby—"one of the worst times in Agency history to become DCI," notes an Agency historian.[3] Colby found himself torn between a White House (under President Gerald R. Ford), which wanted him to be less forthcoming with lawmakers, and the Church Committee, which hounded him each day of the sixteen-month inquiry for more documents, more witnesses, and more candor. He attempted to strike a balance between the two demands, feeling that he had to be reasonably forthright with the Committee or else its members might react angrily by emasculating his beloved Agency. Convinced that lawmakers might even abolish the CIA if Colby failed to cooperate with the investigation, the DCI decided to court the Church Committee and demonstrate to its members that intelligence could be made accountable to Congress. His mantra became another form of the CIA acronym: "Constitutional Intelligence for America," a slogan that seemed to many Ford administration officials as far too conciliatory to the Church panel. One of Colby's predecessors, Richard Helms—highly regarded among members of the CIA's Operations Directorate, where both Helms and Colby had pursued their intelligence careers—scorned Colby's deferential approach, arguing privately among colleagues that the best response to Congress was to hunker down until the storm subsided.

Perilous circumstances were nothing new to Colby, nor was controversy. As a young intelligence officer in World War II, he had joined forces with Norwegian insurgents in parachuting expeditions behind German lines to conduct sabotage operations against the Nazis in Scandinavia. During the Vietnam War, he had headed up Operation PHOENIX from 1968–71, a program designed to "neutralize" (read: apprehend or kill) the Viet Cong infrastructure in South Vietnam. The PHOENIX program led to the death of about 20,000 (Colby's estimate)— some say 60,000—suspected Viet Cong fighters or sympathizers. Colby maintained after the war that these deaths were a necessary part of the conflict, a byproduct of warfare. His critics, though, viewed the program as a massive assassination operation, anathema to American values.[4]

The critics had long memories. In 1979, when I was a staffer member with the House Permanent Select Committee on Intelligence and responsible for organizing a series of hearing for Representative Les Aspin (D-WI) on CIA relations with the media, then-retired Colby came to testify on this subject. Waiting for him in the back row of the hearing room were two young men with buckets of red paint they intended to throw over him in a protest against PHOENIX. The two were apprehended by Capitol Hill police before Colby arrived.

Just as Colby had performed well under fire in Norway and had responded calmly to the criticism rising from Operation PHOENIX, so did he steadfastly take on the task in 1975 of steering the CIA and the other intelligence agencies through the Charybdis of the Ford White House and the Scylla of the Church Committee. Certainly there are legions of intelligence officers who viewed him as too soft during that *annus horribilis*—even a turncoat—but many others inside and outside the intelligence profession admired his skill at navigating this tight strait in rough seas. As Frank Church's assistant during this time, I found Colby charming, bright, more or less cooperative in fulfilling document requests and calls for witnesses, and clearly correct about the need to work with Congress—or face the prospects of an infuriated investigative committee at a time when there was unambiguous evidence that the CIA and other agencies had improperly spied against innocent Americans exercising their First Amendment rights to protest against the war in Vietnam and in favor of the civil rights movement.

From the point of view of the Church Committee, Colby—however charming—was no pushover. For example, he strongly and successfully resisted the Committee's plan to hold public hearings on several covert actions that at the time were (and remain) classified. He negotiated with Senator Church over every step of the inquiry and often persuaded the Committee to back away from some subjects that had nothing to do with illegal domestic espionage. On the subject of domestic improprieties, however, he was forthcoming and personally unhappy that they had occurred.

Colby was born on January 4, 1920, in St. Paul, Minnesota, the son of a U.S. Army officer who traveled with his family in tow to a number of assignments, including a stint in China.[5] A fine student, Colby went to Princeton University and graduated in 1940, then followed his father's footsteps into the Army, volunteering for active duty as a second lieutenant in August 1941. In 1943, he shifted over to the Office of Strategic Services (OSS), operating behind enemy lines in France as well as Norway. He earned a law degree at Columbia University after the war, practiced his profession briefly in New York (1947–49), and then went to work with the National Labor Relations Board in Washington, DC (1949–50). He joined the CIA in 1950. He rose through the ranks of the Operations Directorate, serving as chief, Far East Division, from 1962–67, before becoming director of Civil Operations and Rural Development Support in Saigon and head of the PHOENIX program (under the cover of the Agency for International Development) from 1968–71.

On returning to Agency Headquarters in Langley, he became the executive director and then comptroller from 1972–73 and—the plumb position for an operations officer, Deputy Director for Operations (DDO)—for six months in 1973. At the end of this brief period of work at the pinnacle of the clandestine service within the CIA, Colby was selected as the nation's top spymaster, the DCI, serving in this capacity from September 4, 1973, to January 30, 1976, in the midst of the Watergate and domestic spying scandals.

After his retirement in 1976, Colby authored two well-received books, his memoir, titled *Honorable Men*, and a book on his experiences in Vietnam titled *Lost Victory*.[6] Pointing to the French-language edition of the memoir, the CIA accused him of revealing classified information during his tenure as DCI about an intelligence collection operation that employed a deep-sea mining vessel, the *Glomar Explorer*, to salvage a Soviet submarine that had exploded and sunk in the Pacific Ocean near Hawaii. Colby agreed to pay $10,000 in an out-of-court settlement. For some, it seemed a petty retaliation by certain elements in the Agency against Colby for his "coziness" with the Church Committee. More conspiratorial still, some Colby supporters wondered if his death on a canoeing trip in 1996 might have had sinister causes. Police accounts, though, concluded that he had suffered a stroke or heart attack while canoeing in bad weather near his home at Rock Point, Maryland, with no evidence of foul play.

Five years before his death, as U.S. troops went to war in the first Persian Gulf War against Iraq, I sat down with him in his Washington law office on January 22, 1991, to discuss his career and the evolution of modern intelligence in the United States. Tanned and relaxed, he leaned back in his chair and smiled as I began the recorded conversation with questions about the Church Committee and the system of intelligence oversight it had established in the aftermath of the 1975 investigation.

INTELLIGENCE OVERSIGHT

Johnson: Let me begin by asking you about this "grand experiment" we have been having in intelligence oversight. Do you think it has worked out all right?

Colby: I think it's worked out very well. Of course, there are glitches here and there, and some arguments. I think that Iran-*contra* was a direct violation of the deal, in both the respects of the refusal to send the finding over [to the congressional Intelligence Committees] on the Iranian part, and then coming up with the thesis that the Boland Amendment did not apply to the NSC [National Security Council], which was pure sophistry. I'm surprised [then DCI William J.] Casey didn't pick that up, because the Amendment very clearly says: "*any* agency engaged in intelligence activities." So if you engage, you're automatically included; it doesn't give you it by name. You will have that kind of thing forever: little things that happen here and there.

Johnson: The quality of intelligence oversight often seems uneven.

Colby: It's the same throughout the government. Sometimes people on the Agriculture Committees worry about what is happening in the Agriculture Department, and sometimes they don't. I think that's typical.

Johnson: Do you think that legislators tend to focus in when something goes wrong?

Colby: Oh, sure. That's the way the Hill works, which is fair enough; but they also look at things in the annual budget, which is down to a line-item thing. I remember one incident. Some people came to me with the idea of putting a bug out in one of the trust territories in the Pacific. I sent it up to the lawyers. I said, "Look, this is a trust territory. Is it outside the United States, or is it inside the United States?" And a lawyer came back and said, "It's outside." And I said, "Well, I don't think this will be worth a helluva lot, but okay, let's try it for three months and see what happens." Well, it leaked and Congress complained. I told them the operation had been there all along in the line-item budget. "It was there for you to ask about," I reminded them.

As I say, I never thought it was going to do a helluva lot of good, but I didn't want to put out the word throughout the Agency: "We're going to stop everything because of fear. So let's do the things. If they work, fine; if they don't, the hell with it."

Johnson: How do you develop comity between the branches?

Colby: I don't think you get comity. It's a deliberate separation of powers. I explained our government to a foreigner one time. I said, "Look, you're familiar with establishing a coalition government in your country. You establish a coalition, you agree on a program, and then everything more or less goes through because you have party discipline. You have to realize that in this country we have to establish a new coalition on each issue. There's no party discipline, so each issue has to have its own coalition." So it's consensus that you need, rather than comity.

There was a case here, I noticed in the paper, though it's a little fuzzy, that apparently before the attack in Panama [the United States invaded Panama in 1989] somebody came up with the idea of running a coup against Noriega. The possibility was mentioned in the *PDB* [*President's Daily Brief*]. This idea apparently got all the way to one of the [congressional oversight] committees, as was proper. The committee's members were being briefed on it, as they should have been. And it got into a discussion. If he's killed in the middle of the coup, is that an assassination? And it went back and forth, they mulled it over, and they finally decided not to do it. Instead [of a covert action], they [the first Bush administration] sent 24,000 troops and killed several hundred Panamanians; but I suspect that was the correct decision, because you'd still be hearing about the assassination of Noriega for the next hundred years—and you will not be hearing about the attack on Panama for the next hundred years.

Johnson: I think I've heard you say before that you would not even have ordered an assassination against Hitler before we declared war in 1941.

Colby: Before, no. After, it's an act of war; generals are just as subject to being killed as privates.

Johnson: What about assassinating Saddam Hussein instead of going to war against Iraq and inflicting perhaps thousands of casualties?

Colby: I basically think, no. You have to say, that's what happened in Panama [where the decision was made to arrest rather than kill the president, Manuel Noriega]. It's a tough moral issue. It's a very close call; but I think from the country's point of view, it's better to have a flat prohibition—except in war. And I don't mean to be fancy about war; I mean when our young men are dying, and the other country's young men are dying, then you can go after the top man.

Johnson: Are we likely to have another DCI in the future like Casey who does not appreciate oversight?

Colby: Yeah, sure.

Johnson: There is no way to get around that?

Colby: No, you just count on the tension in the constitutional system to work; and if it doesn't work and gets caught, then there's a back-up [judicial proceedings] that's supposed to work for a while when someone goes off the reservation. It's like the laws against murder: murders take place even though we have laws, and we punish them when it happens.

Johnson: What about the question of access to information by Congress? Is the "sources and methods" argument a bit phony when it's brought up by the Agency in this context, as a means for avoiding the sharing of information with legislators?

Colby: I think it's pretty sincere, though they undoubtedly stretch it. Particularly on agent names, we did convince both [Senator Frank] Church [D-ID] and [Representative Otis] Pike [D-NY] to leave out the names [in their committee reports].[7] We pretty well got through that whole thing without names. It was critical. And the return on it was to be reasonably responsible. There's your comity; even when you're antagonists, you can have comity.

Johnson: Unless you're dealing with Otis Pike and some of his people?[8]

Colby: Oh, they were impossible!

Johnson: A lot of this depends upon personality.

Colby: Yes, of course it does—the character of the person and so forth. Back to sources and methods, the technological people—especially the cryptography people—are hyper about revealing anything, because it's just indoctrinated in them since Year One that if the other side learns you're reading their stuff, then they change their codes and there you are: you're lost. They just learn that from childhood. So that's why they get so upset. And when they have some new whizmo up in the sky that does something new and different, they want to keep a monopoly on the information. But you know, you can buy satellite photography now that is probably better than what we were guarding when I was DCI.

HUMINT

Johnson: If Congress were to examine the quality of HUMINT [human intelligence, collected by agents, as opposed to technical intelligence—TECHINT—gathered by satellites and other machines], wouldn't it have to get into some aspects of sources?

Colby: Yes, but you don't have to get into details. You see, you have undoubtedly seen some of the DDO [Deputy Directorate for Operations] reports and there's a source part: it's descriptive of the source, but it's also fuzzed enough so that you couldn't put it right smack on point. Now if you take the text and it says, "He [the agent] and I were in the garden and we had the following conversation—" and you get that back to the originator, he knows damn well who was in the garden and you've got trouble.

Johnson: No member of Congress would want to know a name anyway, would he or she?

Colby: I don't think so. Once in a while there was a demand for a name of who was receiving subventions [money and other forms of remuneration from the CIA]. There were a few of those, where there were prominent people around the world who were getting help from us. They might also want to know who the intermediary was: "Are you sure these guys don't just pocket the money and run away with it?" This is a legitimate question, and you explain what you do to cross-check with some reasonable control; but quite honestly, you say, "I can't guarantee there isn't any waste here." Yes, it can happen; but still and all, we see the results and the activity that we're paying for, and therefore they [the legislators] seem reasonably happy about it.

CONGRESSIONAL ACCESS TO INFORMATION

Johnson: What about the timing of Congress's access to information?

Colby: I think Stan Turner [Adm. Stansfield Turner, DCI from 1977–81] said it about as well as anyone. He said at one point, when they were talking about this 48-hour stuff,[9] "Look, before Desert One, I had sent people over there [to Iran] in little planes to check out the desert to see whether it would hold the weight of a C-15. I am not able to look a young man like that in the face and tell him that I'm not going to tell ten congressmen [about the mission]; at the same time, I'm not going to lie to him. So, I need that kind of flexibility." I don't think you can write a law to cover it, but I think what you can say is [that] after the event, then Congress would have the right to review whether it was reasonable to withhold the information. In that case, they would have said yes.

But if it had been a jackass operation from the word go, then it might be that it would be reasonable to withhold that individual's involvement and the particular thing he did; but, in the same way, the Congress should have been informed that there was an overall program—as it probably was on the hostage rescue thing. I imagine there was some kind of briefing: that we are going to run some kind of operation some day, without any particular specifics. I would be surprised if [President Jimmy] Carter hadn't arranged for a few of the leadership [in Congress] at least to be brought into the fact that we're going to do something to try to get these people out.

Johnson: And if Congress doesn't like the rationale?

Colby: Then it can raise a fuss.

A GRAND CHARTER FOR INTELLIGENCE

Johnson: What do you think about the idea of a "Grand Charter" for Intelligence?[10] Has that gone the way of the dinosaurs?

Colby: That's gone. I was for it, I was for it. You could diddle with the details, but I've always been interested in getting intelligence a charter—a solid, statutory base—for its functions within the American government. The history of our intelligence is that we use it when we need it, and we throw it away when we don't. We throw away the organization. After World War I, after World War II—Truman tried to throw it away. It's sufficiently institutionalized now that I don't think you can throw it away, but that's part of what the charter proposal was about.

Johnson: I guess we're getting little pieces of the charter.

Colby: You've got little bits of it. I mean, this Agent Identity legislation, the "graymail" thing, the special court [for wiretaps]—that's a fabulous idea.[11] Star chamber! [Laughs.] It's so fascinating that the American citizen carries his constitutional protections with him even when he goes abroad.

FUNDING FOR INTELLIGENCE

Johnson: Does the CIA have access to money outside the appropriations process?

Colby: No.

Johnson: One example might be proprietaries...

Colby: We ran into that when we sold Air America when I was there. I've forgotten how much money we made off that—several millions of dollars, I guess. And I said, "Why don't we save the taxpayers some money? We've got this money; why don't we subtract it from next year's appropriation and use this?" I said, "Go up and talk to the Hill about it." They were interested, and then they ran into this general provision of law that says, "No agency of the government will spend nonappropriated funds." It was determined that the only thing one could do with that money was turn it in to the Treasury as miscellaneous receipts, and you had to get your full appropriation out of Congress, which is basically a good idea, because various intelligence services around the world have gotten into trouble by self-financing and going into their own deals, totally out of control, as the French did at one time.

Johnson: How do we know DCIs have indeed turned such profit over to the Treasury?

Colby: It's set into the rules. Now a proprietary will turn its own money over while it's still alive; in other words, you set up an air transport proprietary, you tell it to go out and do a certain amount of legitimate business so that you have cover for its other business. It'll turn over that basic capital.

Johnson: What if it makes huge profits?

Colby: Huge profits just build up; you can't take it anywhere. Now you may get a bigger airline, which is a little bit what happened to Air America. It got too big, in my mind.

Johnson: In the Iran-*contra* case, private American and foreign governments were willing to give money to pay for our intelligence operations...

Colby: Well, with respect to foreign governments, I don't know if they did or not; I can't answer that question.[12] There is an attempt in Congress now to write law that says, "Thou shall not urge a third country to do what you have not had authority from our Congress to do." President [George H. W.] Bush pocket-vetoed this, because he said it would stop you even from having diplomatic conversation with another country.

Johnson: That seems stretching it to me.

Colby: If you make the distinction that, "Why don't you help those guys?" and it's a direct relationship between those two; but "Why don't you give me money to help those guys?"—no, that's wrong. But I don't object to our government suggesting to the French government that it help the opposition against [Col. Muammar] Qaddafi [the leader of Libya].

Johnson: But should that be reported to the congressional oversight committees?

Colby: You don't have to report everything from a diplomatic exchange. It becomes a matter of whether it's an operation or whether it's just chit-chat. Again, how are you going to define that? If it's cooperation, then clearly you have to report it; but if it's just suggesting that somebody else do something useful, that's not quite the same.

WHITE HOUSE DETAILEES

Johnson: What about this question of detailees?[13] The argument that they run operations against the White House...

Colby: You wouldn't have a Director [DCI] very long.

Johnson: Where is the loyalty of these individuals?

Colby: It's like military officers. In my experience with military officers, you tell them what their chain of command is, and they salute. The same is true with the CIA. Whether there's a little back-channel chatter on what's going on, I'm sure that occurs in the military and everywhere else; but in terms of someone using the position to spy for the Agency, I can't believe that. I would say that if you have a CIA career officer and you send him on TDY [temporary leave to serve as a designee] that you don't put him in the Peace Corps.

Johnson: And you don't make them Fulbright Scholars.

Colby: Right. Obviously we put people undercover all the time. Some of the political sections in the embassies are upset about this.

Johnson: You've spoken about the problem of "vanishing cover."[14]

Colby: Oh, it drives me up the wall. It's a serious problem. . . . So, obviously we've put people undercover, but in those situations they normally have a dual commitment; but what you're referring to is ostensibly, but not actually, a single commitment. I would have doubts that that would be at all feasible. There might be some informal chatter. And old friend calls up and says, "What the hell are you guys doing?" That's part of Washington.

MORE ON HUMINT

Johnson: Is HUMINT valuable?

Colby: It's one of those things, you can't afford to say no, because sometimes it can be. It's a very difficult subject. If in times of crisis, you have an agent in Baghdad, you would have a helluva time communicating to him right now. On the other hand, if he were reasonably close to the Revolutionary Command in the week before the crisis, he might have been able to give us a tip—that "He [Saddam Hussein] really is going [to invade Kuwait in 1990]. This is no bluff." I gather that was the analytical conclusion anyway. And of course, you go through years with nothing much happening, and then you cut off the relationship. We were in the process of closing the stations in El Salvador and Portugal just before [those countries] blew up; nothing had happened there for ten years! [Laughs.] And I was under a lot of pressure to squeeze down in personnel. So it's a tough subject. But I think that . . . well, when the Soviet Union was a monolith, then a little window into this section was quite valuable, because you had a reasonable case that what you saw there was probably typical of what was going on in the rest of the monolith.

    Nowadays, with the Soviet Union spilling all over hell's half-acre and all sorts of voices coming from all sides, using a human agent doesn't have the same value. A human agent in the United States would be absolutely worthless [for a foreign intelligence agency], unless you want some highly technical subject. So, it's a tough subject; but I think you'll always have some, and they'll pay off. And remember that the human agent is also available to somehow manipulate [a foreign government].[15]

THE DISSEMINATION OF INTELLIGENCE

Johnson: What can be done about the dissemination side of intelligence?[16]

Colby: Not very much. You do now pretty well disseminate it—you know, the estimates and that sort of thing to Congress. When [William H.] Webster [DCI from 1987–91] had to say that he thought the situation in Eastern Europe was irreversible, and [Secretary of Defense Dick] Cheney was trying to get a budget for Defense, Cheney was sore as hell. But it had its effect. It didn't have an effect on the administration's budget, but undoubtedly it's going to have an effect on the congressional budget.

Johnson: Where do you come down on the Sherman Kent argument versus those who think intelligence officers ought to be closer to policy makers?[17]

Colby: I think it ought to be closer—not supportive, but it has to be close enough to be related to what the hell is going on. When intelligence was sort of way over here in the early Nixon years [in other words, apart from the interests of decision makers in the government] . . . that was when Henry [Kissinger] was saying, "Oh, what is all this crap?"—it was true.

Johnson: Did [DCI] Casey carry this closeness too far?

Colby: I don't know that any allegation has been made that even Casey was warping the conclusions to fit the policy. I haven't heard that, one way or the other. Some guy [analyst] is always going to say that, if the DCI doesn't agree with him. That's one of the protections you have. The Agency is not a disciplined monolith. If you get something that does upset somebody, it'll come out sooner or later; then, you either defend it or admit that you shouldn't have done it. But that's a pressure point.

INTELLIGENCE COLLECTION AND ANALYSIS

Johnson: Are there any breakthroughs in methodologies for analyzing intelligence?

Colby: I know we were experimenting with some quantitative stuff. As you know, I did break up the Board of National Estimates, because I thought it was so generalist it was lacking in expertise. Then you need some protection against the Agency being the only source of opinion, and I think you get that through the [intelligence] community—having the arguments with the Navy, the Army, or whatever.

Johnson: Do we try to gather too much intelligence?

Colby: Not for a big nation. If I were Israel, I'd spend my time on the neighboring Arab armies and I wouldn't give a damn about what happened in China. We are a big power, and we've got to worry about all of the world.

COVERT ACTION

Johnson: Is covert action really all that useful?

Colby: I think it would be a mistake to get rid of it. Did we overuse it? Probably in some cases. But I think some of the major covert actions were very effective: the Laos case, Western Europe.

Johnson: What about Afghanistan? Was covert action effective there [in the 1980s]?

Colby: Afghanistan, certainly. Even you might say Cambodia. I don't know about Angola. All that was part of the Cold War, the containment policy. The Bay of Pigs was a disaster, of course. But what if it had worked?

DCI–WHITE HOUSE RELATIONS

Johnson: What about DCI access to the White House? Can you mandate it?

Colby: I don't think you can mandate it. I think Casey had too much [during the Reagan years]. I think [Richard] Helms had about the right amount with [President Lyndon B.] Johnson—the Tuesday "lunch group," you know. He was in the circuit. He was quite meticulous about not taking a policy position. But he was still in on the President's agonizing, so he knew how to manipulate the machinery, too. You either support the President, or offer advice that he was on the wrong track. I think the Pentagon Papers are quite a tribute to Helms; you know, Johnson was not the most patient guy in the world.

Johnson: What about your own access?

Colby: I had very little. I had all I wanted to [National Security Adviser] Brent [Scowcroft]. I was on the phone to him every day or so. [Secretary of State] Henry [Kissinger] I'd see fairly frequently. President Nixon was such a retired fellow that you didn't see him very much—though [on those occasions when he did talk to me] he would listen and often disagree, which was fair enough. [President] Ford was more regularized. He'd have the meetings in the NSC on the various issues, so you'd prepare for those. He wasn't very informal on that sort of thing.

Johnson: So Nixon wasn't very interested in meeting with DCIs?

Colby: No, I think one time he called me up and asked me what was happening in China—just out of the blue.

Johnson: Ford didn't seem to treat you well.

Colby: I understood what his problem was. He was taking such a pasting on [intelligence] issues [in 1975–76] that by stepping in and putting his own man in [in other words, Colby as a replacement for DCI James R. Schlesinger]— and, remember, one of the motives of this thing was to conceal the dumping of a vice president [Spiro Agnew]; that was behind the scenario—and, of course, Ford never understood Schlesinger, so he just threw me in as an also-ran.

COUNTERINTELLIGENCE

Johnson: What about the Nosenko case?[18] Did [CIA Chief of Counter-intelligence James J.] Angleton order that confinement?

Colby: No, apparently he did not. Apparently there is even some doubt that he had anything to do with the actual confinement. I don't know. This was before my time. Obviously, he was in the loop of the whole thing, but what he knew about the confinement, I don't know. And I can't name who did. It's the thing that scared me the most. The assassination of a foreign leader may be dumb, but to take someone and put him in jail in the United States . . . what the hell happened to habeas corpus? This is pretty fundamental. For an in-telligence agency to do that in this country—Jesus! Though I gather Nosenko accepted it as "So what's new?" [Laughs]

Johnson: What are the chances that the CIA is currently penetrated at the top? Especially by the Soviets.[19]

Colby: It would be my guess, no. I can't say no absolutely. If it is, you don't know. We did have Alger Hiss, and those punks at various levels; then that Chinese fellow at FBIS, which was a surprise to me.[20] I don't say it's impossible. I just don't think so. Frankly, I think we would have heard about it by now. The big thing we have, which the British did not have, was the security clearances and the polygraph. Now I don't believe in the polygraph either, but it sure as hell helped us. My security people told me that, faced with the polygraph, people told us things that caused us not to hire them. As far as I'm concerned, it paid for itself right there.

Johnson: But the polygraph is no fool-proof system?

Colby: No, and the real weakness was, once you get in [as an employee of a U.S. intelligence agency], there wasn't enough periodic checking.

CIA OVERSIGHT

Johnson: How well has the IG [Inspector General] system worked inside the CIA?

Colby: Well, it's like the IG in the military. They do periodic inspections, and they're a useful investigating team for the director if something is strange. He just tells the IG to look into it. It's a bureaucratic mechanism to get something done; but as a great safety valve, I'm not so sure—any more than the IOB [Intelligence Oversight Board, a panel for intelligence accountability established in the White House in 1976]. I mean, it's there, but I don't think [it always works well] ... Congress is the real safety check.

Johnson: And the press?

Colby: And the press certainly; and the feeling that if something is wrong, people will make it known. I have no idea how many sources someone like Seymour Hersh [a *New York Times* reporter] has, but it must be dozens; they must be all over the place. And so if anything is seriously wrong, it'll come out.

Johnson: Some say the FOIA [Freedom of Information Act] is the most important source of oversight.

Colby: Well, in a way, but now they've exempted the operations files from that—for good reason; it was just a useless exercise. I think it's the press and Congress, and the sort of the traditional feeling that if something is bad you should do something about it. The normal, good, loyal American citizen will think.

THE ROLE OF THE DCI

Johnson: Is the DCI biased toward the CIA?

Colby: If anything, the DCI is inclined to take kind of a position showing that he is not biased. He obviously knows [the CIA] better; his contact with the rest of the services is episodic.

Johnson: Do we need a more powerful DCI?

Colby: I think you've got to have a very close, coordinating mechanism. We use to have weekly meetings of the U.S. Intelligence Board, at which you get the senior representatives of each of the agencies there. This was very useful, because you could argue things out, you know, discuss them. And it was helpful not only in the substantive discussion of what's happening in Argentina (if you're making an estimate or something), but also in the practical sense—you know, how many of these goddamn satellites do we really need? Do we need fifty, or do we only need ten? And you work through those things. You do a lot of staff work beforehand—each agency does.

Johnson: As DCI, does one feel in control of the Agency?

Colby: I think you have to work at it, and that means you have to use your chain of command. You also have to have some independent reporting as to what's going on. You get out of your chair and go out and look . . . talk to people. It's like running General Motors. You're not going to run everything in General Motors; but you can have the auditors and you have the other people to keep it under some semblance of control. I think that business of being in control also has something to do with the attitude of people. When George [H. W.] Bush came into the office [as DCI, following Colby in 1976], there was this wonderful story about him. Three days after he got there, they were having this meeting and somebody said, "Well, there's a story in the press that says we did this or that." And Bush said, "What are they trying to do to us?" *Us* after three days. [After that], he had the place in the palm of his hand.

Turner was at the opposite end. He was afraid of them.

I use to say that one should have an outsider [as DCI], with an insider deputy, because the inside deputy will give the local knowledge and the outsider will give you a little of the independence. You take somebody who comes up through the career [ranks of the CIA]; you're ideas are shaped by what you did during the career. I always thought the best director I ever knew, including myself or anyone else, was John McCone [DCI from 1961–65], and he was an outsider. His first deputy was an outsider, too, General [Charles Pearre] Cabell; but there were other professionals who ran the different directorates.

Johnson: Why was McCone so good?

Colby: He was just such a consummate manager. He would say, "I want this done by tomorrow morning. I want this. I want this. Where is it?" No softness. "Goddamn it, let's get it done!" He had the place totally excited. He'd go down to the White House, and write up six questions on a piece of paper on his way back in the car. He turned this over to [the dean of the CIA's intelligence analysts] Sherman Kent or whoever and say, "I want these answered by 8 o'clock tomorrow morning: 'If we do this, what will China do? If we do that, what will the Soviets do?' Answer those questions." And, of course, they [the analysts] loved it. Absolutely loved it. They worked like hell, and he would then go in and make no bones about what he thought about it [the analytic products].

Johnson: We've drifted away from the notion that we ought to have a military person as DDCIA [deputy director of the CIA, the second in command at the time after the DCI].

Colby: Yeah, we use to feel we had to, but I don't think you do now. I think the reason you don't need to now is that the DIA [Defense Intelligence Agency] fulfills that function—giving senior status to the military. It use to be we thought that to keep some semblance of comity with the military that we had to have a military deputy [at the CIA, as deputy to the DCI]. This is not so important now.

COLBY'S SELF-APPRAISAL

Johnson: What were your most important contributions as DCI?

Colby: Well, I think the thing that will last longest is this constitutional thing—just getting through it alive [the Church Committee inquiry and related investigations]. I think that is the longest term effect that I had. Oh, I fooled around with some of the internal machinery. The other thing I think I started, and Casey finished, was the NIO [National Intelligence Officer] system, which led to the reorganization of the analytical side. Sherman Kent points out in his book, *Strategic Intelligence,* published in 1949 by Princeton University Press, that you organize intelligence either by subject or by area. He said there are arguments for and against both ways. He said that, on balance, "I think it ought to be area," but he wasn't very strong about. So we organized it by discipline: political, economic, scientific, military, all those.

And I got in and I remember one time asking to see some people talk about China, and, Jesus, fifteen people came in! And I realized I was the only central figure of all of those fifteen. I said, "I can't do this for China, for the Soviet Union, and for everything else—this is crazy." We had this Board [of National Estimates], which I had doubts about anyway; so I set up the NIO system. I considered whether we should go ahead and try to reorganize the analysts; and I said, "Christ, we have enough turmoil around here: no, not now."

Casey did, and he did it very quickly after he went into office; he just reorganized. And of course, I often wondered why the hell we did it this way, until somebody pointed out, "That's the way you organize universities"—which have a different function than intelligence. Intelligence is supposed to react to problems and opportunities, and they come largely in geographic terms—not in economic terms or political terms. They come by geographic area.

Johnson: Say, "What are we going to do in China?"

Colby: Sure. This was one of the reasons—that inadequate organization in the early stage—that analysts didn't play a bigger role during those twenty-odd years, because they were all divided up. I remember there was a time, when I was chief of the Far East Division, I was the one going to talk to State or the military about the Far East—not the analysts. I never read NSA [National

Security Agency] traffic, yet here I would be representing intelligence in a meeting on policy, and I was the worst one to do it; it should have been an analyst. Now that is very much the case: the chief of China, he's the guy who goes to the White House meetings for the director.

Johnson: Can you recall any mistakes you made as DCI?

Colby: Obviously, the Yom Kippur War we didn't distinguish ourselves on.[21]

Johnson: I guess there will always be surprises.

Colby: There is that thesis. But my contention—in a way, a mental game—is that if intelligence does its work well and anticipates some problem arising and communicates this to policy makers; and policy makers act so that the thing does not happen in a bad way, but happens in a good way, intelligence turns out to be wrong—but wrong for the right reasons. So I think your record is: How many things do you get policy to move on, and how few bad surprises? I use to say, "I don't mind good surprises, but I don't want any bad surprises." And I think that is a legitimate demand. But you should be braced for the bad. On that Yom Kippur one, we just had convinced ourselves that it didn't make sense. And it didn't! But . . .

LOOKING BACK ON THE YEAR OF INTELLIGENCE

Johnson: Would the CIA have been in big trouble if you hadn't cooperated with the Church and Pike Committees?

Colby: I thought so. I was walking along by the Library of Congress one time—five, maybe eight, years ago—and this fellow who was counsel for the House [Appropriations] Committee crossed the street to me, and he said, "I just want to tell you something. I heard that you thought that, if you weren't cooperative with Congress, they would have gone out to destroy the Agency. I just want to tell you, you're absolutely right. We would have." They were out for blood, so I was throwing things at them, trying to be *reasonably* responsive and trying to protect the Agency. And I considered, really, the greatest victory in that was the Church Committee report, which is not a bad report, it really is not an unbalanced report. It's a little more sanctimonious than I'd like to have had; but when they came down to that part about covert action, I thought we'd come home free—you know, we shouldn't use it very often, but we shouldn't dismiss it. I was really a little surprised, because I thought we'd have a little more antagonistic [report]. The Pike Committee report was useless; but the Church Committee report, if you read it through, hangs together pretty well.[22]

ECONOMIC ESPIONAGE

Johnson: Should the CIA be more involved in economic intelligence and assisting American industry?

Colby: My answer to that is it certainly ought to be more active in the economic analytical area, because economics is going to be a big subject for the next decade or so. It's a major subject and CIA has excellent capabilities in this area. Collection? Overt collection, fine, no problem; covert collection, very rarely and only when there is some strategic reason for it. If you're engaged in illegal espionage in another country, you're entitled to do it for your security; but you really don't [if your objective is simply] to save a few bucks. You don't need to use satellites to count Toyotas.

And what do you do with it [the intelligence]? Suppose you have the information that Toyota is going to come out with a new model, and you got it through a secret penetration—what do you do with it? Both I and Stan Turner experimented with putting out some [public] economic reports, and it was hopeless. It would be met with: "Oh, this is spying!" And it had nothing to do with spies at all. Either they overbelieved it, or just laughed about it—giggled. We did work up a set of relations with the other departments, comparable to the one we have with the Defense Department, where we funneled the information over to Commerce, to Treasury, to Agriculture, I guess, wherever else. Then they absorb it into their business, and they put it out. And they don't just put it out to Ford; they can't. They put it out evenly; and that means it has to go to the foreigners, too, who are by now smart enough to know how much information there is in this city.

But I think the risk factor is such that I would be sort of dubious about this. I won't say never—you know, never say never. But it would have to be something very vital. And of course, controlling the illegal diversion of military related equipment, that sort of thing, proliferation of weapons, all that sort of thing, that's fine, sure.

THE FUTURE OF INTELLIGENCE

Johnson: Will the future mission of U.S. intelligence change much?

Colby: Not a helluva lot. [Colby referred me to a piece he had written recently on intelligence.[23]]

Johnson: Thank you for spending this time with me.

Colby: Thank you.

NOTES

1. For an account of this period, see Loch K. Johnson, *A Season of Inquiry: The Senate Intelligence Investigation* (Lexington: University Press of Kentucky, 1985).

2. The "jewels" included details on CIA assassination plots against foreign leaders, drug testing on unwitting subjects, opening the mail of selected American citizens without a warrant, and spying on Vietnam War protesters.

3. David S. Robarge, "Intelligence in Recent Public Literature," *Studies in Intelligence 47* (2003), available at https://www.cia.gov/csi/studies/vol47no4/article07.html.

4. See, for example, Dale Andradé, *Ashes to Ashes: The Phoenix Program and the Vietnam War* (Lexington, MA: Heath, 1990).

5. For a biography, see John Prados, *Lost Crusader: The Secret Wars of CIA Director William Colby* (New York: Oxford University Press, 2003).

6. William E. Colby with Peter Forbath, *Honorable Men: My Life in the CIA* (New York: Simon & Schuster, 1978); William E. Colby and James McCargar, *Lost Victory: A Firsthand Account of America's Sixteen-Year Involvement in Vietnam* (Chicago: Contemporary Books, 1989).

7. Representative Otis Pike (D-NY) headed up a panel of inquiry in the House of Representatives during 1975. By mutual agreement, the Church Committee focused on questions of intelligence improprieties at home and abroad, whereas the Pike Committee examined questions related to the quality of intelligence collection and analysis.

8. The Pike Committee engaged in a running battle with Colby and the Ford administration during its investigation, whereas the Church Committee attempted to have a more cordial relationship, based on the notion that you catch more flies with honey. The vitriol between the Pike panel and the administration led to the failure of that committee to win the trust of House members, and the investigation faltered in a whirlwind of dissension inside the panel and with the administration. See Frank J. Smist Jr., *Congress Oversees the United States Intelligence Community, 1947–1989* (Knoxville: University of Tennessee Press, 1990).

9. According to the Hughes-Ryan Act of 1974, covert actions were to be reported to Congress "in a timely fashion," which the floor colloquia preceding passage of this law seemed to define as within two days.

10. In 1976–78, the Senate Select Committee on Intelligence attempted to draft an omnibus charter for intelligence to replace the sketchy details of the National Security Act of 1947. This proposed law became long and convoluted and eventually collapsed under its own weight, with the help of lobbying against it by the intelligence bureaucracy. See Loch K. Johnson, "Legislative Reform of Intelligence Policy," *Polity* 17 (Spring 1985), pp. 549–73.

11. In 1982, Congress passed the Intelligence Identities Act to protect intelligence officers and their agents against the disclosure of their names by outsiders, whether newspaper reporters or enemies of the United States seeking to destroy the CIA and the other intelligence services. Four years earlier, in 1978, Congress passed the Foreign Intelligence Surveillance Act (FISA)—a major Church Committee recommendation—that required judicial warrants for intelligence wiretaps and other forms of surveillance, instead of just an order from a president or some other executive branch official. The term "graymail" refers to a threat by a defendant in a court proceeding to expose intelligence operations or other classified information if prosecuted. During the 1980s, the executive

and legislative branches worked together on procedures to conduct trials related to intelligence without exposing classified information.

12. For evidence that money was raised from foreign nations, see Senate Select Committee on Secret Military Assistance to Iran and the Nicaraguan Opposition and House Select Committee to Investigate Covert Arms Transactions with Iran, *Hearings and Final Report* (Washington, DC: Government Printing Office, 1987).

13. Detailees are individuals loaned to the Executive Office of the Presidency from various government agencies around Washington for employment by the President without cost to the White House.

14. See William E. Colby, testimony, "The CIA and the Media," *Hearings*, Permanent Select Committee on Intelligence, U.S. House of Representatives (Washington, DC: Government Printing Office, 1979).

15. That is, human agents don't just gather intelligence, they can also engage in covert actions as well as counterintelligence deception and penetration.

16. This refers to the connection between intelligence professionals and policy makers. Transferring intelligence from the former to the latter is rife with difficulties, perhaps the most important being the distortion of intelligence by policy makers to suit their own political needs.

17. Yale University history professor Sherman Kent served in the CIA as a high-level analyst and argued consistently for a strong barrier between analysts and policy officials, as a means for preserving the neutrality and integrity of analysts (see the chapter by Harold M. Greenberg in Volume 1 of this series).

18. Yuri Ivanovich Nosenko was a Soviet defector banished to the CIA's training facility at Camp Perry (The Farm) in Virginia, where he was confined and interrogated at length to test his bona fides. For one account, see Edward Jay Epstein, *Legend: The Secret World of Lee Harvey Oswald* (New York: Reader's Digest Press, 1978).

19. We now know that Aldrich H. Ames was a Soviet/Russian mole at the time of this interview, as was FBI agent Robert P. Hanssen.

20. Larry Wu-tai Chin became a translator for the United States on Okinawa and later gained employment at the CIA as a translator for its Foreign Broadcast Information Service. See Ronald Kessler, *Inside the CIA* (New York: Pocket Books, 1992), p. 155.

21. This was an unpredicted war between Egypt and Israel in 1973.

22. For the Church Committee Report, see Select Committee to Study Governmental Operations with Respect to Intelligence Activities, *Final Report*, Sen. Rept. No. 94–755, 6 vols., 94th Congress, 2nd sess. (Washington, DC: Government Printing Office, November 20, 1975). The Pike Report leaked to a New York City magazine: "The CIA Report the President Doesn't Want You to Read: The Pike Papers," *Village Voice*, February 16 and 23, 1976. A third investigation in 1975, this one by the White House under the leadership of Vice President Nelson Rockefeller, was expected to whitewash the intelligence abuses, but instead produced a hard-hitting report focused on illegal CIA domestic operations; see Commission on CIA Activities within the United States, *Report to the President* (Washington, DC: Government Printing Office, 1975).

23. William E. Colby, "Intelligence in a New World," *Mediterranean Quarterly* 1 (Fall 1990), pp. 46–59.

4

THE BRITISH EXPERIENCE WITH INTELLIGENCE ACCOUNTABILITY

MARK PHYTHIAN

THIS CHAPTER ASSESSES THE BRITISH EXPERIENCE WITH intelligence accountability through a consideration of the principal mechanism that exists to provide for this—the Intelligence and Security Committee (ISC). In discussing the British experience with intelligence accountability, we are looking at a country whose principal internal security and external intelligence organizations—the Security Service (MI5) and the Secret Intelligence Service (MI6)—trace their origins back to 1909 but whose peacetime existence was only formally acknowledged in the late 1980s and early 1990s. Then, in the wake of a succession of intelligence-linked exposés and in the context of the end of the Cold War and the intrusion of European law into the domestic polity, the Conservative governments of Margaret Thatcher and John Major finally introduced legislation formalizing their existence.

THE EMERGENCE OF OVERSIGHT

A string of revelations and allegations during the 1970s and 1980s created a momentum for greater accountability of the security and intelligence agencies, albeit one that lagged behind similar debates in the United States, Canada, and Australia. The motor driving these concerns was the widespread belief on the Left that in guarding against domestic subversion, MI5 was monitoring and interfering with legitimate political dissent. Left-wing critics argued that MI5 saw its primary allegiance as being to the Crown rather than the elected government of the day. There were suspicions that this extended to undermining Labour governments, reinforced by the revelations contained in former MI5 officer Peter Wright's memoir *Spycatcher*. There were other dimensions to the damage done to the reputation of the security and intelligence services during this period. The public exposure in November 1979 of Sir Anthony Blunt, surveyor of the Queen's Pictures and pillar of the establishment, as a former Soviet spy was quickly followed by the Prime and Bettaney espionage cases, all of which provided fertile ground for Wright's claim that former MI5 Director-General Sir Roger Hollis had been a Soviet spy. By the time of Paul Foot's 1989 book, *Who Framed Colin Wallace?*—at its core an account of the "cowboy" era of military intelligence in the laboratory that was Northern Ireland in the early 1970s—it seemed that there was a reservoir of security and intelligence intrigue and scandal that was in no danger of running dry.

While all of this created heightened parliamentary concern, the existence of what Tony Geraghty has termed the "very public war" in Northern Ireland served as a disincentive for government to act.[1] When Parliament did probe, former ministers were hardly reassuring. For example, when former Prime Minister Jim Callaghan gave evidence to the Treasury and Civil Service Committee in 1986 and was asked if he was satisfied that the agencies were sufficiently accountable, he replied:

> I am not sure what its accountability is to Parliament, I am not sure about ministers. I find it a difficult question to answer, I really do. They are run...as separate departments. They are not in the Minister's office, as it were, not in his headquarters. There is, therefore, all the difficulty of physical separation. When the Minister has to up sticks to ask questions and go somewhere else, that makes for remoteness. There is not immediate day to day closeness. Some Ministers do not want to know a lot: Home Secretary or Foreign Secretary, Prime Minister, others want to know a great deal about what is going on. I am going to give you a very unsatisfactory answer, I do not know. I am certain there must be a very high degree of responsibility among those who serve in MI5 or MI6 because they have great powers...and I think the ethos of those particular services is probably as important as the degree of accountability that you can visit upon them. I am very, very mixed up about this, I do not think I can help you with this.[2]

The most pressing impetus to act from the British government's perspective (although it did not concede this at the time) arose from the impact of European law on the British polity, in particular the European Convention of Human Rights (ECHR). Having fallen foul of this in 1984, the government enacted the Interception of Communications Act the following year. When former MI5 officer Cathy Massiter revealed that future Labour government ministers Harriet Harman and Patricia Hewitt had been placed under surveillance as a consequence of working for the National Council for Civil Liberties, at that time classed by MI5 as a subversive organization, they prepared to take their case to the ECHR. The prospect of further adverse rulings led to the 1989 Security Service Act.

This established MI5 on a legal footing. It created a commissioner, "a person who holds or has held high judicial office," who would review the Home

Secretary's exercise of his powers in signing warrants allowing for interference with private property and produce an annual report for the Prime Minister, who would lay it before Parliament after removing any material considered "prejudicial to the continued discharge of the functions of the Service." The act also created a three-member tribunal to investigate complaints about MI5 from the public which, like the commissioner, had access to MI5 records and personnel. The tribunal would (in conjunction with the commissioner where allegations of property interference were involved) establish whether MI5 had conducted investigations into a complainant and, if so, establish whether the grounds for doing so were reasonable. If the tribunal found against MI5, it could order that any records relating to the complainant be destroyed, further investigations ended, and compensation paid. Out of over 100 cases investigated by the tribunal in its first three years of operation, it did not find for the complainant in a single case. Nevertheless, the commissioner, in his 1992 annual report, suggested that the very existence of the tribunal had acted as a spur to MI5 adopting a more cautious approach to warrants and surveillance.

In mid-1992, Prime Minister John Major, then embarked on a wider "open government" drive, broke with tradition by admitting that MI6 actually existed and undertaking to put it on a statutory footing. Briefings to journalists at this time suggested that parliamentary scrutiny of the services was unlikely to be a feature of this opening. However, when the Intelligence Services Bill was unveiled in 1993, tacked on to the end was provision for a form of parliamentary scrutiny of MI5, MI6, and the Government Communications Headquarters (GCHQ).

Why did Major move to introduce an oversight body at this time? There is no doubt that the end of the Cold War created a political space that made this possible. At the same time this left politicians feeling bolder about removing some of the secrecy surrounding MI5 and MI6, it also affected these organizations' own view of the desirability of a limited degree of accountability. There was a general expectation that the end of the Cold War would bring with it a peace dividend, with clear implications for defense budgets. The intelligence agencies could expect to face similar pressure. In this context, it was felt that agreement to some form of scrutiny was necessary in retaining public confidence and protecting the U.K. intelligence budget (in 1992, £185 million). Moreover, the more perceptive intelligence managers may have appreciated that if oversight was increasingly inevitable, it should be accommodated rather than resisted. After all, scrutineers could also become advocates. They also faced the prospect of a future Labour government seeking to introduce more far-reaching reforms than the agencies were comfortable with. The Labour Party's 1983 election manifesto had spoken in terms of the "now widespread concern about our security services" and committed a future Labour government to introducing legislation that provided for oversight by a select committee, a prospect which must have caused some concern in the agencies. Reinforcing such arguments in favour of cooperation would have been the feedback from foreign counterparts subject to oversight, offering reassurance that it could be accommodated.

Moreover, in searching for a post–Cold War raison d'être, MI5 had assumed the lead role in combating terrorism in Northern Ireland (a role previously occupied by the Metropolitan Police Special Branch) and as such were under some pressure to make themselves as accountable for their part in this as the police had been. At the same time, allegations continued to emerge that strengthened the case for oversight—for example, those emanating from the Scott inquiry into the arms-to-Iraq affair, and concerning the role of MI5 during the 1984–85 miners' strike. Finally, MI6 reportedly took a more relaxed view of the prospect of oversight than MI5, on the basis that its operations abroad were likely to be of less concern to MPs than the domestic operations of MI5, which carried greater concerns over civil liberties. Crucially, legislating from a position of relative strength, rather than being driven by some scandal, allowed the government and agencies to control the agenda. A key dimension of this was the idea, to quote Foreign Secretary Douglas Hurd, that "the past is another country" and not one that the oversight body would be invited to explore.

THE INTELLIGENCE SERVICES BILL

The Intelligence Services Bill included provision for the creation of a committee of six parliamentarians (increased to nine—the only alteration made to the draft bill), hand-picked by the Prime Minister, who would meet in closed session and produce reports for the Prime Minister, who would lay them before Parliament after removing material considered prejudicial to the activities of the agencies. Hence, it was accountable to the executive and only through the executive was it accountable to the legislature. This arrangement would be a continual source of soul searching and debate as to whether the committee should not be a select committee of Parliament, directly accountable to the legislature. To coincide with the introduction of the bill, the head of MI6, Sir Colin McColl, made an unprecedented public appearance to welcome the move toward greater accountability but also reassure former, current, and prospective agents that "Secrecy is our absolute stock in trade. It is important to the people who work for us and risk their lives that we remain a secret service. When the Central Intelligence Agency went open in the 1970s it worried a lot of their people. I want to send our people a signal that we are not going to open everything up."[3]

McColl may have welcomed the bill, but the Labour opposition did not, arguing for scrutiny by a parliamentary select committee rather than the proposed hybrid. As Jack Cunningham, leading for the opposition, put it:

> It is proposed that the committee should not report to Parliament but to the Prime Minister. I do not regard that as parliamentary scrutiny or oversight, because the Prime Minister has the right to veto sections of its report—I call it prime ministerial oversight and scrutiny. If we are to have an effective parliamentary watchdog to oversee such matters and to probe and scrutinise, it should report to Parliament. It cannot legitimately be called a parliamentary committee unless it does so.[4]

Future members of the ISC were among those who expressed concern over the proposed form of oversight. Labour MP John Gilbert called it "far more timid than necessary." He was one of several MPs who could not see that the government had made the case for not granting the proposed oversight committee select committee status, arguing that the existing select committee practice of "sidelining" (i.e., removing) sensitive material would apply. The advantages to the government, it was argued, lay in controlling the timing of publication of the report, and that the proposed committee would not have the same powers as a select committee to send for persons and papers. As future ISC member Allan Rogers put it, "The committee will be a charade, a pretence at accountability."[5] In general, the opposition made it clear that while voting for the bill, they favored select committee status. It would be two years later, with the increasing likelihood that they would form the next government, before the Labour Party began to distance itself from its earlier enthusiasm for genuine parliamentary oversight.

In response to fears that the proposed committee would be toothless, Willam Waldegrave closed the debate by emphasizing the powers that it would possess:

> The committee will be involved in very secret areas that have never before been shared with others outside the Secretary of State's responsibilities. . . . The committee will not only deal with high-level policy in a broad-brush way; it will be able to examine the actual tasking, the money and the organisational structures. The committee will be fully trusted, and fully inside the secret wall. I believe that the result, while it will not establish within the House the parliamentary accountability that . . . we believe would be extremely difficult to organise, will be to spread the reassurance that senior, trusted people on both sides of the House share the secrets of the services, and have a formidable power to cause trouble for the Government. Somebody asked earlier where the teeth were. The teeth consist of the fact that the committee . . . will have the right not to publish stuff that would damage national security—which it would not want to do—but to write a report saying, "We believe that things are not being handled properly, and that Ministers are not responding properly." No Government . . . would want to risk such criticism.[6]

THE ISC UNDER TOM KING, 1994–2001

Nevertheless, the ISC would first of all have to discover that things were not being handled properly, and there remained concerns about its ability to do so. The final Intelligence Services Act stated that the ISC's requests for information would not be met if that information was deemed "sensitive" (and "sensitive" was broadly defined) or because the Home or Foreign secretary "determined that it shall not be disclosed." As with the 1989 act, a commissioner and tribunal were created. The separate tribunals have since been supplanted by a single tribunal under the terms of the Regulation of Investigatory Powers Act 2000, introduced to keep pace with advances in European law. In his brief annual report, the commissioner registers the number of warrants issued in a confidential annex while openly recording the number of complaints investigated by the tribunal, and the number upheld following investigation, usually none.

The ISC's first chairman was former Conservative Secretary of State for Defence and Northern Ireland Tom King, and the committee featured a Conservative Party majority. Its first report was an eleven-paragraph interim report published in May 1995, reporting that "In general terms, we have been encouraged by the openness of the intelligence 'insiders' that we have come into contact with thus far, and in particular by the helpful approach of the Heads of the Agencies themselves."[7] In an eleven-paragraph report, the inclusion of the preambular "in general terms" was not without significance. In terms of the Committee's approach, the report noted that it would "concentrate on major issues rather than, for example, be dawn into every individual intelligence item of current excitement—unless they are of such significance and relevance as to merit exceptional consideration and report to you." The framing of the Committee's interpretation of its mandate inevitably involved a tussle over the question of investigating allegations of past abuses. An attempt by Allan Rogers to raise the question of the agencies' relationship with Soviet defector Oleg Gordievsky, in the context of his contemporaneous allegation that former Labour Party leader Michael Foot was regarded by the KGB as an "agent of influence," were defeated inside the Committee, with Lord Howe echoing Douglas Hurd's earlier intervention and arguing that the ISC should not involve itself in "political archaeology." However, in the United States, Canada, and Australia, the question of past abuses or scandals was among the first to be investigated by the newly formed oversight committees. Having decided that the past is another country and interpreted its mandate as involving broad, strategic policy questions, in its first years of operation the ISC focused on the implications for the agencies of the changed post–Cold War world. Its second report, nine paragraphs long, concerned the decision to move MI5 into the fight against organized crime. Its first annual report was completed in December 1995 and published in March 1996.

There is no doubting the industry of the individual committee members in getting to grips with their task, nor the learning curve they faced. This first annual report revealed what became a pattern of at least weekly meetings and visits to the agencies and abroad (although the agencies have always stressed the limited utility of overseas experiences with accountability, instead emphasizing the unique character of MI5 and MI6). On the basis of its early experiences, the ISC felt able to reassure the Prime Minister that it considered its structure appropriate to the task. However, it would not be long before it requested the addition of an investigative capacity to assist it in its work.

One fundamental early aim of the ISC was to establish the confidence of the agencies themselves. King would subsequently allude to the initial Australian experience with intelligence oversight, wherein what he called the "awkward squad" was selected to sit on the oversight body, and consequently enjoyed little cooperation from the agencies. The ISC sought to reassure the agencies that any information they shared with committee members would be handled securely. In return, the ISC was keen that in turn the agencies

> Understand our needs and are sufficiently frank and open with a new oversight body with whom they have previously not had to relate. These mutual concerns must be met if the Committee is to command the confidence of parliament and the public. This is an essential foundation for our work, particularly if we were at any time required to deal urgently with some specially sensitive or difficult issue.[8]

In comparing the U.S. intelligence agencies' legal obligation to keep their oversight committees informed of their activities with the U.K. agencies' much more limited legal obligation to respond to ISC requests for information, the report later observed that the ISC "does expect to be kept properly and promptly informed." How fully the ISC succeeded in this area is an open question. Nevertheless, it is worth noting that this expectation represented something of an attempted expansion of its role—the Act was silent here. Similarly, its first annual report adopted an expansive interpretation of its financial oversight remit, arguing that this extended to "the clear responsibility to ensure that the Agencies have access to adequate resources for the tasks they are asked to undertake,"[9] and not just how cost-effectively such resources were used.

The second annual report, for 1996, was completed in December 1996 and published in February 1997. This reported that the Committee had faced the first challenges to its decision to focus on major issues (rather than feel obliged to address each and every controversy that might arise) in allegations concerning Menwith Hill and, separately, the alleged surveillance of a meeting between MPs and members of Sinn Fein inside the Palace of Westminster. Having asked the agencies about these matters, "we received . . . categorical assurances, which we accept, that the stories were without foundation."[10] Having no wider investigatory capability, the Committee had little option but to do so.

The third annual report was completed at the end of July 1998, a full nineteen months after the previous one, the intervening period disrupted by the election of a Labour government in 1997 and the subsequent reorganization of the ISC to reflect political retirements and the parliamentary dominance of the Labour Party. King remained as chair of the Committee, reflecting the desire of the Labour government to reassure the agencies that the 1983 election manifesto was long forgotten. With this new membership, the ISC came to see itself as having more of a public education role, opening its third annual report with a lengthy overview of the recent history of the agencies and the evolving nature of the threats they countered. The Committee assured the Prime Minister, Parliament, and public that these new challenges were "real enough" and not "invented to justify the Agencies' continued existence," as some critics had asserted, and moreover that "intelligence and security capabilities cannot be turned on and off like a tap. To meet their responsibilities, they must be maintained, and funded in a sustainable way."[11] To some extent, the ISC was becoming involved in advocacy on the agencies' behalf.

Having taken an interest in the agencies' internal procedures, the now Labour-dominated ISC returned to these in the wake of the August 1997 revelations of former MI5 officer David Shayler, soon to be joined by those of former MI6 officer Richard Tomlinson. Frustrated by what he saw as an antiquated approach to management in general and personnel issues in particular, Shayler had gone public when he failed to secure what he felt was a fair hearing of his grievances internally. Among his revelations, Shayler disclosed the names of a few people on whom MI5 kept personal files, extending to the man to whom they were accountable, Home Secretary Jack Straw, and including other Cabinet members, thereby reviving an issue of particular sensitivity on the Labour left. He also alleged that MI6 had been involved in a plot to assassinate Libyan leader Col. Qaddafi. The ISC responded by returning to the question of personnel policies, vetting, and internal security at relative length.[12] However, it refused to meet or take evidence from Shayler and showed no interest in investigating his allegations of an assassination plot.

The Shayler revelations did, however, lead to a renewed interest in the issue of MI5's files. In its 1997–98 report, the ISC confirmed that MI5 held approximately 250,000 hard copy personal files, with an additional 40,000 held on microfiche, and they outlined the process of opening, storing, and classifying these files—the first time this had been done. Concerned at Shayler's ability as an MI5 officer to call up the files of any politician or celebrity that took his fancy, the ISC recommended that access should be restricted to those "with a clear need to see them" and be accompanied by a detailed audit trail indicating who had seen any file, when, and for what purpose.

From the vantage point of the late 1990s, of even greater concern than MI5's historic maintenance of such an extensive number of personal files was the question of the destruction of those files. The ISC was able to bring considerable light to bear on MI5's approach to file retention/destruction. It revealed that until 1970 MI5 had a policy of weeding and destroying files. However, this had affected its ability to pursue a number of espionage cases. Hence, the policy shifted from destruction to microfiching. However, the ISC revealed that in 1992 MI5 "reconsidered its files policy again in the light of the changing nature of the threat with the end of the Cold War and the decline in the threat from subversion." As a result, MI5 began reviewing and destroying personal files on a case-by-case basis, destroying and concealing aspects of its own history in the process. As ISC member Yvette Cooper argued:

I accept that only the Security Service can make the operational decision whether it still needs to retain a file and continue to use it, but, once the service has decided that it does not need it, there is an historical—not operational—decision to be made. History is not an operational decision. There is absolutely no reason why only the Security Service should be capable of deciding whether something has historical significance for the future. In fact, for the sake of the credibility of history, someone other than the Security Service should make that decision.

It is controversial stuff. We have all heard the allegations about the monitoring of so-called subversives in the 1970s and 1980s. For all I know, none of it may have happened. On the other hand, all sorts of outrageous things may have happened. The point is that future generations have a right to know what happened and how the organs of the state behaved. They have a right to be able to learn from that and to know that what they are looking at is the entire record. They need to be confident about that. For the sake of credibility, it should not be the Security Service that decides that. Future historians should never be able to say that the service was given a licence to write its own history.[13]

By the time the ISC investigated the issue, 110,000 files had either been destroyed or marked for destruction, the "vast majority" of which related to subversion. The ISC found that "Ultimately, the judgement in respect of the review and destruction of individual files is made solely by the Security Service," and recommended that "some form of independent check should be built into the process, particularly in respect of files relating to subversion."[14]

In sum, the 1997–98 report suggested a more assertive ISC, possibly a consequence of having developed greater self-confidence, possibly a consequence of its changed composition, but most likely a combination of the two. Having initially reassured the Prime Minister and Parliament that its structure was well suited to its task, the ISC had by this point become aware of the fact that it had no investigatory capability of its own, and without this it could not "make authoritative statements on certain issues." Hence, it argued that an investigatory arm would "reinforce the authority of any findings that we make, and be an important element in establishing public confidence in the oversight system."[15]

Two innovations followed from this report: firstly the government began the practice of producing a published response; secondly, it granted an annual parliamentary debate on the reports. In its first Response, the government rejected the ISC's proposal that some form of independent check should be built into the process by which MI5 files were reviewed for destruction. It also asserted that access to files was already restricted and subject to audit arrangements, raising the question of why the ISC, assumed to have access to information on such processes, made the recommendation in the first place. It also seemed to resist the introduction of an investigative arm.

There are two further noteworthy dimensions to this response. First, while the ISC was reporting to the Prime Minister on its oversight of the agencies, in formulating its response, the government was clearly working closely with the intelligence agencies in framing their joint rejection of certain of the ISC's proposals. In other words, the government had established the ISC to oversee the agencies but joined forces with the agencies to reject recommendations arising from this oversight. The response found in favor of the agencies and its continued information monopoly rather than in favor of greater openness and accountability. Second, the timing of the government's response was significant. One of the weaknesses of the ISC structure highlighted in the debates over the Intelligence Services Bill had been that the executive would dictate the timing of publication. Here, a report that was published after a nineteen-month gap had to wait a further three months for a government response and parliamentary debate. Hence, Parliament was unable to debate the 1997–98 annual report until November 1998.

Parliamentary debate served to highlight concerns about the ISC on the part of its own members and the House of Commons in general. For example, it quickly exposed concerns about the implication for select committees' ability to oversee matters that now fell under the remit of the ISC. In practice, the existence of the ISC could allow the government to justify a refusal to disclose information to select committees—as, indeed, it would on several occasions in the future, most significantly over the highly sensitive question of intelligence and the case for war in Iraq.

Debate also kept the question of the desirability of a move toward select committee status alive. Allan Rogers referred to the ISC's own "strong debates on the possible adoption of a Select Committee style for our proceedings." Fellow ISC member Dale Campbell-Savours did not "believe that oversight is fully credible while the Committee remains a creature of the Executive—and that is what it is. The problem at the moment is that the Committee considers its relationship with the Prime Minister more important to its operation than its relationship with Parliament. I strongly dissent from that view and find the arguments in favour of Select Committee status utterly overwhelming."[16]

One reason why a narrow majority of ISC members came to believe that select committee status was unnecessary was that they saw an alternative route—further evolution of the ISC, and in particular the idea that an investigatory arm should be established. As Yvette Cooper, one of the most articulate advocates of expanded oversight, argued:

> At the moment, information is provided by agency chiefs and by Ministers at their discretion, which raises a difficult point: how can we have proper oversight if the very people whom we are supposed to be overseeing are determining what information we get? That severely jeopardises the Committee's ability to pronounce with authority on important intelligence issues. Credibility demands knowledge and knowledge demands the power to verify—the power to check what is going on. Until now, the ISC has not had that power, and that reduces its credibility in the public mind, as well as in Parliament's mind.
>
> None of that means that I suspect the agencies of any wrongdoing; it means simply that we on the Committee lack the ability to pronounce with confidence that all is well. We cannot come to the House, put our hands on our hearts and say that all is well, because we do not have the power to know.[17]

By the time the ISC produced its 1998–99 report (in August 1999), the government had consented to the appointment of a single investigator, despite some agency unease at the prospect. The investigator, whose terms of reference were dictated by the Prime Minister rather than the ISC, occupied an interesting position, further inside the "ring of secrecy" than ISC members from whom he could well be obliged to withhold information. Before providing a report on an issue for the ISC, the investigator was required to consult with the agency involved, "so as to allow the Head of the Agency to detemine whether any particular material should be withheld from the Committee."[18]

In its 1998–99 annual report there was further evidence of ISC assertiveness. The Committee argued that it should be granted access to the confidential annexes to the reports of the two commissioners created to investigate warrants in relation to interference with property and complaints referred to them by the tribunals where the tribunal did not uphold a complaint but nevertheless felt that an agency's conduct was unreasonable. On the question of MI5's personal files, its recommendations had contributed toward the creation of a degree of external scrutiny to help ensure that historically valuable documents were not being destroyed. However, the Committee learned that during the period in between the Home Secretary undertaking to review the issue and the announcement that there would be external scrutiny in future rather than suspend file destruction, MI5 destroyed a further 3,000 files.[19] It also continued its campaign to bring greater transparency to the question of the agencies' budgets and expanded its focus on weapons of mass destruction (WMDs), sounding a cautionary note as to the utility of control regimes and treaties and advocating a more proactive approach on the part of MI6 to tracking and frustrating would-be proliferators. In its response, the government refused to make the confidential annexes to the commissioners' reports available to the ISC on the basis that they fell within the category of information defined as "sensitive" in the 1994 Act. It also continued to resist the ISC's attempts to bring greater transparency to the question of agency budgets and rejected the notion that it placed too much faith in control regimes and treaties when it came to countering the spread of WMDs, although its subsqent policy toward Iraq suggested it rapidly lost this faith.

The timing of the report's publication and the government's response was again tardy in the extreme. A report completed in August 1999 was only published in November 1999, the government's response was published at the end of January 2000, and the parliamentary debate finally held in June 2000, almost a year after the report was completed and just two months before the subsequent annual report was presented to the Prime Minister. The delay in publication, response, and scheduling of debate meant that this "annual" debate was held a full twenty months after the previous one.

Although the ISC was established as a self-tasking body, in September 1999 it agreed to the government's request to investigate the policy and procedures employed by the agencies in their handling of information acquired through Soviet defector Vasili Mitrokhin and the events that culminated in the publication of the first volume of his account of Soviet espionage, coauthored with the agencies' favorite academic, Christopher Andrew.[20] This was also interesting in that it was made clear on establishing the ISC that "the past is another country." Now the ISC was being invited to investigate those parts of that country where it could be helpful to the government. Central to this case were issues of agency accountability to ministers and the degree to which ministers were kept informed about espionage issues. The key case was that of Melita Norwood, code-named HOLA, who the Mitrokhin papers allowed to be identified as a Soviet spy as long ago as 1992 but whom MI5 effectively decided against prosecuting. In 1999, when the first volume of the *Mitrokhin Archive* was about to be published, MI5 asked for an opinion on a possible prosecution, only for the attorney general to advise that a court would be likely to view such a prosecution as an abuse of process, given that no action had been taken when Norwood's identity had first become known. The ISC concluded that

> it was a serious failure of the Security Service not to refer Mrs Norwood's case to the Law Officers in mid 1993. This failure to consult the Law Officers resulted in the decision whether or not to prosecute Mrs Norwood effectively being taken by the Security Service. The Committee is concerned that the Service used public interest reasons to justify taking no further action against Mrs Norwood, when this was for the Law Officers to decide. We also believe that the failure of the Security Services to interview Mrs Norwood at this time prevented her possible prosecution.[21]

In a report highly critical of aspects of MI5's performance, the Committee also said that the Norwood case should have been kept under review between 1993 and 1998 and not allowed to "slip out of sight." That it did represented "a further serious failure." MI5 Director General Sir Stephen Lander would subsequently refer to this ISC report as representing a "public kicking" for the agency.[22]

The government had needed to be seen to launch some kind of investigation into the Mitrokhin/Norwood affair. The ISC was the ideal vehicle, given that original documents would remain within the ring of secrecy and not be made public, as was likely under alternative forms of inquiry. However, the ISC had made clear that to undertake the investigation it needed full access to information, including the normally sacrosanct advice to ministers, a development that caused some concern within MI5. As the ISC reported, "Although there was some delay in reaching agreement about the papers, the request was eventually met in full." This access further emboldened the Committee. Nevertheless, despite working to achieve a high level of mutual trust with the agencies, the Committee was never informed of the Mitrokhin/Norwood issue, even after a decision had been taken to publish the *Mitrokhin Archive*. Hence, although this episode demonstrated that the ISC was not afraid to criticize the agencies, and that it was increasingly self-confident, it also left hanging questions about the degree of accountability it was achieving, thereby affecting public confidence in it.

The 1999–2000 Report continued to provide evidence of assertiveness and the beginning of the emphasis that the ISC would henceforth give to the failure of the Prime Minister to regularly convene the Ministerial Committee on the Intelligence Services (CSI), responsible for approving the National Intelligence Requirements, and which would enable senior ministers to take a collective strategic view of the challenges and priorities in the fields of security and intelligence. On investigation, the ISC discovered that this body had not met at all since 1995 and that the civil service committee that shadowed it, the Permanent Secretaries' Committee on the Intelligence Services, had met just three times. The ISC was clear on this issue: "We believe that there should be a clear recognition and demonstration of the lines of responsibility and authority for these important Agencies. We recommend that CSI should meet, under your Chairmanship, at least annually to approve the National Intelligence Requirements and endorse or approve the Agencies' budgets."[23] It also returned to the question of access to the confidential annexes to the reports of the commissioners and the government's decision to refuse their request, giving a clear warning that this refusal was compromising the Committee's ability to carry out its oversight function: "It is still important for us to see the classified annexes to be able to establish the corrective action that the Agencies have introduced following the Commissioners' identification of errors and thus fulfil our statutory requirement to oversee the Agencies' administration processes."[24]

Its analysis of the intelligence contribution to the 1999 Kosovo campaign was so heavily redacted as to be without meaning. Elsewhere, it advocated greater intelligence resources be applied to combating drug trafficking, recommended greater resources be committed to combat tobacco smuggling, and expressed concern at the scale of illegal immigration. In its response, published in December 2000, some four months after the report was submitted, the government accepted the ISC recommendation that the CSI should meet annually. However, it maintained its refusal to allow the ISC access to the annexes to the commissioners' reports.

The ISC produced an interim report in March 2001, in anticipation of the calling of a general election, marking the final contributions of a majority of the Committee, including Chairman King. The report once again criticized the government over the failure of the CSI to meet, despite a government commitment that it should do so, leading the ISC to reiterate that it believed that "it is important for the senior cabinet ministers to be properly briefed on the overall performance of the Agencies and we repeat our recommendation that CSI meets at least annually to review this."[25] Elsewhere, it reiterated its disappointment in the government's refusal to publish fuller agency budget figures (in its response the government again declined) and continued to press for the creation of an employment tribunal capable of hearing the grievances of agency staff to prevent the emergence of further Tomlinsons and Shaylers, something over which the government continued to drag its feet. It again asked the government to reconsider its refusal to grant access to the commissioners' confidential annexes, and the government again declined. In sum, the picture that emerged at the end of the Tom King era was of a Committee that had worked hard to establish itself, had evolved its own terms of reference, had gained a significant degree of trust from the agencies, had been critical of both government and agencies on occasion, and had probed government repeatedly in an attempt to secure access to a full range of information. Yet in the nature of its responses and its handling of the reports, responses, and debates, the government inevitably had the upper hand. Nevertheless, emboldened by its access to material and ability to demonstrate a safe pair of hands over the Mitrokhin affar, the ISC concluded this phase of its development by suggesting a further evolution, in which the past was not necessarily another country. It concluded the interim report by warning:

> One of the characteristics of the intelligence and security field is the frequent, often sensational but unsubstantiated reports that appear in the media. The Committee takes an interest in such matters and seeks to determine which require action by the Committee. A case in point is the allegation of support for a plot to overthrow Colonel Gaddafi. We intended to report to you on this matter but are not yet fully in a position to do so. We believe that the Committee's Report on the Mitrokhin Archive demonstrated our competence in this area, providing an objective view of events with conclusions and recommendations for future work and any necessary changes.[26]

This would represent a significant expansion of the ISC's role, and it remained to be seen whether the significant personnel changes in the wake of the 2001 general election would affect this determination.

THE ISC UNDER ANN TAYLOR, 2001–2005

Following the 2001 general election, the government appointed a new ISC in August comprising five new members and chaired by one of these, Ann Taylor, a former Labour Chief Whip. It produced its first annual report in May 2002, covering the security and intelligence environment in the aftermath of the terrorist attacks of September 11, 2001 (9/11). In it the ISC again pointed to the fact that the CSI had still to meet, although the Prime Minister had convened ad hoc meetings of a similar composition after 9/11. On the question of the 9/11 attacks, a significantly redacted section of the Report showed that, prior to that time, Afghanistan had not been a high priority for the agencies. As the Foreign Secretary, Jack Straw, told the ISC, "the West [had] essentially walked away from Afghanistan, we are trying to get it back."[27] A joint summit of U.S. and U.K. intelligence agencies had spent time discussing Osama bin Laden prior to 9/11, but he remained a "hard target" for the agencies with a specific lack of intelligence on his thinking:

> A JIC assessment in July 2001 suggested that UBL organised attacks were in their final stages of preparation. While US or Israeli interests were the most likely targets, UK interests were at risk, including from collateral damage in attacks on US targets. This lack of intelligence access to a notably hard target meant that the UK and the US did not know who was going to carry out the attacks, how the attacks were going to be mounted or where the attacks were going to take place. Up to that point the West had not foreseen suicide attacks taking place on the USA mainland and certainly not

that the attacks would result in some 3,000 deaths, including the single greatest loss of UK citizens' lives to terrorist attack.[28]

Was this an intelligence failure? The Committee was guardedly ambivalent. The agencies had recognized that there was a "pressing need" to gather intelligence on bin Laden, and ministers had been told that this was in hand; a July 2001 JIC paper had correctly assessed that planning for attacks on Western targets was in the final stages, although it did not present this as a "stark warning" of a threat to the United Kingdom; the conjunction of these facts and Bin Laden's track record "could have warned all concerned that more urgent action was needed to counter this threat." It concluded that with hindsight, "the scale of the threat and the vulnerability of Western states to terrorists with this degree of sophistication and a total disregard for their own lives was not understood."[29] The government's response, drawn up with agency input, defended the agencies' record in relation to the threat from Al Qaeda, declined to make a commitment to follow the ISC's strong and repeated recommendation that the CSI meet at least annually, and continued to refuse to allow the ISC access to the confidential annexes to the commissioners' reports. At this point, the ISC threw in the towel on the question of access to the annexes. If it believed, as it said it did, that access to these was necessary for it to fulfill its mandate, it now appeared to be settling for partial fulfillment.

In October 2002 the ISC was asked by the Foreign Secretary to undertake an inquiry in relation to the adequacy of warnings prior to the Bali bombings of that month, which killed 190 people, including 24 Britons. Its report was critical of the threat assessment produced by MI5. It concluded that MI5 made a "serious misjudgement" and failed to "assess the threat correctly" in not raising the threat level from significant (the third highest level on a six-point scale) to high (the second, behind imminent). At the same time, it reassured Parliament and the public that on the basis of the available intelligence, the attacks could not have been prevented. However, the implication was clear: MI5's threat assessment had been wrong. The ISC also suggested the addition of a further level between significant and high to "allow the threat to be better described for the recipients of the Security Service assessments." As in response to the previous annual report, the government's response included a staunch defense of the agencies and a rejection of the ISC's conclusion that the threat level should have been higher at the time of the bombings. Nevertheless, it also revealed that as a result of a Security Service review rather than ISC recommendations, "threat level definitions have been reworked to give greater definition between levels, to make them more informative to customers and to better support the selection of appropriate protective measures."[30] Similarly, it revealed the establishment of the Joint Terrorism Analysis Centre, an evolution from the multiagency Counter-Terrorist Analysis Centre established after 9/11.

The ISC's 2002–2003 annual report was published in June 2003, in the wake of both the 2003 Iraq war and the controversial case for war presented to the public by Prime Minister Tony Blair and senior Cabinet members. Again, it took up the fact that the Prime Minister had declined to convene a meeting of the CSI despite the repeated strong recommendations of the Committee, offering its opinion that "CSI Ministers are not sufficiently engaged in the setting of requirements and priorities for secret intelligence, nor do they all see the full capability of intelligence collection."[31] Bizarrely, the government's response was to agree "that CSI has an important function especially in relation to the resourcing and future prioritisation of the Agencies' work, and should meet when appropriate to consider this work."[32] In reality, the Prime Minister had given no indication that he attached any importance whatsoever to either the CSI or the ISC's continual highlighting of its failure to meet. However, on December 18, 2003, some eight years after its previous meeting, the CSI finally met, although it was not to be the beginning of the regular series of meetings that the ISC strongly recommended.

The Committee reported separately, in September 2003, on the question of prewar U.K. intelligence on Iraq's WMDs, which had been fundamental to the Prime Minister's case for war in Iraq. In March 2001, Tom King warned, "We must remember that intelligence can be wasted, ignored—especially if it does not accord with the prejudices and preconceptions of the person on whose desk it falls—used for the wrong purposes or misdirected. The Committee exists to monitor those matters and to try to ensure that mistakes are not made."[33] The corollary of this was that intelligence could be exaggerated. This was the charge leveled at Prime Minister Blair in relation to his case for war with Iraq. This also represented the kind of controversial issue that for some observers would represent a litmus test of the ISC's ability to hold the agencies to account and deal objectively with an issue of great political sensitivity. How would the ISC deal with this?

The ISC sought "to examine whether the available intelligence, which informed the decision to invade Iraq, was adequate and properly assessed and whether it was accurately reflected in Government publications."[34] It did not consider the decision to go to war per se. It reported four months later that based on the intelligence it had seen, there was convincing intelligence that Iraq had active chemical, biological, and nuclear programs and the capability to produce chemical and biological weapons. At the heart of the controversy over prewar intelligence on Iraq was a dossier produced by Downing Street in September 2002 and containing intelligence cleared by JIC Chairman John Scarlett.[35] In its 2002–2003 annual report, the ISC had noted this and said that it "supports the responsible use of intelligence and material collected by the Agencies to inform the public on matters such as these." The question here, then, was how far this represented responsible use of the material, and how far it informed the public as opposed to misled them. However, the ISC did not rise to the challenge, offering no commentary on evidence that the political case was in advance of the intelligence case for war. For example, in a draft of Tony Blair's foreword to the dossier, it was acknowledged that there was no threat of nuclear attack on the United Kingdom, but this had been excluded from the published version. This denied the public available reassurance, removed an opportunity to bring some context to bear, and served to heighten the sense of threat posed by Iraq. In a tame criticism, the ISC contented itself with observing that "it was unfortunate that this point was removed from the published version of the foreword and not highlighted elsewhere."

The government's response was a further stage in the presentational game that had begun in earnest with the September 2002 dossier itself. It emphasized those aspects of the ISC report that appeared to support its conduct over the production of the dossier and rejected its criticisms. For example, with regard to the charge that the dossier was misleading, its response was that

> the dossier did present a balanced view of Iraq's CBW capability based on the intelligence available. The dossier made clear (paragraph 14, page 16) that the withdrawal of the United Nations Special Commission (UNSCOM) had greatly diminished the ability of the international community to monitor and assess Iraq's continued efforts to reconstitute its programmes. It also noted (paragraph 13, page 16) that UNSCOM was unable to account for significant quantities of agents, precursors and munitions.[36]

But the government cannot have it both ways. Either—as this and the objective record both suggest—the intelligence picture on Iraq was characterized by a significant degree of uncertainty, or, as Blair wrote in his foreword, it was known that Iraq represented a "current and serious threat to the UK national interest." The ISC was dissatisfied with the government's response, as it "emphasised only four key conclusions while either rejecting or failing to address fully many of our other conclusions and recommendations. We regard this as extremely unsatisfactory. . . . Our dissatisfaction was increased by the Government's decision to allow such little time for parliamentary debate" on its Iraq and annual reports.[37] As a result, the government response to the 2003–2004 annual report began a practice of responding to each of the ISC's conclusions individually. However, it did not deal directly with the core question, simply stating, "We regret that the Committee found [the] response unsatisfactory."[38] This did not amount to effective oversight. Key questions had gone unanswered, and the ISC had effectively run out of options in the face of the government's refusal to engage with it. Its investigation had been limited, its findings dismissed by government, and its credibility damaged.

Moreover, it emerged that although the ISC had stated that it had seen all JIC assessments on Iraq produced between August 1990 and September 2002 and the eight produced in the period October 2002 to March 2003, in fact eight had been withheld—five from the former period, three from the latter. Although the Committee was "satisfied that knowledge of them would not have led us to change the conclusions, including those that were critical, in our Report,"[39] earlier access would have allowed it to include further material, and their conclusions would have been more securely rooted in a fuller picture.

Read in the context of the steady spread of democratic oversight of intelligence in the past thirty years, one thing is very striking about ISC reports published before 2005—the complete absence of explicit reference to human rights. In 2005, however, the ISC reported on an issue at the heart of the global war on terror: the treatment of those detained in Afghanistan, Guantánamo Bay, and Iraq. Paying careful attention to its own boundaries, the ISC investigated any involvement in or witnessing of abuse by intelligence personnel, the adequacy of training as to what to do if it was witnessed, and when ministers were informed of any concerns. Its report rehearsed the relevant conventions on treatment of prisoners, noting that the United States did not regard those detained in Afghanistan as covered by them. The substance of the report was taken up with cases in which intelligence personnel reported their concerns at the treatment of detainees by U.S. personnel; found that these were relatively few (fewer than 15 out of over 2,000 interviews witnessed); criticized the lack of training of staff in convention matters before deployment to Afghanistan, Guantánamo, and Iraq; and noted that when concerns were expressed to U.S. authorities, these were inadequately followed up.

Overall, the report does not provide adequate oversight; certainly the actions of British soldiers lie within the remit of the Defence Select Committee, and the ISC noted that a number were court-martialed, but the Committee did not even explore the issue that soldiers might have prepared detainees for interrogation as U.S. evidence shows. The ISC noted widespread concern about the use of information obtained under torture and briefly noted the pragmatic and principled arguments but did "not attempt to answer these difficult questions." Instead they quoted at length the Foreign Secretary's utilitarian justification for using such information if necessary. Moreover, just as revelations on Iraq subsequent to the ISC investigation left its conclusions there looking thin, so too ongoing revelations about the involvement of U.K. intelligence personnel in the handling and interrogation of detainees have raised questions about the reliability of this investigation.

CONCLUSIONS

In its 1997–98 annual report, the ISC recognized that:

It is vital that public confidence is maintained in the Agencies. At times of grave national threat, their value is readily accepted. At other times, in the face of a bungled operation or security lapse, public confidence can be very fragile. That is the inevitable consequence of operating within the "ring of secrecy", which prevents a more balanced public view of their activities and their value. The public must therefore be confident that there is adequate independent scrutiny and democratic accountability on their behalf, by people within that "ring of secrecy".[40]

How far has the ISC succeeded in this? In attempting to answer this, other questions need to be considered: What was the government's purpose in creating the ISC? Was it to provide accountability or give the appearance of accountability and thereby satisfy growing demands for some form of accountability? Fundamentally, the ISC was set up to serve the executive, and that is what it does. Even disagreements between the ISC and executive, or examples of ISC assertion, serve the executive because they confirm the appearance of accountability and thereby dampen demands for more far-reaching accountability, or the introduction of legislative accountability through a select committee of the House of Commons.

Who guards the guardians? This question needs to be adapted slightly to ask: To whom are the oversight committee accountable? Members are accountable to the Prime Minister, and beyond this to themselves collectively and individually. There is no *parliamentary* accountability. This is significant in that the ISC has proved itself unable to be overly critical of executive failures. It can adequately monitor the financial and administrative dimensions of the agencies on behalf of the executive, but not the actions of the executive on behalf of the legislature. Part of the oversight function should be to do precisely this.

Any assessment of the ISC must consider areas of omission as well as commission. For some observers, the real test for the ISC would come when it was faced with a scandal of comparable gravity to those that had been revealed in the years prior to its establishment. Though the question of politicization of intelligence has emerged as an area of central concern in the post-9/11 environment, it is an issue for which the ISC has shown no appetite. Appointed by the executive, reporting to the executive, and holding membership at the pleasure of the executive (in the majority of cases, also the party leader), it has failed to explore the question of executive responsibility.

There are other areas of omission, for example, regarding the Shayler allegations—particularly relating to his allegation that MI6 was involved in a plot to assassinate Col. Qaddafi. Despite the fundamental nature of the allegations, despite some support within the ISC for undertaking an investigation, and despite the fact that Foreign Secretary Robin Cook had been willing to see the ISC investigate the lesser matter of possible Foreign Office connivance in breaking an arms embargo on Sierra Leone, the ISC has failed to address the issue and thereby offer the public the reassurance of which it spoke in its 1997–98 annual report. Issues relating to Northern Ireland have been largely absent from the ISC's published record but, in the light of the Stevens inquiry report, continue to cause concern. Questions that the case of Katharine Gun might have raised about tasking and policy regarding espionage aimed at the UN Secretary General have been avoided.

Despite the advances made by the ISC, particularly in the years up to 2001, as it stands, the scope of intelligence accountability in the United Kingdom lags behind that of other Western democracies. It even lags behind that of the emerging Eastern European democracies, such as Romania and Poland—as the ISC themselves have acknowledged. A significant component of it should be parliamentary debate, a dedicated opportunity for ISC members to speak in the chamber and offer the reassurances that their oversight function is being carried out to their satisfaction and amplifying areas of concern identified in their reports. However, full parliamentary debate was slow arriving. There was no set debate on the reports until 1998, before the events of 9/11 they were poorly attended, the early debates were held after a significant time had elapsed from the production of the relevant annual report, and when ISC members were critical of the government's response or failure to respond to specific issues, they were effectively ignored.

Oversight of intelligence, whoever carries it out, is inescapably political, and those conducting it must remember that they are engaged in contests of power in which the stakes are high. Shortly after the ISC was established, Peter Gill suggested that a significant indicator of its political will would be "the struggles that take place over access to information. If there are no such battles then we would be justified in concluding that the ISC has failed to challenge central information control."[41] There have been too few of these in the post-9/11 era—the Committee proudly records in the preface to its annual report that it has agreed all government redactions from its annual reports. An oversight committee might be expected to contest at least some of these. This state of affairs suggests a committee too deferential to the executive and too willing to accept deletions. The key area of contest with the executive—over access to the confidential annexes to the commissioners' report—was conceded. To rebuild public and parliamentary trust post-Iraq, the ISC needs to engage in these contests over information.

There are additional limitations or weaknesses that must be considered in any assessment of the ISC. Given the environment in which it must operate, a strong chairman is essential, and in this respect it is worth noting that the elements of role enhancement mentioned in this chapter essentially took place under King's chairmanship. It can be too easily distracted by events, particularly because it is capacity-limited and needs to choose its subjects for inquiry very carefully. In this respect, its decision to dispense with the services of its investigator—after praising his work in successive annual reports—is very disappointing. It was clearly a reaction to his public comments concerning the Blair government's case for war in Iraq. The Committee needs to expand its investigatory and staff base rather than remove it in response to pressure, real or perceived, from agencies or executive. Moreover, there is a very real sense in which post-9/11, the ISC's definition of its role has come to focus more on intelligence management and concern that the agencies are adequately funded at the expense of legislative oversight of the executive branch.

On a more positive note, the ISC was tasked with performing intelligence from scratch, with no more guidance as to how to go about this in practice than that provided by the bare bones of the 1994 Intelligence Services Act. It has put considerable flesh on these in the years since then, expanding its remit in the process. In practice, it has also taken an interest in operational matters, despite these falling outside its remit—for example, in investigating issues relating to the Kosovo campaign, WMD proliferation, Sierra Leone, and the Mitrokhin affair. Moreover, it has introduced significant accountability with regard to the agencies' finances, previously an area of limited transparency even at ministerial level. Indeed, until 1994 there was no external auditing of the agencies' accounts. It is also undoubtedly the case that the very existence of the ISC has given the agencies cause to reflect on proposed actions in advance of undertaking them. At one time, referred King to "a tendency now within the agencies to ask what the Intelligence and Security Committee would think if they embarked on a certain course of action" and suggested that this "could be used in the future against Ministers who want intelligence in areas that the agencies do not think fall within their remit."[42]

Does the ISC represent a first step on the road to fuller accountability, or the best feasible balance between competing demands? During parliamentary debate on the Intelligence Services Bill, MPs were divided on this point. Yet it seems inevitable that the ISC of 1994 will come to be seen as having represented a first step on the road to accountability. As such, in the wake of the division and distrust engendered by the government's presentation of its case for war in Iraq, the time is ripe for an additional step, so that accountability structures retain the confidence of the public they are designed to reassure. In June 2000 ISC member Dale Campbell-Savours told the House of Commons: "The arguments about whether the ISC is a Select Committee will simply be cast aside by history. The process is inevitable; it will happen."[43] However, the treatment of Dr. David Kelly, who committed suicide after a particularly fierce grilling by the Foreign Affairs Committee, has meant that any agency enthusiasm for such a development has been extinguished for now. Nevertheless, it remains a necessary step for the achievement of the fullest feasible degree of accountability.

NOTES

I thank Peter Gill for his comments on an earlier draft of this chapter.

1. Tony Geraghty, *The Irish War: The Military History of a Domestic Conflict* (London: HarperCollins, 1998), chap. 4.

2. *New Statesman*, December 12, 1986, p. 7.

3. John Willman, "Secret Service Open to Scrutiny," *Financial Times*, November 25, 1993.

4. *Hansard*, February 22, 1994, col. 171.

5. *Hansard*, April 27, 1994, col. 351.

6. *Hansard*, February 22, 1994, col. 240.

7. *Interim Report of the Intelligence and Security Committee* (ISC), Cm 2873, May 1995, para. 8.

8. ISC, *Annual Report 1995*, Cm 3198, March 1996, para. 7.

9. Ibid., para. 37.

10. ISC, *Annual Report 1996*, Cm 3574, para. 6.

11. ISC *Annual Report 1997–98*, Cm 4073, November 1998, foreword.

12. Ibid., paras. 24–38.

13. *Hansard*, November 2, 1998, col. 612.

14. ISC, *Annual Report 1997–98*, para. 50.

15. Ibid., para. 69.

16. *Hansard*, November 2, 1998, cols. 596, 618.

17. Ibid., col. 610.

18. *Government Response to the Intelligence and Security Committee's Annual Report 1998–99*, Cm 4569, January 2000, para. 34.

19. ISC *Annual Report 1998–99*, available at http://www.archive.official-docu ments.co.uk/document/cm45/4532/4532.htm, November 1999, para. 79.

20. Christopher Andrew and Vasili Mitrokhin, *The Mitrokhin Archive: The KGB in Europe and the West* (London: Allen Lane, 1999). "The SIS regarded Professor Andrew as a safe pair of hands [who] was also security cleared and had signed the Official Secrets Act." ISC, *The Mitrokhin Inquiry Report*, Cm 4764, June 2000, para. 46.

21. Ibid., para. 34.

22. Sir Stephen Lander, "The Oversight of Security and Intelligence," speech at Royal United Services Institute, London, March 15, 2001.

23. ISC, *Annual Report 1999–2000*, Cm 4897, Nov. 2000, para. 19.

24. Ibid., para. 35.

25. ISC, *Interim Report 2000–01*, Cm 5126, March 2001, para. 15.

26. Ibid., para.34.

27. ISC, *Annual Report 2001–02*, Cm 5542, June 2002, para. 54.

28. Ibid., para. 63.

29. Ibid., para. 65.

30. *Government Response to the Intelligence and Security Committee Inquiry into Intelligence, Assessments and Advice Prior to the Terrorist Bombings on Bali 12 October 2002*, Cm 5765, February 2003, para. 10.

31. ISC, *Annual Report 2002–03*, Cm 5837, June 2003, para. 56.

32. *Government Response to the Intelligence and Security Committee's Annual Report 2002–03*, Cm 5838, June 2003, para. 10.

33. *Hansard*, March 29, 2001, col. 1149.

34. ISC, *Iraqi Weapons of Mass Destruction—Intelligence and Assessments*, Cm 5972, September 2003, para. 11.

35. On this, see Mark Phythian, "Hutton and Scott: A Tale of Two Inquiries," *Parliamentary Affairs* 58, no. 1 (January 1995), pp. 124–37; Peter Gill and Mark Phythian, *Intelligence in an Insecure World* (Cambridge: Polity, 2006), esp. chap. 7.

36. *Government Response to ISC Report on Iraqi Weapons of Mass Destruction—Intelligence and Assessments*, Cm 6118, February 2004, para. 13.

37. ISC, *Annual Report 2003–04*, Cm 6240, June 2004, para. 87.

38. *Government's Response to the Intelligence and Security Committee's Annual Report 2003–04*, Cm 6241, July 2004, para. P.

39. ISC, *Annual Report 2003–04*, Cm 6240, June 2004, para. 146.

40. ISC, *Annual Report 1997–98*, foreword.

41. Peter Gill, "Reasserting Control: Recent Changes in the Oversight of the UK Intelligence Community," *Intelligence and National Security* 11, no. 2 (April 1996), p. 328.

42. *Hansard*, March 29, 2001, col. 1149.

43. *Hansard*, June 22, 2000, col. 512.

5

DOCUMENTARY EVIDENCE FOR DIFFERENCES
BETWEEN AMERICAN AND BRITISH APPROACHES
TO INTELLIGENCE

LAWRENCE J. LAMANNA

THE WAR IN IRAQ, THOUGH TRAGIC, OPENED for scholars and the public a unique window into the world of intelligence: the release of parallel British and American documents related to the prewar intelligence on Iraqi weapons of mass destruction (WMDs). The purpose of this chapter is to exploit this opportunity by comparing these documents to determine what they reveal about differences between British and American approaches to intelligence concepts, structures, methods, purposes, and philosophies. This analysis provides concrete and replicable evidence of differences between the two systems based on directly comparable data. It also provides a convenient and brief description and chronology of the development of these documents.

This study is not, however, an evaluation of the performance or failure of the intelligence apparatus of the United States and the United Kingdom. Neither does it seek to judge whether policy makers and political leaders in either country made proper or improper use of intelligence products. Finally, this chapter is not about Iraq as such.

Among the differences observed in this study are the following:

- When agencies disagree on intelligence findings, the American system allows for the expression of dissent from the majority view, whereas the British system simply excludes the controverted finding.
- American intelligence reports include explicit levels of confidence; British reports do so only vaguely and occasionally.
- British intelligence reports provide greater historical context and take a more narrative form than do American reports.

- The British are more interested in hearing the assessments and analytical opinions of foreign governments and experts than are the Americans. The Americans look to foreigners mostly for collection purposes, not analytical or estimative ones.
- British intelligence agencies and government departments cooperate and collaborate with one another to a high degree, American agencies do not.
- In the American system, the various intelligence agencies come together to produce the most important intelligence reports. In the British system, the intelligence agencies *and* other departments of government come together to produce the most important reports that incorporate intelligence information.
- The American and British political systems (i.e., presidential versus parliamentary) interact with their respective intelligence communities differently, and this may lead to different practices and norms.

METHODOLOGY

The method of the chapter is simple and straightforward. Both sets of documents were read and observations about the systems, concepts, and methods were noted. Then the observations were compared and differences between the two sets were analyzed.

This chapter is deliberately observational: an effort was made to let the documents speak for themselves without bringing theoretical preconceptions to the analysis. In other words, it is not an attempt to find evidence supporting any particular theory of institutions or organization. In this regard, it is a type of case study that Levy refers to as atheoretical or configurative-idiographic: "Idiographic case studies are inductive; they involve a minimum of a priori theoretical preconceptions, and the interpretation emerges from the case itself."[1] The only conscious, working hypothesis is that despite the extremely close cooperation, the shared history, and the "special relationship" between the United States and the United Kingdom intelligence services, there will be some detectable differences in methods, organization, and concepts.

Anyone familiar with intelligence studies will know that there are some generally acknowledged differences between these two national systems. Yet the observation of these differences is frequently personal and impressionistic. The current study is not entirely free from impression either, but the sources of those impressions are publicly available documents. In this respect, therefore, it is concrete and replicable: another researcher could access the same documents and verify or challenge the findings of this study.

BACKGROUND, DEFINITIONS, AND DOCUMENTS

Rarely is there a contemporary glimpse into the workings of the national intelligence apparatus of either the United States or the United Kingdom. Typically, intelligence reports and related documents are released to the public only decades after the events or situations they describe. Memoirs or first-person accounts may be more contemporary, but they are often difficult to verify and are frequently interpretive. Because of the controversies surrounding Iraq, the United States and the United Kingdom both made a remarkable amount of intelligence information available to the public before the war. After the war and because of the subsequent loss of confidence in intelligence capabilities, both nations initiated high-level investigations into their own intelligence apparatus and products. These investigations placed even more information into public view.

Specifically, in fall 2002 the United Kingdom released *Iraq's Weapons of Mass Destruction: The Assessment of the British Government*,[2] and the United States released *Iraq's Weapons of Mass Destruction Programs*.[3] Both documents were written for public consumption, but both were also closely related to one or more classified reports.

By summer 2004, investigations into the quality of the underlying intelligence had been completed in both countries. On July 7, 2004, the U.S. Senate Select Committee on Intelligence (SSCI) released a redacted version of its results, *Report on the U.S. Intelligence Community's Prewar Intelligence Assessments on Iraq*.[4] On July14, the Butler Committee in the United Kingdom released *Review of Intelligence on Weapons of Mass Destruction*,[5] otherwise known as the Butler Report (see Volume 4, Appendix G). In addition to these reports, the Central Intelligence Agency (CIA) also released two heavily redacted versions of a classified intelligence report.

There are three other documents that should be mentioned, although they are not included in the current analysis. First, on September 9, 2003, the Intelligence and Security Committee (ISC) of the U.K. Parliament delivered its investigative report, *Iraqi Weapons of Mass Destruction—Intelligence and Assessments*, to the Prime Minister.[6] This report is excluded because it is not directly comparable to any U.S. report due to its production date. The U.S. and British intelligence estimates were finalized within a few weeks of each other in the fall of 2002. Similarly, the Senate report and the Butler Report were both finalized in July 2004. The Butler Report (BR) acknowledges the usefulness of the ISC report, but it also notes that the Butler Committee had two important advantages over the ISC: the further passage of time and "much wider access to the Government's intelligence and policy papers" (BR 2). The timing of an investigation affects the results, and therefore it is important that the timing match to compare national reports.

Second, the British government released a document to journalists at the beginning of February 2003 that contained some information produced by the intelligence services.[7] This document was excluded from the current analysis because, in addition to information produced by British intelligence, it contained unattributed information from other, nongovernmental sources that made it quite controversial and unusual. On the American side, there is nothing comparable to this document, and its treatment in the British investigative reports is minimal.

Finally, on March 31, 2005, the Presidential Commission on the Intelligence Capabilities of the United States Regarding Weapons of Mass Destruction (the Silberman-Robb Commission) released an unclassified version of its report (see Volume 4, Appendix F).[8] Unfortunately, because this investigation concluded almost nine months later than the other two in the analysis, it also suffers from the mismatched time problem. Furthermore, its findings and characterizations are not independent of the others. The Silberman-Robb Commission acknowledged in its own report that the Butler Report was "an important resource" and the Senate report was "particularly valuable."[9] The report of the Silberman-Robb Commission is an important contribution to understanding what went wrong with U.S. intelligence, but because it was influenced by the Butler Report, it does not represent a purely national perspective.

At this point, a brief explanation of top-level intelligence reports is in order. Both the United States and the United Kingdom have intelligence services that produce information, analysis, and reports for policy makers at the highest levels. In the United States, the epitome of these products is a National Intelligence Estimate (NIE). "NIEs are long-term intelligence products that attempt to estimate (not predict) the likely direction an issue will take in the future. Ideally, NIEs should be anticipatory, focusing on issues that are likely to be important in the near future and for which there is sufficient time to arrive at a community-wide judgment."[10] An NIE may outline several possible directions that events may take, providing a judgment or estimate of the likelihood of each. NIEs are highly classified documents that are normally not released to the public until decades have passed after their production.

Each NIE is prepared under the supervision of a National Intelligence Officer (NIO), of which there are currently twelve.[11] Some NIOs have a geographic responsibility, such as the NIO for Africa, and others have topical responsibilities, such as the NIO for Economics and Global Issues. Together with a chairman and staff, the NIOs make up the National Intelligence Council (NIC). NIEs are systematically and formally circulated and discussed among the sixteen agencies that make up the U.S. intelligence community and finally approved by the Director of Central Intelligence (DCI).[12]

The British product that corresponds to an NIE is an Assessment.[13] Assessments are produced by the Joint Intelligence Committee (JIC) Assessments Staff.[14] The JIC is a Cabinet committee composed of the heads of the three British intelligence and security agencies; the chief of Defence Intelligence; senior policy advisors from the Foreign Office, the Ministry of Defence, the Home Office, the Treasury, and the Department of Trade and Industry; and representatives of other departments as necessary. These civil service policy advisors and department heads report to and assist government ministers in the formulation and execution of policy. The committee meets weekly and provides a key link between policy makers and intelligence services; it both reports intelligence to policy makers and communicates intelligence requirements to the agencies.

Figure 5.1 presents a chronology of the documents examined in this chapter and also notes the abbreviations that will be used to cite them.

THE U.S. ESTIMATE AND WHITE PAPER

The CIA released three related documents that are part of this study. The first of these is the public white paper, *Iraq's Weapons of Mass Destruction Programs*, released on October 4, 2002. Work on this document began in May, but in some ways the drafts were overtaken by events and the final document became a reflection of the classified NIE that was produced on October 1 (SEN 287).

The white paper is twenty-five pages long; contains color pictures, maps, and charts; and is clearly intended to show the danger that was Iraq. It describes nuclear, chemical, biological, ballistic missile, and unmanned aerial vehicle (UAV) programs. It also provides some history of UN resolutions and UN inspection operations related to Iraq. On the one hand, some statements and assertions are plainly speculative and the authors indicate higher or lower levels of confidence for some of their assertions. On the other hand, the document presents no dissenting opinions.

The document is structured in the following way:

1. Key Judgments
2. Discussion—Iraq's Weapons of Mass Destruction Programs
   a. Nuclear Weapons Program
   b. Chemical Warfare Program
   c. Biological Warfare Program
   d. Ballistic Missile Program
   e. Unmanned Aerial Vehicle Program and Other Aircraft
   f. Procurement in Support of WMD Programs

The next relevant U.S. document is the *Key Judgments* text.[15] This document was released by the CIA on July 18, 2003, and contains eight pages photocopied from the original, classified October 1 NIE. Specifically, these are pages 5 through 9, pages 24 and 25, and an amalgamation of pages 74 and 84.[16] Large sections of several pages are masked. The first five pages are the key judgments section of the NIE. These pages are similar (but not identical) to the key judgments section of the white paper.

One of the most important contrasts to the white paper is that the *Key Judgments* text reveals some dissension from the prevailing judgments. At the end of the first paragraph of page one of *Key Judgments*, the reader is directed to a box at the end of the "key judgments" section (KJ 4) which explains the dissent of

Figure 5-1. Chronology of Events and Key to Documents

2002	May 8	Request made in the United States for white paper on Iraq's WMD programs
	September 3	British government requests public dossier on Iraq's WMD programs
	September 9	British assessment most closely associated with the British public dossier is produced
		First request (from Sen. Durbin) for an NIE on Iraq's WMD programs
	September 12	DCI orders the production of a NIE on Iraqi WMDs
	September 24	U.K. government releases *Iraq's Weapons of Mass Destruction: The Assessment of the British Government*, an unclassified dossier based on classified assessments (DR)
	October 1	CIA produces NIE 2002-16HC on *Iraq's Continuing Program for Weapons of Mass Destruction* (NIE)
	October 4	CIA releases *Iraq's Weapons of Mass Destruction Programs*, an unclassified white paper related to the NIE (WP)
2003	February 1–2	British Coalition Information Centre shares *Iraq—Its Infrastructure of Concealment, Deception and Intimidation* with journalists
	March 19	U.S. and U.K. invasion of Iraq begins
	June 20	SSCI announces intention to begin formal review of intelligence on Iraqi WMDs
	July 18	CIA releases *Key Judgments* from NIE 2002-16HC (KJ)
	September 9	Intelligence and Security Committee delivers *Iraqi Weapons of Mass Destruction—Intelligence and Assessments* to the Prime Minister
2004	February 3	British government announces Butler Committee inquiry into September 24, 2002, assessment on Iraqi WMDs
	February 6	President George W. Bush issues Executive Order 13328 creating the Commission on the Intelligence Capabilities of the United States Regarding Weapons of Mass Destruction (Silberman-Robb Commission, SR)
	February 12	SSCI announces expansion of its investigation
	June 1	CIA releases redacted version of NIE 2002-16HC (NIE)
	July 7	SSCI releases redacted version of *Report on the U.S. Intelligence Community's Prewar Intelligence Assessments on Iraq* (SEN)
	July 14	Butler Committee releases *Review of Intelligence on Weapons of Mass Destruction* (BR)
2005	March 31	Silberman-Robb Committee finishes classified and unclassified versions of its *Report to the President of the United States* (SR)

the State Department's Bureau of Intelligence and Research (INR). In this text the INR notes that although it does believe that Saddam Hussein wants to acquire nuclear weapons, it does not believe that the current intelligence makes a compelling case that he is "currently pursuing what INR would consider to be an integrated and comprehensive approach to acquire nuclear weapons" (KJ 4–5).

The INR statement cites the judgment of experts at the Department of Energy who found that a key piece of evidence against Iraq—the aluminum tubes acquired from abroad—were poorly suited for a nuclear program.[17] For this reason and because of the "atypical lack of attention to operational security" on the part of the Iraqis, the INR expresses its dissent from the majority view on the aluminum tubes (KJ 5). INR also states that it finds "highly dubious" the claim that Iraq was seeking to obtain uranium from Africa (KJ 8). Last, within the key judgments section, the text states that the "Director, Intelligence, Surveillance, and Reconnaissance, U.S. Air Force, does not agree that Iraq is developing UAVs *primarily* intended to be delivery platforms for chemical and biological warfare (CBW) agents" (KJ 3, emphasis added). The Air Force believed that the primary role of Iraq's UAVs was for reconnaissance. Although it is not reproduced in *Key Judgments*, further elaboration of this dissent regarding UAVs is included in a footnote at a later point in the NIE. At least part of that footnote has been revealed in the Senate report (SEN 225), in spite of the fact that it is masked in the declassified NIE.

Another notable difference between *Key Judgments* and the white paper is that *Key Judgments* includes caveats such as "we judge" before some assertions (see also SEN 286–89). These phrases have the effect of reminding the reader that a judgment is being expressed, not a statement of indisputable fact. The white paper does not include these caveats and therefore gives the impression that there is no serious doubt about its assertions.[18]

On June 1, 2004, the CIA released yet another version of what can now be identified as NIE 2002-16HC.[19] This final version consists of the original cover, a two-page errata sheet that was referred to in the earlier releases, and the ninety-three pages of the document body. One page of the errata sheet and all but twelve pages of the body of the document are completely masked. Of the pages with text on them, the only new pages are the cover, a title page, and two pages at the end which list the agencies involved in preparing the NIE and all of the NIC officers. In other words, the release is mostly blank pages. The rest of the visible material was available in the *Key Judgments* document. Page numbering is now visible, though, and that reveals the relative positions of the previously released pages.

The NIE states that it was "prepared under the auspices of Robert D. Walpole, National Intelligence Officer for Strategic and Nuclear Programs"; with assistance from the NIOs for Near East and South Asia, Science and Technology, and Conventional Military Issues (NIE title page). This NIE was requested by members of the SSCI, who wanted more information available as they considered authorizing military action against Iraq (SEN 9). The NIE was mainly authored by former CIA Deputy Director John McLaughlin.[20]

THE BRITISH DOSSIER

The British dossier was released by the government on September 24, 2002. It is fifty-one pages long and includes maps and photos. The dossier was commissioned on September 3 and largely based on three classified JIC assessments dated March 15, August 21, and September 9, all of 2002. The September 9 assessment, which focused on various "attack scenarios," was the most influential of the three (BR 79–80, 83).

From the beginning the dossier was conceived of as a document for public consumption to help explain government concerns regarding Iraq. According to the foreword by Prime Minister Tony Blair, the document as published was "based, in large part, on the work of the Joint Intelligence Committee" (DR 3). Subsequent reports indicate that the dossier was in fact authored by the JIC and that the executive summary was authored by the chairman of the JIC, John Scarlett.[21]

In many respects the content is similar to the American documents, which is not surprising given the high level of intelligence and military cooperation between the two countries. Also, both countries were relying heavily on information from the UN inspection teams for a period of time, so they were getting essentially the same information.

The structure of the dossier is as follows:

1. Forward by Prime Minister Tony Blair
2. Executive Summary
3. Iraq's Chemical, Biological, Nuclear, and Ballistic Missile Programs
   a. The Role of Intelligence
   b. Iraq's Programs 1971–1998
   c. The Current Position 1998–2002
4. History of UN Weapons Inspections
5. Iraq under Saddam Hussein

DIFFERENCES BETWEEN THE ESTIMATES

There are a number of differences between the British and the American documents. The British dossier has more historical information and is written in a more narrative style than the American white paper or NIE. It provides more detail about individuals such as Iraqi scientists, government officials, and relatives of Saddam Hussein. In addition to describing Iraq's weapons programs, it lays out a history of Hussein's rule and his many human rights abuses. It also asserts a connection between the threat or use of force and consequent Iraqi cooperation with inspections and the UN Security Council. The dossier gives more detail about what the UN Special Commission (UNSCOM) and the International Atomic Energy Agency (IAEA) teams found and it attributes information to them when appropriate. The dossier more frequently reports the official position of the Iraqi government with respect to each issue, including more mention of the transgressions to which Iraq has admitted.

The U.S. NIE is more explicit than the British document about stating levels of confidence for the various specific estimates. Again, it should be noted that these statements are not explicit in the public 2002 version, but they are there in the unclassified portions of the NIE. Although the British dossier does use words and phrases like "probably" and "may have" to express some uncertainty, there are very few negative statements, such as "we do not know." One of the few statements of this kind is in reference to the aluminum tube question. The dossier states that "there is no definitive intelligence that [the specialized aluminum] is destined for a nuclear programme" (DR 26). Another striking characteristic of the British dossier is the number of statements that in one way or another argue along the lines of "what else could it mean but . . . ?" This could simply be the result of excluding uncertain things from the report.

It is commonly understood that the British assessment system produces reports without dissent.[22] This belief is supported by these documents. In the American documents there are explicit dissents from the main conclusions. Most notably this is seen when reporting on Iraq's nuclear program and capabilities. There is nothing like these alternative views in the British dossier. Of course, the actual, classified British assessments are not available for public inspection, but they were available to the Butler Committee and the Butler Report makes no mention of dissenting opinions.

There is also a difference in preparation time. The NIO for the Near East and South Asia began work on the U.S. white paper in May 2002, although there may have been some adjustment in purpose and focus after a meeting between George Bush and Tony Blair at Camp David in early September 2002 (SEN 55, 287; BR 72). This meeting seems to be the point of origin for the British dossier. On the one hand, the American white paper was worked on for about five months, and the British dossier was produced in fifteen days. On the other hand, the British dossier was largely based on an assessment that had just been completed, whereas the American NIE was hurried through in twenty days and the white paper altered to match it.

There is one last observation about the differences between the British and American estimates worth noting. The British dossier includes at least one case of classic British understatement. Regarding the 1990 invasion of Kuwait it states, "When [Saddam Hussein's] threats and blandishments failed, Iraq invaded Kuwait on 2 August 1990. He believed that occupying Kuwait could prove profitable" (DR 47).

THE REPORT OF THE U.S. SENATE

On June 20, 2003, Senator Pat Roberts and Senator John D. Rockefeller IV, the chairman and vice chairman of the SSCI, respectively, announced that the Committee would investigate the following items:

- the quantity and quality of U.S. intelligence on Iraqi weapons of mass destruction programs, ties to terrorist groups, Saddam Hussein's threat to stability and security in the region, and his repression of his own people;
- the objectivity, reasonableness, independence, and accuracy of the judgments reached by the intelligence community;
- whether those judgments were properly disseminated to policy makers in the executive branch and Congress;
- whether any influence was brought to bear on anyone to shape their analysis to support policy objectives; and
- other issues mutually identified in the course of the Committee's review (SEN 1).

On February 12, 2004, the Committee agreed to add to those terms of reference the following items. Those that are listed as phase one are addressed in the July 7, 2004, report (see Volume 2, Appendix H). Those listed as phase two are to be addressed in a future report.

- the collection of intelligence on Iraq from the end of the Gulf War to the commencement of Operation Iraqi Freedom (phase 1);
- whether public statements, reports, and testimony regarding Iraq by U.S. government officials made between the Gulf War period and the commencement of Operation Iraqi Freedom were substantiated by intelligence information (phase 2);
- the postwar findings about Iraq's WMDs and weapons programs and links to terrorism and how they compare with prewar assessments (phase 2);
- prewar intelligence assessments about postwar Iraq (phase 2);
- any intelligence activities relating to Iraq conducted by the Policy Conterterrorism Evaluation Group and the Office of Special Plans within the Office of the Under Secretary of Defense Policy (phase 1 and 2); and
- the use by the intelligence community of information provided by the Iraqi National Congress (phase 1 and 2) (SEN 2).

Committee staff members had already begun reviewing the intelligence on Iraq several months before the committee announced a formal investigation. The committee staff began with 15,000 pages of material from the intelligence community and subsequently requested and received over 30,000 pages more. The committee was denied access to the relevant *President's Daily Briefs* (*PDBs*). The PDB is a daily report provided to the President of the United States by the Director of Central Intelligence (DCI). Without access to the PDB, the committee could not evaluate the dissemination of intelligence judgments to policy makers (SEN 2–3).

The Committee staff interviewed more than 200 individuals, almost all of whom were officials or employees of the federal government or military services. The staff did interview "nuclear experts with the International Atomic Energy Agency" and former UN inspectors, but it is not clear whether or not these individuals were U.S. citizens. With these individuals as possible exceptions, it seems that the inquiry was conducted entirely within the U.S. government and did not involve information from other governments or non-Americans, except as might exist in the original intelligence products.

The bulk of the work was done by the staff, with the Committee itself holding occasional hearings and giving direction. Part of the method of review was to attempt to ignore and disregard current information on postwar Iraq until an analysis of the prewar information had been complete. The goal was to "replicate the analytical environment [intelligence community] analysts experienced prior to the war" (SEN 4). It is hard to imagine such an attempt being successful.

The report is 511 pages long, all of it text. Although there are quite a few pages with significant portions blacked out, most of the pages are largely in the clear.

The structure of the report is as follows:

1. Introduction
2. Niger
3. Intelligence Community Analysis of Iraq's Nuclear Program
4. Intelligence Community Analysis of Iraq's Biological Weapons Program
5. Intelligence Community Analysis of Iraq's Chemical Weapons Program
6. Intelligence Community Analysis of Iraq's Delivery Systems
7. Iraq WMD Intelligence in Sec. Powell's UN Speech
8. IC Collection Activities Against Iraq's WMD
9. Pressure on IC Analysts Regarding Iraq's WMD Capabilities
10. White Paper on Iraq's WMD
11. Rapid Production of the October 2002 NIE
12. Iraq's Links to Terrorism
13. IC Collection Activities Against Iraq's Links to Terrorism
14. Pressure on IC Analysts Regarding Iraq's Links to Terrorism
15. Powell Speech—Terrorism Portion
16. Iraq's Threat to Regional Stability and Security
17. Saddam's Human Rights Record
18. The IC's Sharing of Intel on Iraqi Suspect WMD Sites with UN Inspectors
19. Appendices, Additional views of particular committee members

The report begins with a description of the training process for CIA intelligence analysts, to put the rest of the discussion into a helpful context for the reader. Particular mention is made of the need to question assumptions and work as a group in which individuals will challenge one another's conclusions.

Of course, the great bulk of the report is about the content and details of the Iraq intelligence and is not especially revealing of American and British intelligence differences. Nevertheless, there are some interesting points for comparison and some points that are simply interesting.

The Senate report reveals that an agency dissenting to some aspect of an NIE can apparently chose how to present its own dissent. In the October 2002 NIE, the INR initially was going to explain its position in footnotes but later "it decided to convey its alternative views in text boxes, rather than object to every point throughout the NIE. INR prepared two separate text boxes, one for the key judgments section and a two-page box for the body of the nuclear section" (SEN 53). Unfortunately, after additional changes to the overall structure of the document, part of INR's dissent on Iraqi efforts to acquire uranium was inadvertently placed in the section dealing with attempts to acquire aluminum tubes, instead of the section dealing with uranium acquisition (SEN 53–54).

The report also reveals that the Department of Energy included at least one extensive text box outlining its dissenting view on the aluminum tubes issue (SEN 95). This text, however, remains classified.

The Senate report notes that managers do not necessarily review the raw intelligence on which an assessment is based. This is especially true if the analyst is more senior and experienced. Editing will be performed, but not necessarily substantial review, and therefore "it is entirely possible that one analyst's views may be presented to high-level officials including the President of the United States without having been reviewed by other analysts with the same depth of knowledge" (SEN 8). This should not be possible for an NIE, however, because it is by definition a collaborative report.

Nevertheless, in the case of the October 2002 NIE on Iraq, the time frame was short and some steps were skipped. The NIE was first requested on September 9, 2002, by Senator Richard Durbin (D-IL), a member of SSCI. This request was followed the next day by another from Senator Bob Graham (D-FL), the chairman of SSCI at that time. By the morning of September 12, the DCI had directed the NIO for Strategy and Nuclear Programs to take the lead in producing an NIE on Iraq's WMD capabilities. Three other NIOs were also directed to work on the NIE. It was understood that the production cycle would need to be fast to meet the congressional need for information prior to voting on legislation. On September 23 the lead NIO circulated a draft to the agencies of the intelligence community, and then two days later held an all-day meeting with community analysts to coordinate changes. A second draft was circulated on September 26. Contrary to standard procedure, the NIO "did not submit the draft for peer review or to a panel of outside experts" (SEN 13).[23] On October 1, the NIE was approved by a meeting of the National Foreign Intelligence Board (NFIB) and printed the same day. The NFIB is chiefly composed of the heads of the various intelligence agencies and is chaired by the DCI. The NFIB normally approves NIEs, but it is not clear how often the board meets in person or whether it met in person to approve this NIE. In all, the process took twenty days. In interviews conducted for the Senate report, NIOs told the staff that they would prefer to have three months to produce an NIE (SEN 11).

Regarding interagency work and collaboration, the report states this: "Depending on the product, the analysis may be coordinated with other [intelligence community] members, but in many instances, each agency produces its own finished products which are subject to review and editing by its own internal management" (SEN 7). The report also identifies agency rivalry and compartmentalization within a single agency (especially the CIA) as problems (SEN 26–29, 268–71). Presumably, some of this is motivated by source protection and some of it by ordinary bureaucratic turf protection. The report finds that this lack of openness between agencies or even within an agency can interfere with what the British call "validation." Validation includes the process of vetting a source, which is a key to giving appropriate weight to the information coming from the source. If an analyst is denied information about a source, it then becomes more difficult to weight that source appropriately.

The dual role of the DCI—head of the CIA and head of the whole intelligence community—is identified as a source of failure. The report asserts that in fact the DCI functions mostly as head of the CIA and that collaboration and sharing of information between agencies suffers as a result. One illustration of this can be seen in the following. The DCI told the committee staff that he does not even expect to learn of dissenting opinions until an issue comes up in the production of an NIE. Prior to that point, "debate about significant national security issues may go on at the analytical level for months, or years, without the DCI or senior policymakers being informed of any opinions other than those of CIA analysts" (SEN 29, 139). Furthermore, the CIA and the DCI are regularly put in the position of presenting information to the President and other policy makers that is supposed to represent the thinking of the whole intelligence community. This means that they must often present dissenting opinions (when they are aware of them) that they do not share, which calls into question the effectiveness of the presentation.

The creation of the Director of National Intelligence (DNI) in December 2004 has, of course, changed this dynamic. The DCI still heads the CIA, but the DNI now has responsibility for overall management of the U.S. intelligence community and for the presentation of intelligence estimates to the President. This should go a long way toward eliminating the overrepresentation of CIA views in intelligence viewed by the President.

The report states that U.S. intelligence "relies too heavily on foreign government services and third party reporting, thereby increasing the potential for manipulation of U.S. policy by foreign interests" (SEN 34). The report is referring to intelligence collection and does not address whether the United States could actually benefit from foreign analysis and assessment help.

Finally, the committee found no evidence that administration officials attempted to coerce or otherwise influence analysts to change their judgments (SEN 272–84).

THE BUTLER REPORT

The Butler Committee was created on February 3, 2004, and consisted of five members led by Lord Butler. The terms of reference for the committee were:

- to investigate the intelligence coverage available in respect of WMD programs in countries of concern and on the global trade in WMDs, taking into account what is now known about these programs; as part of this work;
- to investigate the accuracy of intelligence on Iraqi WMDs up to March 2003, and examine any discrepancies between the intelligence gathered, evaluated, and used by the government before the conflict, and between that intelligence and what has been discovered by the Iraq survey group since the end of the conflict;
- to make recommendations to the Prime Minister for the future on the gathering, evaluation, and use of intelligence on WMDs in the light of the difficulties of operating in countries of concern (BR 1).

Also, the Prime Minister asked that the Committee produce its report before the summer recess. The Committee was charged to follow a method of inquiry modeled on the Franks Committee that investigated the Falklands War.[24] The Committee was to submit its final conclusions "in a form for publication, along with any classified recommendations and material" (BR 1). The main product was meant to be public, with additional classified materials available to the government.

The five Committee members held a total of thirty-six meetings. The Committee interviewed officials within the British government and intelligence services, including the Prime Minister. The Committee also traveled to the United States to meet with senior officials, members of Congress, and the staffs of the CIA and the Defense Intelligence Agency. The Committee traveled to Baghdad to meet with some military leaders and Charles Duelfer, the special advisor to the DCI on Iraq's WMDs. Duelfer's work was important to the Butler Committee because his findings would be the most complete standard against which the Committee could measure the prewar assessments. Unfortunately, the work of the Iraq Survey Group, which Duelfer headed, was not completed before the Butler Committee's deadline. Nevertheless, they were able to obtain preliminary information from Duelfer that allowed them to make some judgments.

The Butler Committee approach was to examine the assessments produced by the JIC and then examine the antecedent and underlying intelligence—both what was accepted and what was rejected. They would then consider "whether it appears to have been properly evaluated" (BR 3). Another method used in the Butler Report was to compare assessments and data that have been made public through some other process, such as a report by the United Nations or the IAEA. Once information entered the public domain in some other way, the Committee had no concerns about drawing attention to it for the purpose of presenting its findings. This allowed it to make its points without revealing more classified material.

The report was issued on July 14, 2004, and consists of 196 pages of text, with nothing blacked out. One of the annexes at the end includes portions of three classified assessments.

The structure of the report is as follows.

1. Introduction
2. Nature and Use of Intelligence
3. Countries of Concern Other than Iraq and Global Trade
4. Terrorism
5. Counter-Proliferation Machinery
6. Iraq
7. Iraq: Specific Issues
8. Conclusions on Broader Issues
9. Summary of Conclusions
10. Annexes

In the introduction, the report thanks the intelligence agencies for their co-operation and work and declares that the Committee is "relatively confident" that they have been provided all of the relevant data. They also note that the British intelligence community coordinated its efforts so that the Committee received a single stream of papers and data, not a separate one from each agency. This would seem to indicate a high level of bureaucratic trust, cooperation, and ability to work together. Consistent with this, the report attributes success in exposing the nuclear proliferation network established by A. Q. Khan, a Pakistani physicist, to "strong integration in the U.K. between all agencies." It notes that a decision was made to share even the most sensitive information at the working level. There was also a "high degree of co-operation between agencies and policy-makers in depart-ments" (BR 20). This integration was further enhanced by the creation of the Joint Terrorism Analysis Centre in June 2003 (BR 36). The center brings together staff from eleven different government agencies and departments.

Like the Senate report, the Butler Report takes some time to describe the intelligence process. The model that the Butler Report lays out consists of four steps: collection, validation, analysis, and assessment.[25] The report explains collection as mainly made up of signals intelligence (SIGINT), information from human sources (HUMINT), and imagery information (IMINT). It describes the other three steps in this way: "Validation should remove information which is unreliable (including reporting which has been deliberately inserted to mislead). Analysis should assemble fragmentary intelligence into coherent meaningful ac-counts. Assessment should put intelligence into a sensible real-world context and identify how it can affect policy-making" (BR 14).

Validation has as much to do with the faithful transmission of the information through the intelligence collection agency as it does with the quality of the source.

In the British system, the Ministry of Defence receives the largest quantity of intelligence and the analysis stage is carried out there by the Defence Intelligence Staff (DIS). The report states that "analysis can be conducted only by people expert in the subject matter" (BR 10). So, though validation looks at both the source and the chain of communication, analysis looks at the factual substance of the information, evaluates it, and tries to make sense of it. The report states that "assessment may be conducted separately from analysis or as an almost parallel process in the mind of the analyst" (BR 10). Furthermore, "in the U.K., assessment is usually explicitly described as 'all-source' " (BR 11). The goal with assessment is to be as objective as possible, unaffected by motives and pressures that might distort judgment (BR 12). The report notes that in the United Kingdom, "central intelligence assessment is the responsibility of the Assessments Staff." This staff is made up of approximately thirty senior and middle-ranking officials on assignment from other departments, along with secretarial and administrative support. The staff is housed within the Cabinet Office.

The JIC brings together the intelligence agencies, the DIS, and important policy departments. The Chief of the Assessments Staff is also a member of the JIC. The JIC meets weekly. In addition to regular attendees, government departments send officials as matters warrant. Representatives from the intelligence communities of Australia, Canada, and the United States also attend on occasion. The chairman of the JIC has at times also been the prime minister's Foreign Policy Adviser. "The JIC thus brings together in regular meetings the most senior people responsible for intelligence collection, for intelligence assessment and for the use of intelligence in the main departments for which it is collected" (BR 13).

In addition to conventional and direct national interests, JIC assessments also support inspection, monitoring, and verification regimes in other parts of the world to prevent the proliferation of nuclear, chemical, and biological weapons (BR 38). This indicates a vision for intelligence that goes beyond immediate state security interests to longer range interests.

As noted earlier, JIC assessments do not contain minority reports or dissents. "When the intelligence is unclear or otherwise inadequate and the JIC at the end of its debate is still uncertain, it may report alternative interpretations of the facts before it such as they are; but in such cases all the membership agrees that the interpretations they are proposing are viable alternatives. The JIC does not . . . characterise such alternatives as championed by individual members who disagree with colleagues' points of view" (BR 13). The JIC has also made the assertion that when intelligence is ambiguous it should not be artificially simplified. The Butler Report includes extensive quotations from JIC assessments.

The report identifies several examples of JIC assessments where the "JIC made clear that much of the assessment was based on its own judgment" (BR 75). By this the authors seem to mean that the assessment was based not on new information but on speculation and logical extrapolation from previously known facts. This type of reporting seems particularly problematic in a context where the providers of intelligence and the consumers of intelligence are working together and are sometimes one and the same. In the absence of hard data, policy preferences are likely to be indistinguishable from assessments. Despite this, the committee found no evidence that senior policy officials on the JIC improperly influenced assessments in a preferred-policy direction (BR 110).

However, there was concern about politicization resulting from publicity. The report notes that the dossier broke new ground in three ways:

- The JIC had never previously produced a public document.
- No government case for any international action had previously been made to the British public through explicitly drawing on a JIC publication.
- The authority of the British intelligence community, and the JIC in particular, had never been used in such a public way (BR 76).

Material from the JIC had been used in public before, but it had never been attributed. To the Butler Committee, this is a major change with worrisome consequences (BR 114). The concern is that bringing intelligence into the public arena will tempt everyone to use it as a political tool and eventually as a partisan political tool. Americans would tend to frame this as an issue of transparency and see attribution as a positive step. To them, the greater danger of politicization arises from the strength of the relationship between intelligence producers and policy makers.

The Butler Committee saw a need to slightly modify the position and choice of the chairman of the JIC. Currently, this person may be outranked by the heads of the intelligence agencies that sit at the JIC. The Butler Committee concludes that the person chosen as chair should be very senior and in the latter stage of his or her career in the government. In sum, the chair should be beyond influence and have more clout in both the intelligence community and the policy community (BR 144).

The committee also suggests expanding and developing both the JIC Assessments Staff and the HUMINT collection capacity of the agencies. There is insufficient collection in some areas. At the same time there is insufficient capacity to analyze the information that is collected.

As mentioned earlier, the public dossier was heavily influenced by the September 9 JIC assessment. According to the Butler Committee, "The most significant difference was the omission of the warnings included in JIC assessments about the limited intelligence base on which some aspects of those assessments were being made" (BR 80).

The committee also suggests that the JIC enhance the ability of assessments to convey levels of confidence, and it draws attention to the U.S. practice of doing this explicitly, along with notes of dissent (BR 145).

In a couple of places the Butler Report mentions compartmentalization as problem, but only very briefly (BR 111, 139). This problem was much more prominent in the Senate report on the American system. In fact, the Butler Report and the British dossier seem relatively comfortable discussing secrets that have already been revealed through some other source.

Finally, the Butler Report notes some management weaknesses with human sources in the Secret Intelligence Service (BR 102–9). These were indirectly the result of staff cuts and could easily be fixed by reversing the cuts and reinstituting previous practices. These do not seem to indicate any major differences in British and American approaches.

DIFFERENCES BETWEEN THE
INVESTIGATIVE REPORTS

First, there are some obvious differences. The Butler Report, which is final, consists of 12 pages of front matter and 196 pages of report. The Senate report is two-and-a-half times longer with 9 pages of front matter and 511 pages of report, and it is only the first of two phases of investigation and reporting. The British report was produced by a Committee of five members: two current members of Parliament (one from the government, the other from the opposition), two former high-ranking civil servants, and one former high-ranking military officer (former chief of defense staff). The Committee had a staff of seven plus additional interview transcribers. The American report was nominally produced by a congressional committee of seventeen members (plus the Senate Majority and Minority Leaders, who are ex officio members of SSCI), no doubt with a much larger staff that did a greater share of the actual work. This disparity in size may be attributable to the disparity between the two nations in resources and international responsibilities, but one suspects that it is at least partly a reflection of relative efficiency.

The British focused their investigation on ensuring validity from the beginning of the evidence chain to the JIC. Because the JIC represents both the producers of intelligence and the consumers of final assessments, it is not subject to some of the assessment problems that occur in the American system. For instance, the Senate report describes the problem of layering (SEN 22–23, 212). This happens when new assessments are based on old assessments, which are based on even older assessments. The key danger with this practice is that the caveats and uncertainties of the earlier assessments may be left out in later ones that almost treat the earlier ones as sources. This causes the reader of the current assessment to think that it rests on a stronger foundation than it does. Previous estimates become conventional wisdom rather than true estimates with particular levels of confidence. When the new estimate reaches the policy maker, he or she is not aware of its true contingency. Although it may still occur, this problem is less likely to occur in a system where those incorporating the intelligence into final policy advice are included in the assessment process. They are more likely to know the history and the genesis of the assessments to which they are contributing and agreeing.

Closely related to the layering problem is that of failing to properly identify assumptions. Both reports are concerned with the possibility that worst-case calculations are mistaken for the prevailing wisdom of what is most likely to develop (BR 46).

Countering the possible benefit the British derive from the JIC system is the danger of politicization of intelligence that most American observers would anticipate from a close proximity of analysis/assessment and policy making.[26] The concern is that known policy preferences will cause analysis to be skewed in favor of supporting those preferences. As one American scholar/practitioner has succinctly put it, "Only by maintaining their [analysts'] distance from policy can they hope to produce intelligence that is objective."[27] The CIA has an Ombudsman for Politicization specifically to deal with the problem of pressure from management or policy makers, and the Senate report includes a chapter on the issue of improper political pressure (SEN 357–65). The Butler Report is not greatly concerned with the relatively close working relationship of intelligence producers and intelligence consumers in the JIC. It notes that "the JIC has always been very conscious" of the need to be objective (BR 16).

Surprisingly, the Senate report does not include a list of recommended changes. This may have fallen outside of their self-determined mandate for political reasons. The Republicans in control of the Committee may have wanted to leave the President's hands free or they simply may not have reached a bipartisan agreement on what changes to recommend. Another explanation is that they did not believe large changes were politically feasible, given the history of the U.S. intelligence community and the great number of individuals and institutions that have a stake in the current arrangements. For instance, all of the various congressional committees and subcommittees that have some control over the intelligence community would likely resist restructuring efforts that would lessen their control. Other departments of government (for example, the military services and the Justice Department) would also fight changes if they meant losing their share of intelligence activities and information sources. Given its public failures and the legislation to reorganize the intelligence community that was passed after these reports were written, it is unlikely that the committee felt that no structural changes were needed.

The Butler Committee did provide explicit recommendations in their report, and this may be a result of the fact that their mandate came from the executive in a parliamentary system where the executive is, of course, also the legislative leader. In such a system, the interest and ability in making changes is much more likely to be consistent.

Both the Senate report and the Butler report identify information sharing within their respective governments and intelligence communities as a problem, but in the British system it is a rather minor anomaly, whereas in the United States it is systemic and normal to refrain from sharing information with other agencies and departments. This is also seen directly in the investigative work of the committees. In the United Kingdom, the investigators eventually had access to all of the information they requested. In fact, the intelligence agencies were able to work together to provide requested information through one source, regardless of its origin. In the United States, the investigators had to negotiate with each agency and the White House. Despite the fact that during the Senate investigation the Senate and SSCI were controlled by the President's political party, they were not granted access to everything that they wanted, most notably the *President's Daily Briefs*.[28] The presidentially appointed Silberman-Robb Commission, though, was granted full access to these documents, which supports the idea that institutional rivalry between the executive and legislative branches in the U.S. system accounts for some differences between intelligence information availability and use in the American and British systems. It is also noteworthy that the American NIE and the first major postinvasion investigation of intelligence were both initiated by American legislators, not by the executive branch. At the least, American intelligence agencies exist in a more complex setting of political institutions than their British counterparts.

Another difference between the two approaches is that the United States suffers from a lack of alternate perspectives. Although the U.S. intelligence community has especially strong relationships and interactions—liaison—with intelligence agencies in the United Kingdom, Canada, Australia, and New Zealand, it is telling that no officials from these countries were interviewed or participated in the investigation leading to the Senate report, even though they are surely involved with and pay close attention to what happens with U.S. intelligence. Indeed, as mentioned, the Senate report views reliance on intelligence collection by foreign governments as a potential source of manipulation. The Butler Committee did not limit its interviews to British government employees or British nationals, but interviewed individuals from a variety of nations, including U.S. government officials.

LIMITATIONS

Before drawing final conclusions, the limitations of this study should be spelled out. First, despite the unusual amount of material released, there are still gaps in the documentary evidence. On the British side, although portions of the actual assessments produced by the government have been made public (BR Annex B 163–76), the percentage of the full assessments these represent is unknown. Also, the Butler Commission delivered some additional classified findings to the government that are not included in their public report. On the American side, most of the text of NIE 2002-16HC is still classified and there are masked-out lines scattered throughout the Senate report. Material that is not available to be read cannot be evaluated. If the unavailable material is selected in some manner that is systematically related to the nation of origin, then the conclusions of the current analysis are biased. Further, even if the still classified material does not skew the analysis, it may include some additional national differences that will not be detected by this study. Nevertheless, it is possible that a great deal of what is still classified would not change the current analysis. For instance, the revelation of protected sources might reveal something about divergent methods, but it is more likely to produce only a list of names.

Second, this chapter looks at only one set of documents for a single time and a single situation that is exceptional in a number of ways. Therefore, there is a question as to whether the evidence reviewed here represents British and American approaches generally. This is a problem of validity—does this data really represent the phenomenon of interest? The data here do provide evidence for the conclusions drawn, but not conclusive evidence. Adding more cases of corresponding British and American documentation would strengthen the conclusions.

Third, there is the question of whether the two investigations and reports are strictly comparable. The American investigation was carried out by the large staff of a legislative committee, the British investigation by a much smaller committee dominated by civil servants. If the Silberman-Robb Committee had formed earlier and finished in the summer of 2004, then it would have more directly corresponded to the Butler Committee. However, as noted, the Silberman-Robb Committee was influenced by both the Senate report and the Butler Report and therefore does not represent a firsthand or exclusively American look at the situation.

As stated at the beginning, this chapter attempts to avoid preconceptions and let the documents speak for themselves. It is, of course, impossible to set aside all preconceptions. The documents examined herein are consistent with some commonly understood differences between American and British intelligence structures, procedures, and attitudes, but they also highlight a few unexamined differences. Even for the former, this chapter provides accessible documented evidence that is sometimes lacking in the literature on intelligence.

CONCLUSIONS

This study has documented a number of significant differences between American and British approaches to intelligence. One of the most noteworthy is the relative ease with which information is shared within the British government. The Butler Committee noted only minor problems along these lines, whereas compartmentalization and information hoarding are major problems in the American system. Without this liberality, the assessments-producing Joint Intelligence Committee would not be possible. The JIC is another important distinguishing structure. In it, the whole government (and sometimes even representatives of foreign governments) is brought together to make assessments, not just the intelligence-producing agencies. This contributes to another distinguishing feature of British intelligence practice, namely, providing greater context for understanding problematic situations. British reports provide more of what anthropologist Clifford Geertz called "thick description," or the detail necessary to understand the meanings and motives of behaviors.[29] This detail might be historical or cultural or even detail about individuals other than the immediate target of interest—detail that reveals not just functional interactions but also the identities and relationships that shape those interactions.

Another important difference made more salient through the documents in this comparison is the way intelligence information is transmitted to the political executive. During the period when these documents were produced, the formal process in the United States was for the DCI to present intelligence produced by the intelligence community to the President. This created a bias toward the views of the CIA over the views of other agencies, and it also created a competition for the President's ear as other agencies tried to find pathways that bypassed the DCI. In the United Kingdom, the JIC system and the generally cooperative attitudes again seem to avoid this problem. All of the intelligence services are represented on the JIC, which meets weekly, and information presented there is taken by the various department heads back to their departments and their political overseers. The Prime Minister also receives his or her information from the JIC. Therefore, individual intelligence services each have the same opportunity to communicate their efforts to the whole government and do not need to compete with one another for access to the leadership of the government.

Furthermore, the British JIC system forces the leaders of different parts of the intelligence community to sit down together on a weekly basis and reconcile their views. This more frequent personal interaction undoubtedly contributes to their willingness to share information with one another, too. The U.S. NFIB structure is similarly collegial on paper, but does not frequently convene in person and serves mainly as a routing list for reports or conference calls. It also lacks the regular interaction with top policy advisors and nonintelligence department heads as a group.

A final major difference comes from the distributed nature of political power in the American system. Because of the separation of the legislative and executive branches of government, intelligence agencies in the United States face a more complicated environment and a different set of pressures than their counterparts in the United Kingdom. As noted, the legislative branch in the American system initiated both the NIE and the postinvasion investigation; the latter despite the lack of partisan division between Congress and the President at the time. In this environment, intelligence agencies can be subjected to conflicting pressures and can also choose to appeal to either of two (or more) masters. In the British parliamentary system, intelligence producers are far less likely to experience these conflicting pressures because the legislative leadership automatically holds the executive power, too. Though there is a parliamentary Intelligence and Security Committee in the United Kingdom, its role is limited and it does not effectively balance against the government the way that the congressional committees balance against the executive branch in the U.S. system.[30] This is evident in the fact of the ISC's restricted access to government documents, its small role in the Butler Report, and its inability to report to Parliament or the public without the prime minister's approval. For the same reasons, the access of opposition or minority political parties to intelligence information and influence is also much less in the British system. One implication of this system is that there is no institutional counterweight to check the executive use or misuse of the intelligence services other than the judiciary, which is not likely to get involved unless there is a domestic abuse of power or some other incident that inflames the public.

Besides these major differences between the two systems, there are also some less sweeping but still important differences. Most significant among these are the American practices of including of notes of dissent and communicating explicit levels of confidence in intelligence estimates. Among other things, the Butler Report recommended that the British JIC assessments staff consider adopting these practices.

In conclusion, the current study is only a basic, observational contribution to intelligence studies. It can be built on in several ways. First, documents from additional nations related to the Iraq WMD problem should be examined. Second, comparable documentation describing other problems (not the Iraq case) should be sought out and examined. Both of these steps would expand the number of cases available and may result in a typology of intelligence systems. Third, theoretical explanations for differences or types found should be explored and tested. Why do the British provide more context in their reports? Why can the British departments share information and the Americans cannot? Some researchers are already engaged in efforts to explain the perceived difference in intelligence—policy maker distance using cultural variables.[31] Additional explanatory power might be found in the broader institutional environment or the historical choices of previous governments. Both the rational choice approach and the less individualistic historical institutionalism approach to explaining norms and patterns of behavior would probably be illuminating.[32] Fourth, the implications of different intelligence systems can be explored, assessing their advantages and disadvantages and thus providing useful information for governments and policy makers. With these steps, further comparative analysis can be applied to the field of intelligence studies to reveal important aspects of intelligence systems that go undetected in the more common, single-country studies. This chapter is a modest contribution to that effort.

NOTES

An earlier version of this chapter was presented at the 2006 International Studies Association conference in San Diego, CA, under the title "A Comparison of the United States and the United Kingdom Inquiries into Intelligence Failure: Mining the Iraq Case."

1. Jack S. Levy, "Qualitative Methods in International Relations," in Frank P. Harvey and Michael Brecher, eds., *Evaluating Methodolgy in International Studies*, Millennial Reflections on International Studies (Ann Arbor: University of Michigan Press, 2002), p. 135.

2. Joint Intelligence Committee, *Iraq's Weapons of Mass Destruction: The Assessment of the British Government* (London: Stationery Office of the United Kingdom, 2002), available at http://www.pm.gov.uk/files/pdf/iraqdossier.pdf (accessed October 13, 2004).

3. CIA, *Iraq's Weapons of Mass Destruction Programs* (2002) available at http://www.cia.gov/cia/reports/iraq_wmd/Iraq_Oct_2002.pdf (accessed September 17, 2004).

4. Senate Select Committee on Intelligence, *Report on the U.S. Intelligence Community's Prewar Intelligence Assessments on Iraq* (Washington: Government Printing Office, 2004), available at http://www.gpoaccess.gov/serialset/creports/pdf/s108-301/ s108-301.zip (accessed September 17, 2004). This report represents the first part of a two-phase investigation. However, there is serious doubt as to whether the full second phase will be carried out, although some aspects were published by the Committee in 2006.

5. Lord Butler, *Review of Intelligence on Weapons of Mass Destruction* (London: Stationery Office of the United Kingdom, July 14, 2004), available at http://www.official-documents.co.uk/document/deps/hc/hc898/898.pdf (accessed October 13, 2004).

6. Intelligence and Security Committee, *Iraqi Weapons of Mass Destruction—Intelligence and Assessments* (London: Stationery Office, September 11, 2003), available at http://www.cabinetoffice.gov.uk/publications/reports/isc/iwmdia.pdf (accessed September 14, 2005).

7. Coalition Information Centre, *Iraq—Its Infrastructure of Concealment, Deception and Intimidation*, (January 2003), available at http://www.pm.gov.uk/files/pdf/Iraq.pdf (accessed September 14, 2005).

8. Commission on the Intelligence Capabilities of the United States Regarding Weapons of Mass Destruction, *Report to the President of the United States* (Washington: Government Printing Office, 2005).

9. Ibid., p. 46.

10. Mark M. Lowenthal, *Intelligence: From Secrets to Policy*, 2nd ed. (Washington, DC: CQ Press, 2003), p. 49.

11. This discussion of the U.S. intelligence community and its products is based on the system in place at the time the Iraq documents were produced. Some features of this system changed with the passage of the Intelligence Reform and Terrorism Prevention Act of 2004 (December 17, 2004). In particular, the creation of the Director of National Intelligence changed the structure and some of the top-level interactions of the intelligence community. This will be discussed further later in this chapter.

12. Lowenthal, *Intelligence*, pp. 102–3. Now, however, the director of National Intelligence has replaced the DCI in this role.

13. Michael Herman, "Assessment Machinery: British and American Models," in David A. Charters, A. Stuart Farson, and Glenn P. Hastedt, eds., *Intelligence Analysis and Assessment*, Studies in Intelligence (London: Frank Cass, 1996).

14. Ibid.; Joint Intelligence Committee, *Iraq's Weapons of Mass Destruction*; Lowenthal, *Intelligence*, p. 236; Jeffrey T. Richelson, *Foreign Intelligence Organizations* (Cambridge, MA: Ballinger, 1988), p. 37.

15. CIA, *Key Judgments (from October 2002 NIE)* (Washington: National Security Archive, 2003), available at http://www2.gwu.edu/~nsarchiv/NSAEBB/NSAEBB129/ nie_judgments.pdf (accessed September 20, 2004).

16. Because none of the pages in *Key Judgments* display page numbers, references to pages in this document will follow an ordinal sequence beginning with the first page as page 1.

17. The Department of Energy, however, did not dissent on the issue of whether Iraq had begun to reconstitute its nuclear weapons program.

18. For another useful comparison of the October 2002 white paper with the *Key Judgments* document, see Parliamentary Joint Committee on ASIO ASIS and DSD, *Intelligence on Iraq's Weapons of Mass Destruction* (Commonwealth of Australia, 2003), available at http://www.aph.gov.au/house/committee/pjcaad/WMD/report/fullreport.pdf (accessed November 26, 2004).

19. CIA, *Iraq's Continuing Programs for Weapons of Mass Destruction: NIE 2002-16hc* (Washington: National Security Archive, 2004), available at http://www2.gwu.edu/~nsarchiv/NSAEBB/NSAEBB129/nie.pdf (accessed August 14, 2004).

20. Michael Hirsh, Michael Isikoff, and Mark Hosenball, "Secret Agent Man," *Newsweek*, July 5, 2004.

21. Butler; Michael Herman, "Intelligence's Future: Learning from the Past," *Journal of Intelligence History* 3, no. 2 (2003), p. 3.

22. Percy Cradock, *Know Your Enemy: How the Joint Intelligence Committee Saw the World* (London: John Murray, 2002), pp. 295–96; Herman, "Assessment Machinery," pp. 19–20; Michael Herman, *Intelligence Services in the Information Age: Theory and Practice*, Studies in Intelligence (London: Frank Cass, 2001), pp. 133–34; Loch K. Johnson, *Secret Agencies: U.S. Intelligence in a Hostile World* (New Haven, CT: Yale University Press, 1996), pp. 128–29.

23. "Outside" in this context appears to mean outside of the group of analysts who prepared it in the first place, not outside of the intelligence community.

24. Lord Butler, *Opening Statement by the Chairman, 14 July 2004* (Butler Committee, 2004), available at http://www.butlerreview.org.uk/news/launchstatement.pdf (accessed December 1, 2004); Butler, *Review*.

25. The report also alludes to requirement setting for collection, but does not treat this formally and perhaps does not consider itself to be evaluating this part of the process.

26. Sherman Kent, *Strategic Intelligence for American World Policy* (Princeton, NJ: Princeton University Press, 1949); H. Bradford Westerfield, "Inside Ivory Bunkers: CIA Analysts Resist Managers' 'Pandering'—Part I," *International Journal of Intelligence and Counterintelligence* 9, no. 4 (1996–97); but for an empirical challenge to the conventional view, see Stephen Marrin, "Does Proximity Between Intelligence Producers and Consumers Matter? The Case of Iraqi WMD Intelligence," paper presented at the *International Studies Association Conference* (Honolulu: International Studies Association, 2005).

27. Lowenthal, *Intelligence*, p. 142.

28. A daily summary of intelligence produced for the president at that time by the DCI.

29. Clifford Geertz, *The Interpretation of Cultures: Selected Essays* (New York: Basic Books, 1973).

30. The ISC consists of nine members appointed by the prime minister in consultation with the leaders of the two main opposition parties. The members come from both houses of Parliament and are not limited to the governing party. The committee is within the "ring of secrecy" of the Official Secrets Act and reports directly to the prime minister.

31. Philip H. J. Davies, "Intelligence Culture and Intelligence Failure in Britain and the United States," *Cambridge Review of International Affairs* 17, no. 3 (2004); Stephen

Marrin, "Why Does Distance Between Intelligence and Decisionmaking Vary? The Impact of Decisionmaking Culture on Intelligence Analysis," working draft, University of Virginia, 2005. See also Michael A. Turner, "A Distinctive U.S. Intelligence Identity," *International Journal of Intelligence and CounterIntelligence* 17, no. 1 (2004).

32. Peter A. Hall and Rosemary C. R. Taylor, "Political Science and the Three New Institutionalisms," *Political Studies* 44, no. 4 (1996); Lawrence J. Lamanna, "Explaining Differences in British and American Intelligence Norms," working draft, University of Georgia, 2005; Paul Pierson, *Politics in Time: History, Institutions, and Social Analysis* (Princeton, NJ: Princeton University Press, 2004); Kathleen Thelen, "Historical Institutionalism in Comparative Politics," *Annual Review of Political Science* 2, no. 1 (1999).

6

MORE PERFECT OVERSIGHT

Intelligence Oversight and Reform

CYNTHIA M. NOLAN

Of all our recommendations, strengthening congressional oversight may be among the most difficult and important. So long as oversight is governed by current congressional rules and resolutions, we believe the American people will not get the security they want and need. The United States needs a strong, stable, and capable congressional committee structure to give America's national intelligence agencies oversight, support, and leadership.[1]

IN 2004, THE NATIONAL COMMISSION ON TERRORIST Attacks Upon the United States (the 9/11 Commission) revealed its research into the events, intelligence, and decision making leading up to the terrorist attacks of September 11, 2001. Among many other recommendations and criticisms, the Commission members concluded that the congressional oversight of intelligence had been insufficient. They argued that the congressional oversight committees—the House Permanent Select Committee on Intelligence (HPSCI) and the Senate Select Committee on Intelligence (SSCI)—required complete reform. According to the Commission members, only a comprehensive overhaul would accomplish clear accountability for the intelligence agencies.[2]

These recommendations imply that stronger, unified, clearer, more efficient oversight would improve the capabilities of the intelligence agencies, their joint relations, their products, and—consequently—foreign policy decision making. According to the members, more comprehensive, far-reaching, actionable, unified, and—most important—accountable intelligence will help prevent future terrorist acts. Though not specifically mentioned by the Commission, its recommendations were based on the conclusion that intelligence oversight is so unique as to require a unique kind of oversight.

With this research, I ask whether this unspoken assumption is correct. Is intelligence oversight so peculiar that it requires exceptional methods? Likewise, I ask whether those who conduct intelligence oversight believe it is unique and therefore believe it requires exceptional methods or whether the overseers believe traditional methods are sufficient.

Examining this question will require a few steps. First, I review the oversight literature to determine the conduct of congressional oversight. Second, I ascertain whether intelligence oversight is conducted differently from the oversight of other bureaucratic offices. Finally, the chapter examines the opinions of congressional insiders; interviews of current and former representatives and senators should shed some light on the extent to which oversight of the intelligence agencies is unique.

CONCEPTUALIZING CONGRESSIONAL OVERSIGHT

Legislative oversight—the review of executive activities by Congress—can take any one of a few forms. Morris Ogul identified a latent and manifest dichotomy of congressional oversight. In his characterization, members of Congress perform oversight indirectly through their many legislative duties, as well as directly through hearings, reporting requirements, and investigations. In his view, much of what is actually congressional oversight has not been called oversight.[3] He concluded that although latent oversight is not well measured, it is most common.

Joel Aberbach distinguished between advocacy and adversarial approaches to oversight. Legislators may seek to protect bureaucratic offices with which they have become very friendly or perhaps criticize these executive-level administrators for some reasons related to political gain, personal preferences, or their home districts. He further asserted that oversight units are more likely to be neutral.[4] He concluded that advocacy oversight, overall, is more often found in the congressional committees.

McCubbins and Schwartz observed centralized and decentralized oversight activities as the most important dividing line between two types of congressional oversight: police patrol style and fire alarm style. They argued that legislators have chosen fire alarm style, a less expensive, decentralized oversight to review the executive branch activities. On the one hand, the centralized oversight (police patrol style) that most researchers expect to find retains most investigative powers within the congressional committee. On the other hand, decentralized oversight empowers outside observers with the ability to initiate necessary "alarms" triggering oversight responsibilities.[5] They observed that decentralized oversight is most likely in Congress.

Ogul and Rockman also observed an active and reactive dichotomy in the academic treatments of congressional oversight. In these characterizations, they argued that McCubbins and Schwartz's treatment of congressional oversight observed active versus reactive activities as well as centralized and decentralized oversight. They modified the police patrol oversight, calling it decentralized and active. In select committees, they asserted that oversight is most likely to be centralized and reactive.[6] They observed that in general, reactive oversight is more likely to be found in congressional oversight.

Ogul and Rockman identified one other dichotomy in the academic treatments of congressional oversight: anticipatory and post hoc oversight. They argued that subtle and anticipatory oversight most certainly occurs, but it is difficult to measure. What may be termed unintended reactions influence bureaucratic officers to change their own actions in anticipation of some form of oversight by Congress in this anticipatory oversight.[7] However, they argued that post hoc oversight is the most likely congressional oversight activity.

DEFINITIONS

Legislative oversight is defined herein as the legislation, hearings, investigations, and activities of Congress that review, study, and report on executive branch agencies and offices.

For my purposes, traditional methods of oversight are defined as the most common ones employed in Congress, as determined by outside researchers. Such observers most often describe legislative oversight as latent, advocacy-oriented, decentralized, reactive, post hoc activities.[8] These common attributes therefore describe the most utilized tools and methods of congressional oversight. By contrast, exceptional methods of oversight are those less commonly identified by outside observers. Such methods might be described as manifest, critical, centralized, and anticipatory.[9]

This research begins by listing and describing the most important factors in determining the character of oversight. This step also includes investigation of these factors in relation to the intelligence agencies with a reference to the oversight of other bureaucratic agencies. Using these comparisons, one can determine whether intelligence oversight in its current state is unique. Using interviews with representatives and senators, I then explore how unique intelligence oversight should be. Finally, the chapter examines reform recommendations related to intelligence oversight and ask whether these reforms are necessary.

DETERMINING OVERSIGHT

As already noted, congressional oversight is traditionally considered latent, friendly, decentralized, reactive, and post hoc. Expectations of what oversight should accomplish have infused the opinions and descriptions of how oversight is conducted. Early researchers on this subject found that congressional oversight of the bureaucracy seldom measured up to these ideals.[10] Later research asserted that the expectations of these researchers had been flawed. For instance, McCubbins and Schwartz argued that the decision is rational to follow fire alarm oversight by building and empowering outside alarms to alert Congress to oversight dangers. Consequently, they found that legislators prefer this type of oversight. Aberbach studied similar concerns in oversight and found that legislators have actually followed a great deal of police patrol oversight because of changes in the congressional context.[11] Thus it is safe to conclude that legislative control of the bureaucracy is some combination of police patrol and fire alarm oversight.

McCubbins and Schwartz emphasize that although Congress will use a variety of methods to oversee the government, they prefer fire alarm oversight because it is most cost-effective. Aberbach agreed that there are many elements of oversight in the legislative arsenal, but nonetheless reached contrary conclusions. Specifically, he decided that the 1970s era of political activism encouraged much more active oversight, and thus more police patrol oversight, than had been prevalent before. The post–Cold War environment likely has encouraged equally active oversight in all areas of government control.

In the area of foreign and defense policy, Christopher Deering asked whether Congress prefers police patrol or fire alarm oversight. Deering first addressed the extent to which these areas of the bureaucracy are unique. He determined that these areas are not so unique as to render the police and fire fighter metaphors inapplicable. He argued that in the House, the National Security and International Relations Committees preferred police patrol oversight during the 104th Congress. The Senate Armed Services and Foreign Relations Committees likewise preferred police patrol oversight during the 104th Congress.[12]

Deering concluded that legislative oversight of foreign and defense policy does not differ significantly from oversight of other bureaucratic offices. In the post–Cold War period, Congress is as willing to participate in defense and foreign policy as it is in other areas of the federal government.[13] Similarly, Aberbach argued in 1990 that the congressional context—relations with the President, resources for the committees and staff, as well as changes in the home districts—changed so dramatically that formal congressional oversight in all areas had increased, making legislators more likely to step publicly into the defense and foreign policy arena.[14]

A few distinct factors stand out in determining this character, quality, and quantity of legislative oversight and how unique or traditional it might be. I now apply them to intelligence oversight.

INFORMATION FLOWS

Lupia and McCubbins examined the decisions of a legislature to delegate policy-making authority to government bureaucrats, as well as the consequences of those decisions. Generally, legislators realize that bureaucrats possess greater expertise than members of Congress. The primary means by which they overcome this deficiency is through oversight. The question for these researchers was as follows: Under what conditions do legislators' efforts at oversight actually achieve their desired outcomes? The main obstacle to legislators gaining their desired policy choices is information.[15]

The quality of any oversight effort relies to some degree on the quality of information the legislators receive. In some areas of government, information flow is easier, more accessible, and much more likely than in others. One can imagine that consumer products, or medical policy decisions and the information surrounding them, is more accessible than defense or intelligence decisions simply because the information is publicly available. For instance, far more of the reports and documents produced by the intelligence agencies are likely to be classified than is the case with respect to the Consumer Products Safety Commission or the surgeon general, although to be sure, the latter offices do not publish every document they produce and Freedom of Information Act requests to these agencies are common.[16]

If the intelligence agencies classify a greater number of documents than other government agencies and offices, this fact would be a significant barrier to legislative oversight, making intelligence oversight unique. To be sure, the intelligence agencies share a great deal of information with Congress—more every year.[17] This classified information may be viewed by legislators on the intelligence oversight committees—the HPSCI and SSCI—in specialized security storage areas only.[18]

However, one can identify other areas of government oversight that require equally secure handling instructions for legislators of government documents, i.e. social security and consumer credit information, individual medical information, weapons specifications, details of defense assignments, FBI files, or perhaps even sensitive information regarding aircraft or other transportation protocols. Moreover, many critics have accused the current administration of President George W. Bush of over-classifying information since the terrorist attacks of September 11, 2001. Indeed, in 2004, twice as many documents—from the entire government—were classified as in 2001.[19]

Increasing classification (both in volume and breadth) of government reveals that the secrecy that previously set the intelligence agencies apart is spreading to other areas of congressional oversight. Moreover, in response to congressional demands, intelligence agencies share more information with legislators. The barriers to information flow within the system of intelligence oversight seemed obvious at first glance, but closer inspection suggests secrecy may not differ as much as previously assumed.

COMMITTEE HISTORY

The HPSCI and SSCI have just passed their thirtieth anniversaries. Established to respond to egregious abuses by the Central Intelligence Agency (CIA) and other intelligence elements in the government, these committees represented a distinct departure from the prior approach to intelligence oversight. That approach had been distant, marginal, and often silent. The establishment of the

HPSCI and SSCI improved intelligence oversight, and the Committees embraced oversight as their primary objectives.

Thus two historical strains of oversight tendencies influenced the history of the Committees. Institutional oversight is supportive of the intelligence agencies, even unquestioning in its advocacy of this government bureaucracy. Investigative oversight questions the intelligence agencies, exposes potential difficulties, criticizes problems, and punishes mistakes and abuses.[20]

According to Seymour Scher's research on congressional oversight, House and Senate committees tend to resist change without significant outside stimuli.[21] Standard operating procedures along with the time pressures to accomplish current legislative business encourage committees to continue their typical patterns. One standard pattern of intelligence oversight was inquisitive because its inception occurred in such difficult circumstances. However, a strong historical strain of advocacy also influences the intelligence committees. A mix of investigative and institutional oversight results. Aberbach argued that committees almost always operate in a non-neutral environment.[22] The intelligence committees are no exception. A mix of advocacy and criticism is probably found in most congressional committees, making the intelligence oversight committees not especially unique.

SUBJECT MATTER/EXPERTISE

Congressional relationships with bureaucratic agencies are rooted in a trade-off between accountability and expertise. By their very nature, bureaucracies possess more expertise than Congress. A member of Congress could certainly obtain considerable expertise with a significant time commitment, but such a decision would preclude learning in other areas of policy necessary to his or her career. As a result, legislators delegate policy-making authority to bureaucratic agencies while retaining some degree of accountability to Congress. That control manifests in the form of oversight, budgetary controls, statutory instructions, initial procedures and structures, and congressional reviews.[23]

According to Ogul, more technical and complex subjects discourage the likelihood of oversight. Only a few members of Congress are likely to become experts in difficult, labyrinthine subjects.[24] The intelligence agencies are one such example. These agencies have acquired their own language, often as a result of secrecy. Although HUMINT may be easy to understand, SIGINT and IMINT are highly technical subjects requiring significant study.[25] Thus intelligence oversight does stand out as unique (although the labyrinthine language and technical details of the Defense Department are probably equally challenging).

Ogul further asserted that if a subject is concentrated in one administrative agency, it is more likely to be overseen than issues that are spread out over more than one bureaucracy.[26] In this context, the intelligence agencies seem to present a rather difficult situation for Congress. On one hand, there are sixteen separate agencies and offices with intelligence duties. On the other hand, the CIA is easily the most visible of these. Thus the CIA often receives the most concentrated attention among intelligence watchers. Congress made its oversight of these agencies even more difficult by spreading its oversight responsibility out over at least four committees when the HPSCI and SSCI were created. Some responsibilities for military oversight were retained by the Armed Services Committees, for instance.[27]

The visibility of the subject matter is also important. Subjects related to one's constituents, personal values, career aspirations, or reelection campaign will in all likelihood attract more congressional attention, according to Ogul.[28] Because of the required secrecy that surrounds intelligence matters, it is not an especially visible subject. However, when some public scandal erupts, the subject becomes highly visible. According to Ogul's criteria, intelligence again seems to both repel and attract oversight.

TRANSPARENCY

Relatedly, Charles Shipan rests his analysis of congressional oversight on transparency that exists where citizens can see how policies are made. The more transparent a subject, the more accountable the bureaucratic agency will be. Certain congressional tools will increase transparency, such as detailed statutes telling bureaucratic agencies exactly what to do; public debates, speeches, reports, and votes; open budget process; and congressional riders that specify individual projects favored by a particular member of Congress. Certain other congressional tools will decrease transparency, such as structures and procedures that establish broad parameters for policy guidelines that are not visible to the public, congressional reviews that follow agency decisions made out of the public view, and general reactive oversight legislation.[29]

Intelligence oversight is quite clearly not very transparent. Consequently, Shipan concludes, Congress will be less involved in the policy making of the intelligence agencies. According to Shipan's categories, intelligence oversight would follow a traditional oversight pattern. Nonetheless, oversight of other bureaucratic agencies is much more open and much more accountable.

INTEREST GROUPS

Transparent bureaucratic agencies are more likely to encourage outside interest groups that will aid congressional oversight. In McCubbins and Schwartz's parlance, outside interest groups can pull metaphorical fire alarms to alert Congress to possible problems in a government office. One can imagine that health subjects, education, or housing issues promote outside observers to form coalitions that lobby Congress much more often than intelligence issues. There are few if any intelligence-related interest groups. Thus intelligence oversight—

unlike most oversight subjects—operates without the benefit of additional view-points, informal watchdogs, or a strong sense of public opinion. Congress operates without interested groups agitating for additional information. This absence gives fewer incentives for legislators to demand more information and involvement and more incentives for intelligence agencies to give less information and involve-ment to Congress. Again, the intelligence agencies seem to both attract and repel congressional scrutiny.

UNCERTAINTY AND CONFLICT

When Congress decides to delegate policy-making authority to bureaucratic agencies, it must assess the level of uncertainty with which it is comfortable. These original decisions regarding the level of delegation influence the future of the relations between the bureaucratic agency and Congress. A high level of uncertainty at the start of a policy-making relationship increases the need for oversight at a later date.[30]

In other words, if legislators start with a low level of information, they will need to make up for that deficiency with traditional oversight methods. The intelligence agencies began as separate bureaucratic offices generally in the post–World War II period. The CIA, for instance, was founded in 1947. The National Security Agency (NSA) was started in 1952. At that time, Congress delegated a great deal of policy-making authority to the agencies. Very little information was shared with Congress beyond budgetary needs.[31] Loch K. Johnson calls this the "era of trust." It ended in 1974, when Congress became enmeshed in a long and detailed investigation of domestic spying by the CIA in direct violation of that agency's original 1947 foundation.[32]

Congress did not assert its general responsibility for oversight in a positive way until the 1946 Legislative Reorganization Act. The act for the first time made all congressional committees responsible for "legislative oversight."[33] This newly introduced term did not hand a new responsibility to Congress, but gave it more power and emphasis. The creation of the CIA and the NSA seem to have missed this trend, however.

The 1970 Legislative Reorganization Act explicitly gave Congress the re-sponsibility to review administrative policy to each standing committee.[34] In to-day's parlance, the goal was to be proactive rather than reactive. A new kind of oversight was thus born. Deering argued that this new oversight was more fully de-veloped in the 1970s, when a popular expression in Congress was, "If we have to be in on the crash landings then we should be in on the takeoffs that precede them."[35]

Despite its short history, intelligence oversight does not differ from the norm insofar as it lacked significant oversight in its early days. The 1970s saw a re-newed interest in oversight of many bureaucratic offices. In this sense, uncertainty in its inception and the predictable response of increased oversight do not seem to be extraordinary for intelligence oversight.

To compensate for not knowing the policy choices—or at least the thinking in the run-up to the decisions— legislators insist on sharing information. As has already been discussed with respect to the classification of intelligence agency documents, greater uncertainty leads to a need for greater information. McCubbins observed another element in that uncertainty. Specifically, he asserted that conflict among legislators—regarding the level of delegation at the original point of policy-making decision—increases the level of uncertainty. As a result, legislators will delegate greater amounts of policy-making responsibility to the bureaucratic agencies, thereby increasing the need for oversight at a later date.[36]

McCubbins concluded that increased conflict among legislators will result in decentralized oversight.[37] In other words, when information is scarce—or otherwise protected by the federal government—and members of Congress disagree over the ways to gain those information flows, congressional committees will be forced to resort to a reactive style of oversight, or fire alarm oversight.

For the intelligence oversight committees, information has been scarce. Information sharing was especially hard to come by at the time the committees were created. As for conflict, however, there have been very few public disagreements. In the era of trust, legislators largely agreed to oversee the intelligence apparatus in a limited way, deferring to the government agencies to conduct themselves within legal limits. During the investigations of the intelligence agencies, although some legislators debated the publicity of the hearings and the form of the response, there was little disagreement over the necessity of an inquiry.

There was a great deal of conflict in the run-up to the establishment of the intelligence oversight committees. The SSCI was created in 1976 with a vote of seventy-two to twenty-two. The HPSCI was created in 1977 with a vote of 227 to 171. In both chambers there was conflict about the creation of the committees, but the vote tallies reveal that the committees were in no real danger of not being created. House Republicans criticized the party ratio in the new committee, which reflected the party ratio of the entire House. They also questioned the new committee's ability to protect secrets. Liberal Democrats viewed the new committee as lacking sufficient tools of oversight.[38] Relying on McCubbins's characterizations, sufficient uncertainty and conflict suggest that intelligence oversight is most likely to receive traditional fire alarm oversight.

CONTEXT

According to Aberbach, the most important variable in determining the quality and quantity of congressional oversight is the context in which the legislators operate. "Congress responds to the changes in its environment."[39] Oversight became a significant goal for legislators in the 1970s throughout Congress because of public interest, resource scarcity, rivalries with the President, committee decentralization, and committee staff size—variables associated with the House's 1973 Subcommittee Bill of Rights.[40] Aberbach perceived a positive result from these variables; they increase police patrol style oversight.

First, public interest in the subject of intelligence does not translate into congressional activity because intelligence has not proven especially salient. Foreign policy does not usually grab the public's attention. Granted, the post-9/11 investigations magnified public salience on this subject, but the secrecy surrounding the investigations generally made intelligence more obscure than other subjects grabbing public attention. On public salience, intelligence is a bit of a mixed picture. Certainly, large-scale scandals and investigations gain public attention and therefore congressional interest, although without front-page newspaper headlines, the topic of intelligence is certainly a low priority for the public.

Second, budget scarcity certainly affects intelligence oversight. Because its details are hidden within the defense budget, the intelligence budget can be limited by its defense counterparts. The defense oversight committees already have some jurisdiction over the intelligence agencies. By keeping the intelligence budget a secret and placing it within the defense budget, the jurisdictional boundaries between the committees get even murkier.

Third, Aberbach asserts that rivalries with the President influence the quality of oversight initiated by Congress. This kind of partisan scoring has been less prominent in the areas of foreign and defense policy. However, partisanship seems to be increasing. Public disagreements from the opposition party were common in the 1990s, producing a highly charged partisan atmosphere.[41] In the area of intelligence, partisanship increased as well. President Clinton faced a more partisan opposition even in areas of defense and foreign policy—traditionally supportive areas for the President.[42]

Finally, the intelligence oversight committees were a product of this increased interest in oversight. They benefited from the changes in the environment. However, one of the most prominent aspects of this change—the Subcommittee Bill of Rights—did not greatly affect the HPSCI and SSCI. These two Committees put more formal emphasis on the committee chairperson than the 1973 bill had demanded.[43] These Committees are more centralized than most of their counterparts. They remain a select committee with strong chairperson influence. They also have smaller staff sizes than other committees due to secrecy requirements.

Regarding Aberbach's four indicators, intelligence faces a murky picture. One factor, partisanship, encourages increased police patrol oversight, whereas the committee environment discourages it. Public interest and resource scarcity lead to mixed results in Aberbach's matrix. Intelligence seems to be both an attractive and a repulsive subject for oversight.

PERSONAL CALCULUS

Fenno determined that individual members of Congress consider their own personal goals in determining their objectives for congressional service. Fenno's

1973 research specified at least three goals for every House member that could be applied to all legislators: (1) reelection, (2) influence within the chamber, and (3) good public policy. Each member of Congress uniquely prioritizes these goals, and each chamber committee yields differing opportunities to achieve these goals. Insofar as each member may join a specific committee to achieve his or her own personal goals, the activities of the committee reflect these three individual objectives.[44]

For example, Fenno's research showed that congressmen seek committee assignments based on their prioritization of these three personal goals. Some committees are better at reelection opportunities than others which focus on power and prestige or policy and oversight. Thus some committees may offer oversight opportunities, and some congressmen may be motivated for personal reasons toward zealous oversight. Others may be less interested in policy goals, and are merely waiting until a more reelection-friendly committee assignment is available.

Members who expressed an interest in the Appropriations and Ways and Means Committees said that power or prestige were their top goals in seeking those committees. For members of the Post Office and Interior Committees, reelection was their top goal. They saw the ability to help their constituents through these committees as advantageous. Members of the Education and Labor and Foreign Affairs Committees expressed the third goal: good public policy.[45]

Foreign affairs or intelligence committees, such as the HPSCI and SSCI, are viewed as prestigious but not especially helpful in home district reelections. Such committees may provide opportunities to make good policy or to use as a platform for some other political ambition, but immediate reelection is not one of them.

David Mayhew's 1974 study of reelection habits supported the prevailing consensus that oversight receives a low priority among members of Congress. Elected legislators are interested in getting reelected. It is the "proximate goal of everyone, the goal that must be achieved over and over if other ends are to be entertained."[46] As a result, individual members of Congress try to engage in "credit claiming," the effort to encourage others to view them as responsible for some desirable activity in government. Similarly, legislators engage in "position taking" by publicly judging anything of interest to residents in their district.[47] Mayhew's election-minded member of Congress may be too preoccupied with fundraising, campaigning, or publicity-seeking activities to engage in behind-the-scenes oversight. Thus intelligence is unlikely to attract oversight.

COST-BENEFIT ANALYSIS

Relatedly, McCubbins and Schwartz argued that fire alarm oversight is more likely because it is less expensive and provides greater returns than police patrol oversight. Congress prefers decentralized, incentive-based oversight that utilizes cost-benefit analysis. Individuals are motivated to oversee administrative decisions mostly based on reelection concerns. Even if legislators are motivated by public interest concerns, they are still more likely to choose the oversight that costs the least for the largest payback. In McCubbins and Schwartz's parlance, this is fire alarm oversight.

Intelligence certainly does not fit into the calculus of purely reelection-minded goals. At least before the events of 9/11, when intelligence was catapulted onto the front pages of all American newspapers, intelligence oversight had not created many opportunities for public speeches and easy claims for reelection bids. Even when the public is highly interested in intelligence, the secrecy demanded by its subject matter presents few options for credit claiming. Thus the cost-benefit analysis surrounding oversight of other administrative areas does not easily translate to the oversight of intelligence.

INTELLIGENCE OVERSIGHT

Intelligence oversight appears to be difficult to characterize using these nine academic criteria—information flows, committee history, subject matter/expertise, transparency, interest groups, uncertainty and conflict, context, personal calculus, and cost-benefit analysis. These diverse measures—at least within the modest descriptions given here—paint intelligence as both an attractive and a repulsive subject for oversight. Does this make intelligence oversight traditional or exceptional? Perhaps its varied characteristics will result in another murky picture here. Indeed, using the five dichotomies identified—latent and manifest, advocate and critical, centralized and decentralized, active and reactive, anticipatory and post hoc—intelligence oversight seems to fit a mix of traditional and exceptional oversight.

First, at first glance, the intelligence oversight committees seem likely to issue manifest legislation because their singular task is oversight. Ogul's distinction between manifest and latent oversight was one of formal and informal oversight. The intelligence communities received the direct attention of about half as many proposed bills from the House and Senate as bills related to Social Security in the 108th Congress.[48] The implication is that intelligence actually receives fewer manifest oversight efforts by Congress. Regarding latent oversight efforts, reporting requirements such as those from the inspector general in the CIA to Congress are quite prolific, according to Frederick Hitz, former inspector general at the CIA.[49] The other intelligence agencies do not have such requirements for their internally created inspectors general. However, other reporting requirements may be equally burdensome. Such a mix of latent and manifest oversight shows that there is no strong tendency for either in the oversight of intelligence.

Second, the intelligence oversight committees, although born out of criticism of the intelligence agencies, have been more friendly than not, according to Johnson.[50] Smist observed both friendly and critical oversight.[51] "Overseeing the intelligence community is like being a good parent. You have to encourage and discipline," according to Representative Norm Dicks (D-WA) who has represented northwestern Washington for almost thirty years, including service on HPSCI.[52] Friendly or critical oversight is probably in the eye of the beholder, but the implication is that there is no single label that can be unquestionably applied to the oversight of intelligence.

Third, intelligence oversight attempts to be active, but it is mostly reactive. Representative Heather Wilson (R-NM) argued that the Committees are driven by crises but that this less-than-systematic approach is inherent in Congress's nature. The annual authorization/appropriation rhythm, the spikes of attention that surround events, and the interests of members drive all oversight, not just intelligence oversight.[53] Dicks agreed that the oversight agenda is event-driven, but he argued that the American culture is crisis-driven. "We like Monday-morning quarterbacking."[54] Any active oversight in the mold of police patrol oversight is hidden behind closed doors in regard to intelligence oversight. Reactive oversight efforts by the intelligence committees are quite public and easily measured. So, are these committees reactive or active? On the whole, they probably look like any other committee in terms of priority setting. If other committees are less likely to engage in active oversight, the intelligence oversight committees are also less likely to do so.

Fourth, the intelligence community is very decentralized. The oversight committees seem to mirror this diversity of agencies. The resulting multiplicity of hearings and committee meetings to which the agencies must respond seems very burdensome. On the other hand, some academic treatments of intelligence oversight have observed a domination of the chairperson of the committee. Indeed, the whole character of the oversight committees might fall on the mood established by the chairs.[55] As a result, the labels of *centralized* or *decentralized* do not seem well suited for intelligence oversight.

Finally, regarding the whole intelligence community, intelligence oversight is mostly post hoc because it is next to impossible to measure anticipatory oversight as defined by Ogul. It is not difficult to imagine some situations where anticipatory oversight has occurred. For instance, the unintended consequences in the wake of various oversight efforts to crack down on law breaking within the intelligence agencies has been risk aversion among the bureaucrats, according to some critics. Relatedly, it can be in the nature of a bureaucracy to produce risk-averse employees. This unintended consequence is not easily measured, but its existence seems to be taken for granted.[56] Congress's post hoc responsibility for oversight is obvious. When Congress established the CIA in 1947, it attached very broad parameters to that organization, requiring post hoc oversight in its future. Congress also recently reorganized the National Geospatial Intelligence Agency with very few ex ante pronouncements. Similarly, the Director of National Intelligence has some fairly broad parameters. The result is a post hoc necessity to ensure that the agencies provide information to Congress, respond to congressional attempts at reform, and follow more specific guidelines on front-page issues. The tools are reporting requirements, legislation, budgeting, informal contacts, and public and private investigations. These are quite common.

Using these dichotomies, it appears that intelligence oversight follows some combination of traditional and exceptional oversight. It is both latent and manifest, both friendly and critical, both centralized and decentralized, but mostly reactive and post hoc. This indicates a tendency toward traditional oversight by the intelligence-related oversight Committees.

However, some attributes of the intelligence oversight system clearly appear unique—paramount secrecy, the term limits under which it has operated and continues to operate, the appointments process, and the history of intelligence oversight in the past. These characteristics are often the most publicly observable—and measurable—aspects of these committees.

First, secrecy plays a significant part in the character of intelligence oversight. Even though all government agencies protect their proprietary information, none assume the secrecy the intelligence agencies do. The rules for observing intelligence information in Congress are unique. Responsibility for intelligence information requires special clearances, restricts the access of staff to the information, and limits note taking. To read classified information from the intelligence agencies, legislators must move to another location altogether. Many choose not to do so. Although other committees have somewhat limited information flows as described herein, the HPSCI and SSCI do currently operate under unique rules. Whether they must have such unique rules is another question. This makes the current system of intelligence oversight unique.

Second, the intelligence oversight Committees have unique rules. HPSCI members abide by term limits, as did SSCI members until recently.[57] Members may serve on HPSCI for no more than eight years, although the chairperson has an unlimited tenure.[58] Until 2004, the SSCI term limit was also eight years. The rules of the committees also require that some portion of their membership simultaneously serve on the Armed Services, Appropriations, Foreign Relations, and Judiciary Committees.[59] These rules make the current system of intelligence oversight unique.

Third, the appointments process follows that of a select committee. These committees are generally set up on an ad hoc basis to address a specific question or problem. Since their inception, the intelligence oversight Committees have been select committees, making them unique even within the world of select committees. A select committee generally means that members are appointed directly by the chamber leadership for a short period of time. Members for standing committees are nominated by the party caucus and then appointed by the House or Senate leadership. According to one insider, selection for a "select" committee indicates a "sign of grace" from the leadership. "You look like one of the cool kids when you get picked."[60] Select committees have clout and prestige. The intelligence Committees, although they are select, are also "permanent," so they act like standing committees even though they are not. These attributes make the current system of intelligence oversight unique.

Finally, partisanship has historically been lacking on the intelligence oversight Committees. Members were originally selected to foster bipartisanship.[61] However, many critics have argued that partisanship on the Committees has increased in recent years.[62] This increase caught significant attention recently.[63] That such recent partisanship stands out suggests a uncommon history of bipartisanship. This makes the current system of intelligence oversight unique.

Intelligence oversight has been treated uniquely in the past. The intelligence committees follow both formal and informal rules that differ from other committees. They also follow both traditional and exceptional patterns of oversight. To illuminate the murky picture created by these academic treatments, the next question is whether intelligence oversight requires such unique approaches. To answer that inquiry, I turn to the participants themselves.

VIEWS OF THE INSIDERS: INTELLIGENCE
OVERSIGHT NOT SO UNIQUE

"Like everything else in Congress, intelligence oversight is messy and imperfect," according to former Representative Charlie Wilson (D-TX).[64] Congressman Wilson served in the House for twenty-four years, representing east Texas. He is probably most remembered for supporting the Afghan resistance during the Cold War to such a degree that some argue he ran "his own war" out of the Appropriations Committee.[65] He argued that there is a general pattern in oversight that applies equally well to intelligence: Congress picks only one issue on which to focus. He said there is no systematic oversight; it is always dependent on the newspaper headlines.[66]

For similar reasons, former Representative Pete Geren concluded that intelligence oversight is "just like any other oversight. It is only when something goes wrong that the system really puts the subject into a crucible to examine it."[67] Geren (D-TX) served on the House Armed Services Committee during his eight-year tenure representing east Texas and currently serves as a special assistant to the Secretary of Defense. He conceded that when an issue like intelligence is shrouded in secrecy, congressional attention is particularly difficult to focus; but he explained that this is generally "the way oversight happens on all issues."[68]

Representative Heather Wilson agreed that HPSCI has a different atmosphere from other committees because of the seriousness of the issues, a sense of responsibility to the rest of Congress, and the additional work.[69] Wilson has represented central New Mexico for the past eight years. Her prior experience in Air Force Intelligence helped prepare her for service on the HPSCI. She remarked that the secrecy requirement presents a different constraint on the committee. Nonetheless, she concluded that "it is not different from any other oversight."[70]

Former Senator Richard Bryan (D-NV) agreed. His twelve years of service in the Senate and two years as vice-chair on SSCI gave him the opinion that intelligence oversight is just like any other oversight.[71] Similarly, former Senator

Malcolm Wallop (R-WY) said that intelligence oversight is same as any other oversight based on his eighteen years in the Senate, including membership on SSCI.[72]

Former Representative Timothy Roemer (D-IN) came to a slightly different conclusion based on his twelve years in the House of Representatives, including membership on HPSCI. "Oversight is not completely unique, but it is very different from oversight in the other committees."[73] He perceived as dissimilar the challenges and tools of intelligence oversight. Namely, the secrecy, the size and diversity of the budget, and the term limits make intelligence oversight somewhat unique. Nonetheless, in Roemer's opinion, the time constraints, the lack of long-range thinking, and the need for more systematic oversight apply equally to all congressional committees.[74]

VIEWS OF THE INSIDERS: UNIQUE OVERSIGHT

Senator Richard Shelby (R-AL) disagreed entirely. Shelby, based on his nearly thirty years of service in the Congress, including eight years in the House, called intelligence oversight unique. He also served as the chair or vice chair of SSCI for three terms (105th through 107th Congresses). He cited the secrecy, compartmentation, and "need to know" as the most distinct challenges of intelligence oversight. The result, in Shelby's opinion, is more work than any other committee. "Intelligence oversight is unique; it's more rigorous, active and involved" than any other committee.[75] In particular, Shelby focused on the reform of the intelligence agencies as such a large task that the Congress must work with the President to get any reform accomplished. He likened the transformation of intelligence to moving "an aircraft carrier down a creek."[76]

Former Senator Slade Gorton (R-WA) seized on the issue of secrecy as the origins of unique oversight. He argued that intelligence issues are "so difficult and so in the dark" that their oversight must be unique. Because the intelligence apparatus is not as transparent as other federal agencies, policy oversight of intelligence is unique.[77] Gorton represented Washington state for eighteen years, during which time he served on SSCI for only three years. He said he asked to leave the Committee because he did not think it was effective. The assignment was too time consuming, the topic was too obscure, and the secrecy prevented discussion in the home districts.[78]

CONGRESSIONAL PERSPECTIVES

This informal and unscientific survey of current and former representatives and senators showed that most believed intelligence oversight is not a unique undertaking. Only Gorton and Shelby argued that intelligence oversight is unique, mostly because of the challenges of secrecy. Their argument cannot be dismissed lightly. The protection of sources and methods—a paramount goal for the intelligence agencies—necessitates certain rules peculiar to the intelligence committees. The requirement of a separate secure location to view certain information is particularly burdensome.

The remaining senators and representatives interviewed agreed that there are some distinct aspects to the task—secrecy in particular—but in the end, they mostly thought that intelligence oversight can be approached in the same way as oversight of other parts of the federal government. As found in the academic treatments of congressional oversight, this duty is often difficult, burdensome, and low on the scale of priorities for legislators. All subjects of oversight suffer from these challenges.

It is in Congress's constitutional power to perform oversight of the federal government. Its enumerated legislative powers, responsibility to declare war, provide for defense, oversee international commerce, and govern the power of the purse, justify oversight of intelligence.[79] Any efforts to increase the amount of scrutiny in any area of government to improve operations or ensure legal transactions would be welcomed by most senators and representatives. Senator Dennis DeConcini (D-AZ) argued that all oversight should be more stringent and more involved. Any legislation or other legislative tool that increases the attention given to the intelligence agencies would be a positive change, according to DeConcini (who represented Arizona for nearly thirty years and served as chair of SSCI from 1993–95).[80] Thus it is possible that any reform of intelligence oversight follow as a consequence of other oversight reform. Similarly, reformers of intelligence oversight may learn some lessons from the reform of other oversight subjects.

REFORM RECOMMENDATIONS

Starting with the broad recommendation to "strengthen congressional oversight of intelligence and homeland security," the 9/11 Commission advanced ten specific proposals for the reform of congressional oversight of intelligence:

1. Scrap the current system and replace it with either a joint committee or one committee in each chamber that combines authorizations with appropriations.
2. Make the intelligence budget public.
3. Grant subpoena authority to the committee or committees.
4. Institute subcommittees specifically dedicated to oversight.
5. The majority party representation should never exceed the minority representation by more than one.
6. Eliminate term limits.
7. If two committees are retained, downsize them.
8. Require that four members of this committee or committee simultaneously serve on the Armed Services, Judiciary, Foreign Affairs/

International Relations, and the Defense Subcommittee of the Appropriations Committee.
9. Staff should be nonpartisan.
10. Consolidate oversight of the Department of Homeland Security (DHS).[81]

Some of these recommendations stand alone; some work only in concert with the others. The first recommendation is the most radical. It is an entirely unique solution to the problems identified in the unity of the oversight of intelligence. Based on the literature review of the most important factors in determining the quality of congressional oversight, these solutions are not necessary. Moreover, none of the legislators interviewed for this research mentioned any inclination to such drastic measures. The Commission's theory was that "tinkering with the existing structure" would not produce the desired improvements. They advocated wholesale restructuring with the goal being to allow a small group of legislators the time and reason to master the intelligence system. It is not obvious, however, why such a radical response instead of a more limited modification—picking and choosing the most important reforms—is necessary to achieve these goals.

For instance, recommendations 3 through 10 could be accomplished with internal rules and probably very little debate. They are the most obvious changes and the least objectionable. In fact, they are not especially unique. Recommendation 3—subpoena authority—can be granted by a vote of the whole chamber and is already a part of some investigative subcommittees. Recommendation 4—investigative subcommittees—already exist in other committees in both the House and Senate. In fact, HPSCI and SSCI previously had investigative subcommittees. Recommendation 5 is not very different from the current system establishing the party ratio of each Congress at the start of the first session. Recommendation 6 has already been accomplished in the Senate. Recommendation 7 could easily be accomplished. To downsize a committee is somewhat against the mainstream. Most committees have been growing rather than shrinking, but it is not outside the usual realm of rules making authority in each chamber. Recommendation 8 is already part of the rules—both formal and informal—of HPSCI and SSCI. Recommendation 9 has been the goal from the start of the committees. Perhaps some new system might ensure a greater sense of nonpartisanship, but it is not a unique situation. Recommendation 10 would only require internal changes. This recommendation might be difficult considering the already murky state of oversight jurisdiction. Some other committees would have to give up their right to oversee this Department, but it could be done. These alterations could stand alone without any reference to the wholesale and very unique change of recommendation 1.

Recommendation 2 would require a change in the administration of intelligence, not an impossible task, but one that has encouraged heated debates in the past. Previous attempts to reveal the intelligence budget publicly and annually have proved unsuccessful. Though Commission members admit disclosure of a number reveals very little, they nonetheless recommended the change in hopes it would foster accountability and allow observers to judge budgeting priorities. They further asserted that making the budget public would generally combat secrecy and complexity—elements that the Commission argue contributed to the series of mistakes behind 9/11.[82]

Contrary to recommendation 1, recommendations 2 through 10 would make intelligence oversight less unique. None of the remaining recommendations are as difficult or as unique as the first one. One unique problem to intelligence oversight—which was created at the very start of HPSCI and SSCI—is jurisdictional. Intelligence-oriented duties are spread throughout sixteen government agencies, and their oversight is spread through many congressional committees—intelligence, armed services, appropriations, international relations, judiciary, homeland security, and government reform.

This overlap requires the intelligence agencies to testify more often before Congress—a time-consuming endeavor—and before more and more committees. With the creation of the DHS and its responsibility to coordinate intelligence on domestic terrorist threats, the jurisdictional ambiguities multiplied. DHS leaders may appear before eighty-eight committees or subcommittees.[83] Thus the Commission recommended consolidation of DHS oversight in recommendation 10. The Commission did not touch on consolidation of intelligence oversight in general, however. It may be an even more daunting task with entrenched turf battles, but it is no less worthwhile to restructure the oversight of the other intelligence agencies. With jurisdictional ambiguity comes multiple responsibilities for the staff to canvass the status and opinions of other involved committees. The current system requires quite a lot of time-consuming checking and cross-checking, particularly regarding budgets.

The Commission's report quite clearly advocates the viewpoint that only a complete overhaul of the system will be helpful. According to the Commission members, choosing one or two of these recommendations without reforming the whole system would be insufficient. Their main argument was that decentralized, relatively weak, divided, superficial, unaccountable oversight contributed to the events of 9/11. These specific recommendations were meant to remedy those deficiencies to create a "strong, stable, capable" structure.[84] Aside from their first recommendation, however, they do not advocate particularly unique solutions. They advocated a wholesale overhaul without dividing that task into unique elements.

CONCLUSIONS

Congressional oversight can be labeled as such, or it can be included among other legislative or constituent-oriented efforts by members of Congress. Ogul argued that oversight can be a part of many of the activities of legislators, whether deliberate or not. He further found that these oversight efforts are more common and thus, for the purposes of this chapter, traditional.

Particularly in the budget process, congressional oversight may be deliberately and generally critical of federal administrations or play the part of the advocates for the government agencies. A committee might fight for an agency's budget to increase even while it is charged with overseeing that agency. In fact, Aberbach found that oversight is most often an advocate rather than a critic. This makes advocating style oversight more traditional than critical oversight.

Congressional oversight may attempt to anticipate events around the world and within the United States, or it may be content to react to these uncontrollable events. McCubbins and Schwartz found that legislators are most often reacting to events around them. This makes reactive oversight more traditional than anticipatory oversight.

Anticipatory oversight attempts to influence federal agencies with the threat of oversight, whereas post hoc oversight demands detailed reports to keep tabs on the administration of its broad mandates. McCubbins found that post hoc oversight is more common than its counterpart, and thus it is considered traditional here.

Using these dichotomies, it appears that intelligence oversight—in these academic characterizations—is a mix of traditional and exceptional oversight. Legislative efforts by the intelligence Committees are often manifest, but legislators also seem to choose informal, less deliberate efforts as well such as reporting requirements, relationships with the inspector general, and informal visits to the agencies themselves. The intelligence oversight efforts by Congress have followed a repeating pattern of advocacy followed by criticism. The intelligence-related Committees seem to be both centralized inside the Committees, but quite decentralized in terms of jurisdiction. Because international, often unpredictable events drive intelligence collection and analysis, they also drive intelligence oversight. So despite the efforts of some legislators to anticipate upcoming events and problems, the Committees are forced to be quite reactive. When creating oversight legislation—both manifest and latent—the Committees may have encouraged some unintended consequences. They have also provided some rather broad mandates to some of these agencies, causing the subsequent use of post hoc oversight tools. This combination of traditional and exceptional provides a very murky picture of the character of intelligence oversight.

Intelligence oversight, as it is currently organized, does operate under some unique oversight rules. Secrecy requirements, term limits, appointments, and bipartisanship do make intelligence oversight unique. Furthermore, the personal calculus and the related cost-benefit analysis of legislators serving on HPSCI or SSCI differs from those on other committees. There are fewer opportunities to benefit one's reelection campaign because the issues are not especially salient and the details are secret.

Relatedly, there are few interest groups in intelligence and very little transparency compared with other oversight subjects. The potential for greater public involvement in intelligence oversight is quite low. One potential exception is the public discussion of weapons of mass destruction in Iraq. Such salient issues do seem to arise every now and then, but typically, with few interest groups to agitate for greater transparency, public demands for change are unlikely to aid congressional inquiries.

There are, however, some characteristics of intelligence oversight that are not especially unique. For instance, information flows from bureaucracies to Congress have been challenging in many areas of oversight. The number of classified documents has increased throughout the government, thus limiting congressional access to the information it needs for oversight. The response of Congress is to use reporting requirements on the bureaucratic agencies throughout the government.

Similarly, although intelligence presents a challenging learning curve, it is not so different from many defense or other technical areas of expertise. The details attending the appropriations to building an aircraft carrier, or following the labyrinthine world of the U.S. tax code are probably equally challenging.

Most important, the surrounding context of all congressional oversight is pervasive. The level of congressional interest in oversight of the federal agencies tends to ebb and flow with the greater political context, and intelligence oversight is no different. This leads to a level of uncertainty and conflict among legislators that is subject to the same outside influences as any other area of oversight.

Following this mixed picture about the unique character of intelligence oversight—both as it is currently practiced and as it compares to other oversight subjects—it may be useful to turn to the legislators themselves. In informal interviews, most of the interviewed representatives and senators involved in intelligence oversight claim it is not unique in comparison with other oversight demands. If their majority view is accurate, this suggests efforts to reform and improve on intelligence oversight structures likewise need not be exceptional. Thus new and reformed congressional efforts to oversee intelligence can follow the same paths of improvement as other oversight efforts. Rather than turn to unique solutions, it may be equally fruitful to study other forms of oversight to find effective solutions to some unique and some not so unique problems.

NOTES

This chapter stems from a paper presented at the International Studies Association (ISA) annual meeting in San Diego, CA, 2006.

1. *The 9/11 Commission Report: Final Report of the National Commission on Terrorist Attacks Upon the United State* (New York: Norton, 2004), p. 419. As of 2006, the intelligence community includes sixteen agencies: Central Intelligence Agency (CIA), Defense Intelligence Agency, National Geospatial-Intelligence Agency, National Reconnaissance Office, National Security Agency (NSA), Air Force Intelligence, Army Intelligence, Coast Guard Intelligence, Marine Corps Intelligence, Navy Intelligence, and elements of the Department of Energy, the Department of Homeland Security, the Department of State, the Department of the Treasury, the Drug Enforcement Agency, and the Federal Bureau of Investigation (FBI).

2. Ibid., p. 420. Some suggestions were: possibly a joint House-Senate committee or a combination of authorization and appropriations in one committee, an end to term limits

in the intelligence oversight committees, a public budget for the intelligence community, subpoena power for the committee members, oversight subcommittees, joint service with related committees for the HPSCI and SSCI members, and a smaller committee to encourage a greater sense of responsibility among committee members.

3. Morris Ogul, *Congress Oversees the Bureaucracy* (Pittsburgh, PA: University of Pittsburgh Press, 1976), p. 180.

4. Joel Aberbach, *Keeping a Watchful Eye: The Politics of Congressional Oversight* (Washington, DC: Brookings Institution, 1990), p. 173.

5. Mathew McCubbins and Thomas Schwartz, "Congressional Oversight Overlooked: Police Patrols Versus Fire Alarms," *American Journal of Political Science* 28 (1984), p. 176.

6. Morris S. Ogul and Bert A. Rockman, "Overseeing Oversight: New Departures and Old Problems," *Legislative Studies Quarterly* 15 (1990), p. 13. The authors credited Aberbach's 1987 review of McCubbins and Schwartz's 1984 article for the original idea of active versus reactive oversight. Ogul and Rockman further refined the concept in this 1990 literature review. See Joel Aberbach, "The Congressional Committee Intelligence System: Information, Oversight, and Change," *Congress and the Presidency* 14 (1987), pp. 51–76.

7. Ogul and Rockman, "Overseeing Oversight," pp. 7, 21.

8. Reactive oversight is distinct from post hoc oversight insofar as it is those efforts that react to outside events beyond the control of individuals, such as natural disasters, acts of terrorism or war, or public scandals. Post hoc oversight refers to the efforts of Congress to control the administrative duties it delegated to a federal agency. In other words, post hoc oversight is necessary to ensure that government agencies act in the way that Congress intended.

9. Anticipatory oversight is distinct from ex ante oversight insofar as it is those efforts that attempt to anticipate outside events beyond the control of individuals. Ex ante oversight is the deliberate, detailed instructions that Congress gives to federal agencies in their creation. When legislators delegate some authorities to government offices, they may be very specific in their guidance (ex ante oversight) or somewhat vague, preferring to look over the shoulders of administrators as they go about the business of broad mandates (post hoc oversight).

10. See for instance, Ogul, *Congress Oversees the Bureaucracy*; Seymour Scher, "Conditions for Legislative Control," *Journal of Politics* 25, no. 3 (1963).

11. Aberbach, *Keeping a Watchful Eye*, p. 190.

12. Christopher J. Deering, "Alarms and Patrols: Legislative Oversight in Foreign and Defense Policy," in Colton C. Campbell, Nicol C. Rae, and John F. Stack Jr., eds., *Congress and the Politics of Foreign Policy* (Upper Saddle River, NJ: PrenticeHall, 2003), p. 134.

13. Ibid.

14. Aberbach, *Keeping a Watchful Eye*, p. 74.

15. Arthur Lupia and Mathew McCubbins, "Learning from Oversight," *Journal of Law, Economics, and Organization* 10 (1994), p. 112. According to the authors, the objective of the legislators is to create institutions that produce learning from oversight. Without this important knowledge from bureaucratic insiders, legislative delegation of authority to government agencies is tantamount to abdication of congressional responsibilities.

16. A quick glance at the websites of these offices reveals the differences. Of course, the Consumer Products Safety Commission and the surgeon general have a primarily

public function, and they attempt to reach as many Americans as possible. Each of the intelligence community members has a website with publicly available information, but far more of their work is quite clearly classified.

17. See generally L. Britt Snider, *Sharing Secrets with Lawmakers: Congress as a User of Intelligence* (McLean, VA: Center for the Study of Intelligence, CIA, 1997), available at http://www.cia.gov/csi/monograph/lawmaker/toc.htm on (accessed February 18, 2006).

18. See U.S. House, Permanent Select Committee on Intelligence, *Publication of the Rules for the Permanent Select Committee on Intelligence* (108; June 12, 2003) (Washington, DC: Library of Congress). Text from *Congressional Record*. Available from Thomas (online service).

19. Scott Shane, "Increase in the Number of Documents Classified by the Government," *New York Times*, July 3, 2005, available at http://www.nytimes.com/2005/07/03/politics/03secrecy.html?ex=1278043200&en=cf5505f95e78680a&ei=5088&partner=rs snyt&emc=rss (accessed February 18, 2006). These classifications are somewhat nebulous, as when labels such as "sensitive security information" are employed.

20. Frank J. Smist, *Congress Oversees the U.S. Intelligence Community*, 2nd ed. (Knoxville: University of Tennessee Press, 1994), pp. 21–24.

21. Scher, "Conditions for Legislative Control," p. 540.

22. Aberbach, *Keeping a Watchful Eye*, p. 162.

23. Charles R. Shipan, "Congress and the Bureaucracy," in Paul J. Quirk and Sarah A. Binder, eds., *The Legislative Branch* (New York: Oxford University Press, 2005), pp. 438–45. Although the legislative veto was declared unconstitutional in *INS v. Chadha* (1983), Congress generally retains the right of congressional review of agency rules. In the Congressional Review Act of 1996, Congress asserted the ability to "disapprove" of certain agency decisions with a congressional joint resolution.

24. Ogul, *Congress Oversees the Bureaucracy*, p. 14.

25. HUMINT is an abbreviation for human intelligence or the people who spy for the United States. SIGINT stands for signals intelligence, a catchall phrase including the collection of conversations by phone or other technical means usually collected by satellite. IMINT is an abbreviation for imagery intelligence—the photography or digital imagery usually collected by satellite.

26. Ogul, *Congress Oversees the Bureaucracy*, p. 14.

27. HPSCI reviews matters related to the National Foreign Intelligence Program (NFIP), Tactical Intelligence and Related Activities (TIARA), and Joint Military Intelligence Programs (JMIP). NFIP, TIARA, and JMIP are budgetary categories for the funding streams into the intelligence community. NFIP includes approximately half the intelligence budget and consists of the civilian parts of the community: the CIA and all its parts; the Director of Central Intelligence; the Bureau of Intelligence and Research in the Department of State; the National Security Agency (NSA); the National Geospatial Intelligence Agency; the Department of Homeland Security (DHS) since 2002; the National Reconnaissance Office; the FBI; the Department of the Treasury; and the Department of Energy intelligence offices; and half of the Defense Intelligence Agency (DIA). JMIP funding covers the defense-related intelligence efforts that do not belong to any one branch of the armed services: half of the DIA, and parts of DOD intelligence offices. TIARA covers the armed services' intelligence branches. The House Armed Services Committee (HASC) shares jurisdiction with HPSCI on TIARA and JMIP as well as the Department of

Energy. HPSCI has exclusive jurisdiction over the NFIP. HASC's responsibilities cover a wide range of defense-related issues. Intelligence is just one small part of its agenda. SSCI also has some responsibility for NFIP, JMIP, and TIARA-related funding, activities, and organizations. However, the Senate Armed Services Committee (SASC) holds exclusive jurisdiction over TIARA and JMIP. Jurisdiction over NFIP is shared by SSCI and SASC. Again, SASC's jurisdiction is so broad that intelligence can only be a small part of it. As such, intelligence only occupies part of the time of the senators on SASC.

28. Ogul, *Congress Oversees the Bureaucracy*, p. 15.

29. Shipan, "Congress and the Bureaucracy," p. 453.

30. Mathew D. McCubbins, "The Legislative Design of Regulatory Structure," *American Journal of Political Science* 29 (1985), p. 737.

31. Loch K. Johnson, *A Season of Inquiry: The Senate Intelligence Investigation* (Lexington: University of Kentucky Press, 1985), p. 7. From its inception in 1947, the CIA was allowed to operate almost completely freely, while Congress's inquiries resembled friendly support—and even awe—rather than meaningful query. The House and Senate Committees on Armed Services and Appropriations oversaw CIA activities. Among these four committees, the CIA was subjected to about twenty-four hours of legislative hearings per year for most of the 1950s and 1960s.

32. Loch K. Johnson, "Accountability and America's Secret Foreign Policy: Keeping a Legislative Eye on the Central Intelligence Agency," *Foreign Policy Analysis* 1 (2005), p. 106.

33. P.L. 79-601 (Legislative Reorganization Act of 1946).

34. P.L. 91-510 (Legislative Reorganization Act of 1970).

35. Deering, "Alarms and Patrols," p. 129.

36. McCubbins, "The Legislative Design of Regulatory Structure," p. 738.

37. Ibid., 739.

38. Smist, *Congress Oversees the U.S. Intelligence Community*, pp. 82, 214–16.

39. Aberbach, *Keeping a Watchful Eye*, p. 104.

40. In this legislation, subcommittees were authorized to meet on their own authority, set their own rules, and enact their own legislation. Thus more incentives to oversee administrative policy evolved.

41. Joel D. Aberbach, "What's Happened to the Watchful Eye?," *Congress and the Presidency* 29 (Spring 2002), p. 19.

42. Stephen F. Knott, "The Great Republican Transformation on Oversight," *International Journal of Intelligence and Counterintelligence* 13 (2000), p. 49.

43. Smist, *Congress Oversees the U.S. Intelligence Community*, p. 217.

44. Richard F. Fenno Jr., *Congressmen in Committees* (Boston: Little, Brown, 1973), pp. 1–2. Fenno studied six committees from the House from 1955 to 1966. These are committees on Appropriations, Education and Labor, Foreign Affairs, Interior and Insular Affairs, Post Office and Civil Service, and Ways and Means. Fenno also briefly examined their Senate counterparts.

45. Ibid., pp. 3–9.

46. David R. Mayhew, *Congress: The Electoral Connection* (New Haven, CT: Yale University Press, 1974), p. 16.

47. Ibid., pp. 49–61.

48. A quick glance by the author at the bills listed in Thomas, an online research service from the Library of Congress, shows these results.

49. Frederick Hitz, interviews with the author, Alexandria, VA, August 18, 2001, and September 12, 2003.

50. See generally Johnson, "Accountability."

51. See generally Smist, *Congress Oversees the U.S. Intelligence Community.*

52. Representative Norm Dicks, interview with the author, October 15, 2003, Washington, DC.

53. Representative Heather Wilson, interview with the author, November 9, 2003, Washington, DC.

54. Dicks interview.

55. Smist, *Congress Oversees the U.S. Intelligence Community.* This kind of personal importance was echoed in an interview conducted by the author with L. Britt Snider, former inspector general of the CIA from 1998 to 2001. Snider said he was struck by how the whole system is still personality-driven. Britt Snider, interview with the author, June 25, 2001, Arlington, VA.

56. Richard A. Posner, "The Danger in 'Fixing' the CIA," *Los Angeles Times*, May 24, 2005, p. B13.

57. In its original documents, the SSCI term limit was eight years. This limit changed in 2004. See Senate, *A Resolution to Eliminate Certain Restrictions on the Service of a Senator on the Senate Select Committee on Intelligence*, 108th Congress, 2nd sess. (2004), S.R. 445.

58. *Rules of the House of Representatives* (109th Congress), 532 (Rule X: Organization of Committees, clause 12k).

59. *Rules of the House of Representatives* (109th Congress), 519 (Rule X: Organization of Committees, Clause 11a) and *Senate Resolution 400 (Rules of Procedure for the Select Committee on Intelligence, United States Senate)*, as amended May 19, 1976, available at http://intelligence.senate.gov/rules%20of%20procedure.htm (accessed March 30, 2006).

60. Mark Lowenthal, interview with the author, February 16, 2006, by phone.

61. Smist, *Congress Oversees the U.S. Intelligence Community*, p. 83.

62. Dana Priest, "Congressional Oversight of Intelligence," *Washington Post*, April 27, 2004, available at http://www.washingtonpost.com/ac2/wp-dyn/A44837-2004Apr26?language=printer (accessed February 21, 2006).

63. L. Britt Snider, "Congressional Oversight of Intelligence after September 11," in Jennifer E. Sims and Burton Gerber, eds., *Transforming U.S. Intelligence* (Washington, DC: Georgetown University Press, 2005), p. 242.

64. Representative Charlie Wilson, interview with the author, July 1, 2004, Washington, DC.

65. See generally, George Crile, *Charlie Wilson's War: The Extraordinary Story of the Largest Covert Operation in History* (New York: Atlantic Monthly Press, 2003).

66. Charlie Wilson interview. The result, according to Wilson, is that much of the intelligence community escapes oversight.

67. Representative Pete Geren, interview with the author, April 26, 2004, Arlington, VA.

68. Ibid. The result, according to Geren, is that legislators must trust the intelligence agency professionals because they cannot see so much of what goes on.

69. Charlie Wilson interview.

70. Ibid.

71. Senator Richard Bryan, interview with the author, November 3, 2003, by phone.

72. Senator Malcolm Wallop, interview with the author, October 16, 2003, by phone.

73. Representative Timothy Roemer, interview with the author, March 15, 2004, by phone.

74. Ibid.

75. Senator Richard Shelby, interview with the author, April 2, 2004, Washington, DC.

76. Ibid.

77. Senator Slade Gorton, interview with the author, September 26, 2003, by phone.

78. Ibid. The result, according to Gorton, was that the intelligence community runs itself.

79. David Everett Colton, "Speaking Truth to Power: Intelligence Oversight," *University of Pennsylvania Law Review* 134 (December 1988), p. 578.

80. Senator Dennis DeConcini, interview with the author, March 6, 2006, by phone.

81. *The 9/11 Commission Report*, pp. 420–21.

82. Ibid., p. 416.

83. Ibid., p. 421

84. Ibid., p. 416.

7

INTELLIGENCE ACCOUNTABILITY

A Comparative Perspective

HANS BORN AND IAN LEIGH

THIS CHAPTER PRESENTS A COMPARATIVE SURVEY OF the accountability for intelligence. Space does not permit an extended description and analysis of the arrangements in different countries.[1] Instead, after a brief historical overview, we take a thematic approach. This emphasizes four factors: the importance of accountability within an agency itself; the role of the executive in accountability; the place of parliamentary or legislative oversight; and finally, independent complaints, inspection, and audit processes.

If spying is the second oldest profession, intelligence accountability is by comparison a modern development. For practical purposes the story begins in the mid-1970s with the official exposure and cataloging of abuses in the U.S. intelligence community by the Church and Pike Committees.[2] This established a pattern for scandal followed by reform that has been repeated in many countries. Similar investigations followed in Canada (the McDonald Commission, 1977–80), Australia (the Royal Commission under Justice Hope, 1974–77), and Norway (the Lund Commission, 1996).[3]

Investigations such as these launched a movement of reform that has steadily spread democratic oversight concerns from the United States to Australia and Canada in 1979 and 1984, respectively, and, within Europe, to Denmark in 1988, the United Kingdom in 1989, Austria in 1991, Greece in 1994, Norway in 1996, and Italy in 1997.[4] So firmly is this now established as part of the good governance agenda that the need for effective democratic oversight has received the backing of international bodies such as the Parliamentary Assemblies of the Council of Europe and of the Western European Union.[5]

The collapse of the Soviet bloc and the resulting constitutional reforms in Eastern and Southern Europe launched another wave of reform. Alongside the establishment of civilian democratic control over the military, there have been established in most of these transitional democracies parliamentary committees whose responsibility is the oversight of the security and intelligence agencies. This was the case for example in Romania, Slovenia, Lithuania, Estonia, Croatia, and Bosnia-Herzegovina. [6] Outside the Anglo-Saxon world and Europe reform has spread also to such transitional countries as South Africa,[7] Argentina,[8] and South Korea.[9]

In these transitional states the domestic security agency had often been tainted by a repressive past. Even among more established liberal democracies, however, there has been a growing recognition that security and intelligence agencies can potentially threaten as well protect democracy. If left unregulated, the propensity of these agencies to systematically invade individual privacy by information gathering and surveillance; manipulate the political process by infiltrating political movements, pressure groups, and trades unions; engage in psychological operations and disinformation; or even, in extreme cases, effect political assassinations and coups in foreign countries is now well documented.

Alongside preventing scandal and cementing constitutional change, a third reason for the spread of intelligence accountability can be mentioned: respect for the rule of law. The absence of an explicit legal basis for the work of its security and intelligence agencies may bring a state into conflict with constitutional or human rights norms, especially where powers affect individuals, for example, surveillance. This has been of particular importance in leading to reform in European states that are parties to the European Convention on Human Rights.[10] In several European states, aspects of the legal basis have been found to be inadequate.[11] This has prompted the passing of legislation that in turn gives security and intelligence agencies legitimacy. In the process, legislators have used the opportunity to address the principles that should govern this important area of state activity and lay down limits to the work of such agencies.

Three recurring issues in the design of oversight procedures can be mentioned at this point. First is the need to establish mechanisms to prevent political abuse while providing for effective governance of the agencies. Overall, the objective is that security and intelligence agencies should be *insulated* from political abuse without being *isolated* from executive governance. Second is upholding the rule of law in the sense of subjecting the agencies to legal control. As in other areas, one key task of the legislature is to delegate authority to the administration but also to structure and confine discretionary powers in law. Third, many countries have been concerned to ensure that the exceptional powers granted to the agencies (such as surveillance and the gathering of personal data) are used in a way proportionate to the threat as a means for protecting civil rights.

With these preliminary remarks in mind we turn to the specific role of the agency, the executive, parliament, and independent review bodies in intelligence accountability.

THE ROLE OF THE AGENCY

The executive and parliament depend for their oversight functions on loyal and professional intelligence agencies. Without a professional agency acting in a disciplined manner, reporting and accountability mechanisms will not function accurately or not at all. Therefore, it is vital that any accountability framework sees the agency not only as an object of control but also as a constituting element of the accountability framework. Furthermore, the internal functioning and organization of the agency is also the first "firewall" against human rights violations by agency officials. Proper mandates, codes of conduct, and other regulations as well as internal complaint mechanisms diminish the risk that officials will be engaged in human rights violations. The focus is here on four important elements of the internal functioning of intelligence agencies: defining the mandate, appointing the director, the use of special powers, and internal direction.

Defining the Mandate

A key aspect of accountability for security and intelligence agencies is that their role and sphere of operation are clearly defined. Therefore, countries that introduced intelligence accountability (as mentioned in the introduction) have enacted legislation to this effect, that is, emphasizing that responsibility for delineating the tasks of a security or intelligence agency lies with parliament and that this role should not be changed without reference to legislators. In transitional states particularly, this may help provide protection from abuse of the agencies by the government. A legal basis is also necessary because of the exceptional powers with which these agencies are often entrusted.

It is also important that security and intelligence agencies are differentiated from other institutions, such as law enforcement bodies, and the legislative mandate can help do so, as is the case in Germany where the *Trennungsgebot* (firewall) is in place between police, military, and intelligence services. Failure to make these clear distinctions will lead to blurred lines of accountability, and to the risk that the special powers that security and intelligence agencies possess are used in routine situations where there is no imminent threat to the state. Post-transition states in particular, for example, Bosnia-Herzegovina, have found it important to clarify, by means of detailed legislation, the various aspects of national security—rather than leaving the mandate of the security and intelligence agencies essentially open-ended through the use of phrases such as "protecting the security of the state."[12]

Four different type of agencies can be distinguished on the basis of the mandate: internal (domestic) service, external (foreign) service, collection and analysis of information services, as well as services that act to counter domestic or foreign security threats. With regard to the first two types, it seems common practice to refer to "intelligence services" for agencies with foreign mandates and to "security services" for agencies with domestic mandates. Both intelligence services and security services can have either a more proactive mandate or be restricted to the gathering and analysis of information. Combining these factors, several different types of institutional arrangements have been adopted by states:

a. A single agency for security and intelligence (both domestic and external), for example, Bosnia and Herzegovina, the Netherlands, Spain, and Turkey.
b. Separate agencies for domestic and external intelligence and security, with either separate or overlapping territorial competences, for example, the United Kingdom, Poland, Hungary, and Germany.
c. A domestic security agency but no acknowledged or actual foreign intelligence agency, for example, Canada.

In post-authoritarian societies, there are often strong memories of security and intelligence services endowed with broad mandates and sweeping powers used to protect dictatorial regimes against rebellions from their own people. Services were used by such regimes to suppress political opposition to prevent any kind of demonstration and eliminate leaders of labor unions, the media, political parties, and other civil society organizations. In doing so, the services intervened deeply in the political and daily life of the citizens. After the transition to democracy, the new leaders were determined to curtail the mandate and powers of the services and guarantee its political neutrality. An example of this practice is given by the Argentine National Intelligence Law of 2001. This law forbids the services to work in areas where they used to be active under the Generals' regime, that is, they are forbidden to be involved in repressive activities; process information on individuals on the basis of race, political ideology, religion, or membership of a trade union or exert influence over the political situation and media in Argentina.[13]

Appointing the Director

A key aspect of the legislation governing intelligence and security agencies is the process for appointing the director. Personal qualities of leadership, integrity, and independence are necessary in the person appointed. This will inevitably be a senior official position, and it is important that the process of appointment reinforces and guarantees the status of the position.

Various countries have adopted the minimum standard that the appointment should be open to scrutiny outside the executive. Constitutional traditions vary, however, in how this takes place in the case of senior government posts. In some countries (for instance, the United Kingdom) the safeguards against abuse rest on customary practice, which, if they were broken, would lead to political criticism and possible censure by independent officials. In other states, a formal confirmation or consultation procedure is common, which enables the legislature to either veto or express their opinion on an appointment. This may be underwritten by a constitutional requirement either that official appointments must be approved by parliament or, alternatively, that they can be blocked by a parliamentary vote (e.g., the practice in the United States). A parliamentary verdict of nonagreement on a proposed nominee may not have the de jure consequences of a veto vote, but often it will de facto. Other noteworthy practices can be found in Belgium, Australia, and Hungary. In Belgium, the director-general is obliged to take the oath before the chairman of the Permanent Committee for Supervision of the Intelligence and Security Services before taking office.[14] In Australia, the prime minister must consult with the leader of the opposition in the House of Representatives concerning the proposed appointment.[15] Considering the executive's involvement in the appointment of the director, the Hungarian law is of interest because it addresses the role of both the respective minister and the prime minister.[16] The goal of all these and similar provisions is to achieve a broad political consensus for the director's appointment.

Apart from the appointment process, in various countries safeguards exist against both improper pressure being applied on the director and abuse of the office. Provisions for security of tenure, subject to removal for wrongdoing, are therefore common, as demonstrated by the legislation example from Poland.[17]

Internal Direction and Control

Essential safeguards within an agency should exist to ensure legality and propriety with regard to its functioning. Inevitably, it is impossible to spell out in legislation every matter of detail concerning the operation of a security and intelligence agency. Moreover it may be undesirable to do so where this would give public notice of sensitive operational techniques. Nonetheless various countries have adopted agency procedures to prevent abuse and offences. In the context of accountability mechanisms, the focus here is on reporting on illegal action and code of conduct.

The most reliable information about illegal action by a security or intelligence agency is likely to come from within the agency itself. Hence, a duty to report illegal action and to correct it is useful and also strengthens the position of staff within the agency in raising concerns that they may have about illegality. For example, the U.S. Department of Defense has created an internal channel for reporting questionable or improper intelligence activities to the assistant secretary of Defense (Intelligence Oversight) and the general counsel.[18] The same is true of so-called whistle-blower provisions, which give protection from legal reprisals to such persons when they raise issues of this kind with the appropriate oversight bodies. In Bosnia and Herzegovina, an employee who believes that he received an illegal order should draw the attention of superior, insist on written confirmation, and eventually report to the next layer of authority.[19] In Hungary, the director-general of the National Security Service is obliged to report unlawful acts immediately to the minister and to the National Security Committee in Parliament.[20] Additionally, staff should be protected in reporting illegality from both disciplinary action and criminal prosecution. A detailed illustration of a public interest defense to criminal liability for unauthorized disclosure protection can be found in Canada.[21]

The formulation of an internal code of conduct is another important manner to ensure proper behavior on the part of intelligence officials. To devise a professional code of ethics and offer training courses for intelligence staffers are useful means to set, communicate, and maintain a minimum level of shared practices among intelligence employees. For example, in the United States, the assistant to the secretary of Defense (Intelligence Oversight) is tasked with, among other issues, the institutionalization of the orientation, awareness, and training of all intelligence personnel in intelligence oversight concepts (e.g., upholding the rule of law, protection of statutory and constitutional rights of U.S. persons).[22] The Republic of South Africa opted for a code of conduct for intelligence workers that gives clear guidance on the ethical scope of their activities.[23]

The Use of Special Powers

Some intelligence bodies are solely concerned with reporting and analysis, for example, the Office of National Assessments in Australia, the Information Board in Estonia, and the U.K. Joint Intelligence Committee. However, where security and intelligence agencies have a proactive, information-gathering capacity they will usually be granted specific legal powers, all the more so where their role includes countering or disrupting threats to national security, actively gathering intelligence, or law enforcement in the field of national security. "Special powers," therefore, refers to the granting of enhanced powers to security and intelligence agencies that directly affect civil liberties, including conducting surveillance and recording information, searching enclosed (private) spaces and objects, using stolen or false identities, monitoring conversations and data transfer, requesting cooperation from providers and public telecommunication networks, as well as having access to all places for installing observation equipment.[24] Typically, greater powers are granted than those normally available to the police or other law enforcement bodies because threats to security are seen to be more serious than ordinary criminality.

Because of the dangers for the rule of law and human rights, the agency's use of special powers needs to be overseen. Helpful practical guidance on what this means in relation to one area of importance—surveillance—was given by the Canadian McDonald Commission of inquiry into abuses by the Royal Canadian Mounted Police, which reported in 1980. To ensure the protection of privacy from intrusive surveillance, the McDonald Commission proposed the following four general principles: the rule of law should be strictly observed; investigative techniques should be proportionate to the security threat under investigation and weighed against the possible damage to civil liberties and democratic structures; less intrusive alternatives should be used wherever possible; and control of discretion should be layered so that the greater the invasion of privacy, the higher

the level of necessary authorization.[25] A fifth point should be added to these principles: legislation governing exceptional powers should be comprehensive. If the
law covers only some of the available techniques of information-gathering there
will be an in-built temptation for an agency to resort to less regulated methods (for
instance those that do not require approval outside the agency itself). Examples of
comprehensive legislation can be found, for instance, in Germany, the Netherlands, and the United Kingdom.[26] It is noteworthy that the latter cover not only
surveillance but also gathering information through human sources.

Prior to surveillance or information gathering, many systems require the authorization of the use of special powers by a person external to the agency. This
may be a judge (as in Bosnia and Herzegovina, Estonia, and Canada) or a specialized court (for example in the Netherlands under the Intelligence and Security
Services Act or the United States under the Foreign Intelligence Surveillance Act of
1978) or a minister (e.g., the United Kingdom). In the latter case, because a minister
is part of the executive, it is important that proper controls against political abuse
exist. In Germany, the law requires that the minister not only approve the use of
special powers but also report them to the parliamentary committee on intelligence
oversight.[27]

THE EXECUTIVE

The importance of the security and intelligence services in supporting the
governments of modern states with the supply and analysis of relevant intelligence
to counter specified threats and advance domestic, defense, and foreign policy is
undeniable. This is equally true of domestic security (especially counterterrorism,
counterespionage, and countering threats to the democratic nature of the state),
as well as in the realm of international relations, diplomacy, and defense. This
pressing need means that the executive branch is entitled to expect unswerving
loyalty from the agencies in implementing the policies of the government in the
nation's interests.

Clear executive control of the agencies is also the antidote to the possibility
of the agencies becoming a law unto themselves in a way that is antidemocratic
and creates a vacuum of accountability. In fact one can go further and argue that,
without information or control, the executive cannot itself be properly accountable to the public within a balanced constitution.

A delicate line must be walked, however, in avoiding the equal and opposite
error that with unchecked executive control governments may be tempted to use
security agencies or their exceptional powers and capacities to gather information
for the purposes of domestic politics, for instance, to discredit domestic political
opponents. Sensitive accountability structures, therefore, attempt to insulate security and intelligence agencies from political abuse without isolating them from
executive governance.

Executive Control in Various Political Systems

The precise form that executive accountability takes in any given country is necessarily relative to the prevailing constitutional arrangements. The differences between presidential executives like the United States, dual executives like France, or Westminster-style parliamentary executives, of course, profoundly affect both the distribution of responsibility for security and intelligence and the corresponding oversight arrangements Even within one type of system, wide variations may exist. For example, quite different patterns of oversight for security and intelligence have emerged in the Westminster family of the United Kingdom, Australia, Canada, and New Zealand.[28]

It is common to find that on the ministerial side, intelligence laws deal with the allocation of responsibility for formulating policy on security and intelligence matters (within, of course, the legislative mandate of the agencies). The laws address, as well, the right to receive reports from the agencies; a reservation of the right to approve matters of political sensitivity (e.g., cooperation with agencies from other countries)[29]; or activities that affect fundamental rights (such as the approval of the use of special powers, whether or not additional external approval is required, for instance, from a judge). Conversely, on the agency side, the following corresponding duties may be codified: the duty to implement government policy, the duty to report to ministers, and the duty to seek approval of specified sensitive matters.

In pure presidential and parliamentary executive systems, however, the safeguards are more likely to take the form of a series of legal checks and balances. These may include security of tenure for the agency heads, legal limits to what the agencies can be asked to do, and independent mechanisms for raising concerns about abuses (e.g., safe routes for whistle-blowing outside the agency for staff who fear improper political manipulation).

At the institutional level the checks and balances model between the executive, the legislature, and the judiciary is, of course, a design feature of the U.S. Constitution. In the intelligence field it takes the form both of powerful congressional committees whose rights extend to timely information about intelligence operations and the blocking powers of the purse and legal controls over the agencies.

Within Westminster-style parliamentary executives, the notion of ministerial accountability to Parliament underpins the design of accountability structures. Effective parliamentary oversight presupposes effective control of the agencies by ministers. Parliaments can only reliably call ministers to account for the actions of the intelligence agencies if ministers have real powers of control and adequate information about the actions taken in their name.

In each of these three systems, however, there are prudential reasons to make a separation between executive oversight and managerial control of the agencies and their operations. If political leaders are too closely involved in day-to-day matters, it will be impossible for them to act as a source of external control, and the whole oversight scheme will be weakened. Equally, if executive control is too close, there is the danger of politicizing the intelligence cycle, especially at the analysis stage, and the end product will be less useful as a consequence.[30] Effectiveness, therefore, suggests distinct but complimentary roles for the executive and agency heads. One provision articulating this principle is the Canadian Security Intelligence Service Act 1984, which refers to the director of the Service having "the *control and management* of the Service" that is "under the direction" of the minister.[31] The Polish intelligence legislation similarly clearly distinguishes between the respective competences of the prime minister and the heads of the agencies.[32]

Transitional societies, wherein previously the line between civilian government and intelligence agencies has been blurred, may find it necessary to provide detailed prohibitions to prevent future executive or ministerial abuses. For instance, in the new Bosnia-Herzegovina legislation, while the chair of the Council of Ministers has a number of detailed policy and review functions,[33] under article 10 he or she is expressly prevented from assuming "in whole or in part" "the rights and responsibilities" of the director-general or deputy director-general. Conversely, the director-general's rights and responsibilities are detailed in a way that makes clear their day-to-day managerial character; these include preparation of the annual budget of the agency; directing analytical, technical, administrative, and partnership cooperation operations; and the external operations of the agency. The same provision lists also protecting intelligence sources, intentions, and operations from unauthorized disclosure as well as obtaining, through the chair, approval and support from the minister of Foreign Affairs for activities that may have a serious impact on the foreign policy of Bosnia and Herzegovina.

Ministerial Knowledge and Control of Intelligence

Within a healthy constitutional order, ministers needs a sufficient degree of control over intelligence agencies and the right to demand information from them to discharge their responsibilities as members of an elected executive acting on behalf of the public. They also need to have adequate control and information to be able to account to parliament for the agencies' use of their legal powers and their expenditure. Effective democratic control and policy support, therefore, depends on a two-way process of access between political members of the executive and officials.

Some of the precise mechanisms for executive control include the following: restrictions on covert action; the formulation of written policies or targets to guide agency priorities; a right to be briefed; the requirement that sensitive matters be approved specifically by ministers; processes of budgetary approval; and regular reporting and audit. In many countries, the minister is often aided in the task of control by an inspector general—an institution most often established by law and endowed with various rights and responsibilities vis-à-vis both the executive and the parliament. In this context, the inspector general monitors whether the government's intelligence policies are appropriately implemented by the services.

International Cooperation

One area in which it is especially difficult for national ministers (or indeed legislatures) to exercise scrutiny lies within the work of international/suprana-tional bodies and bilateral cooperative arrangements.[34] Bilateral cooperation nor-mally involves sharing intelligence information and analysis on topics of mutual interest.[35] The potential of these arrangements to bypass domestic controls on issues such as surveillance and to impinge on international relations suggests that, nevertheless, there is strong case for legal provisions asserting the need for executive approval. A recent example of legislation addressing this issue comes from Bosnia and Herzegovina: Article 64 of the Intelligence Service Act requires approval to be given before the agency enters into an arrangement with in-telligence and security services of other countries. Additionally, the Minister for Foreign Affairs must be consulted before an arrangement is entered with an institution of a foreign state, an international organization of states, or an in-stitution thereof. The Intelligence Committee must also be informed of all such arrangements. It is notable that the Council of Europe has in the context of recent allegations concerning illegal renditions recently argued that parliamentary com-mittees also should assert their power to review the operations of partner agencies within their territory.[36]

Safeguards Against Ministerial Abuse

Alongside powers of executive control there are also various forms of counter-balancing safeguards against political abuse that countries have adopted. In Canada, Hungary, and Australia there is a requirement that certain ministerial instructions be put in writing. Such a stipulation deals with concerns about the executive claiming plausible deniability of certain matters.[37] Ministerial instruc-tions may also be required to be disclosed outside the agency. The Canadian law, for example, requires them to be given to the review body,[38] and Australian law requires them to be given to the Inspector General of Intelligence and Security as soon as practical after the direction is given.[39]

Within a wider frame of checks and balances, the Australian intelligence legislation features another safeguarding provision, namely, the duty of the director-general to brief the leader of the opposition for the purpose of keeping him or her informed on matters related to the agency.[40] Notice that this is also established informal practice in other national settings aiming, inter alia, at the prevention of ministerial abuse. A bipartisan approach to security and intelligence is more likely to be maintained if leading opposition parliamentarians do not feel that they have been wholly excluded from the ring of secrecy. The Australian example operates within a Westminster-style democracy, albeit a federation. In a more complex federal presidential state, there may be a range of actors who should be briefed on a need-to-know basis, as in Bosnia and Herzegovina.[41]

Legislation from Bosnia and Herzegovina and the United Kingdom, for example, includes clear provisions that the intelligence/security services shall not be amenable to any attempts that try to undermine their impartiality—be it by furthering the interests of certain political parties or by undermining the credibility of legitimate political movements within the country.[42]

Finally, the grant to an agency head of a right of access to the prime minister or president can serve as a safeguard. In the United Kingdom, for example, the agency heads of the Security Service, the Secret Intelligence Service, and the Government Communications Headquarters, although responsible to the Home Secretary and Foreign Secretary, respectively, have a right of access to the prime minister.[43]

THE ROLE OF PARLIAMENT

As a consequence of the democratization of intelligence over the past three decades, in liberal democracies it became common to reserve a role for parliament in the oversight of security and intelligence services. Parliamentary involvement can help ensure that security and intelligence organizations are serving the state as a whole and protecting the constitution, rather than narrower political or sectional interests. There are dangers, however, in parliamentary scrutiny. The security sector may be drawn into party political controversy; an immature approach by parliamentarians may lead to sensationalism in public debate and to wild accusations and conspiracy theories aired under parliamentary privilege. Furthermore, effective scrutiny of security is painstaking and unglamorous work for politicians, conducted almost entirely behind the scenes.

In this section we focus on four important aspects of parliamentary oversight: the mandate of the parliamentary oversight body, members of the oversight body, access to classified information, and budget control.

Mandate of the Parliamentary Oversight Body

The international norm is for parliament to establish an oversight body for all the major security and intelligence agencies (a "functional approach" to oversight), rather than having multiple oversight bodies for specific agencies (an "institutional" approach). This functional approach facilitates seamless oversight because, in reality, different parts of the intelligence machinery work closely with each other. There is a risk that an oversight body established on a purely institutional basis may find that its investigations are hampered if they lead in the direction of information supplied by or to an agency outside the legal range of operation. There are some significant divergences from this approach, however. In the United States, there are separate congressional intelligence committees in the House of Representatives and the Senate, each with legal oversight of the agencies. In the United Kingdom, the legal responsibilities of the Intelligence and Security Committee (ISC) cover only part of the intelligence establishment (Defence Intelligence Staff, the Joint Intelligence Committee, and National Criminal Intelligence Service are not included within the legal boundaries of the Committee). In practice, however, and with the cooperation of the government, the ISC has examined their work as well.

Broadly speaking, there are two ways in which a parliamentary oversight committee's role can be set out in law. The first is to give a wide range of responsibility and then detail specific matters that may *not* be investigated; examples of this approach can be found in legislation from the United Kingdom and Australia.[44] The second is to write down in the law a comprehensive list of oversight functions of the parliamentary oversight body, for example, as in the United States.[45]

There is a great variety in types of mandate of the parliamentary oversight body. Some oversight bodies have the power to scrutinize the operations of intelligence agencies. For example, both the U.S. congressional oversight committees as well as the Control Panel of the German Bundestag oversee the operations of their respective nation's intelligence agencies.[46] A parliamentary oversight body able to examine intelligence operations may have greater credibility and may be given greater powers (for example, to compel the production of evidence); however, it will face inevitable restrictions on how it conducts its investigations and on what can be reported to parliament or to the public. It will operate in effect within the ring of secrecy, and that will create a barrier between it and the remainder of parliament.

An alternative approach is to limit the function of the parliamentary oversight body to matters of policy, administration, and finance only (as is the case in the United Kingdom). These are issues that can be more readily examined in the public arena with the need for far fewer restrictions in the national interest on what is disclosed. The difficulty of this approach, however, is that it detracts from one of key tasks of parliamentary scrutiny: to ensure that government policy in a given field is carried out effectively. Without access to *some* operational detail, an oversight body can have or give no assurance about the efficiency of the security and intelligence agency in implementing the published policy. The same applies to auditing issues of legality or the agencies' respect for fundamental rights—tasks that are given to parliamentary oversight bodies in some countries, as in Norway.[47] Such exercises in parliamentary oversight may lack credibility unless founded on some clear evidence about the behavior of the agency concerned.

Members of the Parliamentary Oversight Body

To enjoy legitimacy and command trust, it is vital that parliamentary intelligence oversight bodies have a broad mandate, are appointed by Parliament itself, and represent a cross-section of political parties. Although wherever possible members should have some relevant expertise (say, from previous ministerial service), in our view it is also essential that they be civilian; there must be clear demarcation between the oversight body and the agencies overseen for oversight to be effective. A particular difficulty arises in transition states—the presence of former members of the security agencies on the oversight body. Where the services were implicated in maintaining a repressive former regime, this is bound to undermine confidence in the oversight process and is best avoided, if necessary by a legal prohibition. Equally, to be effective a parliamentary committee must enjoy a relationship of trust with the agencies it oversees. This suggests that to be effective a relatively small committee (without, however, compromising the principle of cross-party membership) is best.

Because the oversight of security and intelligence services requires expertise and time, some parliaments have chosen to set up an outside committee, whose members are not parliamentarians but report to parliament. Examples include the Netherlands, Belgium, Norway, and Canada.[48]

Options for appointing the membership of oversight bodies vary from countries where the head of government appoints (after consultation with the leader of the opposition, in the case of the United Kingdom),[49] to where the executive nominates members but parliament itself appoints (as in Australia),[50] to instances in which the legal responsibility for appointment rests solely with the legislature (as in Argentina,[51] Germany,[52] and Norway).[53]

The chairperson of an oversight body will invariably have an important role in leading it and determining how it conducts its business as well as directing liaison with the services outside formal committee meetings. Traditions within parliamentary systems vary concerning the chairmanship of parliamentary committees. While being sensitive to different traditions, the legitimacy of a parliamentary oversight body will be strengthened if it is chaired by a member of the opposition (as in Hungary),[54] or if the chair rotates between the opposition and the government party. The chairperson should be chosen by parliament or by the committee itself (as in Argentina), rather than appointed by the government (as in the United Kingdom).

Access to Classified Information

The parliament, and particularly the oversight body, needs to have sufficient power to obtain information and documents from the government and intelligence services. The precise extent that a parliamentary oversight body requires access to security and intelligence information and the type of information concerned depends on the specific role that it is asked to play. An oversight body whose functions include reviewing questions of legality, effectiveness, and respect for human rights will require access to more specific information than one whose remit is solely policy. Similarly, it will have a stronger case for a right of access to documents (rather than information or testimony from identified witnesses).

Clearly, however, an oversight body should have unlimited access to the necessary information to discharge its duties, as, for example, in Argentina.[55]

The differences in role explain some of the variations in the extent to which oversight bodies are given access to operational detail in different constitutional systems. Some countries (e.g., the United States) provide that the executive has the legal responsibility to keep the congressional intelligence committees fully and currently informed of the intelligence activities of the United States.[56] Moreover, the U.S. congressional oversight provisions established in 1980 demand that the President keep the two intelligence committees in Congress informed about all covert action operations, including significant failures, before initiation of the covert action authorized by the presidential finding.[57] In the Intelligence Authorization Act of 1991, the President promised to continue to inform Congress in advance in most instances, but he has successfully insisted on flexibility in times of crises—as defined by the White House.[58]

Systems vary in how they handle reporting of sensitive material. In the United States, on the one hand, the onus of being informed rests not only with the oversight body but with the executive as well. In Australia, on the other hand, the parliamentary committee is forbidden from requiring "operationally sensitive information" to be disclosed;[59] requests for documents cannot be made be made by the committee to agency heads, staff members, or the inspector general; and ministers may veto evidence from being given.[60] A power of veto of this kind effectively returns disputes over access to information to the political arena.

Various countries have stipulated that the oversight body is also entitled to obtain information and documents from experts of both the services as well as civil society, for example, think tanks or universities. Such a provision guarantees that parliament is able to receive alternative viewpoints, in addition to the position of the government. For example, in Luxembourg the Parliamentary Control Committee can decide, with two-thirds majority and after having consulted the director of the Intelligence Services, to be assisted by an expert.[61] If parliament lacks clear information or doubts the validity of government information, legislators may have the power to start their own inquiry, for example, in Argentina, Norway, South Africa, South Korea, United Kingdom, and the United States. Of these selected states, the legislative oversight bodies of Norway, South Africa, and the United States possess subpoena powers.[62]

However, because the information and documents are often related to sensitive issues (about persons) and/or about national security, oversight bodies of various countries have made great efforts to protect information from unauthorized disclosure. Unauthorized disclosure of information may harm not only national security interests but also the trust that is necessary for an effective relationship between the oversight body and the services. This is partly a matter of legislation (see the United States and Norway),[63] and partly a matter of proper behavior of the members of the oversight body in dealing with classified information with care and attention.

Parliamentary Budget Control

Budget control is at the heart of parliamentary control. Most countries have developed or are developing a systematic approach to the evaluation and approval of budget proposals. In every country, parliament fulfills a different role in the budgeting and accounting procedures for the security and intelligence services, for example, in terms of the scope of budget control, the power to amend budgets, the power to approve supplementary budget requests, access to classified information, and the disposition of independent financial auditors. The greater the parliament's powers in these areas, the more effective it will be in debates with the government.

Budget control has to be understood in the context of the mandate of the parliamentary intelligence oversight body. In some countries, this body clearly has the power of the purse as the embodiment of the people's voice. In other countries, for example in Norway, parliament has chosen not to give the power of the purse to the oversight committee but to keep it for the plenary or parliamentary budget committee. The reason behind this practice is that budget control would make the oversight committee co-responsible for government policy.

In other parliaments, however, such as in Argentina, the Netherlands, Germany, or the United States, the parliamentary oversight committee has the power of the purse, giving those legislatures control over how money is spent by the services. To be more precise, in the United States as well as, for example, Germany, budgetary power is often divided between the budget committee and the intelligence oversight committee. The former committee focuses on appropriations; the latter focuses on the policy aspects of the services and authorizes funds. Some governments also keep parliament informed about the execution of the intelligence budget during the fiscal year (as in Germany).[64] The state budget concerning the different aspects of the security sector has to be all-inclusive and complete. No expenditure should go unaccounted for. "Black" programs or secret budgets—inaccessible for members of the parliamentary intelligence oversight committee—would be clearly in violation of this principle. Parliamentarians of the intelligence oversight committee and the budget committee should have access to all classified information, as is the case in Hungary.[65]

INDEPENDENT COMPLAINTS, INSPECTION, AND AUDIT PROCESSES

Our third category of oversight structures embraces a variety of concerns, from authorizing the use of special powers, to dealing with complaints brought by citizens, to checking that the services have used their powers with propriety and with financial regularity. What these disparate concerns have in common is that various countries have found it useful to involve politically independent officials and institutions, mostly in ex post facto review, but occasionally in the prior authorization of the work of the agencies.

In other areas of government, this is a task that one would expect to find the judiciary discharging as the third branch, alongside the executive and the legislature. That, however, is rarely appropriate or effective in matters touching national security.[66] Occasionally legal regimes have been constructed that under highly quarantined circumstances involve judges in authorizing or affirming actions based on intelligence, as with the Foreign Intelligence Surveillance Act in the United States, the equivalent role of the Federal Court in Canada, or control orders under the Terrorism Act of 2005 in the United Kingdom. However, the secret nature of the processes involved, difficulties in obtaining evidence, and the legitimate need of these agencies to protect sensitive information from public disclosure can all be cited as objections to adjudication through public hearings in the regular courts.

Nevertheless, there is a clear need for some avenue of redress for individuals who claim to have been adversely affected by the exceptional powers, such as surveillance or security clearance, often wielded by security and intelligence agencies. Complaints may have a broader role to play also in highlighting administrative failings and lessons to be learned, leading to improved performance. Clearly, however, any system for redress needs to be designed to prevent legitimate targets of a security or intelligence agency from finding out about the agency's work. Achieving this balance in a complaints system between independence, robustness, and fairness, on one hand, and sensitivity to security needs, on the other hand, is challenging but not impossible. The requirements of human rights treaties, and especially for European states the European Convention on Human Rights, with its attendant protection of fair trial, respect for private life, and the requirement of an effective remedy, also have a considerable bearing on these matters, but these detailed technical questions cannot be pursued here.[67]

Different oversight systems handle complaints in a variety of ways. An independent official, such as an ombudsman, may have power to investigate and report on a complaint against an agency. This is the case in the Netherlands.[68] In some countries an independent inspector-general of security and intelligence deals in a rather similar way with complaints against the services as part of the office's overall oversight duties. This is the case, for example, in New Zealand (Office of Inspector-General of Intelligence and Security, established in 1996) and South Africa (Office of Inspector General of Intelligence, appointed pursuant to section 12 of the Constitution). In addition, specific offices established under freedom of information or data protection legislation may have a role in investigating complaints against the agencies.

Ombudsman-type systems place reliance on an independent official investigating on behalf of the complainant. They usually exist to deal with an administrative failure rather than a legal error as such. They give less emphasis to the complainant's own participation in the process and to transparency. They typically conclude with a report, and (if the complaint is upheld) a recommendation for putting matters right and future action, rather than a judgment and formal remedies.

Less commonly, complaints and grievances of citizens are may be dealt with by the parliamentary intelligence oversight committee, as is the case, for example, in Germany and Norway.[69] On the one hand, there may be a benefit for a parliamentary oversight body in handling complaints brought against security and intelligence agencies since this will give an insight into potential failures—of policy, legality, and efficiency. On the other hand, if the oversight body is too closely identified with the agencies it oversees or operates within the ring of secrecy, the complainant may feel that the complaints process is insufficiently independent. In cases where a single body handles complaints and oversight, it is best if there are quite distinct legal procedures for these different roles. Generally, it is preferable that the two functions be given to different bodies, but that processes are in place so that the oversight body is made aware of the broader implications of individual complaints.

In some countries not only citizens but also members of the services are permitted to bring service-related issues to the attention of an ombudsman or parliamentary oversight body. For example, in Germany officials may raise issues with the Parliamentary Control Panel,[70] and in South Africa members of the service may complain to the inspector general.

Another method of handling complaints is through a specialist tribunal. This may be established to deal with complaints either against a particular agency or in relation to the use of specific powers, as in the United Kingdom (the Intelligence Services Commissioner and the Commissioner for the Interception of Communications). Or complaints may be handled in a tribunal-type procedure but by a specialist oversight body, as with the Security Intelligence Review Committee (SIRC) in Canada. On the one hand, a tribunal of this kind has some advantages over a regular court in dealing with security- and intelligence-related complaints: it can develop a distinct expertise in the field of security and intelligence, devised for handling sensitive information. In view of the nature of the subject matter, these are unlikely to involve a full public legal hearing. On the other hand, although some tribunals may give the complainant a hearing, he or she is likely to face severe practical difficulties in proving a case, in obtaining access to relevant evidence, or in challenging the agency's version of events. To combat some of these problems special security-cleared counsels have been introduced in Canada and the United Kingdom. These counsels have the task of challenging security-related arguments, especially those aspects not disclosed to the complainant. This can help the tribunal reach a more objective assessment of the evidence and the arguments.

Apart from redress of complaints, a second reason for the creation of independent offices is to provide impartial verification and assurance for the government that secret agencies are acting according to its policies effectively and with propriety. For this reason, a number of countries have devised offices such as inspectors-general, judicial commissioners, or auditors to check on the activities of the security sector and with statutory powers of access to information and staff.[71]

This notion derives from the U.S. intelligence community, which now has around a dozen inspectors general. All are independent of the agencies concerned. There are, however, significant variations among them: some are established by legislation (for example, the inspectors general for the Central Intelligence Agency and the Department of Defense); others are the creatures of administrative arrangements established by the relevant secretary (for example, with regard to the Defense Intelligence Agency and the National Reconnaissance Office, both located within the organizational framework of the Department of Defense). Irrespective of this distinction, some report to Congress as well as to the executive branch. A number of these offices have a responsibility that extends to efficiency, avoiding waste and audit, as well monitoring legality and policy compliance.

A common feature is that inspectors general operate within the ring of secrecy: their function is not primarily to provide public assurance about accountability, rather to strengthen accountability to the executive. The Canadian inspector general is a clear illustration of this type of office and is entrusted with unrestricted access to information in the hands of the Service to fulfill these functions.[72] Likewise in Bosnia and Herzegovina, the inspector general exercises "an internal control function."[73] To this end, the inspector general may review intelligence activities; investigate complaints; initiate inspections, audits, and investigations on his or her own initiative; and issue recommendations. The inspector general has a duty to report at least every six months to the Security Intelligence Committee and keep the main executive actors informed of developments in a regular and timely fashion. The powers of the inspector general include questioning agency employees and obtaining access to agency premises and data.

In other countries—notably South Africa—the role is different, that is, to report to parliament. In effect the office bridges the ring of secrecy: it is an attempt to assure the public through a report to parliament that an independent person with access to the relevant material has examined the activities of the security or intelligence agency. However, inevitably most of the material on which an assessment of the agency's work is made has to remain within the ring of secrecy, although it may be shared with other oversight bodies.

Even some inspectors general whose statutory brief is to report to the executive may maintain an informal working relationship with parliamentary bodies. This is so in Australia for instance, and as noted, a number of the U.S. inspectors general report periodically to Congress.

Whether an office of this kind reports to the government or to parliament, in either case, careful legal delineation of its jurisdiction, independence, and powers are vital. Independent officials may be asked to review an agency's performance against one or more of several standards: efficiency, compliance with government policies or targets, propriety, or legality. In any instance, however, the office will need unrestricted access to files and personnel to be able to come to a reliable assessment. In practice an independent official is unlikely to be able to scrutinize more than a fraction of the work of an agency. Some of these offices work by sampling the work and files of the agencies overseen; this gives an incentive for the agency to establish more widespread procedures and produces a ripple effect. Some also have jurisdiction to deal with individual complaints, as under the Australian scheme.[74]

A third independent review function concerns financial propriety. Both the executive and the legislature have a legitimate interest in ensuring that budgets voted for intelligence are spent lawfully and effectively. However, as with the handling of complaints, it requires some ingenuity to devise systems for protecting secrecy while nevertheless ensuring that auditors have the wide access to classified information necessary to certify whether the services have used government funds within the law. Understandably, limited restrictions to protect the identities of certain sources of information and the details of particularly sensitive operations may be imposed on the access granted to an auditor general.[75]

Primarily what distinguishes the auditing security and intelligence services from regular audits of other public bodies, however, are the reporting mechanisms. To protect the continuity of operations, methods, and sources of the services, special reporting procedures are in place in many countries. For example, in the United Kingdom only the chairs of the Public Accounts Committee and the Intelligence and Security Committee are fully briefed about the outcome of the financial audit. These briefings may include reports on the legality and efficiency of expenditures, occurrence of possible irregularities, and whether the services have operated within or have exceeded the budget. In many countries, the public annual reports of the security and intelligence service (as in the Netherlands) or of the parliamentary oversight body (as in the United Kingdom) include statements about the outcome of the financial audits.[76]

CONCLUSION

In this chapter we have compared the principles, laws, and mechanisms of national intelligence oversight in various democracies; both in old democracies (e.g., the United Kingdom and the Netherlands) as well as in new democracies (e.g., Hungary and South Africa). The purpose was not so much to give a representative overview of intelligence oversight in democracies but to identify approaches that various states have adopted to support democracy, the rule of law, and human rights in this field. A comprehensive approach to accountability was used, which included four layers of accountability: internal control within the agency, the executive, parliament, and independent review bodies such as the ombudsman and national audit offices.

As mentioned in the introduction, intelligence oversight is a very recent development, which started about thirty years ago in liberal democracies. It is not surprising, therefore, that most of the examples we have discussed are based on laws enacted in the late 1980s and the beginning of the 1990s.

The first point to make is that national security is not only a powerful argument against democratic oversight in dictatorial or one-party states but also, until recently, in established democracies such as the United Kingdom and the United States, where oversight legislation was adopted in 1989 and 1974, respectively. According to this argument, national security requires that full secrecy be observed and that the services can be only accountable to a small group of decision makers. This argument, however, goes contrary to the very nature of a democratic polity, which is that all issues vital to the lives of its citizens should be subject to normal democratic decision-making procedures. The mechanisms of intelligence accountability identified and analyzed in this chapter do show clearly that the arguments of national security and democracy can be reconciled. Accountability procedures such as reporting illegal activities within the agency, the practice of consulting the leaders of both opposition and government parties in the appointment of the agency director, access of members of parliament to classified information, independent financial audit as well as ministerial procedures for approving covert action and international intelligence sharing—all show that democratic decision and serious program review can be applied to the area of intelligence. The fear that involving parliament and, above all, members of the opposition would lead to intelligence leaks, seems to be largely unfounded. On the contrary, for example, the recent reports of intelligence leaks in the United States show that not members of the Congress but mostly members of the intelligence agencies and the executive, up to the level of the President, have leaked classified information to the press.

The second point is related to the question of whether these rather young accountability provisions and practices are strong enough to withstand major challenges to intelligence oversight. In particular after 9/11, new developments have challenged and tested the robustness of national intelligence oversight systems. We list some of these problems here. A first issue is the problem of gearing national oversight institutions toward the oversight of *international* intelligence cooperation. This problem is aggravated by the lack of democratic oversight of intelligence on the international level. A second problem is the oversight of the greater powers that governments acquired after 9/11 for dealing with terror (e.g., the new 2004 Civil Contingencies Bill in the United Kingdom and the 2001 USA-PATRIOT Act in the United States). A third danger is the politicization of the services, which refers to the use of intelligence services for personal or political party purposes in both new and old democracies.

The danger of politicization of the intelligence services is the downside of the increasing democratization of intelligence oversight. On one hand, greater transparency and public accountability leads to a better checks and balances of the services. On the other hand, the services and their activities are increasingly becoming part of the normal political debate, which leads to the danger that actors in that political debate will use the services and their work for their own parochial interests.

Whether the systems of checks and balances are strong enough to ensure a proper and lawful control of the services eventually will be known. This brings us to the last and third point. It is important to note that the intelligence agency is included in the framework of the four layers of accountability. The agency, properly understood, is itself not just an object for control.

NOTES

1. Hans Born, Loch Johnson, and Ian Leigh, eds., *Who's Watching the Spies? Establishing Intelligence Service Accountability* (Dulles, VA: Potomac Books, 2005); Hans Born and Ian Leigh, *Making Intelligence Accountable: Legal Standards and Best Practice for Oversight of Intelligence Agencies* (Oslo: Publishing House of the Parliament of Norway, 2005); Jean-Paul Brodeur, Peter Gill, and Dennis Töllborg, *Democracy, Law and Security: Internal Security Services in Contemporary Europe* (Aldershot: Ashgate, 2003); Laurence Lustgarten and Ian Leigh, *In from the Cold: National Security and Parliamentary Democracy* (Oxford: Clarendon Press, 1994).

2. Concerning the United States, see U.S. Senate, *Final Report,* Select Committee to Study Governmental Operations with Respect to Intelligence Activities (the Church Committee), 94th Congress, 2nd sess., Rept. 94-755 (May 1976); Loch K. Johnson, *A Season of Inquiry* (Lexington: University Press of Kentucky, 1985).

3. Respectively, Government of Canada, Commission of Inquiry Concerning Certain Activities of the Royal Canadian Mounted Police, Second Report, *Freedom and Security Under the Law*, 2 vols. (Hull: Ministry of Supply and Services Canada, August 1981) [the McDonald Commission report]; Royal Commission on Intelligence and Security, *Fourth Report* (Canberra, 1977) [the Hope report]; Dok. no. 15 (1995–96) [the Lund report].

4. It has to be noted, however, that parliamentary oversight of the intelligence services was in place in the Netherlands and Germany since 1952 and 1956, respectively.

5. Recommendations 1402/1999 and 1713/2005 of the Council of Europe Parliamentary Assembly; Western European Union Assembly Resolution 113, adopted on December 4, 2002 (9th sitting).

6. Law on the Intelligence and Security Agency of Bosnia and Herzegovina, passed in March 2004. Slovenia: Law on Defense (December 28, 1994), arts. 33–36; The Basics of National Security of Lithuania (1996); Estonia: Security Authorities Act, passed December 20, 2000; RSA, Intelligence Services Act (1994) (as amended).

7. Kevin O'Brien, "Controlling the Hydra: A Historical Analysis of South African Intelligence Accountability," in Born, Johnson, and Leigh, *Who's Watching the Spies?*

8. Eduardo Estevez, "Argentina's New Century Challenge: Overseeing the Intelligence System," in Born, Johnson, and Leigh, *Who's Watching the Spies?*

9. Jonathan Moran, "The Role of Security Services in Democratization: South Korea's Agency for National Security Planning," in Born, Johnson, and Leigh, *Who's Watching the Spies?*

10. Iain Cameron, *National Security and the European Convention on Human Rights* (Uppsala: Lustu Forlag, 2000); Iain Cameron, "Beyond the Nation State: The Influence of the European Court of Human Rights on Intelligence Accountability," in Born, Johnson, and Leigh, *Who's Watching the Spies?*

11. *Harman and Hewitt v. UK* (1992) 14 EHRR 657; *V and Others v. Netherlands,* Commission report of December 3, 1991; *Rotaru v. Rumania,* Appl. No. 8341/95, May 4, 2000.

12. Law on the Intelligence and Security Agency, Bosnia and Herzegovina (2004), art. 5.

13. National Intelligence Law no. 25520, Argentina (2001), art. 4.

14. Act Governing the Supervision of the Police and Intelligence Services (1991), art. 17.

15. Intelligence Service Act, Australia (2001) (Cth), part 3, section 17 (3).

16. Hungarian Law on the National Security Services, Act 125 (1995), section 11.2.

17. The Internal Security Agency and Foreign Intelligence Act, Poland (2002), art. 16.

18. Further information is available at http://www.pentagon.mil/atsdio/mission.html.

19. Law on Intelligence and Security Agency, Bosnia and Herzegovina (2004), art. 14.

20. Hungarian Law on the National Security Services, Act 125 (1995), section 27.

21. Section 15.5 of the Canadian Security of Information Act (2003).

22. Further information available at http://www.pentagon.mil/atsdio/faq.html.

23. Republic of South Africa, *White Paper on Intelligence* (1994), annex A.

24. Richard Best, *Intelligence Issues for Congress* (Washington, DC: Congressional Research Service, 2001).

25. Commission of Enquiry into Certain Actions of the RCMP, *Freedom and Security under the Law* (Ottawa, 1980), vol. 1, pp. 513ff.

26. German Sicherheitsüberprüfungsgesetz (1994); Dutch Intelligence and Security Services Act (2002); U.K. Regulation of Investigatory Powers Act (2000).

27. German Bundesverfassungsschutzgesetz (1990), §9(3) 2.

28. Lustgarten and Leigh, *In from the Cold*, chap. 15.

29. Canadian Security Intelligence Service Act 1984, s. 13

30. Peter Gill, "The Politicization of Intelligence: Lessons from the Invasion of Iraq," in Born, Johnson, and Leigh, *Who's Watching the Spies?*

31. Intelligence Services Act, Canada, R.S. (1985), emphasis added.

32. Internal Security Agency and Foreign Intelligence Agency Act (2002), Poland, art. 7.

33. Law on the Intelligence and Security Agency (2004), Bosnia and Herzegovina, arts. 8 and 9.

34. Note, for example, Art. 85 of the Constitution of Bulgaria, which requires parliamentary approval for treaties with military or political implications.

35. Jeffrey T. Richelson and Desmond Ball, *The Ties That Bind* (London: Allen & Unwin, 1990).

36. "Secretary General's report under Article 52 ECHR on the question of secret detention and transport of detainees suspected of terrorist acts, notably by or at the instigation of foreign agencies," *Council of Europe*, SG/Inf (2006) 5, Strasbourg, pnt. 101, available at http://www.coe.int/T/E/Com/Files/Events/2006-cia.

37. Canadian Security Intelligence Service (CSIS) Act (1984), sections 7(1) and (2); Act on the National Security Services (1995), Hungary, section 11.

38. CSIS Act, s. 6(2).

39. Australian Inspector-General of Intelligence and Security Act (1986), section 32B.

40. Intelligence Services Act, Australia (2001), section 19.

41. Law on the Intelligence and Security Agency, Bosnia-Herzegovina (2004), art. 6.

42. Law on the Intelligence and Security Agency (2004), Bosnia and Herzegovina, art. 39. In the United Kingdom see Security Service Act (1989), s. 2(2)(a); Intelligence Service Act (1994), s. 2(2)(b), 4(2)(b).

43. Security Service Act (1989), s. 2(4); Intelligence Service Act (1994), s. 2(4), 4(4).

44. Concerning Australia: Intelligence Services Act. No. 152 (2001), sections 28 and 29. Concerning the United Kingdom: Intelligence Services Act (1994), s. 10.

45. Section 13, U.S. Rules of the U.S. Senate Select Committee on Intelligence.

46. German Bundestag, Secretariat of the Parliamentary Control Commission, *Parliamentary Control of the Intelligence Services in Germany* (Berlin: Bundespresseamt, 2001)

47. The Act Relating to the Monitoring of Intelligence, Surveillance and Security Services, Act no. 7 (February 3, 1995_, Norway

48. Until 2004 there was no oversight committee in the Canadian Parliament, although the Security Intelligence Review Committee (a statutory body composed of Privy Counsellors) was established under the Canadian Security Intelligence Service Act (1984). A parliamentary oversight committee is soon to be established.

49. Intelligence Services Act (1994), s. 10.

50. Intelligence Services Act (2001), s. 14(2).

51. Estevez, "Argentina's New Century Challenge," in Born, Johnson, and Leigh, *Who's Watching the Spies?*

52. Law on the Parliamentary Control of Activities of the Federal Intelligence Services (PKGrG) (1978; 1992, 1999, and 2001 amended version).

53. Instructions for Monitoring of Intelligence, Surveillance and Security Services (EOS) (1995), section 1.

54. Section 14, 1, Act no. 125 (1995) on the National Security Services, Hungary.

55. Art. 32, National Intelligence Law, no. 25520, Argentina (2001).

56. U.S. Code, Title 50, Section 413 (a).

57. U.S. Code, Title 50, Section 413.

58. Loch K. Johnson, "Governing in the Absence of Angels: On the Practice of Intelligence Accountability in the United States," in Born, Johnson, and Leigh, *Who's Watching the Spies?*, pp. 64–65.

59. Intelligence Services Act (2001), s. 30 (Australia).

60. Ibid., s. 32.

61. Art. 14 (4), Loi du 15 Juin portant organisation du Service de Renseignement de l'Etat, Memorial-Journal Officiel du Grand-Duché de Luxembourg (2004), A-No. 113.

62. Hans Born, "Balancing Operational Efficiency and Democratic Legitimacy," in Born, Johnson, and Leigh, *Who's Watching the Spies?*, pp. 230 and 237.

63. U.S. Code Section 413, General Congressional Oversight Provisions, (d); The Act Relating to the Monitoring of Intelligence, Surveillance and Security Services (1995), Section 9, (Norway).

64. German Bundestag, Secretariat of the Parliamentary Control Commission (PKGr), *Parliamentary Control of the Intelligence Services in Germany* (July 2001).

65. Article 14, 4g, of the 1995 Act on the National Security Services of Hungary.

66. Lustgarten and Leigh, *In from the Cold*, chap. 12.

67. *Klass v. Germany*, para. 15 (regarding Art. 8); *Leander v. Sweden*, para. 68 (regarding Art. 13). See Cameron, *National Security and the European Convention on Human Rights*; Cameron, "Beyond the Nation State."

68. Intelligence and Security Services Act (2002), art. 83.

69. Fredrik Sejersted, "Intelligence and Accountability in a State Without Enemies," in Born, Johnson, and Leigh, *Who's Watching the Spies?*

70. German Bundestag Secretariat of the Parliamentary Control Commission (PKGR), *Parliamentary Control of the Intelligence Services in Germany* (Berlin: Bundespresseamt, 2001), pp. 19–20.

71. For comparison of the powers of inspectors general in different countries, see Intelligence and Security Committee (U.K.), *Annual Report for 2001–2*, Cm 5542, Appendix 3.

72. CSIS Act, 1984, s. 33.2 and 33.3.

73. Law of the Intelligence and Security Agency of Bosnia Herzegovina, art. 32.

74. Inspector-General of Security and Intelligence Act (1986), sections 10–12.

75. These restrictions apply to the U.K. comptroller and auditor general, see Report by the Comptroller and Auditor-General, *Thames House and Vauxhall Cross,* HC Session 1999–2000 (February 18, 2000), point 8, available at http://www.nao.org.uk/publications/nao_reports/9900236.pdf.

76. See, for example, Annual Report of the General Security and Intelligence Services of the Netherlands (2003), available at http://www.minbzk.nl/contents/pages/9459/annual_report_2003_aivd.pdf, pp. 69–70; UK Parliamentary Intelligence and Security Committee Annual Report 2002–2003, presented to Parliament by the Prime Minister by Command of Her Majesty (June 2003), London, pp. 8–13.

8

THE COIN OF INTELLIGENCE ACCOUNTABILITY

A. DENIS CLIFT

THE SETTING

TO PROVIDE A GOVERNMENT OF THE PEOPLE, by the people, for the people, the Constitution of the United States created three separate branches—executive, legislative, and judicial—to exercise the government's lawful powers. By design, each of the three independent branches was given checks and balances against the others. Accountability—the imperative of each individual of government and each organization of government being liable to answer for exercise of duties, responsibilities, and conduct—was at the heart of these checks and balances.

The roles played by print and electronic media and by citizens and private organizations both augment and subdue the role of government, variously sounding alarm and sounding praise, calling for inquiry and challenging any such call. In this era of globalization, this cyber era, this information age, international political, economic, cultural, religious, health, environmental, and security issues must be weighed in the exercise of the government's powers.

If it is the people's government, the people have a right to know. Where the work of intelligence is secret, because it is seeking information that is being hidden, withheld, or denied by foreign sources—or because it is operating covertly to hide U.S. involvement—that secrecy conflicts with the right to know. The work of intelligence must be accountable. The early twenty-first century finds the checks and balances of the American system being applied with broad reach and great depth to the work of U.S. intelligence, which is accorded an importance higher than ever in the work of the nation. Intelligence performs its responsibilities as a member of the executive branch, with the intrusive oversight of the legislative and judicial branches, with periodic examinations by commissions, and under the eyes of the media and the public.

In terms of positive responsibilities, intelligence is held accountable for delivering the highest quality warnings, assessments, analysis, and actions contributing to the effective safeguarding of America and the advancement of U.S. interests. On the reverse side of this coin, intelligence is held strictly accountable for acting within the law and in keeping with the principles of the American democracy, respecting the rights and liberties of U.S. citizens.

The first play of intelligence in U.S. history dates back to the American Revolution. George Washington operated intelligence networks against the British and believed deeply in their value. In a letter to one of his colonels in 1777, he counseled: "The necessity of procuring good intelligence is apparent & need not be furthered urged—All that remains for me to add is, that you keep the whole matter as secret as possible. For upon Secrecy, Success depends in most Enterprizes of the kind, and for want of it, they are generally defeated, however well planned & promising a favorable issue."[1]

Although intelligence figured prominently in the Civil War, for most of the nation's early life, it figured almost not at all. The vast, shielding expanses of the Atlantic and Pacific Oceans were the only protective deterrents needed while the young nation was coming of age. From the late nineteenth century until World War II, U.S. intelligence operated primarily in the separate preserves of the Navy and Army, with small, separate components in the Department of State, Treasury, and Justice, all well shielded from the public eye.

The emergence and rise of importance of intelligence as an instrument of national power dates back no further than the mid-twentieth century. Formal national structures and processes for holding intelligence accountable emerged in the mid-1970s. Throughout the history of U.S. intelligence until the twenty-first century, where there was accountability, it was in the oversight, watchdog role. From the time of the 1878 Posse Comitatus Act, which prohibited the armed forces from engaging in domestic law enforcement unless specifically authorized, it was held in parallel that U.S. intelligence should not operate against U.S. citizens. In a broader sense, to the degree that there was a public awareness of intelligence operations, it was accompanied by skepticism and distrust. In parallel, in American colleges and universities, academic research on intelligence (to the extent there was such research) and teaching on intelligence tended to adopt the oversight, watchdog role focusing on the negative side of accountability.

General of the Army Dwight D. Eisenhower noted the phenomenon of American distrust in his reflections on the challenges the Army and the nation faced at the dawn of World War II. "The American public," he wrote, "has always viewed with repugnance everything that smacks of the spy; during the years between the two world wars no funds were provided with which to establish the basic requirement of an intelligence system—a far-flung organization of factfinders."[2]

Eisenhower's deputy in the 1943 North African campaign, Maj. Gen. Omar Bradley, agreed. Describing the situation at the U.S.-British Allied Force

Headquarters in Algiers, he observed, "In their intelligence activities at [Head-quarters], the British easily outstripped their American colleagues. The tedious years of pre-war study the British had devoted to areas throughout the world gave them a vast advantage which we never overcame. The American Army's long neglect of intelligence training was soon reflected in the ineptness of our initial undertakings."[3]

To help meet World War II intelligence needs, President Franklin D. Roosevelt created the first national civilian U.S. intelligence player in the form of the Coordinator of Information. The Office of Strategic Services (OSS) followed and grew to more than 30,000 strong before being disbanded by President Harry S Truman at the end of the war. One passionate OSS veteran wrote: "President Truman, with complete lack of sophistication, reacted as if espionage were something one shouldn't speak about, like syphilis in the family."[4]

In fact, with the passage of the National Security Act of 1947, signed into law by Truman, the Central Intelligence Agency (CIA) was created and declared a formal arrow, together with defense and foreign policy, in the quiver of American security. The act was born out of the nation's determination never again to have failure of warning as experienced at Pearl Harbor. It was legislation passed at the dawn of the nuclear era creating a National Security Council—with the President, Vice President, Secretary of State, and Secretary of Defense as statutory members—and with the CIA responsible to the Council, a CIA to be headed by a Director of Central Intelligence to be appointed by the President with the consent of the Senate.

The act provided for the intelligence work and responsibilities of the separate military departments and other governmental organizations. Within the framework of the act, new intelligence organizations—for example, the National Security Agency in 1952 and the Defense Intelligence Agency in 1961—joined what has become known as the U.S. intelligence community. The nation, now in a Cold War with the Soviet Union, had a daunting nuclear adversary. Successive Directors of Central Intelligence and intelligence community leaders worked relatively smoothly with Congress in the annual intelligence budget requests, which were acted on, by and large, in the late 1940s, 1950s, and 1960s in a minimally intrusive manner.

In the 1970s, newspaper revelations of intelligence community covert actions and alleged wrongdoings—some against U.S. citizens—coming at the time of national and international turmoil over the conflict in Vietnam and the Watergate scandal, caused Congress to impose itself more firmly. Legislation was passed requiring coordination with Congress on covert actions. Lengthy hearings were held, resulting in the creation of standing Senate and House intelligence committees.[5]

For the balance of the century, the committees shifted and reshifted their oversight priorities as they sought to ensure capable U.S. intelligence while guarding against intelligence excesses and wrongdoings. If there was a constancy to their charge under the Constitution, it could be found succinctly in the words of Senator David Boren (D-OK), chair of the Senate Select Committee on

Intelligence from 1987–93, at the outset of the 1987 confirmation hearings of Judge William H. Webster to be Director of Central Intelligence:

> This Committee and the Senate have a duty to the American people to ensure that the new Director of Central Intelligence will conduct a program of effective intelligence gathering within the framework of our laws and our democratic institutions. It is imperative that the Director of Central Intelligence be a person of exceptional ability and integrity, capable of exercising the independence necessary to protect against possible misuse of the Agency and its resources.[6]

At the same time Boren's words captured the role of the Senate and congressional oversight, they underscored the continuing, dominating puritanism in the nation's late 20th-century approach to intelligence, a quality addressed by British author John Ranelagh. "Intelligence is seen as fun by the British (who in the days of empire called it the 'Great Game')," he wrote, "and without morality. Americans see it as having moral importance, and face real crises of conscience when they find they may have to be involved in immoral activity. In America, power is associated with publicity. In Britain (indeed in Europe), power is associated with secrecy."[7]

When terrorists seized U.S. airliners on September 11, 2001, and crashed them into the twin towers of the World Trade Center, the Pentagon, and a field in Pennsylvania, the history of U.S. intelligence turned to a new chapter. On September 20, 2001, President George W. Bush told a joint session of Congress that an act of war had been committed against the United States and that in a single day a different world had emerged with freedom under attack.[8] Only six weeks later, on October 24, 2001, the Congress passed the USA-PATRIOT Act, signed into law two days later, expanding the government's counterterrorist surveillance powers and expanding cooperation between U.S. foreign intelligence and domestic law enforcement. People across the nation were deeply alarmed. The homeland was vulnerable, without deterrent, to a new form of devastating attack. The cry of "intelligence failure" arose across the land. The search for accountability was mounted.

The National Commission on Terrorist Attacks upon the United States, or the 9/11 Commission, and the Commission on the Intelligence Capabilities of the United States Regarding Weapons of Mass Destruction, or WMD Commission, were formed. Congressional hearings were held. Reform legislation was drafted, and on January 20, 2004, the Intelligence Reform and Terrorism Prevention Act was passed. The act, 235 pages in length, established a new Director of National Intelligence, legislated reorganization and improvement of management of the intelligence community, assigned specific responsibilities for analytic integrity, established a National Counterterrorism Center, a National Counteproliferation Center, and a Privacy and Civil Liberties Oversight Board, among its key provisions.[9]

The act gave expanded intelligence responsibilities to the Federal Bureau of Investigation (FBI) and not only mandated the sharing of information between foreign intelligence and domestic law enforcement agencies at the federal level but also directed the flow of information—down and up—among federal, state, local, and tribal authorities. From the work of the commissions, Congress, and the executive branch, a new concept had emerged and was being enacted—the concept of national intelligence.

In October 2005, in his foreword to *The National Intelligence Strategy of the United States of America*, the first Director of National Intelligence John D. Negroponte underlined the need for a fresh, risk-taking strategy for the intelligence challenges of the twenty-first century and the joining of domestic and foreign intelligence into national intelligence. This new approach, he wrote, did not reflect any change to the nation's commitment to civil liberties and freedom.[10] Accountability would remain clearly engraved on both sides of the Republic's intelligence coin of reform.

THE LAW, THE COURTS, THE WHITE HOUSE

George Washington used intelligence extensively in the American Revolution. As the nation's first President, he requested and received authority from Congress for a Contingency Fund for the Conduct of Foreign Intercourse, placed in the budget of the Department of State, to be available for intelligence purposes. In the years that followed, U.S. Presidents rejected requests from Congress for an accounting of expenditures from the fund. In the 1840s, President James Polk turned down such a request, responding in part: "The experience of every nation on earth has demonstrated that emergencies may arise in which it becomes necessary for the public safety or the public good to make expenditures, the very subject of which would be defeated by publicity. In no nation is the application of such funds to be made public."[11]

Though the National Security Act of 1947 established the Senate's advice and consent role in the appointment of the Director of Central Intelligence, the act prescribed no new legislative oversight structure or process for the work of intelligence. In both the Senate and the House, the Armed Services Committee and the Appropriations Defense Subcommittee became the points of oversight for intelligence. Intelligence budgets would be submitted annually and acted on with few questions asked. From the late 1940s through the 1950s and 1960s, the intelligence community went about its work with few hearings and modest intrusion by the legislative branch. Senator Leverett Saltonstall (R-MA) captured the tone of the relationship in a 1956 comment: "It is not a question of reluctance on the part of CIA officials to speak to us. Instead, it is a question of our reluctance, if you will, to seek information and knowledge on subjects which I personally, as a member of Congress and as a citizen, would rather not have."[12]

In the mid-1970s, news reports and other charges spawned a whirlwind of alleged CIA assassination plots, questionable covert actions, and surveillance of American college students and domestic dissenters. There were allegations of excesses and wrongdoing by other members of the intelligence community, together with allegations of excesses by the FBI, to include charges that the Bureau had acted to discredit the Reverend Martin Luther King Jr. The era of executive-legislative intelligence laissez-faire had passed. The intelligence community would be held to account.

In 1974, Congress passed the Hughes-Ryan Amendment to the Foreign Assistance Act of 1961 requiring the President to review proposed CIA covert actions, to determine—or find—that each such action was in the nation's interest and to submit such findings to six committees of Congress.[13] In 1975, both bodies of Congress established committees to investigate the alleged wrongdoings. The Senate's Select Committee to Study Government Operations with Respect to Intelligence Activities was chaired by Senator Frank Church (D-ID), and was known as the Church Committee. The House's Select Committee on Intelligence, with its second chairman Representative Otis Pike (D-NY), was known as the Pike Committee.

The Church Committee's investigation ran for sixteen months, with the cross-examination of hundreds of witnesses producing thousands of pages of sworn testimony. Several volumes of reports were published, and ninety-six proposals for reform were recommended.[14] The Pike Committee's more sensational report was leaked to the press before publication. This was a tumultuous period, with sensational headlines and sparks flying between the legislative and executive branches. Serving at the time as a senior member of President Gerald R. Ford's National Security Council staff, I can recall in particular the extraordinary rudeness of the Pike Committee staff members I had to deal with. They reminded me of cast members from the film *Lord of the Flies.*

As a result of these investigations, the Senate created the Senate Select Committee on Intelligence in 1976, and the House created the House Permanent Select Committee on Intelligence in 1977. A year later with the passage of the 1978 Intelligence Authorization Act, each committee was given oversight of the intelligence community's budget. Reins of accountability were in the Congress's hands.

• • •

In parallel in 1978, Congress passed the Foreign Intelligence Surveillance Act (FISA), creating the U.S. Foreign Intelligence Surveillance Court in the judicial branch to oversee FBI requests for authority to conduct surveillance against suspected foreign intelligence agents in the United States. Wiretaps would not be permitted unless authorized. This was a very sensitive business. The law provided that the work of the court and its findings would not be available to the public. To provide for situations where a law enforcement agency's request for a surveillance warrant was denied by the court, the Surveillance Act also created a U.S. Intelligence Surveillance Court of Review.

The judicial branch role played by the FISA Court increased significantly both in scope and the volume of court actions after the 2001 terrorist attacks. The number of FBI requests for surveillance warrants rose, as the Bureau drew on its increased counterterrorist surveillance authorities under the USA-PATRIOT Act—including the authority to run checks on an individual's library use. Civil libertarians expressed alarm that the act, which had been passed to protect personal freedoms, was now being used to abuse those freedoms. Law enforcement officials complained that the standard of accountability demanded by the court was still too onerous and high. The nation's checks and balances were functioning as intended.

• • •

From the late 1940s onward, as the executive branch carried out its primary accountability responsibilities, Presidents issued classified and unclassified directives and executive orders making adjustments and interpretations to the 1947 National Security Act. In 1956, the Eisenhower administration created the President's Board of Consultants on Foreign Intelligence Activities, which became the President's Foreign Intelligence Advisory Board, a board of citizens from outside the government charged with providing the President with advice on the performance of the intelligence community and recommendations for improving that performance.[15]

These executive branch changes came into sharper, more prominent focus in the mid-1970s coincident with the congressional hearings and establishment of the House and Senate Committees. Executive Order 11905 on U.S. Foreign Intelligence Activities, signed by President Ford on February 18, 1976, and Executive Order 12036 signed by President Jimmy Carter on January 24, 1978, not only codified the authorities and responsibilities of the DCI and the institutional members of the intelligence community but also included a major section titled "Restrictions on Intelligence Activities." Both orders carried explicit language prohibiting assassination.

Executive Order 11905 established a new Intelligence Oversight Board charged specifically with examining and reporting to the President on an intelligence action or actions that might be either unlawful or contrary to executive branch directives.[16] The Carter executive order retained this new board while eliminating the President's Foreign Intelligence Advisory Board. On December 4, 1981, President Ronald Reagan in signing intelligence Executive Order 12333 stated: "Let us never forget that good intelligence saves American lives and protects our freedom." With the new order, the pendulum of accountability swung from restrictions on intelligence to the importance of the full and effective functioning of intelligence. Section 2.1 of the order stated:

> Accurate and timely information about the capabilities, intentions and activities of foreign powers, organizations or persons and their agents is essential to informed decisionmaking in the areas of national defense and foreign relations. Collection of such information is a priority objective and will be pursued in a vigorous, innovative and responsible manner that is consistent with the Constitution and applicable law and respectful of the principles upon which the United States was founded.[17]

The Reagan administration reestablished the President's Foreign Intelligence Oversight Board, which continues today. Executive Order 12333 remained in effect up to the government's intelligence reform actions in the post-9/11 era.

POLITICIZING AND IRRELEVANCE

The American intelligence professional operating within the framework established by the three separate branches is expected to be a figure of absolute integrity. It was with this in mind that the National Security Act of 1947 made the Director of Central Intelligence, or DCI, an advisor rather than a full member on the National Security Council. The intelligence officer is looked to for both strategic and tactical warning of events that may occur, to offer the best data and best judgments on an intelligence target's capabilities and intentions. The intelligence officer is expected to state what is known, what is not known, and what in his or her judgment is the best estimate of the situation. In this vital role, he or she can expect to be the occasional skunk at the garden party offering advice contrary to that which the policy maker or operational commander would prefer to hear.

Under the U.S. scheme of intelligence accountability, the intelligence professional must not slant or bend data and estimates to suit the preference of the consumer. This is true, as well, during the collection and analysis stages of the work inside the intelligence community. The intelligence cannot be slanted to curry favor or keep the peace with someone more senior in the intelligence chain. To do so is to politicize the intelligence, and this is unacceptable.

During his 1991 Senate confirmation hearings for the post of DCI, Robert M. Gates was met with allegations that as a CIA professional he had politicized intelligence analyses on the Soviet Union. In preparing for his testimony to the Committee, Gates reviewed the scores of intelligence assessments relevant to the charges raised. He wrote:

> After I had dealt with the specific allegations, I told the committee: "... A careful review of the actual record of what was published and sent to policymakers demonstrates that the integrity of the process was preserved. We were wrong at times, but our judgments were honest and unaffected by a desire to please or slant.... I had and have strong views. But ... I'm open to argumentation and there was a lot of that. And I never distorted intelligence to support policy or to please a policymaker."[18]

Gates was confirmed and delivered an address to the CIA's analysts on the importance of guarding against politicizing intelligence early in his tenure as DCI.

Following the 2003 invasion of Iraq, charges and countercharges flew over whether the U.S. intelligence community had distorted intelligence pointing to weapons of mass destruction in Iraq. President Bush established the Commission on the Intelligence Capabilities of the United States Regarding Weapons of Mass

Destruction to investigate. In its covering letter to the President forwarding their findings, the commissioners wrote, in part: "We conclude that the Intelligence Community was dead wrong in almost all of its pre-war judgments about Iraq's weapons of mass destruction. . . . After a thorough review, the Commission found no indication that the Intelligence Community distorted the evidence regarding Iraq's weapons of mass destruction. What the intelligence professionals told you about Saddam Hussein's programs was what they believed. They were simply wrong."[19]

• • •

Although intelligence must not be slanted or distorted to suit the preferences of the consumer, it must have relevance to the needs of the consumer. From 1952 to 1967, Sherman Kent chaired the CIA's Board of National Intelligence Estimates. Kent believed deeply in the integrity of the intelligence estimates process. The work had to be of the best possible quality.

When the estimate was published, the burden, in Kent's view, shifted to the policy maker. "Let things be such that if our policy-making master is to disregard our knowledge and wisdom," Kent said, "he will never do so because our work was inaccurate, incomplete, or patently biased. Let him disregard us only when he must pay greater heed to someone else. And let him be uncomfortable— thoroughly uncomfortable—about his decision to heed the other."[20] In editing Kent's essays on intelligence, Donald Steury examined the decline and eventual demise of the Board of National Intelligence Estimates and found that the board had difficulty focusing on policy makers' priority interests. "The reverse of Sherman Kent's coin of detached objectivity was irrelevance."[21]

If Kent and his board slowly slipped into irrelevance from the 1950s to the 1960s, bear in mind that their decline was set in the printed, hard-copy, pre– information age, when the intelligence community often was the only reliable source on foreign target information. The sources of information available to today's policy-level consumer of intelligence—whether dealing with the Russian Federation rather than the Soviet Union or with any of the current era's closed societies—are far, far greater than forty years ago.

It is almost a given that today's policy-level consumer is quite well informed in his or her area of interest and not dependent on an analyst for a continuing stream of routine, updating information. The analyst no longer sets the pace of the information flow. The web, the media—electronic and hard copy, U.S. and foreign—the telephone, the fax, the interaction with U.S. and foreign colleagues in the professional field, and intelligence reporting available at the consumer's personal, classified, computer keyboard—all play a part.

Today's analyst must not only have a sense of his or her consumer's level of continuing information and knowledge. To provide value-added analysis, today's analyst must focus more sharply on the specific needs and timing of meeting those needs for the policy-level consumer, seek specific tasking, analyze feed-back from analysis already provided, and invite and tackle the consumer's hard questions demanding answers.[22]

Today's combatant commanders place a far higher priority on intelligence and demand far more from intelligence than was the case in the Cold War era. The formerly dominant challenges of understanding force-on-force foreign military capabilities and intentions have been subsumed in a far broader spectrum of intelligence challenges and requirements. In a cyber- and information-era world marked by failed and failing nation-states, religious and cultural conflicts, the proliferation of weapons of mass destruction, and virulent international terrorism, defense intelligence must have an appreciation of regional cultures, religions, and politics, as well as the smoldering tinder of intentions and the sparks of conflict.

In a strategic environment where U.S. forces with their allied and coalition partners are called on to provide forward deterrence, produce forward stability, and ward off threats to the U.S. homeland, there is virtually no geography, no political, cultural, ideological, or religious presence anywhere that is not of relevance. Today's commander holds defense intelligence accountable for the development of increasingly agile, flexible, fused collection and analysis capabilities that allow swift transformation of data into knowledge, for working in partnership with operations, with swift delivery of that knowledge.

UNSAVORY CHARACTERS

The moral dimensions of the work of U.S. intelligence have brought into the focus the question of what types of foreigners Americans should deal with in carrying out the intelligence mission. In espionage, the handling of spies, the turning of agents, and the infiltration and exfiltration of agents are at the heart of intelligence collection and intelligence operations. The challenges such operations pose, the skills they require, the stresses they place on those responsible for their conduct are uniquely challenging. People—however varied, laudable, or sordid their motives and their backgrounds—inform, betray, and ferret out information critical to intelligence successes. Identifying, cultivating, and running such people take time, money, and professional management of the first order. It can be a rough, risky business.

The chair of the House Permanent Select Committee on Intelligence, Representative Porter Goss (R-FL), observed in 2002 that in the mid-1990s,

> The world's remaining superpower—the USA—was losing sight of the contributions made by the Intelligence Community, our first line of defense, our eyes, and ears, and brain.... For example, human intelligence capabilities were hampered by policy guidance that place a higher priority on ensuring that assets weren't tainted with human rights abuses rather than on what information they may have had or may have been able to get.[23]

Goss was referring to a pronouncement by the new DCI John M. Deutch in 1995 that he would be establishing fresh guidelines for CIA dealings with alleged killers, torturers, human rights violators, and other unsavory characters.

Deutch was responding to allegations that CIA agents had been too closely involved with such types and that this contact was not consistent with American interests and values. His critics charged he was producing a risk-adverse atmosphere at the very time when information on terrorist intentions from whatever source was vital to the nation's defenses. Two days after the terrorist attacks of 9/11, Congress directed the DCI to rescind the guidelines. In October 2001, the USA-PATRIOT Act "expressed the sense of the Congress that intelligence officials 'should be encouraged, and should make every effort to establish and maintain intelligence relationships with any person, entity, or group to acquire information on terrorist groups.' "[24]

Here the voice of the late Rebecca West, as expressed in her book *The Meaning of Treason,* provides sage advice for those grappling with accountability. "Not until the Earthly Paradise is established and man regains his innocence, can a power which has ever been at war be blamed if it accepts information regarding the military strength of another power, however this may be obtained; and of course it can be blamed least of all if the information comes to it from traitors, for then it is likely to touch on the truly secret."[25]

DEMOCRATIC PRINCIPLES

The truly secret comes not only from traitors but also from code breakers. The truly secret involves deception on the grand scale. The issues of stealing the communications of and deceiving others find their accountability places in the U.S. intelligence morality play.

In World War I, Herbert O. Yardley, a State Department code clerk, moved to the Army to establish the MI-8 Branch of the Military Intelligence Division, a branch dedicated to collecting and decrypting foreign communications. At the end of the war, Yardley arranged for Army and State jointly to fund a continuation of the code-breaking operations. He and his staff had considerable success, including breaking the Japanese code at the time of the 1921 Washington Naval Conference.

Yardley's success was measured against a fresh standard of accountability in 1929 when a new Secretary of State, Henry L. Stimson, took office. When he became aware of the decryption operations, Stimson was deeply disturbed. "The chief lesson I have learned in a long life is that the only way you can make a man trustworthy is to trust him; and the surest way to make him untrustworthy is to distrust him and show him your distrust. We can do better by being an honest simpleton in the world of nations than a designing Sherlock Holmes. . . . Gentlemen do not read each other's mail." He ordered the State Department's funds for the code breaking stopped immediately. When the *Philadelphia Public*

Ledger learned of Yardley's work, it denounced the decryption of diplomatic messages as discreditable.[26]

Fortunately for the nation, this puritanism stopped short of the separate work under way in the Army and the Navy against Japanese codes that continued throughout the 1930s. Code breaking was extraordinarily difficult, time-consuming work. The Army cracked the Japanese diplomatic code in 1940. The Navy was working hard on the Japanese Fleet General Purpose code. In March 1942 there was a breakthrough allowing current decryption of operational orders to the Japanese fleet.[27] The U.S. Pacific Fleet was still reeling from the December 7, 1941, surprise attack on Pearl Harbor. The Navy needed to know where the Japanese were planning to strike next in the Pacific—possibly New Guinea–Solomons, Australia, Midway Island, or the U.S. mainland.

Cmdr. Joseph Rochefort was the Navy code breaker in charge of a unit serving under Adm. Chester W. Nimitz at Pearl Harbor. In May, a partial decrypt translating as "invasion force" was followed by the geographic designator AF. Rochefort and his team deduced that AF stood for Midway Island. Were the Japanese planning to strike and capture Midway? If the aircraft carriers of the U.S. Pacific Fleet were to be positioned correctly, the Navy needed confirmation.

With Nimitz's approval, Rochefort had a message sent via secure undersea cable from Hawaii to the U.S. forces on Midway instructing them to send a clear, uncoded flash message advising that Midway's water distillation plant had broken. Two days later, the U.S. Navy code breakers decrypted a Japanese fleet message advising that AF had only a two-weeks supply of fresh water. Subsequent Japanese messages indicated the likely date and direction of the attack.[28] This signals intelligence coup allowed Nimitz to surprise the Japanese force under Adm. Chuichi Nagumo. The Battle of Midway was joined on June 4, 1942. By the morning of June 5, all four of the Japanese carriers had been sunk, with the United States losing a single carrier. Signals intelligence (SIGINT) had played a vital role in swinging the tide of battle in the Pacific.[29]

Intelligence had played a crucial role at an extremely fragile point in the nation's history. SIGINT grew into an enormous intelligence discipline in the post–World War II, Cold War era. The Soviet Union was the primary target. The Army and Navy SIGINT services merged into the new National Security Agency (NSA) in 1952. More than fifty years later, NSA's role in the post-9/11 era is crucial, evolving dramatically as the nation blends foreign and domestic intelligence into national intelligence.

In his April 2005 confirmation hearings to become the first principal Deputy Director of National Intelligence, Gen. Michael V. Hayden, who was finishing his sixth year as NSA Director, told the Senate Committee, "American intelligence agencies needed to push 'right up that line,' established under privacy laws in using eavesdropping, surveillance, and other tools to gather information." He told the Committee that it would be vital to ensure "that we are not pulling punches, that we are using all the abilities that Congress has given us under the law. We all know that the enemy may be inside the gates and Job One is to defend the homeland."[30]

• • •

Taking measures to block, prevent, or impair collection of information—*denial* and deliberately manipulating information to mislead, *deception*—have been part of statecraft and warfare from the beginning of states and battles.

Early in World War II, as part of the great game of intelligence, the British exercised tactical deception to considerable advantage. The goal in deception is to influence not only what your opponent thinks but, more important, what your opponent *does*. In the North African campaign and the Battle of Alam Halfa, British intelligence from several sources indicated that the German forces had poor knowledge of the battlefield terrain. "The allies knew that the sands in and around the Ragil depression would not support armored vehicles.... Eighth Army cartographers made a 'false-going' map that showed good hard ground in the Ragil area. The deception was implemented by putting the map in a vehicle deliberately disabled in a minefield. German scouts retrieved the map and delivered it up the chain of command."[31]

When Roosevelt, Churchill, and Stalin met in Tehran, preparations for the 1944 Allied landings in France (Operation OVERLORD), were on the agenda. Churchill asked about the deception and propaganda cover plan, observing that truth deserves a bodyguard of lies.[32] BODYGUARD became the title of the OVERLORD deception plan. When the plan had been drafted, U.S. and British officers flew to Moscow in early 1944 to brief it to the Soviets and obtain their agreement and their plans for cooperation. The Soviet Lt. Gen. Fedor F. Kuznetsov was their principal interlocutor. After weeks of delay, he advised that BODYGUARD was accepted completely. It was when discussion turned to implementation of the deception that the issue of what was acceptable and not acceptable surfaced. The American and British officers "chatted with Kuznetsov about using the press for deception, making it clear that the Western Allies did not do so ... when we said that in a democracy you couldn't use the press to fool your own people, the Soviets said 'Oh, well, we do it all the time.' "[33]

Sixty-one years later, in December 2005, when news stories surfaced that the U.S. command in Baghdad was paying Iraqi newspapers to run positive stories about the state of play in Iraq, feathers immediately flew in Washington. The chair of the Senate Armed Services Committee expressed grave concern and advised that the Department of Defense was looking into the situation. Few disagreed that it would be unethical to run such stories in the U.S. media, but debate was joined on question of "mitigating circumstances justifying such tactics in Iraq."[34] After several weeks of review, an inquiry found in early 2006 that no policy had been violated or laws broken by the news story actions. This said, the Department of Defense announced that it would review whether updated policy guidance was needed.[35]

THE TWO-SIDED COIN

In these early years of the twenty-first century, intelligence is held accountable on the one hand for errors, failures, and wrongdoings and on the other hand for the demonstrated increases in its capabilities and the growing excellence of its performance. During the Balkans conflict, a year after the mistaken 1999 bombing of the Chinese embassy in Belgrade in the belief that it was the headquarters of Yugoslav Army Procurement, the CIA officer responsible for error was dismissed by the DCI, and six other employees were disciplined.[36]

On a grander scale, the House-Senate committee investigating the 9/11 terrorist attacks called on the CIA inspector general "to determine whether and to what extent personnel at all levels should be held accountable for any omission, commission, or failure to meet professional standards." Following his investigation, the inspector general recommended that the CIA Director convene an accountability board. After a lengthy review, Director Porter Goss determined in October 2005 that he would not seek to hold current or former officials responsible for failures leading up to the attacks.[37] In a formal statement, the Director of National Intelligence concurred with this decision, saying he would work with Goss and the CIA to continue to address the systemic issues involved.[38]

The war on terrorism has brought fresh expectations of intelligence—expectations of enormous dimensions. At the same time, the war, which pits nation-states against individuals, cells, and nonstate actors bent on the most murderous of designs, has brought changes to the ground rules for intelligence. New questions, along with differing interpretations of the acceptability (or lack thereof) of intelligence's role in capturing, interrogating, imprisoning, and condoning torture by other nation-states of terrorists, have brought vivid new strokes to the accountability canvas.

In December 2005, Congress entered into a heated debate on renewal of the USA-PATRIOT Act with proponents arguing that the war on terrorism requires continued approval of expanded surveillance authorities and with opponents firm in their belief that such authorities violate basic civil liberties. In the middle of this debate, the *New York Times* reported, in a story it had been holding unpublished for a year, that in 2002 the President had signed an order authorizing—without the requirement for a warrant from the FISA Court—the monitoring of international telephone calls and e-mails of people inside the United States to track suspected terrorist agents and "dirty numbers" linked to Al Qaeda.[39]

The President was firm in underscoring the correctness of his surveillance order, stating that as President and Commander-in-Chief he had the constitutional responsibility and authority to protect the country, that his authorization of the intercept of international communications was consistent with U.S. law and the Constitution, and that "to save American lives, we must be able to act fast and to detect these conversations so we can prevent new attacks."[40] In parallel, the Director of National Intelligence, in a message to intelligence community colleagues, stated, "Last week we witnessed an egregious disclosure of classified information regarding one of our country's major tools in the War on Terror—the interception of al-Qa'ida-related communications. . . . Despite this setback, given the program's continuing utility to the War on Terror and its proven effectiveness in disrupting terrorist threats to the homeland, we will continue to pursue this and other critical efforts."[41] Certain members of Congress challenged the legality of the order; others said that hearings would be held. The nation's checks and balances clearly were in action.

After vigorous debate early in 2006, the Senate and the House voted favorably on renewal of the USA-PATRIOT Act will its provisions largely intact, and on March 9, 2006, the President signed the renewed act into law. In parallel on the issue of wiretap surveillance, by late March 2006, separate pieces of draft legislation had been introduced in the Senate that variously would give the President a set period of time to conduct wiretaps before seeking authorization from other branches of the government or would ease FISA Court restrictions for such wiretapping.[42]

Within the intelligence community, under the leadership of the Director of National Intelligence, the accountability focus is on increased capability and excellence of performance. Top priority is given to bringing foreign and domestic intelligence cultures together to provide the delivery of effective national intelligence. The mindset is on taking risks, not risk avoidance. The strategic mission objectives focus on defeating terrorists at home and abroad, preventing and countering the spread of weapons of mass destruction, bolstering the growth of democracy and democratic states, developing innovative ways to penetrate and analyze the most difficult targets, and providing intelligence that anticipates issues of concern and opportunities for decision makers.[43]

Across the nation, if intelligence was first formally declared an instrument of U.S. national security in the National Security Act of 1947, it did not enter the mainstream of American thinking and discourse until the terrorist attacks of 2001 and their aftermath. With the shock and continuing fear engendered by the attacks, and with the extensive media coverage and debate relating to the post-9/11 commission studies and the passage of the intelligence reform legislation, millions of Americans have come to understand that timely, relevant intelligence is "the air the nation breathes," information essential to our survival and wellbeing.

In a steadily growing number of colleges and universities across the nation, the history, role, and contributions of intelligence are recognized as an important academic field of study and research. The burning of effigies of intelligence leaders on campus is history. It is no longer adequate to relegate the study of intelligence to an examination solely of the negative "rogue elephant" chapters in intelligence history. Intelligence departments are being formed. Intelligence degrees are being offered. The interests of college students extend beyond the classroom to the prospect of intelligence as a career.[44] We are arriving at point in the nation's history where more citizens are coming to the realization that intelligence is too important to be left solely to the government's checks and balances. If Americans are to have the essential contributions that intelligence brings to their safety and security, citizens across the land are accountable for ensuring that the government is providing for that intelligence in full measure.

NOTES

The views expressed are those of the author and do not represent the official views of either the Department of Defense or the U.S. Government.

1. Letter from General George Washington to Col. Elias Dayton, July 26, 1777, original letter in Pforzheimer Collection, as quoted in address by Walter L. Pforzheimer to the Grolier Club of New York, published in Hayden B. Peake and Samuel Halpern, eds., *In the Name of Intelligence, Essays in Honor of Walter Pforzheimer* (Washington, DC: NIBC Press, 1994), p. 73.

2. Dwight D. Eisenhower, *Crusade in Europe* (New York: Doubleday, 1948), p. 32.

3. Omar Bradley, *A Soldier's Story* (New York: Modern Library, 1999), p 33.

4. Robert Hayden Alcorn, *No Bugles for Spies* (New York: David McKay, 1962), p. 195.

5. See A. Denis Clift, *Clift Notes,* 2nd ed. (Washington, DC: Joint Military Intelligence College Press, 2002), pp. 109–11.

6. Boren Hearings for Webster's confirmation as DCI, Senate Select Committee on Intelligence, Washington, DC, April 8. 1987.

7. John Ranelagh, "Through the Looking Glass: A Comparison of United States and United Kingdom Intelligence Cultures," quoted in Peake and Halpern, eds., *In the Name of Intelligence* p. 425.

8. President George W. Bush, Address to a Joint Session of the Congress, Washington, DC, September 20, 2005.

9. Intelligence Reform and Terrorism Prevention Act of 2004, 108th Congress, 2nd sess. (January 20, 2004), Washington, DC.

10. John D. Negroponte, *The National Intelligence Strategy of the United States of America* (Washington, DC, October 2005).

11. James Van Wagenen, "Congressional Oversight: A Look Back," *Studies in Intelligence* 1, no. 1 (1997), quoted in paragraph from Clift, *Clift Notes,* p. 108.

12. Ibid.

13. Ibid.

14. Loch K. Johnson, *A Season of Inquiry: The Senate Intelligence Investigation* (Lexington: University Press of Kentucky, 1985), preface.

15. See http://www.cia.gov/publications/facttell/exectuve_oversight.html 12/8/05.

16. Ibid.

17. See http://www.cia.gov/cia/information/eo12333.html 12/08/05.

18. Robert M. Gates, *From the Shadows* (New York: Simon & Schuster, 1996), pp. 547–50.

19. The Commission on the Intelligence Capabilities of the United States Regarding Weapons of Mass Destruction, *Report to the President of the United States*, March 31, 2005, Forwarding Letter (Washington, DC: Government Printing Office, 2005).

20. *Sherman Kent and the Board of National Estimates, Collected Essays*, edited by Donald P. Steury (Washington, DC: Center for the Study of Intelligence, 1994), p. 34.

21. Ibid., p. xx.

22. See Carmen A. Medina, "What to Do When Traditional Models Fail," *Studies in Intelligence* 45, no. 4 (2001), pp. 35–40, cited in Clift, *Clift Notes*, pp. 203–4.

23. Porter J. Goss, "Commencement Address," Joint Military Intelligence College, Washington, DC, August 9, 2002.

24. Richard A. Best, CRS Issue Brief for Congress, "Intelligence Issues for Congress," Library of Congress (November 9, 2001).

25. Rebecca West, *The Meaning of Treason* (London: Phoenix Press, 2000), p. 192, as cited in A. Denis Clift, "Keynote Address," Swedish National Defense College, Stockholm, Sweden, August 27, 2003.

26. David Kahn, *The Reader of Gentlemen's Mail* (New Haven, CT: Yale University Press, 2004), pp. 98 and 102.

27. Stephen Budiansky, *Battle of Wits* (New York: Free Press, 2000), p. 12.

28. Ibid., pp. 14–16.

29. E. B. Potter, *Nimitz* (Annapolis, MD: Naval Institute Press, 1976), p. 107.

30. Douglas Jehl, "No. 2 Intelligence Nominee Testifies on Privacy Rules," *New York Times* (April 15, 2005), as cited in A. Denis Clift, "Doing Our Work Differently, Doing It Better" Rand Symposium, Washington, DC, June 15, 2005.

31. Neal D. Norman, "British Intelligence and Information Superiority at the Battle of Alam Halfa: Turing the Tide in North Africa," master's thesis, Joint Military Intelligence College, Washington, DC (1997), pp. 78–80, as cited in Clift, *Clift Notes*, pp. 56–57.

32. Keith Eubank, *Summit at Teheran* (New York: William Morrow, 1985), p. 338.

33. Thaddeus Holt, *The Deceivers* (New York: Scribner, 2004), pp. 517–18.

34. Josh White and Bradley Graham, "Military Says It Paid Iraq Papers for News," *Washington Post*, December 3, 2005, p. A1.

35. Thom Shanker, "No Breach Seen in Work in Iraq On Propaganda," *New York Times*, March 22, 2006.

36. Steven Lee Myers, "Chinese Embassy Bombing: A Wide Net of Blame," *New York Times*, April 17, 2000. p. A1.

37. Dafna Linzer and Walter Pincus, "CIA Rejects Discipline for 9/11 Failures," *Washington Post*, October 6, 2005, p. A1.

38. Statement by Ambassador John D. Negroponte, Director of National Intelligence, ODNI News Release No. 1-05, October 5, 2005.

39. James Risen and Eric Lichtblau, "Bush Lets U.S. Spy on Callers Without Courts," *New York Times* (December 16, 2005), p. A1.

40. Press Conference of the President, December 19, 2005, available at http://www.whitehouse.gov/news/releases/2005/12/20051219-2.html.

41. Director of National Intelligence, Letter to Intelligence Community, Washington, DC (December 19, 2005).

42. Eric Lichtblau, "Judges on Secretive Panel Speak Out on Spy Program," *New York Times* (March 29, 2006), p. A19.

43. Negroponte, *The National Intelligence Strategy*, pp. 1–4.

44. See A. Denis Clift, *Learning with Professionals, Selected Works from the Joint Military Intelligence College* (Washington, DC: Joint Military Intelligence College Press, 2005), p. v.

9

A HALF CENTURY OF SPY WATCHING

HARRY HOWE RANSOM

SINCE SEPTEMBER 11, 2001, A PUBLIC PREOCCUPATION and controversy was rekindled about the function, performance, and controls of America's secret intelligence system. Since its creation in 1947, the Central Intelligence Agency (CIA) has periodically been the subject of intense public debate about its proper role and control in American government. Its special status has required it to struggle for legitimacy.

This has prompted me to reflect on my long academic journey as a student of America's intelligence establishment. This chapter will briefly survey my experience of the past half century in attempts to understand this secret side of government and how the CIA has interacted with the American political system and democratic values.

In the face of an accelerating technology and a rapidly changing world, intelligence information has never been more important to national security. And it is to the intelligence establishment we depend on to define and warn of threats to the nation's security. This gives the intelligence system enormous potential power to determine policy and action in foreign affairs. And the unavoidable secrecy protecting the system poses obstacles to the accountability that American democracy demands. The nation's founders created a system of checks and balances—the separation of executive, legislative, and judicial authority—to promote accountability to the people. The dynamic interplay of secrecy and accountability became the focus of my studies.

Many wonder: What do political scientists *do*? The best answer, albeit simplistic, is that we study power in a governmental context. As a sophomore at Vanderbilt University thinking about majoring in political science, I recall choosing as a topic in a public speaking course, Military Intelligence. I must have been intrigued, back in 1941, by the idea of applying information to government security policy and action. I suspected that knowledge—intelligence—is a crucial element in the governmental policy process.

My World War II Army assignments involved no experience with military intelligence. After the war for a few years I was a first lieutenant in Army Intelligence Reserve. But the Army never exposed me to any secrets. I have had no hands-on government experience or access to classified data in intelligence. In my graduate study at Princeton University, I ultimately focused on the broad topic of civil-military relations. My doctoral dissertation was an analysis of the role of Congress in determining military aviation policy after World War I. I was interested in the interplay of congressional politics and armed services politics. The impetus for this choice of topics was a concern with civil-military relations, or as it was sometimes put in the context of American constitutional democracy, "civilian control of the military."

Although this issue was not directly related to intelligence questions, my interest was prompted in 1955, when I was invited to Harvard University to help create a Defense Studies Program supported by a Ford Foundation grant. At Harvard, I began seriously to study the government's foreign intelligence system. It seemed critically important to be informed about how the government was organized for gathering information for Cold War national security policy making. Part of my assignment was to develop reading materials for Harvard graduate students enrolled in a large academic year-long Defense Policy Seminar. Very little literature was available about the CIA, which by the mid-1950s had become a large government organization.

Several dozen students were enrolled from the Harvard graduate schools of Public Administration, Law, and Business. Our charge was not only to operate a year-long seminar in defense policy but also to create and assemble teaching materials on the various segments of the national security establishment. The literature was thin and scattered, especially about strategic intelligence. At this point I undertook the assignment to cover the CIA and other parts of what was called the intelligence community. I soon learned that such a label as "community" was more aspiration than reality. I also learned that very little scholarly information was available on the subject.

As a political scientist studying power, I soon learned that this massive secret intelligence apparatus engaged not only in spying but also in a variety of covert actions, including psychological warfare and political intervention overseas. These activities presented special problems for American constitutional government. Obviously, problems existed of accountability, congressional knowledge and control, and balance between the legislature and executive. Other problems included ethics, morality, civil liberties, and respect for domestic and international law. I shared Lord Acton's concern in his often quoted phrase: "Power corrupts; secret power [Acton said absolute power] corrupts absolutely."

In simplest terms, on the one hand, government espionage and other covert operations require secrecy. Democratic government, on the other hand, requires public accountability. Can these conflicting requirement be accommodated? I wondered. And I still wonder. With this question in mind, I set about to collect information about the CIA for students in the Defense Policy Seminar. I was advised at every turn that this subject could not be studied in a systematic scholarly way because the relevant information is secret. Although secrecy was a major problem, one encounters many other issues inhibiting study of this subject. Let me mention two more complications that obscure a realistic assessment of secret intelligence.

First, there is the semantic entanglement of intelligence terminology. Put simply, we encounter a very ambiguous vocabulary. The principal terms are often used interchangeably and incorrectly. What are these terms? Essentially, *intelligence* means information. Espionage, or spying, is a way of stealing information. Like stealing, espionage is illegal and must be pursued deceptively in secret. Counterintelligence is a police and security activity, aiming to protect the secrets of one's own nation from spies. Covert action, sometimes called covert operations or special activities, means secretly intervening by various means in the political affairs of other nations to produce a desired outcome. Although covert action is not strictly speaking an intelligence function, it is generally performed within an organization called an intelligence agency. Most often misused are the words *agent* and *spy* when referring to a case officer or analyst. But all of these terms often are used interchangeably and imprecisely. Newspaper headlines are particularly prone to confusion of the terms.

A second impediment to public understanding of this subject is the romanticized image of intelligence professionals presented in popular works of fiction. Ian Fleming's novels and movies about James Bond translate secret agentry into heroic deeds. To a reader Bond is a spy. In fact, he rarely engages in espionage. Rather, Bond's adventures resemble counterintelligence or covert action. I argue that covert operations are separate and distinct from the intelligence function. Yet one historian has invented a term, *jamesbonderie*, for a perception that has come to dominate and confuse public understanding of intelligence.[1]

Tom Clancy's fictional protagonist Jack Ryan is another example of a popular hero whose activities further confuse the semantics. The fictional Ryan has a doctorate in history and serves in and out of the CIA in important positions. His exploits as a CIA "superman" bear no more resemblance to reality than the deeds of Clark Kent. Closer to reality, perhaps, are the more subtle novels of British author David Cornwell (who writes under the pen name of John Le Carré). His novels portray intelligence work and espionage as a dull, sordid, immoral, and ultimately pointless game. Although Le Carré's novels may be somewhat more realistic than those of Clancy or Fleming, they are harshly cynical. My point is that government secrecy and disinformation, media sensationalism, imprecise vocabulary, and fictional romanticism combine to obscure comprehension of intelligence, both for the public and even for a scholar who seeks to clarify the subject.

Official secrecy was a major obstacle to my research from the start. Nevertheless, I set about to apply the principles of intelligence analysis—fitting together bits of information—from library resources, newspapers, congressional documents, and from those few leaders within the intelligence system willing to talk with me. My task was to connect the dots. Among the most helpful personal guides to accurate information in the late 1950s were two high CIA officials: William Bundy and Robert Amory. But my primary viewing point of the system was from the ivory tower. I was able to produce publishable manuscripts that passed the test of prior scholarly review. My first book, published by Harvard University Press in 1958, evoked a surprising amount of public attention,[2] which was due less to the book's merit than to the fact that no other serious scholar had attempted to describe in such detail the large intelligence bureaucracy that had grown in the first decade of the Cold War. When my book because a best-seller in the Washington, DC, area during 1958–59, I wondered whether the CIA was buying up copies and burning them. Thirty-five years later, I learned (to my surprise) that my book had received a favorable review in CIA's secret in-house journal. Allen W. Dulles, one of the CIA's founding fathers, once told me that my book had been "useful."

Viewing the CIA and the intelligence system half a century later, the change is dramatic. In 1956, little public knowledge existed about the system. Rarely did the CIA appear in news headlines. Few persons could name the CIA's director or be able to distinguish the agency's function from that of the Federal Bureau of Investigation (FBI). Occasional derring-do articles appeared in the press by investigative journalists under headlines such as "Fighting the Cold War Under Cover." University courses on strategic intelligence were nonexistent. Any attempt to assemble a bibliography of authoritative contemporary publications was virtually impossible.

More than half a century after its creation, the CIA became an almost daily topic in press headlines. This has been especially so since the surprise terrorist attacks on September 11, 2001. Now library shelves bulge with current books on intelligence and various aspects of the "CIA problem." Scores of memoirs and biographies of intelligence officials, including most former Directors of Central Intelligence, are available today.

Today the study of intelligence has become an academic speciality and an extensive, ever-expanding bibliography is available. Early on, the CIA created its own Center for the Study of Intelligence. It publishes informative articles in both classified and nonsecret versions and maintains a website with detailed information about its organization and functions. Also provided is an extensive bibliography of nonsecret publications on intelligence. More recently, a CIA University has been established, as well as the Sherman Kent School of Intelligence Analysis. In Washington, DC, a popular tourist site is the nongovernmental International Spy Museum. Its stated purpose is "to educate the public about espionage in an engaging manner and to provide the dynamic context that offers an understanding of its important role and impact on current and historical events." A CIA program sends selected intelligence officials to serve as visiting faculty at selected universities. The Agency has conducted several conferences at its Langley headquarters to which civilian academic specialists were invited. The CIA maintains a website with detailed information about the agency's organization and functions as well as a CIA's Home Page for Kids. These developments have increased the opportunities for effective oversight, but the record has remained uneven.

Today library shelves are crowded with an almost overwhelming number of studies by presidential, congressional, and private research groups on problems of intelligence policy, organization, and performance. These constitute one of the principal forms of information about the government's secret intelligence apparatus. Few agencies of the federal government have been as perpetually controversial as the CIA. Yet the question persists: How adequate have been efforts at oversight? How truly accountable has the secret intelligence system been to those responsible to the public within the nation's democratic framework?

In spite of the large volume of hearings, studies, and reports, layers of secrecy remain on some of the most critical issues of oversight and accountability. We remain essentially in the dark about some questions of use and abuse of intelligence prior to 9/11. Many of the studies focus on the performance of the intelligence system and how well it served decision makers in an objective fashion. My own interest in this subject evolved from my initial concern about the conflict between our government's desire to gain legitimate information affecting national security and democratic principles of accountability. In spite of the changes in availability of information about the CIA that I have described, this conflict persists.[3]

The American democratic ideal rests on the assumption that the people are the ultimate source of authority and are to be governed with their informed consent. Applying this ideal requires openness and disclosure. But many aspects of national security—military, diplomatic, and intelligence—sometimes require a high degree of secrecy. How can some governmental systems be popularly controlled by those who cannot see? The story of secret intelligence in a democracy has been the story of efforts to reconcile these competing requirements. At this writing, intense controversies exist about various aspects of intelligence programs. Important among these are the prewar information about Iraq, use of torture to obtain information, detention of suspected terrorists, intrusive methods that include spying on Americans, and the persistent issue of politicization of intelligence.

Now I turn to some of my major specific concerns about the CIA as they have changed over the years. I illustrate five major concerns with specific examples from past observation and experience.

The first concern was the absence of effective legislative knowledge and control of the intelligence system. When the CIA was established in 1947, little thought was given to the role of Congress in overseeing intelligence activities. Through the power of the purse, the Constitution gives Congress complete control over all government-funded activities. This is one way democratic accountability is supposed to work. But for two decades Congress was a sleeping, toothless watchdog. A handful of congressional leaders was assigned to monitor the CIA. But there was little payoff in their home districts or party positions for aggressive oversight of a secret entity within the executive branch. They could not publicly discuss their work. They saw their job as primarily to protect the agency. In my earliest writing I had proposed a Joint Congressional Committee on Intelligence with strong monitoring authority over all aspects of intelligence operations. Efforts were made in Congress toward this end. All failed. Similar proposals resurfaced over the years but all have run counter to the culture of Congress. The separation of appropriations and policy authority has been at the heart of the resistance to change, resulting in a system of oversight that is disbursed widely within the House and Senate.

In late December 1974, I was sitting in my office at Vanderbilt University. The telephone rang. On the line was Seymour Hersh, a *New York Times* investigative reporter with whom I was acquainted. "What would you say, Professor Ransom," Hersh queried, "if I told you that the CIA had been involved in a massive program of spying in the United States on Americans?" I expressed disbelief, noting that such activity is clearly prohibited in the CIA's legislative charter. In other words, such activity is illegal. On December 22, a few days after our telephone conversation, Hersh's front-page story detailing the CIA's domestic misdeeds appeared on page 1 of the *Times* and created a firestorm. Because Hersh quoted me in the article, I received many calls for comment from the national media. Surprisingly, few journalists seemed to understand that the CIA had no legitimate domestic security functions.

Within a few months the Senate and House began major investigations, by special committees, of the CIA's past covert activities, both foreign and domestic. The Church Committee in the Senate and the Pike Committee in the House undertook unprecedented hearings on intelligence operations. Additionally, a presidentially appointed commission, chaired by Vice President Nelson Rockefeller, undertook a parallel investigation of the CIA's misdeeds. Reports of these investigations spread details before the public about CIA-attempted assassinations of foreign leaders, opening of private citizens' mail, secret subsidies of foreign political parties, and hundreds of other formerly secret operations. The major consequence of these disclosures was the establishment of permanent committees in the Senate and House to oversee the intelligence establishment. For the first time, the CIA was circumscribed by a variety of controls and requirements that Congress be informed of intelligence and covert operations. Also prescribed was tightened presidential oversight. A clearly defined intelligence accountability to Congress was established. Even so, as later experience demonstrated, true accountability remained dependent on the willingness of Presidents and intelligence leaders to keep Congress properly informed. Secrecy gave special power to those who controlled secret information. So accountability continued to confront secrecy. Over the years it has been aggressive journalists who have forced more accountability than Congress on the intelligence establishment.

My second concern is illustrated by what is known as the U-2 incident of May 1, 1960, when an American spy plane was shot down deep within the Soviet Union and its pilot, Francis Gary Powers, was captured. In a *New York Times Magazine* article published shortly after that event, I pointed out how the risks of such espionage missions and the costs to diplomatic aims might be greater than the benefits.[4] Speculatively, the United States might have achieved detente with the Soviet Union had President Eisenhower canceled U-2 flights prior to an upcoming peace conference in Paris among leaders of the United States, the Soviet Union, Great Britain, and France. Soviet leader Khrushchev canceled the conference because of the U-2 incident. Possibly he had other motives, including political pressures from home, but the spy plane provided an excuse. Biographers tell us that one of Eisenhower's greatest disappointments as President was the failure of the peace conference. Conceivably the Cold War might have ended thirty years earlier if not for this incident. At any rate, this example demonstrates that spying can sometimes conflict with diplomatic goals. The primacy of military espionage over diplomacy can produce unwanted results.

The third concern involves one type of politicization, illustrated by the example of the CIA-sponsored Cuban exiles' attempt to invade Cuba and overthrow the Fidel Castro regime in 1961. Prior to the headlines reporting the CIA's failed Cuban adventure, most Americans probably were only vaguely aware of the Agency's covert action capabilities. History books report this as the Bay of Pigs fiasco. President Kennedy immediately held himself accountable, which Presidents rarely do in such situations. This failed adventure prompted the *New York Times Magazine* editor to request that I write another essay.[5] My article suggested that the CIA failure at the Bay of Pigs was a consequence of housing intelligence analysis and covert action under the same CIA roof, but keeping them isolated from one another. I had long believed that an organizational mistake had been made back in 1947 by combining analysis and action. The Bay of Pigs project was a mistake and a failure because those favoring the invasion project insisted on information favoring its feasibility. In this case the information was cherry picked. And it was wrong. Castro was stronger than the project planners wanted to believe. Reportedly, the intelligence side of the agency was ignored by the covert operators.

Concern number four is closely related to the third: the tendency of intelligence agencies to supply information to please policy makers. I have called this problem politicization of intelligence. This is a somewhat complex matter. In simplest explanation, it involves making policy first and then demanding that the intelligence agency provide facts that support the policy. A long list of apparent intelligence failures have resulted from this tendency of intelligence professionals—particularly when facts are uncertain—to tell policy makers what they want to hear. Or alternatively, sometimes decision makers selectively hear only what they want.

Perhaps it is naive to believe that an agency charged with producing secret information can be insulated from partisan politics. After all, politics is about power, and information conveys potential power. Politicization is not usually a problem if there is broad consensus about foreign policy objectives. When consensus faded in the late 1960s over the Vietnam War, intelligence became a political football. Allen Dulles, one of the early influential intelligence leaders, liked to say, "We give information only, not advice." Perhaps that was once true. Indeed, information objectivity was one of the reasons for creating the CIA as an independent arm of presidency, detached from the military services or the State Department.

Politicization was brought home to me in the early 1980s in a brief conversation I had with then Director of Central Intelligence William J. Casey at CIA headquarters in Langley at an academic conference. I deliberately challenged him with this comment: "You have recently made a foreign policy speech at Westminister College in Missouri. I thought that CIA officials refrained from making foreign policy speeches." Taken aback, Casey hesitated for a moment and then told me, "Well, I have never agreed with that principle of detachment from policy." Then he added, "Besides, I am a member of the president's Cabinet." In my view, Casey and President Reagan had got it seriously wrong, as had some later Presidents. A CIA Director—or a Director of National Intelligence—should not be a member of the Cabinet and should be completely divorced from partisanship. Note that Casey had been Reagan's presidential campaign manager; his appointment as CIA Director was an inappropriate reward. Similarly, George H. W. Bush had been chairman of the Republican National Committee prior to becoming Director of Central Intelligence. Such appointments implied politicization. Casey's later efforts as CIA Director to operate outside of the nation's laws seriously affected the Agency's reputation as nonpartisan. A testimonial in this regard was the following statement by George Schultz, Reagan's Secretary of State: "I felt that the CIA's analysis was distorted by strong views about policy.... I had no confidence in the intelligence community."[6]

My fifth concern is about the future of the CIA. When the Soviet Union collapsed and a half century of Cold War ended, some raised the question, "Do we need the CIA?" In one sense the CIA was created in the mirror image of the Soviet security and intelligence: the KGB. Today there is no Soviet Union and a transformed KGB. One prominent senator, Patrick Moynihan, a former vice chairman of the Senate Select Committee on Intelligence, suggested that the CIA be abolished, proposing to turn over its intelligence functions to the Department of State. Op-ed pieces and newspaper editorials at one time called for the abolition of the CIA. Its reputation had been shattered by a series of scandals and apparent intelligence failures.

In 1994, Congress authorized yet another commission to study the organization, functions, and future of the intelligence system: the Aspin-Brown Commission. This action was precipitated in part by the end of the Cold War but primarily by the CIA's all-time worst internal scandals—the defection of one of its officers, Aldrich Ames. Ames had struck a multimillion-dollar deal with the KGB to reveal bushels of secrets about CIA operations within the Soviet Union. Ames spent his ill-gotten rewards on an expensive home, luxury automobile, and high-end lifestyle. His undetected betrayal cost the lives of some dozen Soviet agents secretly working for the United States within the Soviet Union. CIA operations in Russia and Eastern Europe were virtually destroyed in the mid-1980s as a consequence of Ames's activities.

One is hard-put to explain how Ames's behavior could have been undetected for almost a decade. Perhaps a culture had developed within the Agency resembling a fraternity that assumed its members could do no wrong. Secrecy within the tightly compartmentalized CIA enabled Ames to betray his country undetected over a long period. Public revelation of his case caused a public relations disaster for the CIA. Editorial cartoons ridiculing the Agency numbered in the hundreds. The scandal came at the worst possible time for the CIA, when its competence was already being publicly debated and questions were being raised about its future.

Predictably, the CIA survived the Aspin-Brown Commission's study of its future, although major organizational reforms were proposed. The principle of a central agency independent of the various departments and federal agencies was seen as valid. Keep in mind that the CIA consumes only an estimated 15 percent of the intelligence system's estimated $44 million annual budget. Total budget figures remain secret in spite of widespread belief that budget totals should be made public. I have held the opinion over the years that half the annual budget is wasted. The trouble is, I do not know which half. Such is the price for inevitable secrecy. But certainly nothing is more rational and logical than that national security depends on the fullest degree of information available to decision makers. Yet much of this information inevitably is secret from the public. Intelligence misdeeds can now be reported without public disclosure. And inspectors general within the CIA and the National Security Agency now have authority to report misdeeds directly to Congress. In 1998 Congress passed the Intelligence Community Whistleblower Protection Act. Current or former intelligence employees can report misdeeds to Congress after raising concerns within their agency. Such reports remain secret. Since the Eisenhower administration, a President's Foreign Intelligence Advisory Board has existed. It operates secretly. Nonetheless, imperfections in methods for accountability over the years have left the CIA with a shaky legitimacy.

I have been impressed by an intelligence paradox. Recall that the United States entered World War II as a consequence of a spectacular intelligence failure at Pearl Harbor on December 7, 1941. This disaster was partly the result of various intelligence units failing to share crucial bits of information. There was no intelligence community. Yet World War II ultimately was won in large part because of the success of intelligence agencies in breaking enemy codes.

More recently I developed the controversial, speculative view that the Cold War arose out of a tragedy of faulty perception on both sides. On the one hand, perhaps there was a two-sided intelligence failure in which both the Soviet Union and the United States misread the intentions of one another. On the other hand, accurate strategic intelligence may have prevented a global thermonuclear holocaust. This was the consequence of accurate estimates by each nation of the other's military capabilities. Accuracy of intelligence may be the world's best hope for survival. Clearly, accurate intelligence will become increasingly vital in an age of globalization and an accelerating information technology.

As this is written, ongoing controversies abound about the role and control of secret intelligence. Just as occurred in December 1974, a *New York Times* disclosure in December 2005 of questionable intelligence activities produced a major controversy—and congressional hearings—about the proper limits for spying on Americans in pursuit of strategic information. But in general the public's demand for information, oversight, and accountability will continue to fluctuate, depending on the degree of consensus about security threats and foreign policy goals and programs. In wars people think first about security and then other values. The public's disadvantage is that the intelligence system usually defines the threats.

Meanwhile, the legitimacy of secret intelligence agencies will always be on trial in the absence of all-out war. This may be inevitable, even healthy, for democracy because of the incompatibility of secrecy and accountability.

After extensive hearings, studies and debates, Congress passed the Intelligence Reform and Terrorist Prevention Act of 2004. The act incorporated President George W. Bush's proposals for major restructuring of the national intelligence system and produced the most extensive intelligence reorganization since the CIA's creation by Congress in 1947. In this act the upper-level chairs were rearranged. A new post of Director of National Intelligence (DNI) was created, and the CIA and its director were demoted and charged with the exclusive duties of intelligence collection, analysis, and overseas operations. The DNI was to be the "community" administrator with extensive budgetary and personnel authority. In the process of reform some of the bureaucratic infighting that had occurred prior to the 1947 legislation was evident. At present the real authority of the DNI over sixteen intelligence agencies is uncertain, especially in regard to the role and control of various units of military intelligence. The impact of the 2004 changes will have on more effective accountability remains to be seen. But the new centralized authority offers opportunity for true accountability, which will depend on the aggressive functioning of the major players: the President, Congress, the judiciary, and most important, the press. Above all, effective monitoring and accountability will be a reality only if the President and national intelligence leadership are fully honest and cooperative with the designated congressional watchdogs. Because the requirements of secrecy give the executive the preponderant power, secret intelligence will always put at risk the equilibrium of our constitutional system.

One of the beauties—and perhaps vulnerabilities—of American democracy is that secrets are hard to keep. Undeniably leaks of some very sensitive classified information can do harm. The principle of a free press invites such danger. But an effective intelligence oversight structure will mitigate that danger. What we don't know can harm us. The challenge is always that of knowing what to do with what we do know.

NOTES

1. Robin Winks, *Cloak and Gown: Scholars in the Secret War* (New York: Morrow, 1987).
2. Harry Howe Ransom, *Central Intelligence and National Security* (Cambridge, MA: Harvard University Press, 1958).
3. See a useful contemporary study of accountability in democratic nations: Hans Born, Loch K. Johnson, and Ian Leigh, *Who's Watching* the *Spies?* (Washington, DC: Potomac Books, 2005).
4. Harry Howe Ransom, "How Intelligent Is Intelligence?," *New York Times Magazine* (May 22, 1960), pp. 26, 80–83.
5. Harry Howe Ransom, "Secret Mission in an Open Society," *New York Times Magazine* (May 21, 1961), pp. 20, 77–79.
6. George P. Schultz, *Turmoil and Triumph; My Years as Secretary of State* (New York: Charles Scribner's Sons, 1993).

APPENDIX A

A SENATE SELECT COMMITTEE ON INTELLIGENCE REPORT ON OVERSIGHT EXPERIENCES, 1947–93

I. EARLY EVOLUTION OF THE U.S. SYSTEM OF OVERSIGHT

OVERSIGHT PRIOR TO 1975

Intelligence activities have been conducted by the United States Government since the beginning of the republic. Historically, these activities were carried out by the departments and agencies responsible for U.S. military and foreign policy. Oversight by the Congress was minimal and devolved to the congressional committees responsible for authorizing or appropriating the budget for the department or agency concerned.

It was not until 1946, in the wake of the Second World War, that President Harry S. Truman, mindful of the surprise attack carried out by the Japanese on Pearl Harbor in 1941, chose to create an intelligence agency, independent of the departments charged with the conduct of foreign relations or the preservation of national defense, to assemble the intelligence available to the government as a whole and provide him with an objective assessment of that information. The Central Intelligence Group, as it was first designated by President Truman, retained many of the operational capabilities of the Office of Strategic Services, which had carried out clandestine intelligence activities during the war. In 1947, as part of the legislation enacted by Congress to establish national defense arrangements in the post-war era, the Central Intelligence Agency (CIA) was created by law, and its Director was given the role of pulling together intelligence obtained by the intelligence elements of other departments and agencies.

Congressional oversight over this new agency was the responsibility of the Committees on Armed Services of the House of Representatives and of the Senate, and appropriations for CIA were handled by the defense subcommittees of the respective

---

Source: "Legislative Oversight of Intelligence Activities: The U.S. Experience," *Report*, S. Prt. 103–88, Select Committee on Intelligence, U.S. Senate, 103d Cong., 2d. Sess. (October 1994), pp. 2–26.

Appropriations Committees of each house of the Congress. The budget for the agency was classified, and, for security reasons, was "buried" in non-descript line-items of the defense budget. (It remains so today.) The bulk of U.S. intelligence activities were, and continue to be, carried out by the Department of Defense. Thus, defense appropriations laws provided an appropriate mechanism for funding intelligence activities.

Congressional awareness of CIA activities was limited largely to the Chairmen and Ranking Minority Members of the committees concerned with the defense budget. Staff involvement was limited generally to one or two senior members of the staff of each of these committees who made certain the needs of the intelligence agencies were funded. Oversight concerns were typically worked out between the Director of Central Intelligence (DCI) and a few congressional participants, with little appreciation by the Congress as a whole and virtually none by the public at large. While there were occasional proposals during the 1950s and 1960s to create special committees with responsibility for intelligence, none of these proposals was adopted by the Congress.

The responsibilities of the DCI evolved over time. It was not until the early 1950s that CIA's responsibility for the conduct of "covert actions" (i.e., efforts to influence the course of events abroad) crystalized. Similarly, CIA did not come into its own as a provider of independent analysis until the Korean War in the early 1950s. In the meantime, new intelligence agencies, such as the National Security Agency and the Defense Intelligence Agency, were created within the Department of Defense, and existing intelligence elements within the military departments, the State Department, and the Federal Bureau of Investigation gradually expanded. DCIs played a relatively weak coordinating role with respect to these agencies, however, until the early 1970s when, at the direction of President Richard M. Nixon, the DCI began to bring together the funding for intelligence activities into a single budgetary program which became formally known as the National Foreign Intelligence Program.

Congressional involvement in these developments remained minimal until the mid-1970s, when a series of especially troubling revelations appeared in the press concerning U.S. intelligence activities. Covert action programs involving assassination attempts against foreign leaders and covert efforts to effect changes in other governments were reported for the first time. The efforts of intelligence agencies to collect information concerning the political activities of U.S. citizens during the late 1960s and early 1970s were also documented extensively by the press.

These programs and practices surprised and concerned many Members of the Senate and House of Representatives. Coming on the heels of the Watergate scandal, which had involved efforts to use and manipulate the CIA and FBI for political purposes, these disclosures suggested to many that intelligence activities, long ignored by the Congress and operated without scrutiny outside the Executive branch, had strayed beyond acceptable limits.

The first legislative response to these disclosures was the enactment in 1974 of the Hughes-Ryan amendment to the Foreign Assistance Act of 1961. This amendment addressed the covert action programs of the CIA, prohibiting the use of appropriated funds for "operations in foreign countries, other than activities intended solely for obtaining necessary intelligence unless and until the President finds that each such operation is important to the national security of the United States." The amendment also required that the President report "in a timely fashion, a description and scope of such operation" to the "appropriate committees of the Congress," which was interpreted to include the Committees on Armed Services, Foreign Relations (or Foreign Affairs), and Appropriations of each House of Congress, a total of six committees.

The following year, in 1975, Congress passed legislation which, for the fist time, actually terminated funding for a covert operation: the secret support of military and paramilitary activities in Angola.

In the meantime, additional disclosures began to surface in 1975 with regard to the CIA's domestic operations and the efforts of the FBI to undermine the activities of Rev. Martin Luther King and other civil rights leaders during the 1960s. President Gerald Ford reacted to these disclosures by appointing a special commission headed by Vice President Nelson Rockefeller to look into the alleged improprieties, both foreign and domestic. After an investigation of several months, the Rockefeller Commission issued a report in late 1975 that confirmed many of the reported abuses.

Congress was not willing to rely solely upon the findings of the Rockefeller Commission, however, and during 1975 created special investigating committees to investigate the activities of intelligence agencies across the board. The Senate acted first, creating a special committee which became known as the "Church Committee" after the name of its Chairman, Senator Frank Church of Idaho. The House of Representatives followed suit later in the year, creating a similar committee chaired by Congressman Otis Pike of New York.

In the meantime, while the Church and Pike Committee investigations were proceeding, the Ford administration, in February, 1976, issued the first public Executive Order in history to govern intelligence activities—Executive Order 11905. While the new order did not address the obligations of intelligence agencies with respect to the Congress, it did, for the first time, impose restrictions upon intelligence activities, limiting what might be collected by intelligence agencies regarding "U.S. persons" (i.e. citizens, aliens admitted for permanent residence, and organizations predominantly comprised of such persons) and prohibiting U.S. Government employees from engaging in, or conspiring to engage in, political assassinations.

THE CHURCH AND PIKE COMMITTEES (1975–1976)

The Church Committee began its work in January, 1975, and issued a final report, consisting of five volumes, in April, 1976. As a result of voluminous hearings and a series of concurrent investigations directed at virtually every element of the Intelligence Community, the Committee documented a pattern of misconduct on the part of intelligence agencies which, among other things, strongly suggested the need for more effective congressional oversight. The report showed widespread abuse of the civil rights of American citizens and described activities by intelligence agencies that violated applicable law and executive policy, as well as clandestine undertakings in foreign countries which seemed at odds with U.S. values and foreign policy. At the same time, the report made clear that existing legal and policy constraints on intelligence activities were inadequate and that proper supervision and accountability within the Executive branch and to the Congress were sorely lacking.

While the Church Committee made extensive recommendations for change in its final report, it chose not to develop a legislative proposal to address the problems it had documented. Instead, it recommended the Senate create a new follow-on committee to provide continuing oversight and consider such additional legislation as might be necessary. The Pike Committee made a similar recommendation in its final report.

ESTABLISHMENT OF OVERSIGHT
COMMITTEES (1976–1977)

On May 19, 1976, after review by five committees and ten days of floor debate, the Senate by a margin of 72–22 voted to create the Select Committee on Intelligence. The resolution creating the new committee—Senate Resolution 400, 94th Congress—remains unchanged and in effect today. (See Appendix, p. 27.) Although established as a "select" committee appointed by the Majority and Minority Leaders of the Senate—a practice normally reserved for committees that serve for a limited period—the Senate Select Committee on Intelligence has continued to function with the support of the body as a whole.

While Senate Resolution 400 did not establish binding legal obligations on the part of intelligence agencies with respect to the new Committee, it did include a non-binding "sense of the Senate" provision stating that the heads of intelligence agencies should keep the Committee "fully and currently informed" of their agency's activities, including "any significant anticipated activities," and provide such information as may be requested by the Committee relating to matters within its jurisdiction.

On July 14, 1977, the House of Representatives created its own oversight committee, by a vote of 227–171. The resolution creating the House committee—House Resolution 658—differed in several respects from its Senate counterpart. Notably, it established the committee as a "Permanent Select Committee on Intelligence," indicating its status as a permanent body under the rules of the House. On the other hand, it did not include the "sense of the Senate" provisions pertaining to the responsibilities of intelligence agencies vis-a-vis the new Committee.

Both committees took the position that they were "appropriate committees" for purposes of receiving notice of covert actions pursuant to the Hughes-Ryan amendment (see above), and this position was acquiesced in by the incoming administration of President Jimmy Carter.

II. STRUCTURE AND OPERATION OF THE
OVERSIGHT COMMITTEES

There is no one "right way" to organize legislative oversight of intelligence activities. Indeed, the Senate and House oversight committees are organized differently. The differences reflect both the variation in time—since the Senate committee was the first to be formed and had to overcome more initial resistance—and the difference between the relatively unstructured Senate and the larger House of Representatives, in which rules are followed more rigidly and one political party has had a long period of dominance.

There are, however, some general principles that are worth keeping in mind for any intelligence oversight committee. One is the need to have access to, and to handle properly, very sensitive information on intelligence capabilities and activities. Access to information is the lifeblood of intelligence oversight. Tight security is both an end unto itself and also a means to justify and maintain the committee's access to information. A second need, in many cases, is to limit the role of partisan politics in the operation of the committee. In part, this is one more means of reducing the risk of security lapses that could affect the national security and/or the committee's access to information. It may also serve, however, to moderate the pace of changes wrought by legislative oversight and thereby to give typically conservative intelligence institutions more time to adjust to a world in which they are accountable to elected representatives of the people.

Key to the effectiveness of the U.S. system has also been control over the budgets of intelligence agencies. As explained below, the oversight committees of the U.S. Congress are involved in funding a myriad of intelligence programs and activities, from large to small. While such a system may not be readily adaptible by other legislatures, some form of budgetary control is essential to encouraging cooperation with the committees responsible for oversight, to obtaining access to information held by intelligence agencies, and generally to encourage compliance with law and direction by the oversight committees.

MEMBERSHIP OF AN OVERSIGHT COMMITTEE

Most committees of the U.S. Senate and House of Representatives distribute their membership in proportion to each political party's membership in that house of congress. Some House committees have been weighted even more strongly in favor of the majority party, however, and occasionally a committee is organized with nearly equal membership for the minority party in order to foster a more bipartisan ethic.

The House intelligence committee's membership has generally been apportioned in the traditional manner, which has given the majority party in the House a substantial majority on the committee as well. By contrast, Senate Resolution 400 apportions the Senate committee's membership in a more bipartisan manner, with the majority party having only a 1-vote margin. The intended effect of that structure, which has been generally borne out in practice, is to limit the ability of any party to count on a bipartisan committee majority to take legislative actions. The need to seek support from members of more than one party, in order to attain a secure majority for legislative action also tends to lessen the likelihood that the committee will approve proposals for radical change.

Both the 19-member House committee and the Senate committee, which has ranged between 13 and 17 members, are structured to include members (at least one from each party) who also serve on each of several other committees that have a legitimate interest in intelligence matters: the Appropriations Committees, the Armed Services Committees, the Judiciary Committees, and the Committees on Foreign Relations (in the Senate) and Foreign Affairs (in the House of Representatives). This membership requirement has almost always been fully implemented, with the result that those related committees have a direct channel of communication with the Intelligence Committees. This has helped to allay the concerns of those committees that the intelligence oversight committees might take (or approve) secret actions that would seriously affect their areas of interest in adverse ways.

Both intelligence committees have limits on the number of years a member may serve before having to leave the committee. The Senate limit is eight years of consecutive service, and the House limit is six years. These limits are designed to ensure a steady rotation of membership, which brings in members with new ideas and approaches, and, over time, to acquaint more members of Congress with this area of government activity.

The selection of members for the Senate committee is also handled in an unusual manner. Most committee memberships are decided by each party's members of the Senate. For the Intelligence Committee, however, members are named by the Majority Leader and the Minority Leader. The intent of this approach is to remove this committee's membership selection from the normal political process and to permit the leadership of the Senate to select Members whose duties and experience lend themselves to service on the oversight committee.

Each member of the House committee, including members from the minority party, is appointed by the Speaker of the House. Members from the minority party are nominated by the House Minority Leader, and such nominations have heretofore been accepted by the Speaker. The selection process in the House is not specified in the House committee's charter, Rule XLVIII of the Rules of the House, as it is in the resolution creating the Senate Committee.

LEADERSHIP OF AN OVERSIGHT COMMITTEE

As with any legislative committee, there is a premium on strong leadership of an intelligence oversight committee. By and large, the leadership of both the Senate and House committees have been chosen from the members of each party with the longest service on the committee. This serves to maximize the chairman's and vice chairman's familiarity with intelligence oversight, without requiring a background in those agencies.

On rare occasions, an unusual loss of members (through retirements, electoral losses or deaths) and a limit on terms of service on an intelligence oversight committee can result in one party having no experienced members to serve as chairman. Both the Senate and the House of Representatives can handle these or other rare circumstances by agreeing in a particular case not to observe the normal limit on terms of service.

There is often a premium on leadership that reaches across the boundaries of both party and ideology. One organizational measure used by the Senate to foster bipartisanship has been to have the minority party's leading member on the committee serve as vice chairman— and, in the absence of the chairman, as acting chairman—of the committee. Both the chairman and the vice chairman may be substantially deterred from partisan posturing by the knowledge that on any given day, the absence of the chairman may result in a member from the opposition exercising the chairman's powers. This arrangement generally leads to a close working relationship between the chairman and vice chairman, especially in their handling of the most extremely sensitive matters, which may be withheld from other members of the committee.

The House committee has no such formal procedure for shared leadership and has generally been organized on a more partisan basis.

SECURITY

Security is absolutely vital to the operation of an intelligence oversight committee. Although it is also vital for such a committee to have a means of forcing disclosure of information in extremis, day-to-day security is the means by which the committee assures the intelligence agencies—and by which those agencies can assure their sources and co-operative counterparts overseas—that release of information to the committee will not inevitably lead to public disclosure. The experience of the Senate and House committees is that no law or resolution can substitute for the trust that is built upon years of secure handling of sensitive information.

The resolutions establishing each Intelligence Committee provide that classified information and other information received by the committee in confidence may not be disclosed outside the committee other than in a closed session of the Senate or House of Representatives, respectively, unless the committee votes to release such information and such vote does not prompt an objection from the Executive branch. Failure of members to abide by this restriction subjects them to investigation and, where appropriate, to referral to the Ethics Committee of each House for disciplinary action. In addition, the chairmen of each committee routinely advise their members that anyone who fails to protect such information will be asked to leave the committee. There have, in fact, been instances in which members have left the intelligence committees, either because of an infraction of security rules or because they were unwilling to remain bound by these limits on their actions.

Each committee has the power under its respective charter to release classified information. It must give the President time to object to such disclosure, however, and, if such objection is filed in writing, must vote again on the issue and then take the matter to a closed session of its respective House of Congress, which will make the final determination. In practice, the committees and the Executive branch have reached agreement on disclosures; no President has ever filed a formal objection.

Members of each committee receive access to classified information held by the committee by virtue of their elective office, i.e., they are not subjected to background investigations. Committee staffs, on the other hand, are subjected to background investigations (and reinvestigations) that are carried out by the Federal Bureau of Investigation. (Although a polygraph examination is used as a condition of employment in some intelligence agencies, it is not used with regard to congressional staff appointments.) The results of these investigations are provided to the Committees, who, in turn, seek a "security opinion" from the Director of Central Intelligence (DCI) and Secretary of Defense concerning each potential staff member. While each committee, as a matter of principle, reserves the right to hire its own staff, it is rare that any person is hired for the staff over the objection of the DCI or Secretary of Defense. Indeed, there have been occasional cases in which the committees have declined to hire a potential employee on security grounds despite the absence of objection from the DCI or Secretary of Defense.

Intelligence Committee staff members are required to sign "nondisclosure agreements" pledging not to reveal secret information to which they have access, and they are similarly advised that failure to do so will result in their dismissal. The nondisclosure agreements, by adding a contractual obligation, may open an offending staff member to various civil actions, such as denial of pension rights or recovery of any profits from the improper use of committee information. The agreements also require the pre-publication review (by the committee, which in turn relies upon Executive branch experts) of materials that current or former staff members may wish to publish, unless such materials are clearly unrelated to intelligence matters or the author's service on the committee.

Each committee has established its own security procedures, consistent with (and, in some respects, exceeding) the requirements of the Executive branch. In the Senate committee, the location of each document is controlled every day; all readers of each document are recorded; and there are severe restrictions on the removal of documents from the committee's office spaces or hearing rooms. Thus, if a person attending a closed hearing should take notes, those notes must be surrendered before leaving the room to security staff, who arrange for the secure transportation of the notes to the author's agency. Secure office spaces, including hearing rooms and conference areas, have been constructed for the Intelligence Committees and certified by appropriate security authorities within the Executive branch.

ACCESS TO INFORMATION HELD BY THE
INTELLIGENCE COMMUNITY

U.S. intelligence agencies are required by law to furnish to the oversight committees "any information or material concerning intelligence activities . . . which is in their custody or control and which is requested by either of the intelligence committees in order to carry out its authorized responsibilities." The law specifically provides that even information which reveals intelligence sources and methods shall not be denied the committees. In short, the committees, as a matter of law and principle, recognize no limitation on their access to information.

As noted earlier, however, no law can readily compel full access to information if intelligence agencies are convinced that such access will result in catastrophic disclosures of information on their sensitive sources and methods. As a matter of practice, therefore, the committees have been willing to accommodate legitimate concerns for the security of intelligence secrets, either by limiting the scope of their requests or by limiting the manner in which sensitive information is handled, so long as their oversight responsibilities can be fulfilled. Thus, the committees do not ordinarily request the identities of intelligence agents or the details concerning anticipated collection operations where such information is not necessary to the conduct of oversight. Similarly, the committees have refrained from inquiries involving what U.S. intelligence agencies may know about sensitive activities undertaken by their foreign counterparts (other than activities in, or directed at, the United States) where such information is not relevant to the oversight of U.S. agencies. Moreover, the committees have ordinarily been willing to limit access to particularly sensitive information to members and/or a few senior staff, to limit the number of committee members with access to especially sensitive information, or to permit intelligence agencies to retain custody of such information rather than maintaining copies at the committee themselves.

Intelligence agencies typically advise the committees when particularly sensitive information is being requested or provided, and ask that the committees limit the scope of their request or the manner in which such information is to be handled. The committees, for their part, typically satisfy themselves that such requests are legitimate and, once satisfied, negotiate appropriate access or handling arrangements on a case-by-case basis. As a practical matter, instances in which committee access could not be arranged have been extremely rare.

RELATIONS BETWEEN THE CONGRESSIONAL
OVERSIGHT COMMITTEES

In general, each of the oversight committees pursues its own agenda during the course of a year in terms of holding hearings, briefings, inquiries, or investigations on subjects of its choosing. Occasionally, events drive both committees to pursue the same objective at the same time and, when this occurs, informal arrangements are often made for both committees to be briefed concurrently, or perhaps for one committee to handle one aspect of an inquiry and for the other to handle a different aspect. Often this will depend upon the level and intensity of member interest in a particular topic.

Generally, it is the practice of intelligence agencies to provide identical information of an oversight nature to the two committees, regardless of which committee actually takes the lead in terms of the inquiry or investigation at issue.

Where the two committees necessarily must come together is over legislation and the annual budget. Because each committee is charged by its respective body with authorizing appropriations for intelligence activities, each year the two committees are responsible for "conferencing" the differences in the annual intelligence authorization bill, as passed by their respective Houses. (The budget process is described in greater detail in the sections that follow.)

While conference on the authorization bill takes place after the bill has cleared each House, typically late in the session, in practice the committees consult quite closely regarding their respective actions on the budget long before conference. Indeed, the committee which reports its bill first may do so based upon its understanding of what the other committee is likely to do when it reports its own version of the bill. The committee which reports its bill last not only has the benefit of seeing what the other committee did, but is able to gauge its own actions in terms of likely trade-offs later in conference.

Both committees must also ultimately agree with respect to any legislation regarding intelligence which may be offered by either committee. Typically, legislative items are included in the public portion of the annual authorization bill (see below), but sometimes they are handled as "freestanding" bills. In either case, since agreement between the two committees will ultimately be required, each committee understands that if it wishes to get legislation enacted, it must ensure not only that the other committee is informed of and appreciates its actions, but also is given an adequate opportunity to examine the legislative initiative in its own process (via hearings or other means) if it chooses to do so. Thus, of necessity, there is close coordination regarding both substance and timing on all legislative initiatives. In practice, this often means that legislation first proposed in one session is not finally enacted until a later session of Congress.

RELATIONS WITH OTHER CONGRESSIONAL COMMITTEES

The resolution establishing the Senate oversight committee provides that the committee will have jurisdiction over the CIA and the "intelligence activities" of other departments and agencies of the Executive branch. The term "intelligence activities" is defined, however, to exclude "tactical foreign military intelligence serving no national policymaking function." The practical effect of these definitions is (1) to leave the CIA and DCI structure within the sole jurisdiction of the intelligence committee; (2) to leave defense intelligence activities other than solely tactical activities to shared jurisdiction between the intelligence and armed services committees; and (3) to leave tactical military intelligence within the sole jurisdiction of the Committee on Armed Services. (Despite this latter limitation, the Senate oversight committee has historically reviewed the annual budget request for tactical military intelligence activities and provided recommendations regarding the request to the Committee on Armed Services.) Standing committees of the Senate whose jurisdiction encompasses departments or agencies which conduct intelligence activities are given the right to seek referral for a period of 30 days of any legislation reported by the Senate intelligence committee pertaining to any matter within the standing committee's jurisdiction. Conversely, the oversight committee is given the right to seek referral for the same period of any legislation reported by other committees which pertains to "intelligence activities" within the jurisdiction of the oversight committee.

A somewhat different arrangement exists in the House of Representatives, where the oversight committee is given jurisdiction over the CIA and the "intelligence *and intelligence-related* activities" (emphasis added) of other departments and agencies. This term does not exclude "tactical intelligence," and, thus, the House oversight committee retains jurisdiction over this category while the Senate oversight committee does not. Similar provisions apply to the right of other House committees to seek referral of legislation pertaining to matters within their jurisdiction, but the time period for such referral is made a matter of discretion with the Speaker rather than the 30-day period called for by the Senate resolution. The House oversight committee is also authorized to seek referral of legislation covering matters within its jurisdiction which is reported by other committees.

As a practical matter, both oversight committees seek the concurrence of other committees before reporting legislation which contains provisions which might trigger a request for referral. Where concurrence cannot be obtained, the oversight committee has the option of reporting a bill with a provision in dispute (and risking a request for referral or other actions to delay or oppose passage of the bill) or dropping the provision so as to avoid referral.

Both oversight committees also become involved in deliberations concerning legislation in other committees which involve or may affect intelligence agencies. Indeed, intelligence agencies frequently request the assistance of the oversight committees in dealing with legislation in other committees which is believed to adversely affect intelligence operations. The oversight committees typically provide such assistance if they believe a legitimate concern is posed by the legislation under consideration.

Occasionally, the assistance of the oversight committees is sought by other congressional committees. Since other committees often lack staff who are cleared for intelligence matters or otherwise lack the expertise necessary to pursue a particular inquiry, the intelligence committees are asked to conduct investigations or provide their assessments in particular circumstances. For example, an intelligence committee might be asked by its house's Foreign Affairs Committee for an assessment of the behavior of a particular foreign country—based upon information available to intelligence agencies—as part of the Foreign Affairs committee's consideration of legislation to impose sanctions upon the foreign government concerned.

Finally, due to the complex nature of the budget process within the Congress, special coordination occurs between the oversight committees and the respective Armed Services and Appropriations Committees of each House with regard to the annual intelligence authorization. This coordination is explained below in the discussion of the budget process.

RELATIONSHIPS WITH OVERSIGHT MECHANISMS IN THE EXECUTIVE BRANCH

In addition to the oversight provided by the congressional committees, there is an elaborate system of oversight for intelligence activities within the Executive branch. The President's Foreign Intelligence Advisory Board (PFIAB) conducts oversight investigations on an ad hoc basis, reporting its results directly to the President, and requires periodic reports from the Inspectors General at intelligence agencies. Each of the intelligence agencies, in fact, maintains an internal Inspector General who reports to the agency head concerned. Where there are intelligence elements at departments and agencies which are not intelligence agencies per se, e.g., the Department of State, such elements are covered by the Inspector General of the department or agency concerned. The Inspector General at the CIA is appointed by the President and is subject to Senate confirmation, as are the

Inspectors General of departments and agencies which are not intelligence agencies. Inspectors General at other intelligence agencies are typically appointed by the agency head.

The oversight committees have historically had no relationship with the PFIAB, which, as part of the Executive Office of the President, has occupied a privileged status vis-a-vis the Congress under the American system of separation of powers. Nothing prevents elements of the Executive Office of the President and the intelligence committees from cooperating on particular matters, however, where both branches consider it advantageous to do so. For example, the Senate committee contributed to the work of the Vice President's Task Force on Combatting Terrorism in the 1980s.

Moreover, with the exception of the Inspector General at the CIA, there are no formal links between the oversight committees and the Inspectors General at other intelligence agencies. In practice, however, the oversight committees review the activities of the Inspectors General as part of the committees' own oversight responsibilities and occasionally request, via the agency head concerned, that these offices conduct oversight inquiries or investigations in appropriate circumstances and report their results to the oversight committees. The heads of intelligence agencies have historically been responsive to such requests. The CIA Inspector General is required by law to provide reports to the committees on a semi-annual basis and to report "particularly serious or flagrant problems, abuses or deficiencies" within seven days.

In the case of the Inspector General at the CIA, the law creating this office (see Appendix, page 60) also provides that in several unusual circumstances, the Inspector General will report directly to the oversight committees: (1) when the Inspector General is unable to resolve differences with the CIA Director affecting the execution of his or her responsibilities; (2) when the Director or Acting Director is the focus of the Inspector General's activities; and (3) when the Inspector General is unable to obtain significant documentary information in the course of an investigation.

III. FUNCTIONS AND POWERS OF THE OVERSIGHT COMMITTEES

The following sections set forth the functions of the oversight committees. In some cases—particularly where the budget process is concerned—the explanation, while accurate, is somewhat oversimplified in the interests of preserving clarity for the reader with respect to the key points.

AUTHORIZATION OF APPROPRIATIONS FOR INTELLIGENCE: THE BUDGET PROCESS

Both Senate and House resolutions creating the oversight committees empower them to authorize appropriations for intelligence activities. (The House resolution provides for authorization of appropriations for "intelligence and intelligence-related activities.") This means that, consistent with the two-step funding process utilized in the U.S. Congress generally, the oversight committees each year must report legislation to their respective bodies which "authorizes" a certain level of funding for all U.S. intelligence activities. This legislation, in theory, becomes the basis upon which the appropriations committees in each

House then determine how funds are to be appropriated to the department or agency concerned for the next fiscal year (which runs from October 1st until September 30th of each year). Appropriations for intelligence and intelligence-related activities are contained largely in the Department of Defense appropriations bill.

In addition, title V of the National Security Act of 1947 (see Appendix, page 42) provides that intelligence agencies may not spend funds available to them unless they have been both authorized and appropriated. This provision was adopted by Congress in 1985 to ensure that the oversight committees would have a voice in all resource decisions affecting intelligence activities.

Both oversight committees begin with the level of funds requested in the President's budget for intelligence and intelligence-related activities, which typically arrives in February or March of each year. The budget for intelligence activities is contained in the President's National Foreign Intelligence Program (NFIP) budget, which is submitted and justified to the Congress by the Director of Central Intelligence. The budget for "intelligence-related activities" is contained in a budget aggregation known as the Tactical Intelligence and Related Activities (TIARA) budget which is justified by the Secretary of Defense. (Although the Senate committee does not have authorizing authority over TIARA, it receives and analyzes the TIARA budget request and recommends actions on the Administration request to the Committee on Armed Services, which retains authorizing jurisdiction.)

The budget requests for NFIP and TIARA are very detailed funding plans, broken down first into major program categories (e.g., the General Defense Intelligence Program, the National Reconnaissance Program, the Consolidated Cryptologic Program, the FBI Foreign Counterintelligence Program, etc.), and then into specific elements under each major grouping. Specific allocations for both funding and personnel are made for each element. Both budget requests are highly classified.

Once the Administration request has been received, each committee engages in its own elaborate review of the request. These reviews typically are accomplished between February and May of each year and consist of formal hearings, staff visits or briefings, the submission of questions for written response by the agencies, and occasionally in-depth audits or investigations with respect to areas of particular concern to the committee.

On the basis of these reviews, the staffs of each committee formulate recommended positions on the Administration's request which are presented to their respective committees for review, modification, and approval. This takes place in a business meeting of each committee, referred to as the "mark-up" of the annual authorization bill. Typically, the views of the Administration on the proposal are made available to each committee prior to their taking action. Once the committee has "marked up," the bill is formally reported to the parent body, i.e., the House or Senate.

While the authorization bill reported to each parent body is public, the funding and personnel levels being recommended are classified by the Executive branch. The committees deal with this problem by giving legal effect, in the public bill, to a classified "schedule of authorizations" which is incorporated by reference in the public bill and is made available to the Executive branch. Members of the House and Senate are invited to review the schedule at the offices of each committee, but are not provided copies.

The public bill not only authorizes the intelligence budget for the next fiscal year, but also contains numerous legislative measures dealing with such intelligence matters as pension rights, health plans, authority to engage in business activities to provide cover for intelligence operations, etc. These legislative provisions are further explained in a committee report that, while not carrying the force of law, is still treated both by judges and by the Executive branch as a significant indicator of congressional intent.

There is no secret legislation in the intelligence authorization bill, but the classified "schedule of authorizations" is amplified by a classified report. This report gives the reasons for particular changes that the committee proposes to make in the budget submitted by the President. It also contains direction to the intelligence agencies, ranging from requests for particular studies to direction that particular programs or operations be undertaken, revised, or ended. These provisions are viewed by each committee and understood by the Executive branch to be the basis for the committee's willingness to authorize the intelligence budget. Although as report language they do not carry the force of law, they are generally obeyed by intelligence agencies in order to avoid antagonizing the oversight committees and risking a hostile reaction in the next year's budget cycle.

Once the committees have reported their bills to the floor, they are subject to sequential referral to other committees which have jurisdictional interests in the subject matter of the bill. Historically, in both Houses, the Committee on Armed Services has sought sequential referral of the intelligence authorization bill inasmuch as most of the funding and personnel levels being recommended pertain to elements within the Department of Defense. Other committees may also seek referral should they desire an opportunity to consider specific provisions.

Once the referrals to other committees have been completed, the bills are reported back to the floor by the committee which sought the referral and placed on the calendar for floor action. Historically, this has occurred between June and September of each year. On the floor, the bills are subject to amendment, according to the rules of each House, as is any piece of legislation. Any amendments to the classified "schedule of authorizations" are considered in a closed session of the House concerned, but such amendments have been very rare.

When both Houses have acted on their respective versions of the authorization bill, the body which acted last requests a "conference" with the other body to resolve the differences between the two bills. Typically, all members of the oversight committees in both Houses are appointed as "conferees." Preliminary to a meeting of the conferees, the staffs of both committees develop, where possible, a proposed resolution of the differences in funding between the two bills which is submitted to the conferees for their consideration. Where differences cannot be unresolved in the context of the staff proposal, items of disagreement are placed on the agenda for discussion between conferees. Again, the views of the Administration on the proposed staff resolution and on the issues remaining in dispute are made available to the conferees prior to the conference meeting.

In addition, there is close coordination at this stage with the Appropriations Committees in each House to ensure that the actions of the authorizing committees are generally consistent with those anticipated by the appropriating committees. If the authorizing committees provide authorization where the appropriating committees do not provide appropriations, the authorization is "hollow" or meaningless since funds cannot be spent that have not been appropriated. On the other hand, if the authorizing committees do not provide authorization where the appropriating committees provide appropriated funds, the intelligence agencies are precluded by law from spending the money appropriated. Thus, close coordination with the appropriations committees is essential at this juncture, prior to action by the conferees on the intelligence authorization.

Once agreement has been reached between the conferees, the conference agreement is reported, by a majority vote of the conferees from each House, back to each House for final action. Usually approval of the conference report occurs in September or October of each year, without substantial debate. The conference report contains both the final text of the bill and a "statement of conference managers" that explains the actions taken in conference. The conference report is also accompanied by the final "schedule of authorizations" and a classified explanation, which, like the reports of the individual committees, often contains specific directions to intelligence agencies.

The bill is then enrolled and sent to the President. Once signed, it becomes law. Should the bill be vetoed by the President, a two-thirds vote in each House is required to enact the bill into law.

LEGISLATION

Both oversight committees are legislative committees; that is, they are authorized to have bills within their area of jurisdiction referred to them for disposition and can report legislation to their respective bodies.

Traditionally the oversight committees have used the annual intelligence authorization bill as their primary legislative vehicle, not only for purposes of authorizing appropriations (described above), but also to enact other public law relating to intelligence. The CIA Inspector General Act of 1990, the Intelligence Oversight Act of 1991, and the Intelligence Organization Act of 1992, were each enacted as a separate title to the intelligence authorization bill for the fiscal year concerned. As alluded to above, the committees have also historically used the annual authorization bill to enact administrative authorities needed by intelligence agencies in order to carry out their functions. Indeed, the Administration routinely requests such legislation from the Congress.

Occasionally, the oversight committees have chosen to report "freestanding" bills—outside the context of the annual authorization—where it appears that legislation is needed before the authorization bill can be enacted or where another committee has a significant interest in the legislation, or where the legislation appears so consequential or controversial that the committees believe it preferable to handle such legislation separately. The Foreign Intelligence Surveillance Act of 1978, the Intelligence Identities Protection Act of 1983, and the CIA Voluntary Separation Incentive Act of 1993 were each processed by the committees as separate, "freestanding" bills.

INVESTIGATIONS, AUDITS, AND INQUIRIES

In addition to their legislative functions, the oversight committees are authorized to conduct investigations, audits and inquiries regarding intelligence activities as may be required. These may be prompted by a variety of circumstances: allegations in the news media; confidential communications by employees or former employees of intelligence agencies; or matters that have arisen in the course of the committee's hearings, briefings, or trips.

The committees may also institute investigations or inquiries involving matters that have been reported to the committees through official channels. Such reports come to the committees through a variety of sources. For example, pursuant to various statutes or agreements with Executive agencies, the committees receive periodic reports from the CIA

Inspector General describing his activities; from the Attorney General describing the use of court-ordered electronic surveillance for intelligence purposes; and from the Secretary of Defense advising of the deployment of intelligence assets in particularly sensitive circumstances. Frequently these reports lead to follow-on inquiries and perhaps full-fledged investigations.

Often, these inquiries and investigations involve classified matters which the committees cannot discuss publicly. However, both committees attempt, where possible, to issue public reports where the allegations of improprieties have themselves been public. In recent years, for example, the Senate committee has issued public reports of its investigation into allegations of improper domestic surveillance by the FBI; of its investigation of allegations that CIA may have intentionally withheld pertinent information from a federal court; and of its investigation into allegations that the Reagan White House had improperly withheld documents from the congressional Iran-contra committees.

Generally, the oversight committees refrain from involvement in individual cases unless the facts of a particular case appear to indicate systemic problems or policy shortcomings at the department or agency concerned. And, even here, the committees typically decline involvement when the complainant's case is before the courts or is being considered by the department or agency concerned.

ASSESSING WORLD EVENTS

Although not specifically required by their "charters," both oversight committees attempt to monitor and assess world events where U.S. interests are involved. Typically, this occurs in the form of briefings or hearings where representatives of intelligence agencies testify regarding the significance of these events and respond to questions from the members. In some cases, these briefings involve events which may be the subject of legislation pending before the Congress. Both committees, for example, received numerous briefings by intelligence agencies prior to the votes in each body in 1991 to commit U.S. armed forces to the liberation of Kuwait.

In some cases, the committees look back on events that have already taken place to assess the value of the intelligence support to U.S. policymakers or military commanders. Such assessments took place, for example, in both committees after the U.S. actions in Panama in 1989 and in Kuwait in 1991.

By making these assessments, the committees are able to test and evaluate the quality and timeliness of the intelligence analysis performed by elements of the Intelligence Community and come to understand the strengths and shortcomings of U.S. intelligence-gathering capabilities. This, in turn, affects the committees' respective actions on the budget and may suggest legislative initiatives as well.

CONFIRMATION OF PRESIDENTIAL APPOINTEES

Under the U.S. Constitution, certain Government officers are appointed by the President, "by and with the advice and consent of the Senate." Such positions include the Director of Central Intelligence, the Deputy Director of Central Intelligence, and the CIA Inspector General. In the Senate, the Select Committee on Intelligence reviews the nominations of individuals appointed to these positions.

The Senate Committee routinely explores the background of all nominees to assess the fitness of the nominee concerned as well as to identify possible conflicts of interest. It routinely investigates all allegations of improper conduct which might be made regarding the nominee either in the press or to the committee privately. The Chairman and Vice Chairman of the Committee are also provided access to the background investigation performed on the nominee by the FBI.

Public hearings are then conducted on the nomination where the nominee and others who have pertinent information to share regarding the nominee testify before the Committee. Depending upon the circumstances, these hearings have been the occasion for in depth inquiries into events of the past, as in the Robert Gates confirmation hearings in 1991, and typically provide an opportunity to learn the nominee's vision of the future, as was the case with the R. James Woolsey confirmation hearing in 1993.

In either event, the Senate committee has traditionally used these occasions not only to ascertain the views of the nominee with regard to intelligence, but also to obtain commitments from nominees towards the oversight process itself. Confirmation hearings not only serve to acquaint the Senate committee with the leaders of the Intelligence Community with whom it must closely work, but also to inform the nominee with respect to the views and concerns of the committee itself.

CONSIDERATION OF TREATIES

Under the U.S. Constitution, the President may ratify a treaty only if the Senate has consented to it. While treaties are typically referred to the Senate Committee on Foreign Relations, the Select Committee on Intelligence is routinely asked to evaluate arms control treaties and other similar agreements where the ability of the United States to determine violations by the other signatories is an issue for the Senate as a whole.

Typically, the Senate committee holds extensive hearings on the verification aspects of such treaties, and issues both classified and unclassified reports regarding its findings and recommendations. Such reports were issued with regard to the ability of the United States to verify the SALT II treaty in 1979; the INF treaty in 1988; the Threshold Test Ban Treaty and Treaty on Peaceful Nuclear Explosions in 1990; the CFE treaty in 1991; the START treaty in 1992; and the Open Skies treaty in 1993. The findings and recommendations contained in these reports are, in turn, ordinarily addressed in the reports issued by the Committee on Foreign Relations regarding the treaties themselves.

IV. OVERSIGHT IN PRACTICE: (1977–1995)

OVERSIGHT DURING THE CARTER ADMINISTRATION (1977–1980)

Coming to office on the heels of the Church and Pike Committee investigations, the Carter Administration sought to establish a clear legal framework for U.S. intelligence activities by working at two levels: first, by drafting a new Executive Order on intelligence activities; and second, in consultation with the two newly-formed congressional oversight committees, by developing legislation to establish in law the mission and functions of U.S. intelligence agencies.

Among the most important provisions of the new Executive order—Executive Order 12036 of January 26, 1978—was a requirement that the restrictions on intelligence-gathering contained in the order be implemented in regulations of each intelligence agency that would have to be approved by the Attorney General. This not only ensured consistency in approach throughout the Intelligence Community but also provided legal review external to intelligence agencies of the rules governing their activities.

Executive Order 12036 also, for the first time, directed the Director of Central Intelligence and the heads of intelligence agencies to keep the two congressional intelligence committees "fully and currently informed" of intelligence activities, including "significant anticipated activities," and to provide pertinent information in their possession to the oversight committees—subject to the constitutional authorities of the President and the statutory duty of the Director of Central Intelligence to protect intelligence sources and methods. This was the first binding direction to intelligence agencies to cooperate with their congressional oversight committees.

The effort to craft "charter legislation" for U.S. intelligence agencies did not fare so well. In 1978, the Senate committee introduced a detailed bill which not only set forth missions and functions for each agency, but also proposed complex restrictions and limitations upon the operations of each agency. After months of consultation and after ever-increasing objections from the intelligence agencies that the proposed restrictions would hamper them in accomplishing their missions, the Carter Administration eventually abandoned its effort to develop a bill agreeable to both itself and Congress, preferring instead to rely upon the new Executive order to provide the fundamentals of control.

Unable to reach agreement with the Administration on the "missions and functions" portion of the legislation, and deeply concerned over the Administration's failure to inform them of intelligence operations relating to the failed attempt to rescue U.S. hostages in Iran, the oversight committees turned their attention to the portion of the bill that would establish the legal obligations of intelligence agencies towards the two oversight committees. Months of negotiation eventually resulted in an agreement between the oversight committees and the Administration, ultimately enacted into law as Title V of the National Security Act of 1947, also known as "the Intelligence Oversight Act of 1980." (See appendix, p. 42.) Significantly, this legislation established as a matter of law (consistent with the constitutional responsibilities of the President) the obligation of intelligence agencies—

To keep the congressional intelligence committees "fully and currently informed";

To report "significant anticipated intelligence activities" to the committees;

To provide prior notice of covert actions to the committees and, where prior notice could not be provided, to provide notice "in a timely fashion"; and

To report violations of law and "significant intelligence failures" to the committees "in a timely fashion."

In return for the Administration's agreement to make the obligations of intelligence agencies to the oversight committees a matter of law, the Hughes-Ryan amendment was changed to require notice of covert actions only to the two intelligence committees (i.e., the legal requirement to notify six other committees was eliminated).

During this period, the committees continued to consolidate their positions within their respective bodies. In 1977, the Senate committee, with the agreement of the Committee on

Armed Services, assumed responsibility for reviewing presidential nominations of the Director and Deputy Director of Central Intelligence. In 1978, the committees produced the first bill authorizing appropriations for intelligence activities ever enacted by the Congress. (Previously, appropriations for intelligence were drawn from defense appropriations without systematic congressional review of intelligence activities.) Both committees held public hearings during this period on the issue of whether the dollar figure for the total intelligence budget should be made public. Investigations and inquiries were conducted by both bodies. While confusion with respect to the obligation of intelligence agencies to provide information to the committees remained considerable—notwithstanding the new 1980 law—it did not prevent either committee from carrying out investigations requiring access to highly sensitive information.

The committees also played a major role during this period in the enactment of legislation related to intelligence. Acting in concert with the Judiciary Committees in each House, the committees developed legislation known as the Foreign Intelligence Surveillance Act of 1978 (see appendix p. 65) which, for the first time, required that a court order be obtained from a special court established under the Act as a condition for undertaking electronic surveillances for intelligence purposes within the United States. Heretofore, such surveillances had been carried out without a search warrant or court order, pursuant to the asserted constitutional authority of the President. The committees were also instrumental in the enactment of the Classified Information Procedures Act of 1980, which established statutory procedures for handling classified information involved in a federal criminal proceeding. The law provided an in camera process for determining the relevance of classified information that a defendant might wish to use at trial and required federal judges to consider a variety of alternatives to protect national security information from being publicly disclosed during a criminal trial, rather than posing an "all or nothing" dilemma for the Government, i.e., reveal a secret or give up a prosecution.

OVERSIGHT DURING THE REAGAN ADMINISTRATION (1981–1988)

The Reagan Administration came to office with the express intent of reducing where appropriate the bureaucratic constraints placed upon intelligence agencies and increasing the level of resources available to these agencies, which had been sharply reduced during the 1970s.

It began by revising the Carter Executive order on intelligence, issuing Executive Order 12333 (see Appendix, p. 87) on December 4, 1981. The specific obligations of intelligence agencies contained in the Carter order pertaining to congressional oversight were replaced simply by a reference to the new oversight statute enacted the year before (see above). The new Administration also requested increased resources for intelligence, and these requests were generally supported by the oversight committees.

The new Administration also brought in a controversial Director of Central Intelligence, William J. Casey, and, for the first time, the oversight committees—particularly the Senate committee—took an aggressive role in investigating allegations concerning a sitting Director. Although DCI Casey had only recently been confirmed, the Select Committee on Intelligence opened an intensive investigation of allegations of improper conduct on the part of the new Director while he had been in the private sector, concluding that Casey was "not unfit to serve" as head of the CIA.

During the first Reagan Administration, new legislation—favorable to intelligence agencies—was enacted. In 1982, the Intelligence Identities Protection Act became law, making it a crime to reveal the identity of intelligence agents under certain circumstances. In 1984, the Central Intelligence Agency Information Act was passed, exempting certain CIA operational files from being searched in response to requests received by CIA under the Freedom of Information Act. The committees also looked closely at the implementation of the Foreign Intelligence Surveillance Act to assure themselves and the public that it was being administered properly.

During this period, the oversight committees became increasingly concerned with the role of U.S. intelligence agencies in Central America. Investigations were conducted into allegations that CIA may have been involved in political violence in El Salvador and Guatemala. Yet the issue which clearly caused the greatest concern was the CIA's role in the civil war taking place in Nicaragua. In one highly publicized incident which occurred in 1984, the Chairman and Vice-Chairman of the Senate Committee, Senators Goldwater and Moynihan, respectively, severely chastized Director Casey for failing to advise the Committee that CIA had participated in mining a harbor in Nicaragua. This led to renewed discussions with the Administration in terms of keeping the Committees "fully and currently informed" of developments in covert action operations which had previously been briefed to the Committees. Ultimately, an informal agreement, referred to as "the Casey Accords," was agreed to which provided that "memoranda of notification" would be provided the oversight committees to advise them of significant changes or developments in ongoing covert operations.

The committees also became increasingly involved during this period in congressional efforts to limit U.S. assistance to the Nicaraguan rebels. A series of funding restrictions— known collectively as the "Boland Amendments" (after the name of the original sponsor of the first such restriction, Congressman Edward Boland, Chairman of the House Permanent Select Committee on Intelligence)—placed limits on U.S. assistance by both intelligence and military elements of the U.S. Government and were enacted as part of annual authorization or appropriation bills.

Alarmed by a spate of serious espionage cases in 1985 and 1986 (e.g., the Walker-Whitworth case, the Pelton case, and Pollard case), both committees also undertook extensive reviews of U.S. counterintelligence and security policies and practices during this time period.

The second Reagan Administration produced what the committees regarded as the most serious breach of the oversight arrangements since the committees were created: the so-called Iran-contra affair. In November, 1986, the oversight committees learned for the first time that the President had approved a covert action finding ten months earlier authorizing the sale of arms to Iran in an effort to obtain the release of American hostages being held in Lebanon and had specifically ordered that the oversight committees not be notified. The committees also learned that Administration officials had used the proceeds of these sales to provide assistance to the Nicaraguan rebels at a time when the use of appropriated funds for such purpose was prohibited by law. It also came to light that certain officials in the Administration had entertained the idea of funding covert action programs with funds other than those which had been authorized and appropriated by the Congress, avoiding the congressional oversight process altogether. Both committees undertook intensive investigations of these events during November-December, 1986. These inquiries were followed by the appointment of special investigating committees in each House in January, 1987.

While the Iran-contra investigation was proceeding, both committees sought to shore up the existing oversight arrangements in light of what they had learned. While the Reagan Administration adopted new procedures recommitting itself to the oversight arrangements, bills were introduced in both Houses calling for notice to the committees of all covert actions within 48 hours of their approval without exception, and hearings were held on the bills in the fall of 1987.

In the meantime, with DCI Casey incapacitated by illness, the Administration nominated Deputy DCI Robert M. Gates to be the new Director in February, 1987. After a series of confirmation hearings by the Senate committee which highlighted the role of the nominee in the Iran-contra affair—then under investigation by the special investigating committee and by a special prosecutor—Gates asked that his nomination be withdrawn. The Administration then nominated Judge William H. Webster, who was then serving as Director of the FBI, to be the new Director of Central Intelligence. A second round of confirmation hearings ensued with Webster ultimately being confirmed by the Senate in May, 1987, after pledging to restore the trust and cooperative working relationship shattered by the Iran-contra affair.

Subsequently, the work of the special investigating committees ended and in October, 1987, the final report of the committees was issued, endorsing, among other things, the 48-hour bills then pending.

In the spring of 1988, the Senate passed a bill requiring 48-hour notice of covert actions by a vote of 71–19, but no action was taken in the House. The 48-hour bill thus died without being enacted, at a time when a new Administration was coming into office.

In the summer of 1988, the Senate committee undertook an extensive oversight inquiry into the FBI's investigation of a domestic political group, the Committee in Solidarity with the People of El Salvador (CISPES) during the early 1980s, finding several violations of existing guidelines for such investigations. As a result of this and an internal inquiry conducted by the FBI Inspection Division, six FBI agents were disciplined by the Director of the FBI.

OVERSIGHT DURING THE BUSH
ADMINISTRATION (1989–1992)

Met with pledges of commitment to the oversight process from the incoming Administration, the intelligence committees did not immediately press for enactment of the 48-hour bill, but sought instead to obtain a formal, written explanation from the new President with respect to how he intended to implement the statutory requirement to provide notice of covert actions "in a timely fashion." After several months of discussion, President Bush wrote to the oversight committees in October, 1989, saying that he would ordinarily provide prior notice of covert actions to the committees, but where that was not possible, he would provide notice "within a few days." Should notice be withheld for a longer period, the President stated, he would rely upon his authorities under the Constitution. In its version of the intelligence authorization bill for fiscal year 1990, the Senate adopted language which would have incorporated this formulation into the oversight statute itself, but this language was dropped from the bill in conference after the House committee disagreed with this proposal.

The oversight committees were able to agree, however, on one proposal growing out of the Iran-contra affair by including in the fiscal year 1990 intelligence authorization bill a provision calling for the creation of an independent Inspector General at the Central

Intelligence Agency appointed by the President rather than the Director with responsibilities to report directly to the oversight committees under certain circumstances. (See Appendix, p. 60.) This legislation marked the first time Congress had created by law an oversight mechanism within an intelligence agency.

During 1990, both committees renewed their efforts to modify the oversight statute to incorporate the understandings they believed had been reached with the President in terms of reporting covert actions to the Congress and to deal with other problems which had surfaced in the course of the Iran-contra affair. Relying upon informal assurances from senior Administration officials that the proposed language on these points was agreeable, the committees adopted language in the intelligence authorization bill for fiscal year 1991 which included a substantial revision of the Intelligence Oversight Act of 1980. The Administration subsequently had second thoughts regarding the proposed legislation and, after Congress had adjourned for the year, the President vetoed the bill.

This action led to further negotiations during the early part of 1991 to resolve the concerns of the Administration, and, after months of negotiation, a compromise was finally achieved, allowing for passage of the fiscal year 1991 intelligence authorization bill in August, 1991. (See Appendix, p. 42.) The bill revised the Intelligence Oversight Act of 1980 in its entirety and, among other things, provided that:

> Presidential approvals of covert actions must be in writing and cannot retroactively authorize such actions;
>
> Reports to the Congress must identify all government entities participating in the operation and state whether third parties outside of government control are involved;
>
> Covert actions cannot not be used to influence U.S. politics or domestic opinion;
>
> Covert actions cannot violate the laws of the United States or the U.S. Constitution; and
>
> Significant changes to ongoing operations must be approved by the President and reported to the committees in the same manner as the original operation.

Insofar as the longstanding issue of "timely" notice was concerned, the compromise left intact the existing statutory formulation requiring prior notice ordinarily and, where that is not possible, requiring notice "in a timely fashion." But for the first time, report language was included which said that the committees interpreted the phrase "in a timely fashion" as meaning "within a few days," consistent with the position previously taken by the President. While the report acknowledged that the President may assert authority under the Constitution to withhold for longer periods, the committees expressed the view that the Constitution did not provide such authority to the President. The issue was left at this philosophical impasse.

While the negotiations over the changes to the oversight statute were taking place during the summer of 1991, DCI Webster resigned, and the President nominated Robert M. Gates, whose nomination had been withdrawn four years earlier, to replace him. The Senate Committee held extensive hearings regarding the nomination, focusing particularly on the role of Gates in the Iran-contra affair and on allegations that he had slanted intelligence analysis at the CIA to conform to a particular political viewpoint. Indeed, the Gates hearings constituted the first in-depth exploration of the intelligence analytical process which had ever taken place in a public forum.

Despite the controversial nature of the hearings themselves, the Committee voted 11–4 to report the nomination, and Gates was confirmed by the Senate by a vote of 64–31 in October, 1991.

The new DCI immediately undertook an extensive reexamination of the role of the Intelligence Community in the post-Cold War era. The committees, for their part, followed suit. In January, 1992, the chairmen of both committees introduced far-reaching bills to reorganize the Intelligence Community, and extensive hearings on the legislation were undertaken by both bodies.

In the fall of 1992, after several months of negotiation between the Administration and the oversight committees, agreement was reached on "The Intelligence Organization Act of 1992," which amended the National Security Act of 1947 to provide explicitly for the responsibilities and authorities of the Director of Central Intelligence. (See Appendix, page 48.) Although the new law did not, as a practical matter, represent a radical departure from the status quo, it did represent a substantial change in the legal framework for U.S. intelligence activities. Among other things, the new law:

Recognized the role of the DCI as statutory advisor to the National Security Council;

Recognized the three roles of the DCI as (1) principal intelligence advisor to the President, (2) head of the U.S. Intelligence Community, and (3) head of the CIA;

Established in law the National Intelligence Council as the highest authority for developing and publishing intelligence analysis;

Gave the DCI responsibility for establishing priorities for U.S. Government intelligence-gathering and for coordinating all collection involving human sources, both overt and clandestine;

Gave the DCI authority to approve the budgets of intelligence agencies and provided that once approved, funds could not be reprogrammed to other purposes without the approval of the DCI; and

For the first time in statute, defined the term "Intelligence Community."

Indeed, the new law represented the first successful effort by the Congress to enact organizational legislation for the U.S. Intelligence Community since 1947.

In the fall of 1992, both committees undertook extensive investigations into allegations that CIA had provided false or misleading information to a federal criminal proceeding in Atlanta, Georgia, involving a branch manager of the Banca Nazionale Del Lavoro (BNL), headquartered in Rome, Italy. The Senate committee produced a lengthy report of its inquiry contained numerous recommendations for improving the relationship between intelligence agencies and law enforcement authorities.

OVERSIGHT IN THE CLINTON ADMINISTRATION (1993–)

The Clinton administration has continued the commitment to the congressional oversight process, but has as of this writing (mid-1994) undertaken no significant organizational or structural change within the Intelligence Community.

In 1993, freestanding legislation was enacted permitting the Director of Central Intelligence to offer financial incentives to senior employees to retire at an earlier date, in an effort to assist the CIA in meeting its manpower reduction objectives.

In 1994, in the wake of the arrest of a CIA employee and his wife for espionage, both committees conducted oversight inquiries into CIA security practices and reported legislative proposals to improve the U.S. counterintelligence and security posture. Supported by the Clinton administration, certain of the legislative proposals were enacted as part of the intelligence authorization bill for fiscal year 1995.

In particular, legislation was enacted to expand the Foreign Intelligence Surveillance Act to impose the same court order procedure to authorize physical searches for intelligence purposes as had existed for electronic surveillances since 1978. The legislation also contained provisions requiring improved coordination of counterintelligence matters with the FBI and provisions to enhance the investigative authorities of federal counterintelligence agencies.

The Congress also enacted legislation to create a new commission to review the roles and missions of U.S. intelligence agencies in the post-Cold War era, and charged it with producing a report to the President and the Congress by March 1, 1996. In essence, the commission was asked to reexamine the basic assumptions underlying the intelligence function. It was envisioned that this review, once completed, would provide the basis for subsequent actions by the intelligence committees for years to come.

THE FOREIGN INTELLIGENCE SURVEILLANCE ACT OF 1978

Editor's note: Congress passed another important intelligence oversight bill in between the Hughes-Ryan Act of 1974 (with its attention to covert action) and the Intelligence Oversight Act of 1980 (with its concern for prior notification about all significant foreign intelligence operations). It was called the Foreign Intelligence Surveillance Act—FISA, for short—and it set up a special court where the intelligence agencies or the White House could go to obtain a warrant for electronic or other forms of surveillance against suspected terrorists or other threats to the nation. The FISA warrant procedure became controversial in 2004 when the *New York Times* reported that the second Bush administration had been using the National Security Agency for electronic surveillance against terrorist suspects without first acquiring a warrant, as required by FISA. The language of the law is reprinted in this appendix.

FOREIGN INTELLIGENCE SURVEILLANCE

Section
1801. Definitions
1802. Electronic surveillance authorization without court order; certification by Attorney General; reports to congressional committees; transmittal under seal; duties and compensation of communication common carrier; applications; jurisdiction of court
1803. Designation of judges
    (a) Court to hear applications and grant orders; record of denial; transmittal to court of review
    (b) Court review; record, transmittal to Supreme Court
    (c) Expeditious conduct of proceedings; security measures for maintenance of records
    (d) Tenure

§ 1801. Definitions

As used in this title [50 USCS §§ 1801 et seq]:
    (a) "Foreign power" means—
      (1) a foreign government or any component thereof whether or not recognized by the United States;
      (2) a faction of a foreign nation or nations, not substantially composed of United States persons;

(3) an entity that is openly acknowledged by a foreign government or governments to be directed and controlled by such foreign government or governments;

(4) a group engaged in international terrorism or activities in preparation therefor;

(5) a foreign-based political organization, not substantially composed of United States persons; or

(6) an entity that is directed and controlled by a foreign government or governments.

(b) "Agent of a foreign power" means—

(1) any person other than a United States person, who—

(A) acts in the United States as an officer or employee of a foreign power, or as a member of a foreign power as defined in subsection (a)(4);

(B) acts for or on behalf of a foreign power which engages in clandestine intelligence activities in the United States contrary to the interests of the United States, when the circumstances of such person's presence in the United States indicate that such person may engage in such activities in the United States, or when such person knowingly aids or abets any person in the conduct of such activities or knowingly conspires with any person to engage in such activities; or

(2) any person who—

(A) knowingly engages in clandestine intelligence gathering activities for or on behalf of a foreign power, which activities involve or may involve a violation of the criminal statutes of the United States;

(B) pursuant to the direction of an intelligence service or network of a foreign power, knowingly engages in any other clandestine intelligence activities for or on behalf of such foreign power, which activities involve or are about to involve a violation of the criminal statues of the United States;

(C) knowingly engages in sabotage or international terrorism, or activities that are in preparation therefor, for or on behalf of a foreign power; or

(D) knowingly aids or abets any person in the conduct of activities described in subparagraph (A), (B), or (C) or knowingly conspires with any person to engage in activities described in subparagraph (A), (B), or (C).

(c) "International terrorism" means activities that—

(1) involve violent acts or acts dangerous to human life that are a violation of the criminal laws of the United States or of any State, or that would be a criminal violation if committed within the jurisdiction of the United States or any State;

(2) appear to be intended—

(A) to intimidate or coerce a civilian population;

(B) to influence the policy of a government by intimidation or coercion; or

(C) to affect the conduct of a government by assassination or kidnapping; and

(3) occur totally outside the United States or transcend national boundaries in terms of the means by which they are accomplished, the persons they appear intended to coerce or intimidate, or the locale in which their perpetrators operate or seek asylum.

(d) "Sabotage" means activities that involve a violation of chapter 105 of title 18, United States Code, [18 USCS §§ 2151 et seq.], or that would involve such a violation if committed against the United States.

(e) "Foreign intelligence information" means—

(1) information that relates to, and if concerning a United States person is necessary to, the ability of the United States to protect against—

(A) actual or potential attack or other grave hostile acts of a foreign power or an agent of a foreign power;

(B) sabotage or international terrorism by a foreign power or an agent of a foreign power; or

(C) clandestine intelligence activities by an intelligence service or network of a foreign power or by an agent of a foreign power; or

(2) information with respect to a foreign power or foreign territory that relates to, and if concerning a United States person is necessary to—

(A) the national defense or the security of the United States; or

(B) the conduct of the foreign affairs of the United States.

(f) "Electronic surveillance" means—

(1) the acquisition by an electronic, mechanical, or other surveillance device of the contents of any wire or radio communication sent by or intended to be received by a particular, known United States person who is in the United States, if the contents are acquired by intentionally targeting that United States person, under circumstances in which a person has a reasonable expectation of privacy and a warrant would be required for law enforcement purposes;

(2) the acquisition by an electronic, mechanical, or other surveillance device of the contents of any wire communication to or from a person in the United States, without the consent of any party thereto, if such acquisition occurs in the United States;

(3) the intentional acquisition by an electronic, mechanical, or other surveillance device of the contents of any radio communication, under circumstances in which a person has a reasonable expectation of privacy and a warrant would be required for law enforcement purposes, and if both the sender and all intended recipients are located within the United States; or

(4) the installation or use of an electronic, mechanical, or other surveillance device in the United States for monitoring to acquire information, other than from a wire or radio communication, under circumstances in which a person has a reasonable expectation of privacy and a warrant would be required for law enforcement purposes.

(g) "Attorney General" means the Attorney General of the United States (or Acting Attorney General) or the Deputy Attorney General.

(h) "Minimization procedures," with respect to electronic surveillance, means—

(1) specific procedures, which shall be adopted by the Attorney General, that are reasonably designed in light of the purpose and technique of the particular surveillance, to minimize the acquisition and retention, and prohibit the dissemination, of nonpublicly available information concerning unconsenting United States persons consistent with the need of the United States to obtain, produce, and disseminate foreign intelligence information;

(2) procedures that require that nonpublicly available information, which is not foreign intelligence information, as defined in subsection (e)(1), shall not be disseminated in a manner that identifies any United States person, without such person's consent, unless such person's identity is necessary to understand foreign intelligence information or assess its importance;

(3) notwithstanding paragraphs (1) and (2), procedures that allow for the retention and dissemination of information that is evidence of a crime which has been, is being, or is about to be committed and that is to be retained or disseminated for law enforcement purposes; and

(4) notwithstanding paragraphs (1), (2), and (3), with respect to any electronic surveillance approved pursuant to section 102(a) [50 USCS § 1802(a)], procedures that require that no contents of any communication to which a United States person is a party shall be disclosed, disseminated, or used for any purpose or retained for longer than twenty-four hours unless a court order under section 105 [50 USCS § 1805] is obtained or unless the Attorney General determines that the information indicates a threat of death or serious bodily harm to any person.

(i) "United States person" means a citizen of the United States, an alien lawfully admitted for permanent residence (as defined in section 101(a)(20) of the Immigration and Nationality Act [8 USCS § 1101(a)(20)]), an unincorporated association a substantial number of members of which are citizens of the United States or aliens lawfully admitted for permanent residence, or a corporation which is incorporated in the United States, but does not include a corporation or an association which is a foreign power, as defined in subsection (a)(1), (2), or (3).

(j) "United States," when used in a geographic sense, means all areas under the territorial sovereignty of the United States and the Trust Territory of the Pacific Islands.

(k) "Aggrieved person" means a person who is the target of an electronic surveillance or any other person whose communications or activities were subject to electronic surveillance.

(l) "Wire communication" means any communication while it is being carried by a wire, cable, or other like connection furnished or operated by any person engaged as a common carrier in providing or operating such facilities for the transmission of interstate or foreign communications.

(m) "Person" means any individual, including any officer or employee of the Federal Government, or any group, entity, association, corporation, or foreign power.

(n) "Contents," when used with respect to a communication, includes any information concerning the identity of the parties to such communication or the existence, substance, purport, or meaning of that communication.

(o) "State" means any State of the United States, the District of Columbia, the Commonwealth of Puerto Rico, the Trust Territory of the Pacific Islands, and any territory or possession of the United States.

(Oct. 25, 1978, P. L. 95–511, Title I, § 101, 92 Stat. 1783.)

HISTORY; ANCILLARY LAWS AND DIRECTIVES

Short titles:
Act Oct. 25, 1978, P. L. 95–511, § 1, 92 Stat. 1783, provided: "this Act [50 USCS §§ 1801 et seq., generally; for full classification of this Act, Consult USCS Tables volumes] may be cited as the 'Foreign Intelligence Surveillance Act of 1978'.".

Other provisions:
Effective date of Act Oct. 25, 1978; exception. Oct. 25, 1978, P. L. 95–511, Title III, § 301, 92 Stat. 1798, provided: "The provisions of this Act [50 USCS §§ 1801 et seq., generally; for full classification of the Act, consult USCS Tables volumes] and the amendments made hereby shall become effective upon the date of enactment of this Act [enacted Oct. 25, 1978], except that any electronic surveillance approved by the Attorney General to gather foreign intelligence information shall not be deemed unlawful for failure to follow the procedures of this Act, if that surveillance is terminated or an order approving that surveillance is obtained under title I of this Act [50 USCS §§ 1801 et seq.] within ninety days following the designation of the first judge pursuant to section 103 of this Act [50 USCS § 1803]."

RESEARCH GUIDE

Law Review Articles:
Shapiro, Foreign Intelligence Surveillance Act: Legislative Balancing of National Security and the Fourth Amendment. 15 Harvard Journal of Legislation 119, December, 1977.

United States v Butenko (494 F2d 593): Executive Authority to Conduct Warrantless Wiretaps for Foreign Security Purposes. 27 Hastings L J 705, January, 1976.

Nesson, Aspects of the Executive's Power Over National Security Matters: Secrecy Classifications and Foreign Intelligence Wiretaps. 49 Ind L J 399, Spring, 1974.

Wiretapping of an Alien Spy for Foreign Intelligence Purposes Does not Violate Communications Act of 1934 or Fourth Amendment. 8 NYU Journal of International Law and Politics 479, Winter, 1976.

Present and Proposed Standards for Foreign Intelligence Electronic Surveillance. 71 Northwestern L Rev 109, March-April, 1976.

Presidential Power to Conduct Electronic Surveillance for Foreign Affairs Purposes. 20 Villanova L Rev 833, March, 1975.

Fourth Amendment and Executive Authorization of Warrantless Foreign Security Surveillance. 1976 Washington U L Q 397, Spring, 1978.

Fourth Amendment and Judicial Review of Foreign Intelligence Wiretapping: Zweibon v. Mitchell (516 F2d 594). 45 George Washington L Rev 55, November, 1976.

§ 1802. Electronic surveillance authorization without court order; certification by Attorney General; reports to congressional committees; transmittal under seal; duties and compensation of communication common carrier; applications; jurisdiction of court

(a) (1) Notwithstanding any other law, the President, through the Attorney General, may authorize electronic surveillance without a court order under this title [50 USCS §§ 1801 et seq.] to acquire foreign intelligence information for periods of up to one year if the Attorney General certifies in writing under oath that—

(A) the electronic surveillance is solely directed at—

(i) the acquisition of the contents of communications transmitted by means of communications used exclusively between or among foreign powers, as defined in section 101(a) (1), (2), or (3) [50 USCS § 1801(a)(1), (2), or (3)]; or

(ii) the acquisition of technical intelligence, other than the spoken communications of individuals, from property or premises under the open and exclusive control of a foreign power, as defined in section 101(a) (1), (2), or (3) [50 USCS § 1801(a)(1), (2), or (3)];

(B) there is no substantial likelihood that the surveillance will acquire the contents of any communication to which a United States person is a party; and

(C) the proposed minimization procedures with respect to such surveillance meet the definition of minimization procedures under section 101(h) [50 USCS § 1801(h)]; and

if the Attorney General reports such minimization procedures and any changes thereto to the House Permanent Select Committee on Intelligence and the Senate Select Committee on Intelligence at least thirty days prior to their effective date, unless the Attorney General determines immediate action is required and notifies the committees immediately of such minimization procedures and the reason for their becoming effective immediately.

(2) An electronic surveillance authorized by this subsection may be conducted only in accordance with the Attorney General's certification and the minimization procedures adopted by him. The Attorney General shall assess compliance with such procedures and shall report such assessments to the House Permanent Select Committee on Intelligence and the Senate Select Committee on Intelligence under the provisions of section 108(a) [50 USCS § 1808(a)].

(3) The Attorney General shall immediately transmit under seal to the court established under section 103(a) [50 USCS § 1803(a)] a copy of his certification. Such certification shall be maintained under security measures established by the Chief Justice with the concurrence of the Attorney General, in consultation with the Director of Central Intelligence, and shall remain sealed unless—

    (A) an application for a court order with respect to the surveillance is made under sections 101(h)(4) and 104 [50 USCS §§ 1801(h)(4) and 1804]; or

    (B) the certification is necessary to determine the legality of the surveillance under section 106(f) [50 USCS § 1806(f)].

(4) With respect to electronic surveillance authorized by this subsection, the Attorney General may direct a specified communication common carrier to—

    (A) furnish all information, facilities, or technical assistance necessary to accomplish the electronic surveillance in such a manner as will protect its secrecy and produce a minimum of interference with the services that such carrier is providing its customers; and

    (B) maintain under security procedures approved by the Attorney General and the Director of Central Intelligence any records concerning the surveillance or the aid furnished which such carrier wishes to retain.

The Government shall compensate, at the prevailing rate, such carrier for furnishing such aid.

(b) Applications for a court order under this title [50 USCS §§ 1801 et seq.] are authorized if the President has, by written authorization, empowered the Attormy [Attorney] General to approve applications to the court having jurisdiction under section 103 [50 USCS § 1803] and a judge to whom an application is made may, notwithstanding any other law, grant an order, in conformity with section 105 [50 USCS § 1805], approving electronic surveillance of a foreign power or an agent of a foreign power for the purpose of obtaining foreign intelligence information, except that the court shall not have jurisdiction to grant any order approving electronic surveillance directed solely as described in paragraph (1)(A) of subsection (a) unless such surveillance may involve the acquisition of communications of any United States person.

(Oct. 25, 1978, P. L. 95–511, Title I, § 102, 92 Stat. 1786.)

HISTORY; ANCILLARY LAWS AND DIRECTIVES

Explanatory notes:

The bracketed word "Attorney" was inserted in subsec. (b) to denote word probably intended by Congress.

Effective date of section:

Act Oct. 25, 1978, P. L. 95–511, Title III, § 301, 92 Stat. 1798, provided that this section is generally effective on Oct. 25, 1978. For exception, see note containing Act Oct. 25, 1978, § 301, located at 50 USCS § 1801.

Other provisions:
Foreign intelligence electronic surveillance. Ex. Or. No. 12139 of May 23, 1979, 44 Fed. Reg. 30311, provided:

"1-101. Pursuant to Section 102(a)(1) of the Foreign Intelligence Surveillance Act of 1978 (50 U.S.C. 1802(a)) [subsec. (a)(1) of this section], the Attorney General is authorized to approve electronic surveillance to acquire foreign intelligence information without a court order, but only if the Attorney General makes the certifications required by that Section.

"1-102. Pursuant to Section 102(b) of the Foreign Intelligence Act of 1978 (50 U.S.C. 1802(b)) [subsec. (b) of this section], the Attorney General is authorized to approve applications to the court having jurisdiction under Section 103 of that Act [50 USCS § 1803] to obtain orders for electronic surveillance for the purpose of obtaining foreign intelligence information.

"1-103. Pursuant to Section 104(a)(7) of the Foreign Intelligence Surveillance Act of 1978 (50 U.S.C. 1804(a)(7)) [50 USCS § 1804(a)(7)], the following officials, each of whom is employed in the area of national security or defense, is designated to make the certifications required by Section 104(a)(7) of the Act in support of applications to conduct electronic surveillance:

"(a) Secretary of State.

"(b) Secretary of Defense.

"(c) Director of Central Intelligence.

"(d) Director of the Federal Bureau of Investigation.

"(e) Deputy Secretary of State.

"(f) Deputy Secretary of Defense.

"(g) Deputy Director of Central Intelligence.

"None of the above officials, nor anyone officially acting in that capacity, may exercise the authority to make the above certifications, unless that official has been appointed by the President with the advice and consent of the Senate.

"1-104. Section 2–202 of Executive Order No. 12036 is amended by inserting the following at the end of that section: 'Any electronic surveillance, as defined in the Foreign Intelligence Surveillance Act of 1978, shall be conducted in accordance with that Act as well as this Order.'.

"1-105. Section 2–203 of Executive Order No. 12036 is amended by inserting the following at the end of that section: 'Any monitoring which constitutes electronic surveillance as defined in the Foreign Intelligence Surveillance Act of 1978 shall be conducted in accordance with that Act as well as this Order.' "

§ 1803. Designation of judges

(a) Court to hear applications and grant orders; record of denial; transmittal to court of review. The Chief Justice of the United States shall publicly designate seven district court judges from seven of the United States judicial circuits who shall constitute a court which shall have jurisdiction to hear applications for and grant orders approving electronic surveillance anywhere within the United States under the procedures set forth in this Act, except that no judge designated under this subsection shall hear the same application for electronic surveillance under this Act which has been denied previously by another judge designated under this subsection. If any judge so designated denies an application for an order authorizing electronic surveillance under this Act, such judge shall provide immediately for the record a written statement of each reason for his decision and, on motion of the United States, the record shall be transmitted, under seal, to the court of review established in subsection (b).

(b) Court of review; record, transmittal to Supreme Court. The Chief Justice shall publicly designate three judges, one of whom shall be publicly designated as the presiding judge, from the United States district courts or courts of appeals who together shall comprise a court of review which shall have jurisdiction to review the denial of any application made under this Act. If such court determines that the application was properly denied, the court shall immediately provide for the record a written statement of each reason for its decision and, on petition of the United States for a writ of certiorari, the record shall be transmitted under seal to the Supreme Court, which shall have jurisdiction to review such decision.

(c) **Expeditious conduct of proceedings; security measures for maintenance of records.** Proceedings under this Act shall be conducted as expeditiously as possible. The record of proceedings under this Act, including applications made and orders granted, shall be maintained under security measures established by the Chief Justice in consultation with the Attorney General and the Director of Central Intelligence.

(d) **Tenure.** Each judge designated under this section shall so serve for a maximum of seven years and shall not be eligible for redesignation, except that the judges first designated under subsection (a) shall be designated for terms of from one to seven years so that one term expires each year, and that judges first designated under subsection (b) shall be designated for terms of three, five, and seven years.(Oct. 27, 1978, P. L. 95–511, Title I, § 103, 92 Stat. 1788.)

HISTORY; ANCILLARY LAWS AND DIRECTIVES

References in text:
"This Act," referred to in this section, is Act Oct. 25, 1978, P. L. 95–511, 92 Stat. 1783, popularly known as the Foreign Intelligence Surveillance Act of 1978, which is generally classified to 50 USCS §§ 1801 et seq. For full classification of this Act, consult USCS Tables volumes.

Effective date of section:
Act Oct. 25, 1978, P. L. 95–511, Title III, § 301, 92 Stat. 1798, provided that this section is generally effective on Oct. 25, 1978. For exception, see note containing Act Oct. 25, 1978, § 301, located at 50 USCS § 1801.

§ 1804. Applications for court orders

(a) **Submission by Federal officer; approval of Attorney General; contents.** Each application for an order approving electronic surveillance under this title [50 USCS §§ 1801 et seq.] shall be made by a Federal officer in writing upon oath or affirmation to a judge having jurisdiction under section 103 [50 USCS § 1803]. Each application shall require the approval of the Attorney General based upon his finding that it satisfies the criteria and requirements of such application as set forth in this title [50 USCS §§ 1801 et seq.]. It shall include—

(1) the identity of the Federal officer making the application;

(2) the authority conferred on the Attorney General by the President of the United States and the approval of the Attorney General to make the application;

(3) the identity, if known, or a description of the target of the electronic surveillance;

(4) a statement of the facts and circumstances relied upon by the applicant to justify his belief that—

(A) the target of the electronic surveillance is a foreign power or an agent of a foreign power; and

(B) each of the facilities or places at which the electronic surveillance is directed is being used, or is about to be used, by a foreign power or an agent of a foreign power;

(5) a statement of the proposed minimization procedures;

(6) a detailed description of the nature of the information sought and the type of communications or activities to be subjected to the surveillance;

(7) a certification or certifications by the Assistant to the President for National Security Affairs or an executive branch official or officials designated by the President from among those executive officers employed in the area of national security or defense and appointed by the President with the advice and consent of the Senate—

(A) that the certifying official deems the information sought to be foreign intelligence information;

(B) that the purpose of the surveillance is to obtain foreign intelligence information;

(C) that such information cannot reasonably be obtained by normal investigative techniques;

(D) that designates the type of foreign intelligence information being sought according to the categories described in section 101(e) [50 USCS § 1801(e)]; and

(E) including a statement of the basis for the certification that—

(i) the information sought is the type of foreign intelligence information designated; and

(ii) such information cannot reasonably be obtained by normal investigative techniques;

(8) a statement of the means by which the surveillance will be effected and a statement whether physical entry is required to effect the surveillance;

(9) a statement of the facts concerning all previous applications that have been made to any judge under this title [50 USCS §§ 1801 et seq.] involving any of the persons, facilities, or places specified in the application, and the action taken on each previous application;

(10) a statement of the period of time for which the electronic surveillance is required to be maintained, and if the nature of the intelligence gathering is such that the approval of the use of electronic surveillance under this title [50 USCS §§ 1801 et seq.] should not automatically terminate when the described type of information has first been obtained, a description of facts supporting the belief that additional information of the same type will be obtained thereafter; and

(11) whenever more than one electronic, mechanical or other surveillance device is to be used with respect to a particular proposed electronic surveillance, the coverage of the devices involved and what minimization procedures apply to information acquired by each device.

(b) Exclusion of certain information respecting foreign power targets. Whenever the target of the electronic surveillance is a foreign power, as defined in section 101(a)(1), (2), or (3) [50 USCS § 1801(a)(1), (2) or (3)], and each of the facilities or places at which the surveillance is directed is owned, leased, exclusively used by that foreign power, the application need not contain the information required by paragraphs (6), (7)(E), (8), and (11) of subsection (a) [50 USCS § 1801(a)(6), (7)(E), (8) and (11)], but shall state whether physical entry is required to effect the surveillance and shall contain such information about the surveillance techniques and communications or other information concerning United States persons likely to be obtained as may be necessary to assess the proposed minimization procedures.

(c) **Additional affidavits or certifications.** The Attorney General may require any other affidavit or certification from any other officer in connection with the application.

(d) **Additional information.** The judge may require the applicant to furnish such other information as may be necessary to make the determinations required by section 105 [50 USCS § 1805].

(Oct. 25, 1978, P. L. 95–511, Title I, § 104, 92 Stat. 1788.)

HISTORY; ANCILLARY LAWS AND DIRECTIVES

Effective date of section:
Act Oct. 25, 1978, P. L. 95–511, Title III, § 301, 92 Stat. 1798, provided that this section is generally effective on Oct. 25, 1978. For exception, see note containing Act Oct. 25, 1978, § 301, located at 50 USCS § 1801.

Other provisions:
Foreign intelligence electronic surveillance. For provisions governing electronic surveillance to acquire foreign intelligence information, see Ex. Or. No. 12139 of May 23, 1979, 44 Fed. Reg. 30311, located at 50 USCS § 1802 note.

§ 1805. Issuance of order

(a) **Necessary findings.** Upon an application made pursuant to section 104 [50 USCS § 1804], the judge shall enter an ex parte order as requested or as modified approving the electronic surveillance if he finds that—

(1) the President has authorized the Attorney General to approve applications for electronic surveillance for foreign intelligence information;

(2) the application has been made by a Federal officer and approved by the Attorney General;

(3) on the basis of the facts submitted by the applicant there is probable cause to believe that—

(A) the target of the electronic surveillance is a foreign power or agent of a foreign power: *Provided,* That no United States person may be considered a foreign power or an agent of a foreign power solely upon the basis of activities protected by the first amendment to the Constitution of the United States; and

(B) each of the facilities or places at which the electronic surveillance is directed is being used, or is about to be used, by a foreign power or an agent of a foreign power;

(4) the proposed minimization procedures meet the definition of minimization procedures under section 101(h) [50 USCS § 1804(h)]; and

(5) the application which has been filed contains all statements and certifications required by section 104 [50 USCS § 1804] and, if the target is a United States person, the certification or certifications are not clearly erroneous on the basis of the statement made under section 104(a)(7)(E) [50 USCS § 1804(a)(7)(E)] and any other information furnished under section 104(d) [50 USCS § 1804(d)].

(b) **Specifications and directions of orders.** An order approving an electronic surveillance under this section shall—

(1) specify—

(A) the identity, if known, or a description of the target of the electronic surveillance;

(B) the nature and location of each of the facilities or places at which the electronic surveillance will be directed;

(C) the type of information sought to be acquired and the type of communications or activities to be subjected to the surveillance;

(D) the means by which the electronic surveillance will be effected and whether physical entry will be used to effect the surveillance;

(E) the period of time during which the electronic surveillance is approved; and

(F) whenever more than one electronic, mechanical, or other surveillance device is to be used under the order, the authorized coverage of the devices involved and what minimization procedures shall apply to information subject to acquisition by each device; and

(2) direct—

(A) that the minimization procedures be followed;

(B) that, upon the request of the applicant, a specified communication or other common carrier, landlord, custodian, or other specified person furnish the applicant forthwith all information, facilities, or technical assistance necessary to accomplish the electronic surveillance in such a manner as will protect its secrecy and produce a minimum of interference with the services that such carrier, landlord, custodian, or other person is providing that target of electronic surveillance;

(C) that such carrier, landlord, custodian, or other person maintain under security procedures approved by the Attorney General and the Director of Central Intelligence any records concerning the surveillance or the aid furnished that such person wishes to retain; and

(D) that the applicant compensate, at the prevailing rate, such carrier, landlord, custodian, or other person for furnishing such aid.

(c) Exclusion of certain information respecting foreign power targets. Whenever the target of the electronic surveillance is a foreign power, as defined in section 101(a)(1), (2), or (3) [50 USCS § 1801(a)(1)(2), or (3)], and each of the facilities or places at which the surveillance is directed is owned, leased, or exclusively used by that foreign power, the order need not contain the information required by subparagraphs (C), (D), and (F) of subsection (b)(1) [50 USCS § 1801(b)(1)(C), (D), and (F)], but shall generally describe the information sought, the communications or activities to be subjected to the surveillance, and the type of electronic surveillance involved, including whether physical entry is required.

(d) Duration of order; extensions; review of circumstances under which information was acquired, retained or disseminated. (1) An order issued under this section may approve an electronic surveillance for the period necessary to achieve its purpose, or for ninety days, whichever is less, except that an order under this section shall approve an electronic surveillance targeted against a foreign power, as defined in section 101(a)(1), (2), or (3) [50 USCS § 1801(a)(1), (2) or (3)], for the period specified in the application or for one year, whichever is less.

(2) Extensions of an order issued under this title [50 USCS §§ 1801 et seq.], may be granted on the same basis as an original order upon an application for an extension and new findings made in the same manner as required for an original order, except

that an extension of an order under this Act for a surveillance targeted against a foreign power, as defined in section 101(a)(5) or (6) [50 USCS § 1801(a)(5) or (6)], or against a foreign power as defined in section 101(a)(4) [50 USCS § 1801(a)(4)] that is not a United States person, may be for a period not to exceed one year if the judge finds probable cause to believe that no communication of any individual United States person will be acquired during the period.

(3) At or before the end of the period of time for which electronic surveillance is approved by an order or an extension, the judge may assess compliance with the minimization procedures by reviewing the circumstances under which information concerning United States persons was acquired, retained, or disseminated.

(e) **Emergency orders.** Notwithstanding any other provision of this title [50 USCS §§ 1801 et seq.], when the Attorney General reasonably determines that—

(1) an emergency situation exists with respect to the employment of electronic surveillance to obtain foreign intelligence information before an order authorizing such surveillance can with due diligence be obtained; and

(2) the factual basis for issuance of an order under this title [50 USCS §§ 1801 et seq.] to approve such surveillance exists;

he may authorize the emergency employment of electronic surveillance if a judge having jurisdiction under section 103 [50 USCS § 1803] is informed by the Attorney General or his designee at the time of such authorization that the decision has been made to employ emergency electronic surveillance and if an application in accordance with this title [50 USCS §§ 1801 et seq.] is made to that judge as soon as practicable, but no more than twenty-four hours after the Attorney General authorizes such surveillance. If the Attorney General authorizes such emergency employment of electronic surveillance, he shall require that the minimization procedures required by this title [50 USCS §§ 1801 et seq.] for the issuance of a judicial order be followed. In the absence of a judicial order approving such electronic surveillance, the surveillance shall terminate when the information sought is obtained, when the application for the order is denied, or after the expiration of twenty-four hours from the time of authorization by the Attorney General, whichever is earliest. In the event that such application for approval is denied, or in any other case where the electronic surveillance is terminated and no order is issued approving the surveillance, no information obtained or evidence derived from such surveillance shall be received in evidence or otherwise disclosed in any trial, hearing, or other proceeding in or before any court, grand jury, department, office, agency, regulatory body, legislative committee, or other authority of the United States, a State, or political subdivision thereof, and no information concerning any United States person acquired from such surveillance shall subsequently be used or disclosed in any other manner by Federal officers or employees without the consent of such person, except with the approval of the Attorney General if the information indicates a threat of death or serious bodily harm to any person. A denial of the application made under this subsection may be reviewed as provided in section 103 [50 USCS § 1803].

(f) **Testing of electronic equipment; discovering unauthorized electronic surveillance; training of intelligence personnel.** Notwithstanding any other provision of this title [50 USCS §§ 1801 et seq.], officers, employees, or agents of the United States are authorized in the normal course of their official duties to conduct electronic surveillance not targeted against the communications of any particular person or persons, under procedures approved by the Attorney General, solely to—

    (1) test the capability of electronic equipment, if—

        (A) it is not reasonable to obtain the consent of the persons incidentally subjected to the surveillance;

        (B) the test is limited in extent and duration to that necessary to determine the capability of the equipment;

        (C) the contents of any communication acquired are retained and used only for the purpose of determining the capability of the equipment, are disclosed only to test personnel, and are destroyed before or immediately upon completion of the test; and:

        (D) *Provided,* That the test may exceed ninety days only with the prior approval of the Attorney General;

    (2) determine the existence and capability of electronic surveillance equipment being used by persons not authorized to conduct electronic surveillance, if—

        (A) it is not reasonable to obtain the consent of persons incidentally subjected to the surveillance;

        (B) such electronic surveillance is limited in extent and duration to that necessary to determine the existence and capability of such equipment; and

        (C) any information acquired by such surveillance is used only to enforce chapter 119 of title 18, United States Code [18 USCS §§ 2510 et seq.], or section 605 of the Communications Act of 1934 [47 USCS § 605], or to protect information from unauthorized surveillance; or

    (3) train intelligence personnel in the use of electronic surveillance equipment, if—

        (A) it is not reasonable to—

            (i) obtain the consent of the persons incidentally subjected to the surveillance;

            (ii) train persons in the course of surveillances otherwise authorized by this title [50 USCS §§ 1801 et seq.]; or

            (iii) train persons in the use of such equipment without engaging in electronic surveillance;

        (B) such electronic surveillance is limited in extent and duration to that necessary to train the personnel in the use of the equipment; and

        (C) no contents of any communication acquired are retained or disseminated for any purpose, but are destroyed as soon as reasonably possible.

(g) Retention of certifications, applications and orders. Certifications made by the Attorney General pursuant to section 102(a) [50 USCS § 1802(a)] and applications made and orders granted under this title [50 USCS §§ 1801 et seq.] shall be retained for a period of at least ten years from the date of the certification or application.

(Oct. 25, 1978, P. L. 95–511, Title I, § 105, 92 Stat. 1790.)

HISTORY; ANCILLARY LAWS AND DIRECTIVES

Reference in text:

"This Act," referred to in subsec. (d)(2), is Act Oct. 25, 1978, P. L. 95–511, 92 Stat. 1783, popularly known as the Foreign Intelligence Surveillance Act of 1978, which is generally classified to 50 USCS §§ 1801 et seq. For full classification of this Act, consult USCS Tables volumes.

Effective date of section:
Act Oct. 25, 1978, P. L. 95–511, Title III, § 301, 92 Stat. 1798, provided that this section is generally effective on Oct. 25, 1978. For exception, see note containing Act Oct. 25, 1978, § 301, located at 50 USCS § 1801.

§ 1806. Use of information

(a) **Compliance with minimization procedures; privileged communications; lawful purposes.** Information acquired from an electronic surveillance conducted pursuant to this title [50 USCS §§ 1801 et seq.] concerning any United States person may be used and disclosed by Federal officers and employees without the consent of the United States person only in accordance with the minimization procedures required by this title [50 USCS §§ 1801 et seq.]. No otherwise privileged communication obtained in accordance with, or in violation of, the provisions of this title [50 USCS §§ 1801 et seq.] shall lose its privileged character. No information acquired from an electronic surveillance pursuant to this title [50 USCS §§ 1801 et seq.] may be used or disclosed by Federal officers or employees except for lawful purposes.

(b) **Statement for disclosure.** No information acquired pursuant to this title [50 USCS §§ 1801 et seq.] shall be disclosed for law enforcement purposes unless such disclosure is accompanied by a statement that such information, or any information derived there-from, may only be used in a criminal proceeding with the advance authorization of the Attorney General.

(c) **Notification by United States.** Whenever the Government intends to enter into evidence or otherwise use or disclose in any trial, hearing, or other proceeding in or before any court, department, officer, agency, regulatory body, or other authority of the United States, against an aggrieved person, any information obtained or derived from an electronic surveillance of that aggrieved person pursuant to the authority of this title [50 USCS §§ 1801 et seq.], the Government shall, prior to the trial, hearing, or other proceeding or at a reasonable time prior to an effort to so disclose or so use that information or submit it in evidence, notify the aggrieved person and the court or other authority in which the information is to be disclosed or used that the Government intends to so disclose or so use such information.

(d) **Notification by States or political subdivisions.** Whenever any State or political subdivision thereof intends to enter into evidence or otherwise use or disclose in any trial, hearing, or other proceeding in or before any court, department, officer, agency, regulatory body, or other authority of a State or a political subdivision thereof, against an aggrieved person any information obtained or derived from an electronic surveillance of that aggrieved person pursuant to the authority of this title [50 USCS §§ 1801 et seq.], the State or political subdivision thereof shall notify the aggrieved person, the court or other authority in which the information is to be disclosed or used, and the Attorney General that the State or political subdivision thereof intends to so disclose or so use such information.

(e) **Motion to suppress.** Any person against whom evidence obtained or derived from an electronic surveillance to which he is an aggrieved person is to be, or has been, introduced or otherwise used or disclosed in any trial, hearing, or other proceeding in or before any court, department, officer, agency, regulatory body, or other authority of the United States, a State, or a political subdivision thereof, may move to suppress the evidence obtained or derived from such electronic surveillance on the grounds that—

(1) the information was unlawfully acquired; or

(2) the surveillance was not made in conformity with an order of authorization or approval.

Such a motion shall be made before the trial, hearing, or other proceeding unless there was no opportunity to make such a motion or the person was not aware of the grounds of the motion.

(f) In camera and ex parte review by district court. Whenever a court or other authority is notified pursuant to subsection (c) or (d), or whenever a motion is made pursuant to subsection (e), or whenever any motion or request is made by an aggrieved person pursuant to any other statute or rule of the United States of any State before any court or other authority of the United States or any state to discover or obtain applications or orders or other materials relating to electronic surveillance or to discover, obtain, or suppress evidence or information obtained or derived from electronic surveillance under this Act, the United States district court or, where the motion is made before another authority, the United States district court in the same district as the authority, shall, notwithstanding any other law, if the Attorney General files an affidavit under oath that disclosure or an adversary hearing would harm the national security of the United States, review in camera and ex parte the application, order, and such other materials relating to the surveillance as may be necessary to determine whether the surveillance of the aggrieved person was lawfully authorized and conducted. In making this determination, the court may disclose to the aggrieved person, under appropriate security procedures and protective orders, portions of the application, order, or other materials relating to the surveillance only where such disclosure is necessary to make an accurate determination of the legality of the surveillance.

(g) Suppression of evidence; denial of motion. If the United States district court pursuant to subsection (f) determines that the surveillance was not lawfully authorized or conducted, it shall, in accordance with the requirements of law, suppress the evidence which was unlawfully obtained or derived from electronic surveillance of the aggrieved person or otherwise grant the motion of the aggrieved person. If the court determines that the surveillance was lawfully authorized and conducted, it shall deny the motion of the aggrieved person except to the extent that due process requires discovery or disclosure.

(h) Finality of orders. Orders granting motions or requests under subsection (g), decisions under this section that electronic surveillance was not lawfully authorized or conducted, and orders of the United States district court requiring review or granting disclosure of applications, orders, or other materials relating to a surveillance shall be final orders and binding upon all courts of the United States and the several States except a United States court of appeals and the Supreme Court.

(i) Destruction of unintentionally acquired information. In circumstances involving the unintentional acquisition by an electronic, mechanical, or other surveillance device of the contents of any radio communication, under circumstances in which a person has a reasonable expectation of privacy and a warrant would be required for law enforcement purposes, and if both the sender and all intended recipients are located within the United States, such condents shall be destroyed upon recognition, unless the Attorney General determines that the contents indicate a threat of death or serious bodily harm to any person.

(j) Notification of emergency employment of electronic surveillance; contents; postponement, suspension or elimination. If an emergency employment of electronic surveillance is authorized under section 105(e) [50 USCS § 1805(e)] and a subsequent order approving the surveillance is not obtained, the judge shall cause to be served on any United States person named in the application and on such other United States persons subject to electronic surveillance as the judge may determine in his discretion it is in the interest of justice to serve, notice of—

(1) the fact of the application;

(2) the period of the surveillance; and

(3) the fact that during the period information was or was not obtained.

On an ex parte showing of good cause to the judge the serving of the notice required by this subsection may be postponed or suspended for a period not to exceed ninety days. Thereafter, on a further ex parte showing of good cause, the court shall forego ordering the serving of the notice required under this subsection.

(Oct. 25, 1978, P. L. 95–511, Title I, § 106, 92 Stat. 1793.)

HISTORY; ANCILLARY LAWS AND DIRECTIVES

Reference in text:
"This Act," referred to in subsec. (f), is Act Oct. 25, 1978, P. L. 95–511, 92 Stat. 1783, popularly known as the Foreign Intelligence Surveillance Act of 1978, which is generally classified to 50 USCS §§ 1801 et seq. For full classification of this Act, consult USCS Tables volumes.

Effective date of section:
Act Oct. 25, 1978, P. L. 95–511, Title III, § 301, 92 Stat. 1798, provided that this section is generally effective on Oct. 25, 1978. For exception, see note containing Act Oct. 25, 1978, § 301, located at 50 USCS § 1801.

§ 1807. Report to Administrative Office of the United States Court and to Congress

In April of each year, the Attorney General shall transmit to the Administrative Office of the United States Court and to Congress a report setting forth with respect to the preceding calendar year—

(a) the total number of applications made for orders and extensions of orders approving electronic surveillance under this title [50 USCS §§ 1801 et seq.]; and

(b) the total number of such orders and extensions either granted, modified, or denied.

(Oct. 25, 1978, P. L. 95–511, Title I, § 107, 92 Stat. 1795.)

HISTORY; ANCILLARY LAWS AND DIRECTIVES

Effective date of section:
Act Oct. 25, 1978, P. L. 95–511, Title III, § 301, 92 Stat. 1798, provided that this section is generally effective on Oct. 25, 1978. For exception, see note containing Act Oct. 25, 1978, § 301, located at 50 USCS § 1801.

§ 1808. Report of Attorney General to congressional committees; limitation on authority or responsibility of information gathering activities of congressional committees; report of congressional committees to Congress

(a) On a semiannual basis the Attorney General shall fully inform the House Permanent Select Committee on Intelligence and the Senate Select Committee on Intelligence concerning all electronic surveillance under this title [50 USCS §§ 1801 et seq.]. Nothing in this title [50 USCS §§ 1801 et seq.] shall be deemed to limit the authority and responsibility of the appropriate committees of each House of Congress to obtain such information as they may need to carry out their respective functions and duties.

(b) On or before one year after the effective date of this Act [50 USCS § 1801 note] and on the same day each year for four years thereafter, the Permanent Select Committee on Intelligence and the Senate Select Committee on Intelligence shall report respectively to the House of Representatives and the Senate, concerning the implementation of this Act. Said reports shall include but not be limited to an analysis and recommendations concerning whether this Act should be (1) amended, (2) repealed, or (3) permitted to continue in effect without amendment.

(Oct. 25, 1978, P. L. 95–511, Title I, § 108, 92 Stat. 1795.)

HISTORY; ANCILLARY LAWS AND DIRECTIVES

References in text:
"This Act," referred to in subsec. (b), is Act Oct. 25, 1978, P. L. 95–511, 92 Stat. 1783, popularly known as the Foreign Intelligence Surveillance Act of 1978, which is generally classified to 50 USCS §§ 1801 et seq. For full classification of this Act, consult USCS Tables volumes.

Effective date of section:
Act Oct. 25, 1978, P. L. 95–511, Title III, § 301, 92 Stat. 1798, provided that this section is generally effective on Oct. 25, 1978. For exception, see note containing Act Oct. 25, 1978, § 301, located at 50 USCS § 1801.

§ 1809. Criminal sanctions

(a) Prohibited activities. A person is guilty of an offense if he intentionally—
(1) engages in electronic surveillance under color of law except as authorized by statute; or
(2) discloses or uses information obtained under color of law by electronic surveillance, knowing or having reason to know that the information was obtained through electronic surveillance not authorized by statute.

(b) Defense. It is a defense to a prosecution under subsection (a) that the defendant was a law enforcement or investigative officer engaged in the course of his official duties and the electronic surveillance was authorized by and conducted pursuant to a search warrant or court order of a court of competent jurisdiction.

(c) Penalties. An offense described in this section is punishable by a fine of not more than $10,000 or imprisonment for not more than five years, or both.

(d) Federal jurisdiction. There is Federal jurisdiction over an offense under this section if the person committing the offense was an officer or employee of the United States at the time the offense was committed.

(Oct. 25, 1978, P. L. 95–511, Title I, § 109, 92 Stat. 1796.)

HISTORY; ANCILLARY LAWS AND DIRECTIVES

Effective date of section:
Act Oct. 25, 1978, P. L. 95–511, Title III, § 301, 92 Stat. 1798, provided that this section is generally effective on Oct. 25, 1978. For exception, see note containing Act Oct. 25, 1978, § 301, located at 50 USCS § 1801.

§ 1810. Civil liability

An aggrieved person, other than a foreign power or an agent of a foreign power, as defined in section 101(a) or (b)(1)(A) [50 USCS § 1801(a) or (b)(1)(A)], respectively, who has been subjected to an electronic surveillance or about whom information obtained by electronic surveillance of such person has been disclosed or used in violation of section 109 [50 USCS § 1809] shall have a cause of action against any person who committed such violation and shall be entitled to recover—
(a) actual damages, but not less than liquidated damages of $1,000 or $100 per day for each day of violation, whichever is greater;
(b) punitive damages; and
(c) reasonable attorney's fees and other investigation and litigation costs reasonably incurred.
(Oct. 25, 1978, P. L. 95–511, Title I, § 110, 92 Stat. 1796.)

HISTORY; ANCILLARY LAWS AND DIRECTIVES

Effective date of section:
Act Oct. 25, 1978, P. L. 95–511, Title III, § 301, 92 Stat. 1798, provided that this section is generally effective on Oct. 25, 1978. For exception, see note containing Act Oct. 25, 1978, § 301, located at 50 USCS § 1801.

§ 1811. Authorization during time of war

Notwithstanding any other law, the President, through the Attorney General, may authorize electronic surveillance without a court order under this title [50 USCS §§ 1801 et seq.] to acquire foreign intelligence information for a period not to exceed fifteen calendar days following a declaration of war by the Congress.
(Oct. 25, 1978, P. L. 95–511, Title I, § 111, 92 Stat. 1796.)

HISTORY; ANCILLARY LAWS AND DIRECTIVES

Effective date of section:
Act Oct. 25, 1978, P. L. 95–511, Title III, § 301, 92 Stat. 1798, provided that this section is generally effective on Oct. 25, 1978. For exception, see note containing Act Oct. 25, 1978, § 301, located at 50 USCS § 1801.

INDEX

An index to material contained in this title will be found at the end of 50 USCS Appendix; see subsequent volume.

APPENDIX C

THE INTELLIGENCE OVERSIGHT ACT OF 1980

Editor's note: The first important statute since 1947 to improve congressional supervision of America's secret services was the Hughes-Ryan Amendment of 1974 (see Appendix A of Volume 3). That law, however, dealt only with covert action. By 1980, Congress had decided to address all intelligence activities, including sensitive collection operations and counterintelligence. Initially, lawmakers had considered passing an omnibus act over 200 pages long, but backed away from such a comprehensive piece of legislation when the intelligence agencies strenuously objected and lobbied effectively to dismantle the "grand charter." In its place came the much abbreviated 1980 act. Though short, it nonetheless had teeth—particularly displayed in its provision that required advance notification of all important intelligence activities, going far beyond the "in a timely manner" reporting requirement embedded in the Hughes-Ryan Act.

(b)(I) The National Security Act of 1947 (50 U.S.C. 401 et seq.) is amended by adding at the end thereof the following new title:

"TITLE V—ACCOUNTABILITY FOR INTELLIGENCE ACTIVITIES

"CONGRESSIONAL OVERSIGHT

"SEC. 501. (a) To the extent consistent with all applicable authorities and duties, including those conferred by the Constitution upon the executive and legislative branches of the Government, and to the extent consistent with due regard for the protection from unauthorized disclosure of classified information and information relating to intelligence sources and methods, the Director of Central Intelligence and the heads of all departments, agencies, and other entities of the United States involved in intelligence activities shall—

"(I) keep the Select Committee on Intelligence of the Senate and the Permanent Select Committee on Intelligence of the House of Representatives (hereinafter in this section referred to as the 'intelligence committees') fully and currently informed of all intelligence activities which are the responsibility of, are engaged in by, or are carried out for or on behalf of, any department, agency, or entity of the United States, including any significant anticipated intelligence activity, except that (A) the foregoing provision shall not require approval of the intelligence committees as a condition precedent to the initiation of any such anticipated intelligence activity, and (B) if the President determines it is essential to limit prior notice to meet extraordinary circumstances affecting vital interests of the United States, such notice shall be limited to the chairman and ranking minority members of the intelligence committees, the Speaker and minority leader of the House of Representatives, and the majority and minority leaders of the Senate;

"(2) furnish any information or material concerning intelligence activities which is in the possession, custody, or control of any department, agency, or entity of the United States and which is requested by either of the intelligence committees in order to carry out its authorized responsibilities; and

"(3) report in a timely fashion to the intelligence committees any illegal intelligence activity or significant intelligence failure and any corrective action that has been taken or is planned to be taken in connection with such illegal activity or failure.

(b) The President shall fully inform the intelligence committees in a timely fashion of intelligence operations in foreign countries, other than activities intended solely for obtaining necessary intelligence, for which prior notice was not given under subsection (a) and shall provide a statement of the reasons for not giving prior notice.

"(c) The President and the intelligence committees shall each establish such procedures as may be necessary to carry out the provisions of subsections (a) and (b).

"(d) The House of Representatives and the Senate, in consultation with the Director of Central Intelligence, shall each establish, by rule or resolution of such House, procedures to protect from unauthorized disclosure all classified information and all information relating to intelligence sources and methods furnished to the intelligence committees or to Members of the Congress under this section. In accordance with such procedures, each of the intelligence communities shall promptly call to the attention of its respective House, or to any appropriate committee or committees of its respective House, any matter relating to intelligence activities requiring the attention of such House or such committee or committees.

"(e) Nothing in this Act shall be construed as authority to withhold information from the intelligence committees on the grounds that providing the information to the intelligence committees would constitute the unauthorized disclosure of classified information or information relating to intelligence sources and methods."

(2) The table of contents at the beginning of such Act is amended by adding at the end thereof the following:

"TITLE V—ACCOUNTABILITY FOR INTELLIGENCE ACTIVITIES

"Sec. 501. Congressional oversight."

APPENDIX D

THE INTELLIGENCE OVERSIGHT ACT OF 1991

Editor's note: In the aftermath of the Iran-*contra* affair, lawmakers tried again to improve the statutory framework for intelligence accountability. The result was the Intelligence Oversight Act of 1991, reprinted here, which defined covert action more sharply; required the President to sign all "findings" (oral approvals, as used by President Ronald Reagan, would no longer suffice); and clarified the reporting requirements for covert actions, with a slight congressional concession in favor of presidential delay in reporting during times of acute national emergencies. In such cases, the president could postpone reporting for a couple of days, rather than honoring the "prior notice" provision of the 1980 Intelligence Oversight Act.

TITLE V—ACCOUNTABILITY FOR INTELLIGENCE ACTIVITIES[1]

GENERAL CONGRESSIONAL OVERSIGHT PROVISIONS

SEC. 501. [50 U.S.C. 413] (a) (1) The President shall ensure that the intelligence committees are kept fully and currently informed of the intelligence activities of the United States, including any significant anticipated intelligence activity as required by this title.

(2) As used in this title, the term "intelligence committees" means the Select Committee on Intelligence of the Senate and the Permanent Select Committee on Intelligence of the House of Representatives.

---

[1] This title is also set out *post* at page 409 along with other materials relating to congressional oversight of intelligence activities.

(3) Nothing in this title shall be construed as requiring the approval of the intelligence committees as a condition precedent to the initiation of any significant anticipated intelligence activity.

(b) The President shall ensure that any illegal intelligence activity is reported promptly to the intelligence committees, as well as any corrective action that has been taken or is planned in connection with such illegal activity.

(c) The President and the intelligence committees shall each establish such procedures as may be necessary to carry out the provisions of this title.

(d) The House of Representatives and the Senate shall each establish, by rule or resolution of such House, procedures to protect from unauthorized disclosure all classified information, and all information relating to intelligence sources and methods, that is furnished to the intelligence committees or to Members of Congress under this title. Such procedures shall be established in consultation with the Director of Central Intelligence. In accordance with such procedures, each of the intelligence committees shall promptly call to the attention of its respective House, or to any appropriate committee or committees of its respective House, any matter relating to intelligence activities requiring the attention of such House or such committee or committees.

(e) Nothing in this Act shall be construed as authority to withhold information from the intelligence committees on the grounds that providing the information to the intelligence committees would constitute the unauthorized disclosure of classified information or information relating to intelligence sources and methods.

(f) As used in this section, the term "intelligence activities" includes covert actions as defined in section 503(e).

REPORTING OF INTELLIGENCE ACTIVITIES
OTHER THAN COVERT ACTIONS

SEC 502. [50 U.S.C. 413a] To the extent consistent with due regard for the protection from unauthorized disclosure of classified information relating to sensitive intelligence sources and methods or other exceptionally sensitive matters, the Director of Central Intelligence and the heads of all departments, agencies, and other entities of the United States Government involved in intelligence activities shall—

(1) keep the intelligence committees fully, and currently informed of all intelligence activities, other than a covert action (as defined in section 503(e)), which are the responsibility of, are engaged in by, or are carried out for or on behalf of, any department, agency, or entity of the United States Government, including any significant anticipated intelligence activity and any significant intelligence failure; and

(2) furnish the intelligence committees any information or material concerning intelligence activities, other than covert actions, which is within their custody or control, and which is requested by either of the intelligence committees in order to carry out its authorized responsibilities.

PRESIDENTIAL APPROVAL AND REPORTING
OF COVERT ACTIONS

SEC 503. [50 U.S.C. 413b] (a) The President may not authorize the conduct of a covert action by departments, agencies, or entities of the United States Government unless the

President determines such an action is necessary to support identifiable foreign policy objectives of the United States and is important to the national security of the United States, which determination shall be set forth in a finding that shall meet each of the following conditions:

(1) Each finding shall be in writing, unless immediate action by the United States is required and time does not permit the preparation of a written finding, in which case a written record of the President's decision shall be contemporaneously made and shall be reduced to a written finding as soon as possible but in no event more than 48 hours after the decision is made.

(2) Except as permitted by paragraph (1), a finding may not authorize or sanction a covert action, or any aspect of any such action, which already has occurred.

(3) Each finding shall specify each department, agency, or entity of the United States Government authorized to fund or otherwise participate in any significant way in such action. Any employee, contractor, or contract agent of a department, agency, or entity of the United States Government other than the Central Intelligence Agency directed to participate in any way in a covert action shall be subject either to the policies and regulations of the Central Intelligence Agency, or to written policies or regulations adopted by such department, agency, or entity, to govern such participation.

(4) Each finding shall specify whether it is contemplated that any third party which is not an element of, or a contractor or contract agent of, the United States Government, or is not otherwise subject to United States Government policies and regulations, will be used to fund or otherwise participate in any significant way in the covert action concerned, or be used to undertake the covert action concerned on behalf of the United States.

(5) A finding may not authorize any action that would violate the Constitution or any statute of the United States.

(b) To the extent consistent with due regard for the protection from unauthorized disclosure of classified information relating to sensitive intelligence sources and methods or other exceptionally sensitive matters, the Director of Central Intelligence and the heads of all departments, agencies, and entities of the United States Government involved in a covert action—

(1) shall keep the intelligence committees fully and currently informed of all covert actions which are the responsibility of, are engaged in by, or are carried out for or on behalf of, any department, agency, or entity of the United States Government, including significant failures; and

(2) shall furnish to the intelligence committees any information or material concerning covert actions which is in the possession, custody, or control of any department, agency, or entity of the United States Government and which is requested by either of the intelligence committees in order to carry out its authorized responsibilities.

(c)(1) The President shall ensure that any finding approved pursuant to subsection (a) shall be reported to the intelligence committees as soon as possible after such approval and before the initiation of the covert action authorized by the finding, except as otherwise provided in paragraph (2) and paragrap (3).

(2) If the President determines that it is essential to limit access to the finding to meet extraordinary circumstances affecting vital interests of the United States, the finding may

be reported to the chairmen and ranking minority members of the intelligence committees, the Speaker and minority leader of the House of Representatives, the majority and minority leaders of the Senate, and such other member or members of the congressional leadership as may be included by the President.

(3) Whenever a finding is not reported pursuant to paragraph (1) or (2) of this section, the President shall fully inform the intelligence committees in a timely fashion and shall provide a statement of the reasons for not giving prior notice.

(4) In a case under paragraph (1), (2), or (3), a copy of the finding, signed by the President, shall be provided to the chairman of each intelligence committee. When access to a finding is limited to the Members of Congress specified in paragraph (2), a statement of the reasons for limiting such access shall also be provided.

(d) The President shall ensure that the intelligence committees, or, if applicable, the Members of Congress specified in subsection (c)(2), are notified of any significant change in a previously approved covert action, or any significant undertaking pursuant to a previously approved finding, in the same manner as findings are reported pursuant to subsection (c).

(e) As used in this title, the term "covert action" means an activity or activities of the United States Government to influence political, economic, or military conditions abroad, where it is intended that the role of the United States Government will not be apparent or acknowledged publicly, but does not include—

(1) activities the primary purpose of which is to acquire intelligence, traditional counterintelligence activities, traditional activities to improve or maintain the operational security of United States Government programs, or administrative activities;

(2) traditional diplomatic or military activities or routine support to such activities;

(3) traditional law enforcement activities conducted by United States Government law enforcement agencies or routine support to such activities; or

(4) activities to provide routine support to the overt activities (other than activities described in paragraph (1), (2), or (3)) of other United States Government agencies abroad.

(f) No covert action may be conducted which is intended to influence United States political processes, public opinion, policies, or media.

FUNDING OF INTELLIGENCE ACTIVITIES

SEC 504. [50 U.S.C. 414] (a) Appropriated funds available to an intelligence agency may be obligated or expended for an intelligence or intelligence-related activity only if—

(1) those funds were specifically authorized by the Congress for use for such activities; or

(2) in the case of funds from the Reserve for Contingencies of the Central Intelligence Agency and consistent with the provisions of section 503 of this Act concerning any significant anticipated intelligence activity, the Director of Central Intelligence has notified the appropriate congressional committees of the intent to make such funds available for such activity; or

(3) in the case of funds specifically authorized by the Congress for a different activity—

(A) the activity to be funded is a higher priority intelligence or intelligence-related activity;

(B) the need for funds for such activity is based on unforseen requirements; and

(C) the Director of Central Intelligence, the Secretary of Defense, or the Attorney General, as appropriate, has notified the appropriate congressional committees of the intent to make such funds available for such activity;

(4) nothing in this subsection prohibits obligation or expenditure of funds available to an intelligence agency in accordance with sections 1535 and 1536 of title 31, United States Code.

(b) Funds available to an intelligence agency may not be made available for any intelligence or intelligence-related activity for which funds were denied by the Congress.

(c) No funds appropriated for, or otherwise available to, any department, agency, or entity of the United States Government may be expended, or may be directed to be expended, for any covert action, as defined in section 503(e), unless and until a Presidential finding required by subsection (a) of section 503 has been signed or otherwise issued in accordance with that subsection.

(d)(1) Except as otherwise specifically provided by law, funds available to an intelligence agency that are not appropriated funds may be obligated or expended for an intelligence or intelligence-related activity only if those funds are used for activities reported to the appropriate congressional committees pursuant to procedures which identify—

(A) the types of activities for which nonappropriated funds may be expended; and

(B) the circumstances under which an activity must be reported as a significant anticipated intelligence activity before such funds can be expended.

(2) Procedures for purposes of paragraph (1) shall be jointly agreed upon by the intelligence committees and, as appropriate, the Director of Central Intelligence or the Secretary of Defense.

(e) As used in this section—

(1) the term "intelligence agency" means any department, agency, or other entity of the United States involved in intelligence or intelligence-related activities;

(2) the term "appropriate congressional committees" means the Permanent Select Committee on Intelligence and the Committee on Appropriations of the House of Representatives and the Select Committee on Intelligence and the Committee on Appropriations of the Senate; and

(3) the term "specifically authorized by the Congress" means that—

(A) the activity and the amount of funds proposed to be used for that activity were identified in a formal budget request to the Congress, but funds shall be deemed to be specifically authorized for that activity only to the extent that the Congress both authorized the funds to be appropriated for that activity and appropriated the funds for that activity; or

(B) although the funds were not formally requested, the Congress both specifically authorized the appropriation of the funds for the activity and appropriated the funds for the activity.

NOTICE TO CONGRESS OF CERTAIN TRANSFERS OF
DEFENSE ARTICLES AND DEFENSE SERVICES

SEC 505. [50 U.S.C. 415] (a)(1) The transfer of a defense article or defense service, or the anticipated transfer in any fiscal year of any aggregation of defense articles or defense services, exceeding $1,000,000 in value by an intelligence agency to a recipient outside that agency shall be considered a significant anticipated intelligence activity for the purpose of this title.

(2) Paragraph (1) does not apply if—

(A) the transfer is being made to a department, agency, or other entity of the United States (so long as there will not be a subsequent retransfer of the defense articles or defense services outside the United States Government in conjunction with an intelligence or intelligence-related activity); or

(B) the transfer—

(i) is being made pursuant to authorities contained in part II of the Foreign Assistance Act of 1961, the Arms Export Control Act, title 10 of the United States Code (including a law enacted pursuant to section 7307(b)(1) of that title), or the Federal Property and Administrative Services Act of 1949, and

(ii) is not being made in conjunction with an intelligence or intelligence-related activity.

(3) An intelligence agency may not transfer any defense articles or defense services outside the agency in conjunction with any intelligence or intelligence-related activity for which funds were denied by the Congress.

(b) As used in this section—

(1) the term "intelligence agency" means any department, agency, or other entity of the United States involved in intelligence or intelligence-related activities;

(2) the terms "defense articles" and "defense services" mean the items on the United States Munitions List pursuant to section 38 of the Arms Export Control Act (22 CFR part 121);

(3) the term "transfer" means—

(A) in the case of defense articles, the transfer of possession of those articles; and

(B) in the case of defense services, the provision of those services; and

(4) the term "value" means—

(A) in the case of defense articles, the greater of—

(i) the original acquisition cost to the United States Government, plus the cost of improvements or other modifications made by or on behalf of the Government; or

(ii) the replacement cost; and

(B) in the case of defense services, the full cost to the Government of providing the services.

APPENDIX E

HOUSE PERMANENT SELECT COMMITTEE ON INTELLIGENCE CONCLUSIONS ON INTELLIGENCE OVERSIGHT, 1996

Editor's note: In 1995–96, both the White House and the U.S. House conducted inquiries into the state of intelligence, prompted by the revelations about the Aldrich Ames counterintelligence failure as well as a sense that the end of the Cold War meant dramatic changes would be necessary in America's global intelligence activities. The Aspin-Brown Commission led the White House inquiry. The House Permanent Select Committee on Intelligence named its investigation "IC21," standing for the Intelligence Community in the 21st century. This appendix offers the summary conclusions of the House Committee on how to improve intelligence oversight.

CONGRESSIONAL OVERSIGHT

The modern system of congressional oversight of intelligence—select committees in the House and in the Senate specifically devoted to intelligence—is almost twenty years old. Reviewing the strengths and weaknesses of this system, as well as the contribution that congressional oversight can and should make to intelligence is appropriate as part of the larger *IC21* study.

Issues regarding congressional oversight fall into two large categories: the general nature of how Congress carries out oversight and specific issues of organization and process related to intelligence oversight. Although this report touches on some generic issues of intelligence oversight, its findings and recommendations are restricted to the way in which the House of Representatives handles this function.

Source: "IC21: Intelligence Community in the 21st Century," *Staff Study*, Permanent Select Committee on Intelligence, House of Representatives, 104th Cong. 2d Sess. (1996), pp. 313–330.

BACKGROUND: EVOLUTION OF CONGRESSIONAL OVERSIGHT OF INTELLIGENCE

It is important to recall how the current intelligence oversight system came into being. The two select committees were the direct result of the congressional (and executive) investigations into U.S. intelligence activities in 1975–76. Both Houses came to the conclusion that the past oversight system had been inadequate in terms of both the vigor with which it was carried out[1] and the very limited number of Members who were privy to intelligence-related information. That older system reflected the gentleman's agreement nature of oversight that evolved during the Cold War. It accepted the necessity of intelligence—and especially of intelligence activities (i.e., covert action), but treated them in an extraordinary manner because of their highly classified and extremely sensitive nature.

The House Permanent Select Committee on Intelligence (HPSCI) was established on July 14, 1977 by H. Res. 658 of the 95th Congress and is governed by Rule XLVIII of the Rules of the House. The current system attempted to correct the main flaws in the older system in two major ways. First, the House decided that a committee with specific oversight over intelligence (albeit with different jurisdictions in the House and Senate) was necessary to ensure more vigorous and regular oversight. Second, in order to broaden the oversight base, each committee has "cross-over" Members from other committees that have an interest in intelligence or intelligence related issues: Appropriations; International Relations; Judiciary; and National Security.

However, and this is perhaps ironic, the House continued to treat intelligence as something extraordinary, rather than as an accepted function of government similar to any others that are subject to oversight. This is reflected in two aspects of HPSCI. First, it is a select committee rather than a standing committee. Second, and derived from the first, are the rules limiting the length of consecutive service on the Committee. These tenure rules arose from the perception that the past intelligence overseers had grown "too cozy" with the intelligence agencies, thus becoming less vigorous in their oversight. Rotating the membership on a regular basis, it was believed, would avoid this type of overly close and potentially less critical relationship in the future.

THE NATURE OF OVERSIGHT: ADVERSARY VS. ADVOCATE

Each committee charged with congressional oversight has a dual responsibility. The most obvious is to oversee the various agencies under its mandate, approve their budgets, investigate known or suspected problems, and report back to the House on these matters. Recognizing the impossibility of each Member being conversant with (or intensely

---

[1] The most-oft cited example of the problem was the quote from Senator Leverett Saltonstall, a member of the Armed Services Committee, which was responsible for intelligence oversight. When asked by Senator Mike Mansfield why there had only been two committee meetings with the CIA in the past year, Senator Saltonstall replied: "... it is not a question of reluctance on the part of the CIA officials to speak to us. Instead, it is a question of our reluctance, if you will, to seek information and knowledge on subjects which I personally, as a Member of Congress and as a citizen, would rather not have, unless I believed it to be my responsibility to have it because it might involve the lives of American citizens." *Congressional Record,* April 9, 1956, p. 5924.

interested in) all issues, the committee system delegates responsibility to the committees and accepts their leadership in specific areas. Given the checks and balances nature of the congressional-executive relationship, each committee has, at some level, an adversarial role with its Executive Branch opposites. The relationship need not be overtly or continuously hostile, but there is inevitably a certain amount of friction involved.

The responsibility for being the House's resident experts on given programs and agencies also gives rise to a second role for each oversight committee, that of advocacy for those agencies and programs. It is only natural that those Members most interested in and most conversant with agencies and programs will also, on occasion, be their advocates. Increasingly constrained debates over budget shares, disinterest or outright hostility from other Members about agencies or programs for a wide variety of reasons, all put oversight committees in this advocacy role as well.

Oversight, if carried out properly, should be a combination of these two roles. An excessive concentration on either will damage the ability of the committee to handle its issues effectively and can undermine the credibility of that committee among its colleagues.

However, it is not clear that this norm of oversight behavior is widely accepted as proper for HPSCI. The fact that intelligence continues to be handled as an extraordinary issue in terms of oversight—by virtue of a select committee and tenure limits—suggests that it was at least expected at its origin that HPSCI would largely eschew advocacy role and that this expected emphasis on adversary rather than advocate has been tacitly accepted over the last twenty years.

There remains a lingering uneasiness about intelligence and its role in the U.S. government that will never be completely resolved. At some level, the concept of secret agencies with classified budgets runs counter to some deeply felt view of what and how the U.S. government should behave. However, this less than full acceptance may actually be heightened rather than pacified by the current oversight system, which treats intelligence in a manner different from other government activities.

Interestingly, several witnesses who appeared before HPSCI during *IC21* hearings made the same point: intelligence, unlike virtually all other functions of government, has no natural advocates in the public at large. Its direct effect on the lives of most citizens is largely unfelt or unseen; its industrial base is too rarefied to build a large constituency in many areas; it is largely an "inside the Beltway" phenomenon in terms of location, logistics, budget and concern. The only places where intelligence can hope to find some base level of support are from its Executive Branch masters and its congressional overseers.[2]

By having HPSCI as a select committee, Congress is, in effect, *elevating* intelligence. It is seen as an extraordinary issue requiring congressional organizational responses that depart from the norm. At some levels, this view of intelligence is accurate, but this also adds to the mystique that too often surrounds intelligence and often engenders wariness about it on the part of some Members. By making HPSCI a standing committee, intelligence would be treated like other "normal" functions of government. Making intelligence a less extraordinary issue might actually have positive effects, in that by being seen as less unique the very *raison* of the IC might not be questioned as much.

---

[2] Testimony of Richard Helms and James Schlesinger before House Permanent Select Committee on Intelligence on May 22, 1995.

THE PROPRIETY OF CONGRESSIONAL OVERSIGHT OF INTELLIGENCE

Not surprisingly, we believe that the modern oversight system for intelligence residing in committees specifically devoted to that task has worked well. The House and Senate committees have achieved the two main goals of their founders in the 94th and 95th Congresses, creating a system that is more vigorous and more rigorous and is more broadly based than the previous system. All oversight is imperfect and is always limited by the degree to which the Executive Branch will be forthcoming with information. Given the highly classified and often compartmented nature of intelligence information, this may be a more exacting problem for the intelligence committees. Nonetheless, we continue to believe that the current system has largely been effective.

We also do not see that any alternative to having a distinct committee oversee intelligence is preferable. Each oversight committee finds itself with a full agenda. Returning oversight to the House National Security Committee (HNSC) would act to the detriment of both those Members charged with intelligence oversight and the intelligence agencies themselves.

We also understand that there will always be some in the intelligence agencies who will question, resent and perhaps resist the idea of Congress having extensive oversight powers. This view is not unique to intelligence. It is unlikely that there is any Executive agency or department that does not harbor similar sentiments at some time. Still, this feeling may run deeper in the Intelligence Community. Sharing information with "outsiders," even if they are elected officials, runs counter to the ethos of intelligence as some understand it. We are also aware of repeated complaints by intelligence agency heads about the amount of time they must spend either before Congress or responding to Congress. Again, this sentiment is not unique, and we are also not convinced that the burden is any more onerous for intelligence agencies than for any others.

Effective oversight and an informed Congress are now considered among the expected norms of our system of government. We believe that oversight, if carried out seriously and with a modicum of support from intelligence agencies, not only helps ensure greater Executive branch effectiveness and propriety, but can also be a substantial force in rebuilding a sorely needed consensus to support intelligence agencies, prorams and activities.

A JOINT COMMITTEE

The issue of a joint congressional committee to oversee intelligence has been proposed in virtually every Congress since 1976. The main arguments in favor of a joint committee are:

- It would restrict the number of Members and staff (currently 33 Members and 50 staff in the House and Senate Committees) with access to highly classified information, thus limiting the possibility of unauthorized disclosures.
- It would underscore the seriousness with which Congress views intelligence, by handling it in this manner, similar to how atomic energy (i.e., nuclear weapons development and proliferation) issues were overseen from 1946–1977 by the Joint Committee on Atomic Energy.

The main arguments against a joint committee are:

- Concern over restricting the number of Members and staff with access to intelligence information implies that Congress cannot be trusted with such information. Although the record of Congress with regard to safeguarding such information is not perfect, it remains far better than Executive Branch agencies. Congress must be vigilant in this regard, but this does not argue that current number need to be further restricted.
- By creating a joint committee, Congress would further heighten the view that intelligence is an extraordinary, rather than an accepted, function of government. No other executive branch agencies or functions are overseen by a joint committee, thus raising the issue of why intelligence needs to be overseen in this manner.
- The oversight scope of the two current intelligence committees are not identical. Intelligence programs are currently divided into three broad groups: *NFIP: the National Foreign Intelligence Program*, which includes the Director of Central Intelligence; CIA; and the national foreign intelligence or counterintelligence programs of the Defense Department, DIA, NSA, the Central Imagery Office, NRO, Army, Navy and the Air Force, the Departments of State, Treasury and Energy, the FBI and DEA; *JMIP: the Joint Military Intelligence Program*, covering intelligence for defense-wide or theater-level consumers; and *TIARA: Tactical Intelligence and Related Activities*, covering service unique and tactical intelligence needs. HPSCI oversees all of these intelligence programs, sharing oversight of TIARA with the HNSC. The Senate Select Committee on Intelligence (SSCI) oversees only the NFIP. To create a joint committee, one House or the other would have to make substantial changes in the scope of oversight accorded to this new committee.
- It is highly questionable that the establishment of a joint committee would significantly reduce the number of Members and staffers that currently have access to classified information. No committee system will make Congress "leak proof." Even with a joint committee, there still would be a substantial number of Members and staff with access to intelligence information across several House Committees (Appropriations, National Security, Judiciary, International Relations), as well as their Senate counterparts.
- The joint committee structure is not suitable to an authorizing committee as it would complicate Congressional efforts to conduct our necessary oversight activities. By shrinking the number of Members familiar with the Intelligence Community, an inevitable result will be a diminution in Members' knowledge of the complexities of intelligence oversight. Additionally, the current system of two separate intelligence committees provides a more effective system of Constitutional checks and balances on Executive Branch activities.

Finding: There is no compelling reason to convert the current system to a joint committee. As noted, Congress's record regarding safeguarding highly classified information is not perfect, but does not warrant this step. Creating a joint committee would also require either the House or the Senate to alter its current arrangements for intelligence oversight, which has not had significant support in the past. Finally, and most importantly, creating a joint committee for intelligence would continue to heighten the view that intelligence is something other than an accepted function of government, which tends to increase rather than complement oversight issues and problems.

SELECT COMMITTEE/APPOINTMENT AND TENURE LIMITS

The reasons for these two aspects of the current oversight structure are described above. Although specific provisions for a standing intelligence committee could be established, changing HPSCI into a standing committee would *most likely* (but not necessarily) affect the process of assignment and lengths of service.

The main arguments in favor of the current select committee arrangement relating to assignment procedures are: [still-classified section missing text]

CONCLUSION: FINDINGS AND RECOMMENDATIONS

FINDINGS

- The current intelligence oversight system arose from a view that intelligence had to be handled in a manner that was extraordinary when compared to other functions of government. Although that view may have been warranted in the aftermath of the investigations in 1975–76, it is not warranted any longer. Indeed, by continuing to view intelligence in this manner, oversight and the work of the Intelligence Community are likely made more difficult.
- Advocacy for overseen agencies is legitimate and to some extent necessary. This has not been an accepted stance for the intelligence committees. We agree with the view of former DCIs that intelligence is such a restricted issue that Congress must be more active in building the necessary political consensus.
- The current oversight system has been largely effective, and clearly has responded to those problems that prompted the creation of the current committees.
- There is no compelling reason to convert the current system to a joint committee. As noted, Congress's record regarding safeguarding highly classified information is not perfect, but does not warrant this step. Creating a joint committee would also require either the House or the Senate to alter its current arrangements for intelligence oversight, which has not had significant support in the past. Finally, and most importantly, creating a joint committee for intelligence would continue to heighten the view that intelligence is something other than an accepted function of government, which tends to increase rather than complement oversight issues and problems.
- Although the reasons for which the current committee was made a select committee with tenure limits may have been valid in 1977, these may no longer be compelling or valid. There are equally compelling arguments in terms of the general effect of these arrangements on oversight to warrant reconsidering them.
- Unauthorized disclosures of classified information by Members or staff should trigger thorough investigations relying on strict enforcement of the applicable Federal statutes and House rules. Any individual who is conclusively determined to be the source of such unauthorized disclosures should be subject to the full range of penalties prescribed by the law. The rules promulgated by the Committee on Standards of Official Conduct on July 12, 1995 should be strictly and consistently enforced by HPSCI.
- The current oversight structure puts intelligence—as both a government function and as an issue—at a distinct disadvantage. Unlike other national security functions, congressional oversight of intelligence is neither unified nor clearly delineated. The

prime effect of this arrangement is seen in the degree to which intelligence programs are subjected to budget cuts largely because of *how* they are dealt with (i.e., as part of the defense authorization and appropriations process), rather than on their own merits.

RECOMMENDATIONS

- It is important that the House act to "normalize" the way in which it oversees intelligence. By continuing to handle intelligence as an extraordinary function, the current oversight system predicates an approach that may be overly adversarial and may actually make effective oversight more difficult.
- The House should give serious consideration to converting HPSCI to a standing committee, with no limits on terms of service for Members. This would help "normalize" intelligence and greatly improve expertise and continuity on the Committee.
- The House should consider allowing HPSCI to have exclusive jurisdiction over all aspects of intelligence that are part of the larger intelligence architecture, while the HNSC has exclusive jurisdiction over those aspects of intelligence solely related to military intelligence needs but that are not part of this larger architecture. Second, the House should consider creating a separate appropriations subcommittee exclusively for intelligence.
- The House should seek to better protect Intelligence Community equities by erecting legislative "firewalls" between HPSCI and HNSC during the authorization phase; similarly, efforts should be made to establish mechanisms for better legislative consultation and coordination with the House Appropriations Committee during the appropriations phase.
- Establish a semi-annual strategic intelligence review meeting between the new Committee on Foreign Intelligence (CFI) and the intelligence committees.

9/11 COMMISSION CONCLUSIONS ON INTELLIGENCE OVERSIGHT, 2004

Editor's note: Eight years after the IC21 Report, the 9/11 Commission also took a look—albeit brief—at the state of intelligence accountability. Its conclusion was blunt: the whole system of oversight had become "dysfunctional." This appendix provides the language of the Commission on the subject of weaknesses in the legislative supervision of America's intelligence agencies.

13.4 UNITY OF EFFORT IN THE CONGRESS

STRENGTHEN CONGRESSIONAL OVERSIGHT OF INTELLIGENCE AND HOMELAND SECURITY

Of all our recommendations, strengthening congressional oversight may be among the most difficult and important. So long as oversight is governed by current congressional rules and resolutions, we believe the American people will not get the security they want and need. The United States needs a strong, stable, and capable congressional committee structure to give America's national intelligence agencies oversight, support, and leadership.

Few things are more difficult to change in Washington than congressional committee jurisdiction and prerogatives. To a member, these assignments are almost as important as the map of his or her congressional district. The American people may have to insist that these changes occur, or they may well not happen. Having interviewed numerous members of Congress from both parties, as well as congressional staff members, we found that dissatisfaction with congressional oversight remains widespread.

The future challenges of America's intelligence agencies are daunting. They include the need to develop leading-edge technologies that give our policy-makers and warfighters

Source: *The 9/11 Report*, The National Commission on Terrorist Attacks Upon the United States (the Kean Commission), Washington, D.C., 2004, pp. 419–423.

a decisive edge in any conflict where the interests of the United States are vital. Not only does good intelligence win wars, but the best intelligence enables us to prevent them from happening altogether.

Under the terms of existing rules and resolutions the House and Senate intelligence committees lack the power, influence, and sustained capability to meet this challenge. While few members of Congress have the broad knowledge of intelligence activities or the know-how about the technologies employed, all members need to feel assured that good oversight is happening. When their unfamiliarity with the subject is combined with the need to preserve security, a mandate emerges for substantial change.

Tinkering with the existing structure is not sufficient. Either Congress should create a joint committee for intelligence, using the Joint Atomic Energy Committee as its model, or it should create House and Senate committees with combined authorizing and appropriations powers.

Whichever of these two forms are chosen, the goal should be a structure—codified by resolution with powers expressly granted and carefully limited—allowing a relatively small group of members of Congress, given time and reason to master the subject and the agencies, to conduct oversight of the intelligence establishment and be clearly accountable for their work. The staff of this committee should be nonpartisan and work for the entire committee and not for individual members.

The other reforms we have suggested—for a National Counterterrorism Center and a National Intelligence Director—will not work if congressional oversight does not change too. Unity of effort in executive management can be lost if it is fractured by divided congressional oversight.

Recommendation: Congressional oversight for intelligence—and counterterrorism— is now dysfunctional. Congress should address this problem. We have considered various alternatives: A joint committee on the old model of the joint Committee on Atomic Energy is one. A single committee in each house of Congress, combining authorizing and appropriating authorities, is another.

- The new committee or committees should conduct continuing studies of the activities of the intelligence agencies and report problems relating to the development and use of intelligence to all members of the House and Senate.
- We have already recommended that the total level of funding for intelligence be made public, and that the national intelligence program be appropriated to the National Intelligence Director, not to the secretary of defense.[19]
- We also recommend that the intelligence committee should have a subcommittee specifically dedicated to oversight, freed from the consuming responsibility of working on the budget.
- The resolution creating the new intelligence committee structure should grant subpoena authority to the committee or committees. The majority party's representation on this committee should never exceed the minority's representation by more than one.
- Four of the members appointed to this committee or committees should be a member who also serves on each of the following additional committees: Armed Services, Judiciary, Foreign Affairs, and the Defense Appropriations subcommittee. In this way the other major congressional interests can be brought together in the new committee's work.

- Members should serve indefinitely on the intelligence committees, without set terms, thereby letting them accumulate expertise.
- The committees should be smaller—perhaps seven or nine members in each house—so that each member feels a greater sense of responsibility, and accountability, for the quality of the committee's work.

The leaders of the Department of Homeland Security now appear before 88 committees and subcommittees of Congress. One expert witness (not a member of the administration) told us that this is perhaps the single largest obstacle impeding the department's successful development. The one attempt to consolidate such committee authority, the House Select Committee on Homeland Security, may be eliminated. The Senate does not have even this.

Congress needs to establish for the Department of Homeland Security the kind of clear authority and responsibility that exist to enable the Justice Department to deal with crime and the Defense Department to deal with threats to national security. Through not more than one authorizing committee and one appropriating subcommittee in each house, Congress should be able to ask the secretary of homeland security whether he or she has the resources to provide reasonable security against major terrorist acts within the United States and to hold the secretary accountable for the department's performance.

Recommendation: Congress should create a single, principal point of oversight and review for homeland security. Congressional leaders are best able to judge what committee should have jurisdiction over this department and its duties. But we believe that Congress does have the obligation to choose one in the House and one in the Senate, and that this committee should be a permanent standing committee with a nonpartisan staff.

Improve the Transitions between Administrations

In chapter 6, we described the transition of 2000–2001. Beyond the policy issues we described, the new administration did not have its deputy cabinet officers in place until the spring of 2001, and the critical subcabinet officials were not confirmed until the summer—if then. In other words, the new administration—like others before it—did not have its team on the job until at least six months after it took office.

Recommendation: Since a catastrophic attack could occur with little or no notice, we should minimize as much as possible the disruption of national security policymaking during the change of administrations by accelerating the process for national security appointments. We think the process could be improved significantly so transitions can work more effectively and allow new officials to assume their new responsibilities as quickly as possible.

- Before the election, candidates should submit the names of selected members of their prospective transition teams to the FBI so that, if necessary, those team members can obtain security clearances immediately after the election is over.
- A president-elect should submit lists of possible candidates for national security positions to begin obtaining security clearances immediately after the election, so that their background investigations can be complete before January 20.
- A single federal agency should be responsible for providing and maintaining security clearances, ensuring uniform standards—including uniform security

questionnaires and financial report requirements, and maintaining a single database. This agency can also be responsible for administering polygraph tests on behalf of organizations that require them.

- A president-elect should submit the nominations of the entire new national security team, through the level of under secretary of cabinet departments, not later than January 20. The Senate, in return, should adopt special rules requiring hearings and votes to confirm or reject national security nominees within 30 days of their submission. The Senate should not require confirmation of such executive appointees below Executive Level 3.
- The outgoing administration should provide the president-elect, as soon as possible after election day, with a classified, compartmented list that catalogues specific, operational threats to national security; major military or covert operations; and pending decisions on the possible use of force. Such a document could provide both notice and a checklist, inviting a president-elect to inquire and learn more.

NOTE

19. This change should eliminate the need in the Senate for the current procedure of sequential referral of the annual authorization bill for the national foreign intelligence program. In that process, the Senate Armed Services Committee reviews the bill passed by the Senate Select Committee on Intelligence before the bill is brought before the full Senate for consideration.

DOCUMENTS ON INTELLIGENCE FUNDING

Editor's note: In 1995–96, the Aspin-Brown Commission Report examined a wide range of intelligence issues in the United States. This appendix contains the Commission's main findings about intelligence funding—a key aspect of maintaining accountability for the secret agencies.

THE NEED FOR AN EFFECTIVE BUDGET STRUCTURE AND PROCESS

The annual budgets for U.S. intelligence organizations constitute one of the principal vehicles for managing intelligence activities. They reflect decisions on whether to expand or cut existing activities and whether to initiate new ones, thereby molding future capabilities. How effectively and efficiently the Intelligence Community operates is to a large degree a function of how these budgets are put together and how they are approved and implemented.

The budget process for most departments and agencies is relatively straightforward. A budget is prepared in accordance with the funding level approved by the President and submitted to Congress as part of the President's annual budget. After its review, the Congress appropriates funds for the agency concerned.

Where intelligence—a function, rather than an agency—is concerned, the budget process is more complex. This complexity exists essentially for two reasons. The DCI is

Source: *Preparing for the 21st Century: An Appraisal of U.S. Intelligence,* Report of the Commission on the Roles and Capabilities of the United States Intelligence Community (the Aspin-Brown Commission, led first by former Secretary of Defense Les Aspin and then, when he passed away during the inquiry, by former Secretary of Defense Harold Brown), Washington, D.C., March 1, 1996, pp. 71–82, 131–138.

charged by law with developing and approving a budget for "national" foreign intelligence activities that cut across departmental and agency lines. In addition, the budget developed by the DCI for "national" intelligence activities is but one of three resource aggregations that make up the overall intelligence budget. The other two aggregations are funded separately by the Department of Defense.

The implications of this arrangement for the DCI and the intelligence function are explained below.

THE NATIONAL FOREIGN INTELLIGENCE PROGRAM BUDGET

The budget for national intelligence programs is known as the National Foreign Intelligence Program (NFIP) budget. In theory, the NFIP funds all of the foreign intelligence and counterintelligence activities of the Government that respond to "national" needs, as opposed to the needs of a single department or agency. Put another way, it funds the activities of the U.S. Intelligence Community, as defined in law and described in this report.[1]

Intelligence activities compete with other funding priorities of the parent department or agency that manages the intelligence unit(s). The funds appropriated for NFIP activities are made available to the parent department or agency and not to the DCI.[2] Thus, intelligence funds represent a part of the budgets of the several departments and agencies which maintain intelligence elements with national responsibilities. In developing a single "national" foreign intelligence budget, the DCI must first accommodate the funding levels and priorities of the department or agency that "owns" the intelligence element(s) concerned. At the same time, the DCI must devise an overall intelligence program to satisfy national needs.

DoD "owns" the preponderance of national intelligence capabilities and its intelligence spending accounts for about three-fourths of the NFIP. When DoD spending is combined with CIA spending (which also is funded in the Defense budget for secrecy reasons), they constitute virtually all of the total budget for national intelligence. For all practical purposes, therefore, the amount determined by the Secretary of Defense, in consultation with the DCI, for "national" intelligence activities within the Defense budget *is* the National Foreign Intelligence Program budget.

From the overall level established for the NFIP, the DCI establishes funding levels for certain component "programs," each of which is administered by a separate "program manager."[3] These program managers perform the detailed work of assembling the budgets for each program which are ultimately reviewed and submitted to the DCI for approval. To succeed in their task, program managers must understand the information requirements

---

[1] The intelligence organizations of the Departments of the Army, Navy, and Air Force also receive significant funding outside of the NFIP.

[2] Funding for the CIA is appropriated to the Department of Defense, which transfers it to the CIA.

[3] As generally used in this report, "program managers" refers to those individuals who formulate the budget of a particular subcomponent, or program, within the NFIP. For example, the program managers of the four largest NFIP subcomponents are the Director, NRO (for the National Reconnaissance Program); the Director, NSA (for the Consolidated Cryptologic Program); the Executive Director, CIA (for the Central Intelligence Agency Program); and the Director, DIA (for the General Defense Intelligence Program). However, there are other intelligence program managers, such as the Director, Defense Airborne Reconnaissance Office (for the Defense Airborne Reconnaissance Program, a subcomponent of DoD's Joint Military Intelligence Program).

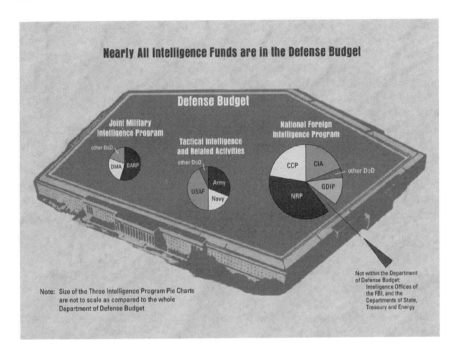

Nearly All Intelligence Funds are in the Defense Budget

Defense Budget

Joint Military Intelligence Program

Tactical Intelligence and Related Activities

National Foreign Intelligence Program

other DoD

DMA DARP

other DoD

USAF Army Navy

CCP CIA

NRP GDIP

other DoD

Not within the Department of Defense Budget: Intelligence Offices of the FBI, and the Departments of State, Treasury and Energy

Note: Size of the Three Intelligence Program Pie Charts are not to scale as compared to the whole Department of Defense Budget

likely to be placed on them and decide how best to satisfy them. For the costly technical disciplines, program managers must try to divine what technological capabilities are likely to be available and needed during the next five to 10 years so that funding can be included in their budget requests. They also must decide, given the amount of funding they have to work with, where tradeoffs have to be made, for example, should more be allocated to collection or processing? To personnel or investments in new technology?

INTELLIGENCE PROGRAMS SEPARATELY FUNDED BY THE
DEPARTMENT OF DEFENSE

The NFIP budget at present comprises about two-thirds of the total spending for U.S. intelligence. The remainder is funded in one of two separate aggregations within DoD's budget:

- The Joint Military Intelligence Program (JMIP), managed by the Deputy Secretary of Defense, is composed of several separate sub-programs each managed by a different DoD official. They respond to defense-wide intelligence needs as opposed to the needs of a particular military service.
- Tactical Intelligence and Related Activities (TIARA) is an after-the-fact aggregation of funding for tactical military intelligence projects and combat support units which are not centrally managed. Within DoD, each military service and the U.S. Special Operations Command budget for its own tactical intelligence capabilities within the context of its annual budget. These decisions are reported to the Office of

the Secretary of Defense, which aggregates them for purposes of providing them to the Congress and others within the Executive branch.

In order to assess sensibly what should be spent on national intelligence programs funded in the NFIP, many of which principally support military requirements, the DCI and the NFIP program managers must understand which military intelligence capabilities are being separately funded by DoD in the JMIP and TIARA. Heretofore this was accomplished on a largely *ad hoc* basis, with the Assistant Secretary Defense for Command, Control, Communications and Intelligence (ASD(C³I)) serving as the principal bridge between national, defense-wide, and tactical programs. Recently, however, the DCI and the Secretary of Defense agreed that all intelligence programs that support military operations would be reviewed together. After this joint review, the DCI and the Deputy Secretary of Defense would recommend an overall intelligence program and budget to the Secretary of Defense for his decision. The Secretary would then submit the defense budget, including intelligence funding, to the White House for inclusion as part of the President's budget.

The new joint budget review is clearly desirable to identify waste and duplication and improve overall efficiency among intelligence activities. However, some have urged the Commission to go further and recommend that JMIP and TIARA funds be consolidated with the NFIP. This one intelligence budget would be under the DCI's control to bring more coherence and efficiency to intelligence spending. The Commission does not, however, think that such consolidation is either necessary or desirable. DoD and its subordinate military departments have separate needs, apart from national needs, that they have a right—and indeed, an obligation—to fund. For example, the DCI is not the most appropriate official to decide how many (or which) reconnaissance aircraft are appropriate for Army units in Korea. This is not to say the military departments should act without regard to the overall needs of the nation, but only that they have separate needs which they attempt to satisfy within the funds available to them. The Commission's recommended changes to the budget process, described later, would effectively achieve the same result without unduly interfering with the independent authorities of the Secretary of Defense or those of the military departments.

The Commission also found numerous and significant shortcomings in the way the NFIP is structured and in the way it is prepared. The remainder of this chapter is devoted to these topics.

PROGRAM AND BUDGET STRUCTURE

BUDGETING BY "BUSINESS AREA"

As noted above, the NFIP is composed of separate "programs," each with its own "program manager" (e.g. the Consolidated Cryptologic Program is managed by the Director, NSA). These component programs are not, however, grouped around a consistent organizing principle. Some fund a type of intelligence activity; others fund a particular agency; and others fund a combination of both. As a result, no single program manager has budgetary responsibility for a given intelligence "business area" or discipline (such as signals intelligence or imagery). Instead, activities within a particular discipline are funded in several component programs. In simple terms, like activities are not grouped together for purposes of resource allocation or program execution. This structure makes it very difficult to identify wasteful activities, decide where tradeoffs should be made, and determine where cuts should be taken, if required. As the DCI recently observed, the "Intelligence Community has been relatively free from the systematic planning, programming, and budgeting process that is the hallmark of efficient government . . . The present system does not permit resource-saving trade-off analysis: for example, the possibility of substituting satellites for aircraft imagery or signals collection. . . ."

The existing structure also increases the likelihood that like activities funded in different programs will not interoperate or otherwise complement each other once deployed. The Commission was provided several examples by senior military officials and intelligence officers of redundant systems, funded in different programs, which were either inefficient or not interoperable. The problems with disseminating imagery during Operation Desert Shield/Storm, for example, were attributed to funding numerous imagery dissemination systems in different programs without coordination between them. Further, despite large expenditures on technical collection systems, the Intelligence Community's inability to process data collected by existing systems is attributable in part to the funding of these activities in different programs.

Given that like activities in each of the intelligence disciplines are also funded by DoD's JMIP and TIARA aggregations, and that the same situation exists with respect to each of them, the scope and effects of the problem are multiplied.

The commission concludes that the current program budget structure and diffused responsibilities over basic business areas have resulted in unnecessary duplication, interoperability problems, and other inefficiencies. These problems exist within the NFIP, and among NFIP, JMIP and TIARA activities, creating a substantial obstacle to the efficient use of intelligence resources.

7–1. The Commission recommends that:

(1) The budget for the National Foreign Intelligence Program be restructured by creating new discipline-oriented programs for SIGINT, IMINT, MASINT and HUMINT, each with a single program manager (see Table 7.1 below). The budgets (but not operational control) for all SIGINT activities in NFIP programs would be transferred to the new SIGINT program; the budgets for all IMINT activities to the new IMINT program, and so forth. In addition to these discipline-oriented program budgets, the DCI should allow for agency-oriented infrastructure programs to fund activities that provide general support to the disciplines (e.g., CIA Headquarters building).

(2) The Secretary of Defense vest authority in the national program managers for SIGINT, IMINT, and MASINT, respectively, to perform the initial budgetary review of investments in defense-wide and tactical intelligence capabilities that may be funded outside of the NFIP. The Secretary of Defense would continue to have final approval on these DoD investment projects. The Director, NSA has already been placed in this position by the Secretary of Defense with respect to SIGINT activities. The Commission recommends extending this concept to the two other DoD officials who also would serve as national program managers. Each discipline or business area would then have a single authoritative program and budget manager for its intelligence activities. Responsibility for carrying out the various intelligence activities funded by any of these programs would not change under this proposal whether such responsibility now rests with national intelligence agencies or DoD elements.

The Commission believes that if these steps were taken, program managers would be able to develop cohesive programs involving all assets within a particular discipline, as well as trade off capabilities within a particular discipline (regardless of where the funds are

Table 7-1. Increasing Budget Formulation Responsibility for NFIP Program
Managers in each of the Intelligence Disciplines

Intelligence Discipline	Proposed NFIP Program Manager	Percentage of *national* (NFIP) discipline activity budgeted by each program manager	
		Today	Commission's Plan
Imagery Intelligence	Director, National Imagery and Mapping Agency	3%	100%
Signals Intelligence	Director, NSA	52%	100%
Measurement and Signature Intelligence	Director, DIA	87%	100%
Clandestine Human Intelligence	Deputy DCI for CIA	96%	100%

Notes: Two proposed managers—the Director, National Imagery and Mapping Agency and the
Deputy DCI for CIA—are positions which do not currently exist, but have been endorsed
by the Commission.
The 3% figure, associated with imagery intelligence, refers to funds currently budgeted by
the Director, CIO.
The 96% figure, associated with clandestine human intelligence, refers to funds currently
budgeted by the Executive Director, CIA.

spent). These managers also would be able to better determine investment priorities, eliminate unwarranted duplication, and significantly improve end-to-end interoperability within their discipline.

These changes should also facilitate tradeoffs between disciplines, and between NFIP and Defense programs, substantially helping the DCI and the Secretary of Defense reach sensible, cost-effective decisions. They will also help OMB and the Congress perform their respective reviews and assessments of intelligence spending.

It was suggested to the Commission that intelligence budgets be constructed not around disciplines but around missions, e.g. support to military operations, support to policymaking, similar to the program "packages" used in the planning, programming, and budgeting process of the Department of Defense. The Commission agrees that examining tradeoffs among the various capabilities within each discipline (SIGINT, IMINT, etc.) in terms of how they satisfy mission categories is an effective way to make *program* decisions.

However, most intelligence capabilities can be used to support a variety of missions and the missions themselves are constantly in flux. It does not appear feasible, therefore, to build an intelligence *budget* according to how the intelligence capabilities being funded may or should be ultimately used. Clearly, those building intelligence budgets must understand the capabilities of the systems and activities being funded in terms of how well they can be expected to satisfy the requirements of a variety of missions. Moreover, once intelligence capabilities have been fielded, they must be managed in such a way as to achieve the missions of intelligence in the most efficient and effective way. (Thus, intelligence capabilities might be evaluated in terms of how they satisfy the requirements of particular missions by arraying them on a matrix, with "missions" as columns and capabilities within "disciplines" as rows.) It is difficult, however, for the Commission to see how intelligence *budgets,* in the first instance, could be constructed according to particular missions.

FUNDING FOR DEPARTMENTAL ANALYSIS IN THE NATIONAL
FOREIGN INTELLIGENCE PROGRAM

The NFIP includes three small programs[4] that fund the analysis of intelligence at the Departments of State, Treasury, and Energy. Each is developed within its parent department and competes against the other funding priorities of that department. After the Secretary of each department approves his or her proposed budget, including funding for intelligence analysis, the request is sent to OMB for review and adjustment in light of Presidential priorities.

Budget estimates for these intelligence elements also are sent to the DCI. But because the programs are small and have competed internally within their own departments, the DCI typically accepts the estimates without change.

The NFIP also includes the General Defense Intelligence Program (GDIP) managed by the Director, DIA. The GDIP funds an array of activities that provide for:

- military intelligence analysis at DIA, nine Unified Commands, and the military intelligence commands of the Army, Navy, and Air Force;
- infrastructure for DIA and the military service intelligence commands;
- intelligence openly collected by Defense Attaches and other DoD personnel;
- intelligence clandestinely collected by DoD personnel; and
- certain technical collection efforts (e.g. characterizing foreign nuclear testing).

Under the Commission's recommended structure for the NFIP, the GDIP's clandestine human intelligence activities and technical activities would be moved to the new consolidated national programs for clandestine human intelligence and measurement and signature intelligence, respectively. This would leave the GDIP composed essentially of intelligence activities that serve principally departmental purposes.

In light of this, the Commission considered whether the budgets for the small departmental intelligence elements and the reduced GDIP should remain within the NFIP. DCIs have historically played a limited role with respect to these budgets, but their budgetary role has been, and continues to be, a key element of their authority with respect to other elements of the Intelligence Community. *To maintain the DCI's cognizance over these intelligence programs, the Commission concluded that the budgets for the small departmental elements and for the GDIP should remain under the DCI's authority as part of the NFIP.*

COUNTERINTELLIGENCE FUNDING

As discussed in Chapter 2, counterintelligence is a critical part of nearly all intelligence activities. When performed properly, the counterintelligence function is integral

---

[4] As a group, these three programs constitute less than one-half of one percent of the NFIP.

to the intelligence activity itself and part of the overall security of the organization. As the Ames case demonstrated, the consequences of poor counterintelligence can be disastrous and deadly.

The FBI has a mission to "protect the U.S. from the intelligence activities of foreign powers and international terrorists through neutralization of activities inimical to our national security interests." By law and Presidential directives, the FBI has been designated as the federal government's lead agency for counterintelligence investigations and operations. Outside the U.S., the FBI coordinates its counterintelligence efforts with the CIA. Within other elements of the Intelligence Community, counterintelligence principally involves providing internal security to the parent organization at a level consistent with the needs of the organization.

Given these factors, the counterintelligence function is not readily amenable to budgetary tradeoffs among the various agency counterintelligence staffs. There is, however, a need for an independent review of counterintelligence budgets to ensure that adequate resources are being allocated to the function consistent with national objectives and priorities. In the past, funding for counterintelligence activities has occasionally been a convenient place for agencies under budget pressures to find money for other activities. This must be assiduously prevented. Funding for counterintelligence activities is now provided by the NFIP subject to the DCI's approval. Separate authority to conduct reviews of counterintelligence budgets is also lodged by Presidential Directive in the National Counterintelligence Policy Board, created in 1994 in the wake of the Ames case. The Board reports to the Assistant to the President for National Security Affairs and includes senior representatives from the FBI; CIA; the Departments of Defense, Justice, and State; the military services; and the National Security Council staff.

The Commission believes that funding for counterintelligence activities should remain a part of the National Foreign Intelligence Program. At the same time, it is useful to have the National Counterintelligence Policy Board perform a separate review of counterintelligence budgets. Together, they should provide assurance that funding is adequate to achieve national objectives and priorities as well as prevent counterintelligence funds being used for other purposes.

THE BUDGET PROCESS

In addition to the problems found in the existing budget structure, numerous problems appeared to exist with the process used to develop and implement the budget.

PROGRAM GUIDANCE AND EVALUATION

The DCI is charged by law to "provide guidance to elements of the Intelligence Community for the preparation of their annual budgets."[5] Usually, this guidance is issued by the DCI's staff or jointly with the Office of the Secretary of Defense after an overall level of funding has been decided by the Secretary of Defense and the DCI, and takes into account presidentially directed needs and priorities, statements of national security strategy, analyses of intelligence "gaps" and future needs, and other pertinent direction. Often, however, this guidance comes after the program and budget process has begun, and the program

---

[5] Public Law 102–496, Sec. 705.

managers have already incorporated their own assumptions about intelligence requirements into budget estimates. In the view of the Commission, the current quality and timeliness of program guidance is far from optimal.

Furthermore, according to many who spoke with the Commission, it is rare, if ever, that a program manager will have adequate evaluations from customers of how well the activities funded by his or her program respond to their information needs. Without such evaluations, it is difficult for program managers to identify and give priority to their most effective intelligence capabilities when building programs.

On the whole, the Commission believes that evaluations of intelligence by users should be relied upon to a far greater extent in the budget process. In Chapter 3, the Commission recommends that a "consumers committee" be established as part of a "Committee on Foreign Intelligence" under the National Security Council with ongoing responsibility to identify intelligence requirements and priorities, and to evaluate the Intelligence Community's response to policymakers' requirements. Inputs from this Committee, along with the fiscal decisions which he develops with the Secretary of Defense, should help the DCI to issue effective and timely guidance to support program and budget building. These evaluations also should enable program managers to know what intelligence support is, and is not, working well.

Strengthen Community-Wide Analysis of Intelligence Budget Items

Historically, the program and budget submitted by each NFIP program manager has been changed little, if at all, by the DCI's staff. There are several reasons for this, including the lack of a sufficiently capable analytical staff permanently assigned to the DCI, the DCI's focus on other important responsibilities, and prior agreements between the DCI and DoD which excluded certain staff offices of the Secretary of Defense (e.g. Comptroller and Program Analysis and Evaluation) from reviewing NFIP programs, as they do for Defense programs. In the view of the Commission, these bureaucratic arrangements must be changed if economy and efficiency are to be achieved. While the new DCI has taken initial steps in this regard, they have not yet been implemented fully.

7–2. The Commission recommends that the DCI establish a permanent cadre of analysts reporting to the Deputy DCI for the Intelligence Community to analyze and evaluate intelligence programs, identify inefficiencies within those programs, and assess trade-offs among programs. These analysts should include some with experience in the intelligence agencies and some with experience principally outside of intelligence. Further, current plans to include the DoD Comptroller, the Secretary of Defense's Program Analysis and Evaluation staff, and OMB staff in the review of national intelligence programs should be carried out.

Information on intelligence programs has not been organized to facilitate decision-making by the DCI or to provide outside reviewers, such as OMB, with an informed view. Although the DCI and DoD each maintain classified databases that track intelligence resources, they do not allow decisionmakers to have their questions readily answered at a meaningful level of accurate detail. Furthermore, 60 percent of NFIP funds are obscured by lumping them into a category called "base" which is minimally described, even in budget books sent to the Congress. It is these types of vague accounting and budgeting practices that permitted the accumulation of large NRO reserves, reported recently in the media, to go undetected.

The Commission understands that commercially-available computer technology would permit existing agency data files to be aggregated and analyzed without re-keying or manually re-formatting the data, allowing for the creation of a consolidated Community-wide data base that encompasses national, defense-wide, and tactical resources. However, despite the power of available technology, implementing this management information system may require one to two years to achieve the desired results.

Ideally, the building blocks of such a database would be individual "projects" or "activities" that accomplish a single purpose, rather than large amounts attributed to "base" that do not inform decisionmaking. Such a change would be in line with the private sector trend toward "activity accounting" to improve decision-making.

In the Commission's view, a Community-wide database of national, defense-wide, and tactical intelligence resources is feasible and highly desirable. Such a tool would allow the Secretary of Defense, the DCI, program managers, and other stakeholders to identify program issues, analyze all related resources, and improve the chances for implementing the most cost-effective intelligence program. An improved budget process, as recommended above, should allow the DCI and Secretary of Defense to identify excesses or shortfalls within each intelligence discipline and facilitate tradeoffs among the intelligence disciplines to optimize the government's intelligence posture. For example, the DCI and Secretary would be able to track funding for new technological innovations regardless of program and funding source. Better and more accessible resource data would allow program managers to design and fund a more efficient end-to-end system for each intelligence discipline and facilitate a matrix approach to budget analysis that would allow program managers to evaluate how particular intelligence capabilities were contributing to the missions of intelligence.

7–3. The Commission recommends that the DCI, in consultation with the Secretary of Defense, develop and implement a database to provide timely and accurate information on the purposes, amounts, and status of resources for national, defense-wide, and tactical intelligence activities. To minimize time and expense, this database should build upon existing data files from the agencies involved and be available for use by all appropriately cleared resource management officials and decisionmakers. A goal should be established to have such a database in place prior to developing the budget for fiscal year 2000.

MONITORING EXPENDITURES

In the normal course of the budget process, once Congress authorizes and appropriates funds, OMB apportions the funds to DoD for all programs included in the DoD budget. The DoD Comptroller then transfers to the military services, defense agencies, and the CIA the authority to spend money in accordance with the congressional direction. In turn, the agencies build their financial plans and display in detail the manner in which they intend to spend money. Deviations from these plans that exceed stated thresholds are subject to "reprogramming" actions, usually requiring the approval of Congressional committees, the DCI, the Office of the Secretary of Defense and OMB. The DCI, program managers, and other review authorities must remain apprised of the status of expenditures in order to ensure that programs are being implemented according to the intent of the original requests and Congressional mandates. Currently the DCI must be notified by agencies of reprogramming actions that exceed Congressional thresholds. *The Commission found that the*

DCI and his staff, some program managers, and other review authorities such as OMB, are not always given sufficiently detailed information to stay abreast of how agencies are spending money. Knowledge of current spending in any one area is critical to formulate and review requests for new spending in that area.

7–4. The Commission recommends that all intelligence agencies provide the DCI, program managers, and other review authorities with budget execution (spending) reports in sufficient detail to follow budget implementation and analyze reprogramming requests. The budget spending reports should be periodic, timely, and at a meaningful level of detail (e.g. by major project).

THE IMPACT OF THE COMMISSION'S RECOMMENDATIONS

The Commission believes that if the recommendations proposed in this chapter are adopted, they would provide a far more effective framework for the allocation of intelligence resources. They would facilitate the identification of wasteful activities, promote interoperability among systems and programs, and provide a better basis for streamlining and consolidation. The public would have greater assurance that the Intelligence Community of the future was operating effectively and efficiently. The budget structure and process which exist today do not provide such assurance.

The Commission's recommendations on the budget process, particularly building a Community-wide resource data base, would require an initial (though not large) outlay of funds, but should pay for themselves many times over in terms of the efficiency brought to the budget process.

IMPROVING INTELLIGENCE ANALYSIS

The *raison d'etre* of the Intelligence Community is to provide accurate and meaningful information and insights to consumers in a form they can use at the time they need them. If intelligence fails to do that, it fails altogether. The expense and effort invested in collecting and processing the information have gone for naught.

Assessing how well the Intelligence Community accomplishes this fundamental task is a complicated matter. A great deal of analysis is published; much of it is timely and of excellent quality. The Intelligence Community has many analysts who are recognized experts in their respective fields and whose professional judgments are valued and relied upon. Clearly, intelligence analysis has substantial value to many consumers.

The Commission found especially close ties between the producers and users of military intelligence. Within the military there is a long history of respect for, and reliance upon, intelligence. Intelligence is factored into strategic and tactical planning, is exercised in war gaming, and is integral to operations. As a result, military requirements are better defined, in large part, because of the close and continuing dialogue between intelligence analysts and the military commands they support.

Where policy agencies are concerned, however, consumers more often take a jaundiced view of the analytical support they receive. The President and senior cabinet officials appear to be relatively well served, but many decisionmakers at lower levels find that intelligence analysis comes up short. Often what they receive fails to meet their needs by being too late or too unfocused, or by adding little to what they already know.

In fact, only a small percentage of the resources allocated to intelligence goes to "all-source" analysis. Relatively few resources are devoted to developing and maintaining expertise among the analytical pool. Intelligence lags behind in terms of assimilating open source information into the analytical process, and it continues to struggle with how to avail itself of expertise in the private sector. Analysis that is not responsive to consumer needs continues to be produced.

The Intelligence Community is not entirely to blame. Consumers have a responsibility not only to engage in the process but, more important, to drive it. Often, they are uncooperative or too busy to engage at all. Since most are political appointees, many enter and leave government never appreciating what intelligence might have done for them. Clearly, consumers need to be better educated about the value of intelligence.

The Commission did find numerous instances where there was a close working relationship with policymakers. Intelligence producers were able to focus on issues of significance and to make information available when needed. Analysts understood the consumer's level of knowledge and the issues he or she wanted help on. Their analysis was read and relied upon. The consumer, for his part, developed an understanding of what intelligence could do for him and—equally important—what intelligence could not do. Many considered the support vital to meeting their responsibilities and actively engaged in [still-classified section missing here]

[still-classified section missing here] has no capability of its own to collect or to analyze information. While the United States presently provides the majority of the information that the UN receives in support of its operations, this support remains relatively limited. Other nations reportedly contribute very little.

In general, the Commission believes the United States should use its broad experience in intelligence matters to arrange for appropriate information support to multinational bodies as well as international coalitions, where important interests of the United States are at stake. The Commission is persuaded that this can be accomplished without jeopardizing the security of U.S. intelligence activities. It may require "sanitizing" information produced by intelligence agencies to ensure protection of sources or methods and/or limiting this sanitized information to particular topics or operational activities. These actions do place extra burdens on U.S. intelligence agencies to assess the particular needs of foreign recipients, to create "sanitized" versions of their reports, and to set up separate dissemination channels and/or communication systems for the foreign recipients. But, in the Commission's view, it is essential that the effort be made. Good information support is ordinarily critical to the success of any multilateral or coalition operation in which the U.S. is involved and, as a practical matter, the United States may be best positioned to take a leadership role.

In providing such support, U.S. intelligence agencies ordinarily should not deal directly with multinational organizations or coalitions, but rather should work through other elements of the U.S. Government (e.g. the Department of State for diplomatic actions, appropriate military channels for military coalitions). The U.S. agency charged with overall responsibility for the relationship with the multinational organization or coalition being supported will usually be in the best position to understand the needs of the recipients and balance risk versus gain.

The Commission's impression is that the arrangements for information support to multinational organizations or coalitions are often constructed and tailored to meet particular situations. While a certain amount of tailoring will inevitably be needed for each organization or coalition supported, new policies, procedures and capabilities (e.g. communications systems) should be developed to provide the standard means and methods for providing support in a multinational environment, similar to those in existence with NATO. Deviations could be authorized as appropriate.

12–1. The Commission recommends that the DCI and the Secretaries of State and Defense jointly develop a strategy that sets forth the policies, procedures, and capabilities that will normally serve as the basis for sharing information derived from intelligence in a multinational environment as well as how deviations from these policies, procedures, or capabilities may be authorized. To achieve maximum effectiveness, this strategy should build upon the extensive set of bilateral and multilateral relationships already maintained by the United States.

THE COST OF INTELLIGENCE

Viscerally, in the wake of the Cold War, many Americans believe the costs of intelligence should go down. Indeed, since 1989, the resources allocated to intelligence have gone down—by about 21 percent in real terms—but, nonetheless, they remain substantial. Budget projections show spending for intelligence holding relatively constant in real terms through the rest of the decade. Reflecting a sense of unease, Congress asked this Commission to determine ". . . whether the existing levels of resources allocated for intelligence collection and intelligence analysis are seriously at variance with United States needs. . . ."

To answer this question, the Commission undertook an extensive review of the intelligence budget and analyzed the changes to that budget since 1980. In doing so, the Commission attempted to ascertain what basis, if any, had been used over time to arrive at the resource level for intelligence. Was there a discernable standard or criteria that might help those responsible for resource allocations in the future to determine how much intelligence is enough?

Recognizing that pressure to reduce spending is apt to continue, the Commission attempted to assess whether and how the costs of the existing intelligence capability could be reduced without damaging the nation's security.

THE RECENT HISTORY OF INTELLIGENCE FUNDING, IN BRIEF

In recent decades, intelligence funding has been treated preferentially when compared to other parts of the Defense budget. As Figure 1 illustrates, non-intelligence defense funding in real (constant dollar) terms grew by 40 percent from 1980 to 1986, leveled off, and then declined to its current level, four percent below its 1980 level. In contrast, total intelligence funding grew by 125 percent in real (constant dollar) terms from 1980 to 1989 but declined thereafter to its current level of 80 percent above 1980. Reductions taken in the intelligence budget since 1989 have been at a rate to allow the intelligence agencies to continue most of their basic activities. Each agency has taken its share of the reduction from 1989, but no major structural change was required.

Personnel strength at NSA, CIA, and DIA has also remained significantly above the 1980 level despite across-the-board reductions over the last four years. NSA is 22 percent above its 1980 level; CIA, 8 percent; and DIA, 80 percent, primarily because DIA assumed major new functions which involved the transfer of additional personnel. In 1991, Congress in concert with the Bush Administration imposed a 17.5 percent across-the-board reduction in intelligence personnel to be accomplished between 1991 and 1997. This is less than 3 percent per year and has already largely been accomplished through attrition. This agreement had the Intelligence Community already on track when President Clinton directed that overall government personnel be reduced by 12 percent from 1993 to 1997, or about 3 percent per year. The Community has, in fact, extended these reductions through 2001, resulting in an anticipated total reduction from 1991 to 2001 of about 24 percent. This pace of reduction is consistent with the level of reductions that the President has directed for non-intelligence agencies.

Although intelligence funding remains classified, Figure 2 depicts the relative funding levels of the major intelligence agencies and their personnel levels for FY 1996. NSA, CIA, and DIA (and the Service intelligence units) have the largest number of personnel; the NRO, on the other hand, has the highest level of funding of any program in the Community,

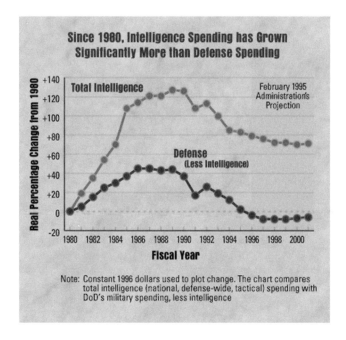

Since 1980, Intelligence Spending has Grown Significantly More than Defense Spending

Total Intelligence

February 1995 Administration's Projection

Defense (Less Intelligence)

Real Percentage Change from 1980

+140
+120
+100
+80
+60
+40
+20
0
-20

1980 1982 1984 1986 1988 1990 1992 1994 1996 1998 2000

Fiscal Year

Note: Constant 1996 dollars used to plot change. The chart compares total intelligence (national, defense-wide, tactical) spending with DoD's military spending, less intelligence

but virtually no federal workforce. Its work is accomplished primarily by contractors in the private sector.

The Community Management Staff (CMS) is the small staff of the DCI used to assist in the execution of his Community functions.

WHAT CONCLUSIONS CAN BE DRAWN FROM RECENT EXPERIENCE?

In general, from 1980 until the present, intelligence grew at a faster rate than defense when defense spending was going up and decreased at a slower rate when defense spending was going down. As a result, intelligence funding is now at a level 80 percent above where it was in 1980, while defense overall (other than intelligence) is now 4 percent below its 1980 level.

Because the Secretary of Defense in consultation with the Director of Central Intelligence has largely determined[1] the size of the annual budget for intelligence vis-à-vis the remainder of the defense budget, one conclusion that might be drawn is that successive Secretaries since 1980 have believed that intelligence should be funded at a somewhat higher rate than defense (regardless of the rate of increase or decrease for defense as a whole). Based upon the Commission's interviews, it appears that, in practice, most Secretaries have begun with the amount appropriated for intelligence the previous year, taken into account whether the overall defense number is increasing or decreasing, examined the additional initiatives needed for intelligence, and arrived at a somewhat preferential number for intelligence spending. Compounded over a period of years, this practice has led

---

[1] Congress annually makes adjustments to the President's budget request.

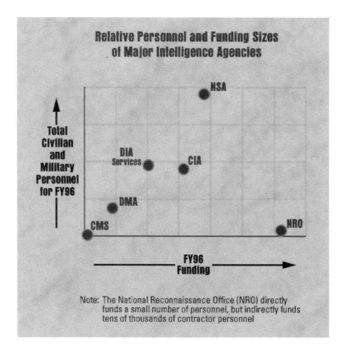

Relative Personnel and Funding Sizes of Major Intelligence Agencies

Note: The National Reconnaissance Office (NRO) directly funds a small number of personnel, but indirectly funds tens of thousands of contractor personnel

to the relatively large disparity between where intelligence is now funded, relative to its 1980 level, as compared with where defense spending other than intelligence is now funded relative to its 1980 level.

The Commission does not conclude the practice followed by successive Secretaries of Defense is necessarily right or wrong, but only that it has been the case. Nor does the Commission conclude that the wide disparity between intelligence spending and defense spending, relative to their 1980 levels, necessarily means that intelligence spending should be cut. But what, then, should be used to gauge the level of spending for intelligence?

The Commission struggled to find a substantive standard or criteria that might serve as a basis for answering this question. Some suggested that the spending level for intelligence should be what is needed to support the military operational requirements of a particular Administration, e.g. the "two major regional conflicts" strategy of the current Administration, and all other intelligence needs should be met by the same intelligence capabilities. The capabilities needed to support military operations, however, will not satisfy all intelligence needs. For example, the President and other users (including defense officials) rely on information produced by intelligence capabilities that are not principally used to support military operations, e.g., HUMINT, some imagery, and some signals intelligence activities. Moreover, the operational needs of the military provide no real limits to intelligence spending. As military commanders seek to win battles while minimizing casualties by knowing where the enemy is at all times—what the Pentagon has been referring to as "dominant battlespace awareness"—the need for intelligence grows exponentially. The costs of collecting signals and imagery intelligence from satellites, processing it at ground stations, and transmitting it to foxholes, tanks and aircraft in the "battlespace," all in a matter of seconds, are potentially unlimited and, regardless of how much capability is available, it may never provide total coverage.[2]

The Commission found it is equally difficult to assess the overall resource level for intelligence based upon the perception of the "threat" at any given point in time. If one target is no longer considered a "threat," intelligence collectors usually can be moved to others that are. Indeed, since intelligence collection capabilities, both human and technical, take years to deploy once resources for them have been provided, they are designed to be flexible in order to adapt to new needs.

Ultimately, the Commission concluded that developing a precise criterion for measuring the right level of intelligence resources would inevitably be too simplistic and perhaps unwise. The reality, as for many functions of government, is that intelligence capabilities are determined by whatever the nation chooses to spend on them, not by some rigorous calculation which attempts to precisely balance threats against capabilities. Like the conduct of diplomacy, controlling commercial air traffic, monitoring weather, or defending our borders, there is always more that could be done. Unlike the precision that the government can attach to the cost of delivering a letter, or printing and delivering a Social Security check, there is no precise means to determine how much the nation should spend on intelligence. Just as with other aspects of our national security, determining the appropriate level for intelligence funding requires an assessment of various criteria such as foreign threats and the advantages a particular capability can provide against such threats. These must then be weighed against what the nation can afford, given other government spending requirements and priorities.

In any event, how much the nation can afford to spend on intelligence has been and will continue to be constrained. While the need for such capabilities is compelling, so too is the need to reduce Government spending. Over the next decade, there is likely to be strong and persistent pressure to reduce the costs of Government across the board. Given the fact that the President and the Congress have now agreed in principle to balance the federal budget by the year 2002, deficit reduction casts a particularly long shadow over future intelligence investments. Though the calculations thus far agreed upon for balancing the budget assume that defense spending is capped and intelligence funding remains flat within this cap, changes in the economy or other spending priorities could re-open the debate on the level of spending for defense and hence impact intelligence. Therefore, reducing intelligence funding due to external pressures may be unavoidable in the long run. Furthermore, internal Defense Department pressures to reduce intelligence are also growing as the military services vie for funds to modernize their forces, maintain current levels of readiness, and pay for an increasing number of peacekeeping missions. Even within the existing cap for intelligence in the projected budget, there will be pressures to hold costs down in some areas and increase them in others.

WHAT NEEDS TO BE DONE

In view of these pressures, it behooves those with responsibility for intelligence resources to begin planning how such resources might be further reduced and/or reallocated

---

[2] There is, in fact, a process within DoD for trading off intelligence expenditures needed for the support of military operations against non-intelligence expenditures needed to support military operations within the overall limits of the DoD budget. Support to military operations does provide, in any case, the principal justification for the overall level of expenditure for intelligence within DoD.

to meet future intelligence requirements. Unfortunately, while the Commission found evidence of such planning in a few agencies, most intelligence agencies seemed to lack a resource strategy apart from what is reflected in the President's current six-year budget projection. Indeed, until the Intelligence Community reforms its budget process, it is poorly positioned to implement such strategies. The Commission's recommended actions to improve the budget process, set forth in Chapter 7, are thus a necessary first step towards more rational resource planning. The Commission also believes that certain of its other recommendations, if implemented, would produce costs savings:

- The one-time personnel authority outlined in Chapter 9 to "rightsize" to meet the needs of the Intelligence Community could save an estimated $2–3 billion in personnel costs over a ten-year period.
- The infrastructure costs associated with maintaining the existing level of personnel (e.g. buildings, communications, recruitment, security, training) could also be reduced, as noted in Chapter 9.
- Increased international cooperation in space reconnaissance, as recommended in Chapter 11, could, in time, also achieve savings.

In addition, there are a number of developments external to the Intelligence Community which offer promise of cost reductions:

- Aggressive implementation of the acquisition reforms recommended by the Defense Science Board would reduce the burden on industry and government of excessive red-tape and unnecessary oversight, and should reduce the costs of contract administration for most DoD intelligence components;
- Capabilities under development in the private sector, such as commercial imaging systems, might prove sufficiently reliable that intelligence capabilities could be reduced; and
- Potential savings could also stem from greater use of commercial technology for intelligence purposes, such as using commercial communication systems to disseminate intelligence to consumers around the world.

The Commission also explored the feasibility of reducing costs by allowing intelligence agencies to charge their consumer departments and agencies for the support they receive. Many witnesses pointed out that intelligence is a "free good" to most departments and agencies. Whether the support provided by intelligence is a map for a State Department analyst, an intelligence report on the economic conditions in a particular country for a Treasury analyst, or imagery necessary for precisely targeting Air Force cruise missiles, the cost of producing these intelligence products is free to the user. Because it is free, the appetite of consumers is essentially insatiable and undisciplined. Consumers who appeared before the Commission conceded that if they had to pay for intelligence support out of their agency budgets, they would, in fact, be more judicious in the number and type of requests they levied.

While charging for intelligence support may, indeed, bring greater discipline to the system, the Commission found many practical difficulties in implementing such a system. One is assigning cost to intelligence support. How does one assign a monetary value to an intelligence analysis, or a map, or a photograph? Another is providing intelligence support to departments and agencies who need it but have not asked for it. What do intelligence agencies do when they have crucial information for a particular department or agency, but the customer agency has used up its annual allocation for intelligence support? How would such a system be administered? Would each intelligence producer keep its own accounts? Would departments and agencies who were delinquent in their payments have their intelligence spigots turned off?

The Commission concluded that the benefits of bringing greater discipline to the current system by permitting intelligence agencies to charge for their services were far outweighed by the difficulties apparent in implementing such a proposal.

The Commission did, however, make one additional effort to assess intelligence costs by undertaking a review of the projected budget for intelligence from FY 1996–2001 in order to ascertain whether there appeared to be intelligence programs that were duplicative or providing marginal value. The conclusions of this review are set forth in the next section.

THE COMMISSION'S BUDGET REVIEW

The purpose of the Commission's review was to determine whether there were existing intelligence capabilities, developed during the Cold War, which appeared to be duplicative of each other or of other government capabilities, or which otherwise provided capability excess to the country's needs in the post-Cold War era. The intent of this review was not to arrive at recommendations for cuts to specific programs, but rather to judge whether such problems were apparent, and, if so, to what extent.

To perform this review, the Commission's staff organized the President's FY 1996 to FY 2001 budget for national and tactical intelligence programs into seven "business areas:" 1) signals collection and processing, 2) imagery collection and processing, 3) human source collection and processing, 4) measurement and signature collection and processing, 5) production and analysis of intelligence products, 6) multidisciplinary intelligence (those programs that contribute to multiple intelligence disciplines), and 7) intelligence infrastructure (buildings, support staffs, telecommunications, etc.). All intelligence programs and activities funded by the National Foreign Intelligence Program, the Joint Military Intelligence Program, and the Tactical Intelligence and Related Activities aggregation were included.

Within each of the business areas identified above, further divisions were made to identify the end use, target, or ultimate purpose of the expenditure. For example, the business area of "imagery collection and processing" was divided into three further categories: 1) imagery of the battlefield; 2) imagery for indications and warning intelligence, science and technological developments, and other needs; and 3) imagery management and dissemination. The purpose of this approach was to align expenditures for intelligence programs with their ultimate purpose or target in order to make informed decisions concerning possible duplication or excess capability.

Ultimately, the Commission staff assessed the contributions made by each intelligence program or activity with respect to each of the selected end uses or targets, and judged whether the programs were appropriate given the end of the Cold War, whether they duplicated other programs, and whether they provided excessive capability. These were necessarily subjective judgments based upon the staff's appreciation of the Government's need and what the respective programs and activities contributed in particular areas.

The Commission nonetheless believes the staff's review demonstrated that reductions to the existing and planned intelligence resources may be possible without damaging the nation's security. Indeed, finding such reductions is critical if funds are to be found for the investments in intelligence capabilities that the nation will need in the future, capabilities that are not now funded in the proposed program and budget. Precisely where such reductions should be made and at what level are judgments which the Commission is not in a position to make. Nonetheless, it is clear a more rigorous analysis of the resources budgeted for intelligence is required. In the Commission's view, this analysis should be performed jointly by the DCI, the Secretary of Defense, and the Director, OMB. It should span all three sources of intelligence funding (NFIP, JMIP, and TIARA) and assess the total U.S. intelligence capability against particular targets or types of targets.

In sum, the Commission believes cost savings can be achieved if the Intelligence Community adopts the management practices and implements the cooperative arrangements summarized earlier in this chapter. Those actions, together with pruning unnecessary requirements and unproductive systems and activities, could free significant resources. At the same time, the Commission recognizes that its proposed reforms to the budget review process could result in the identification of shortfalls between programmed resources and needed capabilities, or identify areas where new developments and investments are needed but are not now programmed. This might require the expenditure of most, perhaps all, of the funds freed up by cost saving measures. The Commission itself is not in a position to make this assessment.

REMARKS ON INTELLIGENCE OVERSIGHT, DCI ROBERT M. GATES, 1993

AMERICAN INTELLIGENCE AND CONGRESSIONAL OVERSIGHT

Today marks the last speech that I will give as Director of Central Intelligence. I have decided to use this opportunity to talk with you about Congressional oversight of intelligence and how it can be strengthened.

The idea of Congressional oversight of intelligence first came up a year after CIA was created by the National Security Act when, in 1948, there was a motion to establish a joint committee to oversee intelligence. This motion, which failed to get out of committee, was the first of nearly 150 proposals concerning intelligence oversight that would follow over the next 25 years. Just two of those proposals made it to the floor for action and both were defeated by greater than 2 to 1 margins.

Not that CIA was totally without Congressional oversight in the first quarter century of its existence. The Armed Services Committees and Defense Subcommittees of the Appropriations Committees had authorizing and appropriating jurisdiction for the Intelligence Community.

However, there were never more than a few Members of either House that actually participated in this oversight of intelligence. The number of hearings was limited and, according to one expert on Congress and intelligence, there were several years where the Senate oversight bodies met only once or twice.

By the early 1970s, the Director or Deputy Director averaged some 30 to 35 committee

---

Source: Remarks by Robert M. Gates, Director of Central Intelligence, Before the World Affairs Council of Boston, Massachusetts (January 15, 1993), reprinted in "Legislative Oversight of Intelligence Activities: The U.S. Experience," *Report*, S. Prt. 103–88, Select Committee on Intelligence, U.S. Senate, 103d Cong., 2d Sess (October 1994), Appendix 10.

appearances annually. There were even briefings for the Congress on covert action. For example, Foreign Relations Committee Members were briefed as early as 1962 on covert assistance to the Myong in Laos and during the ensuing years Foreign Relations and Armed Services Committees of the Senate were briefed on a total of 28 occasions on this effort alone.

Even so, Chairman of the Intelligence Subcommittee of the House Armed Services Committee Lucien Nedzi accurately described the overall state of Congressional oversight in a talk to the CIA Senior Seminar in November 1973, when he said, "It is a sobering experience for me, as Chairman of the House Intelligence Subcommittee, to find our Subcommittee still in the process of defining ourselves, still exploring (or worse yet, just beginning to explore) what we can do and what we must do."

The pattern of oversight just described was not a product of CIA or Intelligence Community reluctance to appear before the Committees or inform the Congress. The Subcommittees were regularly informed of the most significant covert programs and routinely briefed on the intelligence budget. As one observer put it, "The mechanism for oversight clearly existed; what was missing was an interest in using it—or more properly speaking, a consensus that would legitimize its use."

By the mid-1970s, a broad consensus emerged for the creation of a permanent and more effective Congressional oversight capability. Both the Rockefeller Commission and the Church Committee separately recommended creation of committees to oversee intelligence, and those recommendations were enacted into law by the Senate in May 1976 through Senate Resolution 400. The House acted a little over a year later in July 1977 with House Resolution 658.

In the early 1980s, Congress demonstrated its support for good intelligence and also its interest in stronger oversight both with support for increased funding and with three major pieces of legislation affecting intelligence. First was the Classified Information Procedures Act that provided for the protection of classified information—especially intelligence information—in courtrooms. Second was the Intelligence Identities Protection Act. Following the assassination of CIA Station Chief Richard Welch, the Congress moved to make it illegal to publicly identify a CIA officer who was under cover.

Finally, and most significantly, the Intelligence Oversight Act of 1980 reduced the number of Committees overseeing the Intelligence Community from eight to two—the Select Committees of the House and Senate, but also established certain obligations on the part of CIA and the Intelligence Community: to keep the Committees fully and currently informed of all intelligence activities, to furnish information deemed necessary by the Oversight Committees, and to report illegal or failed intelligence activities in a timely fashion. The legislation also revised the notification procedures for covert action, again reducing the number of Committees notified from eight to two.

So where do we stand today? Over the past sixteen years, CIA accountability and legislative oversight have grown enormously. With this oversight, CIA and the other intelligence agencies have become the most scrutinized intelligence services in the world. It would be difficult for any secret intelligence organization to be placed under this microscope of intense review. And yet, I believe, under these circumstances we not only remain effective and capable, we enjoy a legitimacy and an acknowledged role in our government not shared by any foreign intelligence service. It is fair to say today that there is not a single planned or ongoing activity in the Intelligence Community that it is not in some way or another subject to review by at least two Committees of the Congress.

To give you some insight into the breadth of this relationship, let me cite a few statistics. In 1992, representatives of the agencies of the American Intelligence Community met more than 4000 times with Members and staff of the Congress in either briefings or other meetings. We provided over 50,000 documents to the Congress and responded to almost 1200 questions for the record or Congressionally-directed queries.

Now, let me address two areas of special interest to Congress. First, the budget. The Intelligence and Appropriations Committees of the House and Senate take seriously their oversight responsibility to review the Intelligence Community budget and examine planned intelligence expenditures into the billions of dollars. They scrutinize budget line items in the thousands. In so doing, they pass judgment on virtually every plan and program. And Congressional oversight of the intelligence budget does not end after funds have been appropriated. We must gain the approval of up to six Congressional Committees when we reprogram money beyond a minimal amount and we must notify four Congressional Committees of any withdrawal of money from the CIA's reserve fund for contingencies. Furthermore, both intelligence authorizing committees and the House Appropriations Committee have created their own audit units and these have access both at Headquarters and in the field to our books and our expenditures.

The second area of special interest to Congress is covert action—actions which support the foreign policy objectives of the United States but cannot be achieved by overt means. The United States has the most elaborate set of checks and balances on its covert activities of any country on earth.

Few realize that most covert action proposals originate in the National Security Council or the State Department. But before any proposal for covert action moves forward, it is subject to intense scrutiny inside the CIA. The Covert Action Review Group—which includes the Executive Director of the Agency, the four Deputy Directors, the General Counsel, the Directors of Congressional and Public Affairs and the Comptroller—examines the critical legal issues of the covert action and also asks an important question: "If this program becomes public, will it make sense to the American people?"

Under the laws governing the oversight of intelligence, covert actions are conducted only after the proposal has been reviewed and approved by the National Security Council, the Attorney General, and finally, the President. The President's approval is embodied in a written Presidential Finding—which explicitly acknowledges that this operation is important to the national security of the United States. For the last seven years, every finding has been briefed to the Congress within 48 hours of signature.

The intelligence committees hold hearings to review new covert actions approved by the President, and they regularly examine all on-going actions. These two committees not only know the nature of the covert action that we are undertaking, but they know exactly how we are doing it, and they monitor every dime that is spent on it. This is no pro forma exercise. Congress can—and has—exercised control over CIA covert actions by denying us the funds needed to carry them out—just as it approves funds for all covert action that are undertaken.

Contrary to the image sometimes portrayed, most American intelligence officers welcome Congressional oversight—and all are subject to it. We see these Congressional mechanisms as surrogates for the American people, ensuring that our intelligence services operate within the law but also in ways consistent with American values. Congressional oversight is a protection against misuse of the Agency by Executive authorities and Congressional review of our intelligence publications helps guard our objectivity. Intelligence professionals believe that effective oversight is vital if intelligence is to have a future in this most radically democratic country in the world.

The vast majority of CIA employees have grown up under Congressional oversight. More than 75% of the Agency's population has entered on duty since the creation of the oversight Committees. They understand the rules and appreciate the value of and reasons for oversight.

Having said that, the process by which American intelligence agencies became accustomed to and positive about Congressional oversight was a long, and often difficult, one. Especially in the first half of the 1980s—and occasionally afterward—there were periodic crises of confidence brought on by concern on the part of the Oversight Committees that they were not being dealt with candidly, in a full and forthcoming manner. These concerns were too often justified, at least in some measure. However, in recent years the relationship between American intelligence and the Congress has improved steadily to reach its current excellent state.

Yet, just as we have focused in recent years on improving our performance in this relationship, today I would like to reflect from our perspective on several problems on the Congressional side which, if addressed, could strengthen and enhance oversight while contributing to the further improvement of our intelligence.

My first and most important concern is that very few Members of the Intelligence Oversight Committees (or the Appropriations Committees) appear to devote much effort or time to their intelligence oversight responsibilities. Only a handful of Members in both Houses have taken the time to visit the intelligence agencies and to make the effort required to gain some knowledge and understanding of what is a very complicated and sophisticated undertaking. This places an enormous burden on the Chairmen and Ranking Minority Members. Individual Members from time to time will develop an interest in one or another aspect of our work and acquire some knowledge of that, but the number of those with broad understanding and real knowledge in my judgment can be counted on the fingers of one hand—and that is after 15 years of continuous oversight. At the same time, there are too many instances of members of our committees having important misunderstandings, misconceptions or just wrong facts about U.S. intelligence, including their own legislation governing our activities.

Most Members of Congress are among the hardest working people I have ever met. But they have many Committee assignments, must carry out their responsibilities to constituents, and they have a multitude of other obligations. The sad result is that Committee hearings and briefings are usually not well attended and it is my experience that the record is getting worse, not better.

Let me give you one example. We had a single budget hearing for Fiscal Year 1993 in the Senate Intelligence Committee last spring. The heads of all of the intelligence agencies were present. Of the 15 Members of the Committee, the Chairman and a handful of members, perhaps three or four, showed up. A half-hour or so into the hearing, it was recessed for a vote and when the hearing resumed a short while later, the Chairman and only two or three members returned. All but the Chairman were gone within 20 minutes. The result is that for the single most important hearing of the year—on the budget of the entire Intelligence Community—only Chairman Boren was present throughout.

By the same token, the next day there was a hearing on covert action and 12 out of 15 Senators attended and stayed throughout—and that for a covert program that is but a fraction of one percent of our total budget, and that is just one-tenth the size of the program two years ago, and where there are virtually no controversial activities under way. Budget hearings on the House side were often attended only by the Chairman, the Ranking Minority Member, and a very small number of others, typically dropping in for a few minutes at a time.

I know that the Members can read the record of the hearing, but how many really do? The result is that enormous responsibility then falls to the staffs of the Committees. They are neither elected nor confirmed by anyone, and yet they acquire enormous influence over the structuring of issues, as well as the attitudes and votes of the members.

My concern, then, is not oversight, but the lack of attention and knowledge and time on the part of too many members of the intelligence and Appropriations Committees. This, in turn, means that in this most sensitive area of American government, anonymous staff members with little or no experience in intelligence or its use by the Executive acquire enormous power over the programs and directions of American intelligence.

To make matters worse, Congressional rules approved in the mid-1970s established time limits on Members' service on the Intelligence Committees—eight years in the Senate, six years in the House. As a result, just when an interested or concerned member begins to acquire some knowledge and understanding of our work, he or she is rotated off the Intelligence Committee—unlike most other Committees of the Congress.

So my major complaint with Congressional oversight of intelligence is that there is not enough of it—that is, by the Members of Congress themselves. Now, I am not naive. I know how the system in Congress works, and I know that the situation that I describe prevails in nearly all other areas of government as well. But, as we reduce the size of our military and contemplate major changes in the structure and size of American intelligence, I would argue strongly that these decisions are too important to be left to staff. Those in Congress who are selected for these Committees—and I am told that there is high interest in joining these Committees in both Houses—should be expected to invest the time necessary to gain an understanding of the intricate and fragile system that they seek to change. Our national security depends upon it.

The second concern that I have involves the way in which Congress is organized to deal with our budget. Again, we are on the receiving end of a larger problem identified by Congressional reformers. In past years, the Chairmen of our two Intelligence Committees have devoted enormous effort to reviewing our budget in great detail and making recommendations with respect to that budget. Until recently, the Appropriations Committees were willing to defer in considerable measure to the Intelligence Committees—and would usually see to it that the Appropriations bills paralleled the recommendations of the Intelligence Authorizing Committees. However, in the last two years or so, the appropriators have shown considerably less willingness to defer to the Intelligence Committees with the result that these two bills—the intelligence authorization bill and the separate appropriations bill—are often very different. As a result, when the appropriators tell us to do one thing and the Intelligence Committees have not acted or disagree, we are paralyzed—caught in the middle.

Let me give you an example. Last year, the Appropriations Committees approved several hundred million dollars more for intelligence than did the authorizing Intelligence Committees. We went back to all of the Committees in the spring and asked that a substantial portion of that money be approved by the Committees so that we could enhance our efforts on nonproliferation, counternarcotics and certain other high priorities. Everyone agreed with our intended use of the money, but because of minor differences and procedural squabbles among the Appropriations, Intelligence and Armed Services Committees, it took us five months of intense effort to get these transfers approved. I don't know anyone in Congress who believes that is how the system is supposed to work.

We in intelligence also are becoming vulnerable to another common practice but one from which heretofore we have largely been protected—insistence by individual Members on funding of pet projects before they will approve our budget. At a time of significantly declining resources, this is a dangerous trend that threatens to weaken our intelligence capabilities by forcing us to spend money for programs that we do not seek and that we find wasteful.

Let me conclude by making three recommendations for strengthening Congressional oversight:

—First, Congress should end the practice of rotating Members on the Intelligence Committees. The fear in 1976 that Members of the Committees would be co-opted by the intelligence services and lose their ability to be critical has proven unfounded. At the same time, the rotation has contributed to a lack of expertise, knowledge and understanding on the part of Members of the Oversight Committees of what U.S. intelligence does, how it does it, and how it can be improved. If it is too hard to end the rotation, at a minimum the period of service should be extended substantially. As Representative Lee Hamilton said in an address at the University of Virginia on 16 December 1986, "The large turnover of Committee Membership every six years produces a loss of institutional memory {that} hinders effective oversight."

—Second, I urge the returning Members of the Intelligence Committees and the new Members to take especially seriously their responsibilities on the Oversight Committees and give them high priority. For the good of the country, they must make the time available to learn about the intelligence agencies that they oversee—how they do their work, how well they perform, the quality of the people, how they can be improved, and what intelligence capabilities this country will need in the future.

—Third, and finally, although I realize that it is a naive request, I hope that the Congressional leadership can do something about the conflict between the authorizing committees and the appropriators because the problems created by the disparity in their respective legislation is imposing a great cost on the Intelligence community both in terms of effective management and the ability to deal with high priority issues.

In the first nine months of 1992, I personally had some 120 meetings, briefings and hearings on Capitol Hill. Building on the efforts of my predecessor, Judge Webster, over several years to improve our relationship with Congress, one of the achievements of the past year about which I am the most proud was the absence for the first time of a single major problem, incident or controversy in our dealings with the Intelligence Oversight Committees.

I have just issued guidance to every employee of CIA and the Intelligence Community who may appear before Congress that stresses four principles of testifying first articulated by my predecessor, Judge William Webster: candor, completeness, correctness and consistency. I am confident that my successor will devote the same effort, in collaboration with the other leaders of the Community, to extending this period of cooperation and confidence-building between the Intelligence Community and the Congress.

I strongly support Congressional oversight of intelligence activities. I believe it is a needed check in our system. But it is also a measure of how far we have come that it is the intelligence professionals who now call for a further strengthening of Congressional oversight—that is, by the Members of Congress who accept that responsibility.

GLOSSARY

ACCM	Alternative or Compensatory Control Measure
AFIO	Association of Former Intelligence Officers
AG	Attorney General
Aman	Agaf ha-Modi'in (Israeli military intelligence)
ANC	African National Congress
BDA	Battle Damage Assessment
BfV	Bundesamt für Verfassungsschutz (German equivalent of the FBI)
BMD	Ballistic Missile Defense
BND	Bundesnachrichtendienst (German foreign intelligence service)
BSO	Black September Organization
BW	Biological Weapons
CA	Covert Action
CAS	Covert Action Staff (CIA)
CBW	Chemical/Biological Warfare
CCP	Consolidated Cryptographic Program
CDA	Congressionally Directed Action
CE	Counterespionage
CHAOS	Code name for CIA illegal domestic spying
CI	Counterintelligence
CIA	Central Intelligence Agency
CIFA	Counterintelligence Field Activity
CIG	Central Intelligence Group
CMS	Community Management Staff
CNC	Crime and Narcotics Center (CIA)

COINTELPRO	FBI Counterintelligence Program
COMINT	Communications Intelligence
Corona	Codename for first U.S. spy satellite system
COS	Chief of Station (CIA)
COSPO	Community Open Source Program Office
CPA	Covert Political Action
CPSU	Communist Party of the Soviet Union
CSI	Committee on Intelligence Services (Britain)
CT	Counterterrorism
CTC	Counterterrorism Center (CIA)
CW	Chemical Weapons
D & D	Denial and Deception
DARP	Defense Airborne Reconnaissance Program
DAS	Deputy Assistant Secretary
DBA	Dominant Battlefield Awareness
DC	Deputies Committee (NSC)
DCD	Domestic Contact Division (CIA)
DCI	Director of Central Intelligence
D/CIA	Director of Central Intelligence Agency
DDA	Deputy Director of Administration (CIA)
DDCI	Deputy Director for Central Intelligence (DDCI)
DD/CIA	Deputy Director, Central Intelligence Agency
DDO	Deputy Director for Operations (CIA)
DDP	Deputy Director for Plans (CIA)
DDS&T	Deputy Director for Science and Technology (CIA)
DEA	Drug Enforcement Administration
DGSE	Directorie Génerale de la Sécurité Extérieure (French intelligence service)
DHS	Department of Homeland Security
DI	Directorate of Intelligence (CIA)
DIA	Defense Intelligence Agency
DIA/Humint	Defense Humint Service
DINSUM	*Defense Intelligence Summary*
DNI	Director of National Intelligence
DO	Directorate of Operations
DoD	Department of Defense
DOD	Domestic Operations Division (CIA)
DOE	Department of Energy
DOJ	Department of Justice
DOT	Department of Treasury
DOS	Department of State
DP	Directorate of Plans (CIA)
DST	Directoire de Surveillance Territore (France)
ECHR	European Convention of Human Rights

ELINT	Electronic Intelligence
ENIGMA	Code machine used by the Germans during World War II
EO	Executive Order
EOP	Executive Office of the President
ETF	Environmental Task Force (CIA)
FARC	Fuerzas Armadas Revolucionarias in Colombia
FBI	Federal Bureau of Investigation
FBIS	Foreign Broadcast Information Service
FISA	Foreign Intelligence Surveillance Act (1978)
FNLA	National Front for the Liberation of Angola
FOIA	Freedom of Information Act
FRD	Foreign Resources Division (CIA)
FSB	Federal'naya Sluzba Besnopasnoti (Federal Security Service, Russia)
GAO	General Accountability Office (Congress)
GCHQ	Government Communications Headquarters (the British NSA)
GEO	Geosynchronous Orbit
GEOINT	Geospatial Intelligence
GRU	Soviet Military Intelligence
GSG	German Counterterrorism Service
HEO	High Elliptical Orbit
HPSCI	House Permanent Select Committee on Intelligence
HUAC	House Un-American Activities Committee
HUMINT	Human Intelligence (assets)
I & W	Indicators and Warning
IAEA	International Atomic Energy Agency
IAF	Israel Air Force
IC	Intelligence Community
ICS	Intelligence Community Staff
IDF	Israeli Defense Force
IG	Inspector General
IMINT	Imagery Intelligence (photographs)
INR	Bureau of Intelligence and Research (Department of State)
INTELINK	An intelligence community computer information system
INTs	Collection disciplines (IMINT, SIGINT, OSINT, HUMINT, MASINT)
IOB	Intelligence Oversight Board (White House)
ISA	Israeli Security Agency
ISC	Intelligence and Security Committee (U.K.)
ISI	Inter-Services Intelligence (Pakistani intelligence agency)
IT	Information Technology
JCAE	Joint Committee on Atomic Energy
JCS	Joint Chiefs of Staff
JIC	Joint Intelligence Committee (U.K.)

JSOC	Joint Special Operations Command
JSTARS	Joint Surveillance Target Attack Radar Systems
KGB	Soviet Secret Police
KH	Keyhole (satellite)
LTTE	Tamil Tigers of Tamil Elam
MAGIC	Allied code-breaking operations against the Japanese in the World War II
MASINT	Measurement and Signatures Intelligence
MI5	Security Service (U.K.)
MI6	Secret Intelligence Service (U.K.)
MON	Memoranda of Notification
MONGOOSE	Code name for CIA covert actions against Fidel Castro of Cuba (1961–62)
Mossad	Israeli Intelligence Service
MPLA	Popular Movement for the Liberation of Angola
NAACP	National Association for the Advancement of Colored People
NBC	Nuclear, Biological, and Chemical (Weapons)
NCS	National Clandestine Service
NCIC	National Counterintelligence Center
NCTC	National Counterterrorism Center
NED	National Endowment for Democracy
NFIB	National Foreign Intelligence Board
NFIC	National Foreign Intelligence Council
NFIP	National Foreign Intelligence Program
NGA	National Geospatial-Intelligence Agency
NGO	Nongovernmental organization
NIA	National Intelligence Authority
NIC	National Intelligence Council
NID	*National Intelligence Daily*
NIE	National Intelligence Estimate
NIO	National Intelligence Officer
NOC	Nonofficial Cover
NPIC	National Photographic Interpretation Center
NRO	National Reconnaissance Office
NSA	National Security Agency
NSC	National Security Council (White House)
NSCID	National Security Council Intelligence Directive
NTM	National Technical Means
OB	Order of Battle
OC	Official Cover
ODNI	Office of the Director of National Intelligence
OMB	Office of Management and Budget
ONI	Office of Naval Intelligence

OPC	Office of Policy Coordination
OSD	Office of the Secretary of Defense
OSINT	Open-Source Intelligence
OSS	Office of Strategic Services
P & E	Processing and Exploitation
PDB	*President's Daily Brief*
PFIAB	President's Foreign Intelligence Advisory Board (White House)
PFLP	Popular Front for the Liberation of Palestine
PIJ	Palestinian Islamic Jihad
PLO	Palestine Liberation Organization
PM	Paramilitary
PRO	Public Record Office (U.K.)
RADINT	Radar Intelligence
RFE	Radio Free Europe
RL	Radio Liberty
SA	Special Activities Division (DO/CIA)
SAS	Special Air Service (U.K.)
SBS	Special Boat Service (U.K.)
SDO	Support to Diplomatic Operations
SHAMROCK	Code name for illegal NSA interception of cables
SIG	Senior Interagency Group
SIGINT	Signals Intelligence
SIS	Secret Intelligence Service (U.K., also known as MI6)
SISDE	Italian Intelligence Service
SMO	Support to Military Operations
SMS	Secretary's *Morning Summary* (Department of State)
SNIE	Special National Intelligence Estimate
SO	Special Operations (CIA)
SOCOM	Special Operations Command (Department of Defense)
SOE	Special Operations Executive (U.K.)
SOG	Special Operations Group (DO/CIA)
SOVA	Office of Soviet Analysis (CIA)
SSCI	Senate Select Committee on Intelligence
SVR	Russian Foreign Intelligence Service
TECHINT	Technical Intelligence
TELINT	Telemetry Intelligence
TIARA	Tactical Intelligence and Related Activities
TPED	Tasking, Processing, Exploitation, and Dissemination
UAV	Unmanned Aerial Vehicle (drone)
ULTRA	Code name for the Allied operation that deciphered the German ENIGMA code in World War II
UN	United Nations
UNITA	National Union for the Total Independence of Angola

UNSCOM	United Nations Special Commission
USIB	United States Intelligence Board
USTR	United States Trade Representative
VCI	Viet Cong Infrastructure
VENONA	Code name for SIGINT intercepts against Soviet spying in America
VOA	Voice of America
VX	A deadly nerve agent used in chemical weapons
WMD	Weapons of mass destruction

INDEX

ABOUT THE EDITOR AND CONTRIBUTORS

EDITOR

Loch K. Johnson is Regents Professor of Public and International Affairs at the University of Georgia and author of several books and over 100 articles on U.S. intelligence and national security. His books include *The Making of International Agreements* (1984); *A Season of Inquiry* (1985); *Through the Straits of Armageddon* (1987, coedited with Paul Diehl); *Decisions of the Highest Order* (1988, coedited with Karl F. Inderfurth); *America's Secret Power* (1989); *Runoff Elections in the United States* (1993, coauthored with Charles S. Bullock III); *America as a World Power* (1995); *Secret Agencies* (1996); *Bombs, Bugs, Drugs, and Thugs* (2000); *Fateful Decisions* (2004, coedited with Karl F. Inderfurth); *Strategic Intelligence* (2004, coedited with James J. Wirtz); *Who's Watching the Spies?* (2005, coauthored with Hans Born and Ian Leigh); *American Foreign Policy* (2005, coauthored with Daniel Papp and John Endicott); and *Seven Sins of American Foreign* Policy (2007). He has served as special assistant to the chair of the Senate Select Committee on Intelligence (1975–76), staff director of the House Subcommittee on Intelligence Oversight (1977–79), and special assistant to the chair of the Aspin-Brown Commission on Intelligence (1995–96). In 1969–70, he was an American Political Science Association Congressional Fellow. He has served as secretary of the American Political Science Association and President of the International Studies Association, South. Born in New Zealand and educated at the University of California, Johnson has taught at the University of Georgia since 1979, winning its Meigs Professorship for meritorious teaching and its Owens Award for outstanding accomplishments in the field of social science research. In 2000, he led the founding of the School of Public and

International Affairs at the University of Georgia. He is the senior editor of the international journal *Intelligence and National Security*.

CONTRIBUTORS

Matthew M. Aid is Managing Director in the Washington, DC, office of Citigate Global Intelligence and Security and coeditor of *Secrets of Signals Intelligence During the Cold War and Beyond* (2001).

James E. Baker sits on the U.S. Court of Appeals for the Armed Forces. He previously served as Special Assistant to the President and Legal Adviser to the National Security Council and as Deputy Legal Adviser to the NSC. He has also served as Counsel to the President's Foreign Intelligence Advisory Board, an attorney at the Department of State, a legislative aide to Senator Daniel Patrick Moynihan, and as a Marine Corps infantry officer. He is the coauthor with Michael Reisman of *Regulating Covert Action* (Yale University Press, 1992).

David M. Barrett is Associate Professor of Political Science at Villanova University and author of *Congress and the CIA* (Kansas, 2005).

Hans Born is a senior fellow in democratic governance of the security sector at the Geneva Centre for Democratic Control of the Armed Forces (DCAF). He is an external member of the crisis management and security policy faculty of the Federal Institute of Technology and a guest lecturer on governing nuclear weapons at the UN Disarmament Fellowship Programme. He has written, co-authored, and co-edited various books on international relations and security policy, including the Inter-Parliamentary Union Handbook on *Parliamentary Oversight of the Security Sector: Principles, Mechanisms and Practices* (Geneva: IPU/DCAF, 2003, translated in 30 languages); *Making Intelligence Accountable: Legal Standards and Best Practice for Oversight of Intelligence Agencies* (Oslo: Publishing House of the Parliament of Norway, 2005, translated in 10 languages); *Who is Watching the Spies? Establishing Intelligence Agency Accountability* (Dulles, VA: Potomac Publishers, 2005); *Civil-Military Relations in Europe: Learning from Crisis and Institutional Change* (London: Routledge, 2006); and *The Double Democratic Deficit: Parliamentary Accountability and the Use of Force under International Auspices* (London: Ashgate Publishers: Aldershot).

A. Denis Clift is President of the Department of Defense Joint Military Intelligence College. He was born in New York City and educated at Friends Seminary, Phillips Exeter Academy (1954), Stanford University (B.A., 1958), and the London School of Economics and Political Science (M.Sc., 1967). He began a career of public service as a naval officer in the Eisenhower and Kennedy administrations and has served in military and civilian capacities in ten administrations, including thirteen successive years in the Executive Office of the President and the White House. From 1971–76, he served on the National Security

Council staff. From 1974–76, he was head of President Ford's National Security Council staff for the Soviet Union and Eastern and Western Europe. From 1977–81, he was Assistant for National Security Affairs to the Vice President. From 1991–94, he was Chief of Staff, Defense Intelligence Agency. From 1963–66, he was the editor of the U.S. Naval Institute *Proceedings*. His published fiction and nonfiction include the novel *A Death in Geneva* (Ballantine Books, Random House), *Our World in Antarctica* (Rand McNally), *With Presidents to the Summit* (George Mason University Press), and *Clift Notes: Intelligence and the Nation's Security* (JMIC Writing Center Press).

William J. Daugherty holds a doctorate in government from the Claremont Graduate School and is Associate Professor of government at Armstrong Atlantic State University in Savannah, Georgia. A retired senior officer in the CIA, he is also the author of *In the Shadow of the Ayatollah: A CIA Hostage in Iran* (Annapolis, 2001) and *Executive Secrets: Covert Action and the Presidency* (Kentucky, 2004).

Jack Davis served in the CIA from 1956 to 1990 as analyst, manager, and teacher of analysts. He now is an independent contractor with the Agency, specializing in analytic methodology. He is a frequent contributor to the journal *Studies in Intelligence*.

Stuart Farson is Lecturer, Political Science Department, Simon Fraser University, Vancouver/Surrey, Canada. He is a former Secretary-Treasurer of the Canadian Association for Security and Intelligence Studies, and served as Director of Research for the Special Committee of the House Commons (Canada) on the Review of the Canadian Security Intelligence Service Act and the Security Offences Act. He has numerous articles on security, intelligence, and policing issues and is the coeditor of *Security and Intelligence in a Changing World* (with David Stafford and Wesley K. Wark, Cass, 1991).

Timothy Gibbs is a final-year doctoral student in history at Robinson College, Cambridge University, and a member of the Cambridge University Intelligence Seminar. He is also a former Visiting Scholar at the University of Georgia. His doctoral dissertation, titled *British and American Intelligence and the Atom Spies*, was submitted in the summer of 2006 and was supervised by Professor Christopher Andrew.

Peter Gill is Reader in Politics and Security, Liverpool John Moores University, Liverpool, United Kingdom. He is coauthor of *Introduction to Politics* (1988, 2nd ed.) and *Intelligence in an Insecure World* (2006). He is currently researching the control and oversight of domestic security in intelligence agencies.

Harold M. Greenberg graduated with a B.A. in history from Yale University in 2005. At Yale, he participated in the Studies in Grand Strategy program, and he has recently published research on CIA covert action in the 1950s. He now works as a legislative aide in the U.S. House of Representatives.

Daniel S. Gressang IV is Professor at the Joint Military Intelligence College (JMIC) in Washington, DC, and serves concurrently as the National Security Agency/National Cryptologic School of Liaison to JMIC. He has researched, written, and lectured extensively on terrorism and counterinsurgency. His research focuses primarily on the application of complex adaptive systems perspectives to understanding the dynamics of terror and other forms of unconventional warfare. In 2004, he was designated Intelligence Community Officer by the Director of Central Intelligence.

Glenn Hastedt received his doctorate in political science from Indiana University. Until recently he was Professor and Chair of the Political Science Department at James Madison University. He is now chair of the Justice Studies Department there. Among his publications is *American Foreign Policy: Past, Present, Future*, 6th ed. (Prentice Hall).

John Hollister Hedley, during more than thirty years at CIA, edited the *President's Daily Brief*, briefed the *PDB* at the White House, served as Managing Editor of the *National Intelligence Daily*, and was Chairman of the CIA's Publications Review Board. Now retired, Hedley has taught intelligence at Georgetown University and serves as a consultant to the National Intelligence Council and the Center for the Study of Intelligence.

Michael Herman served from 1952 to 1987 in Britain's Government Communications Headquarters, with secondments to the Cabinet Office and the Ministry of Defence. Since retirement he has written extensively on intelligence matters, with official clearance. He has had academic affiliations with Nuffield and St. Antony's Colleges in Oxford and is Founder Director of the Oxford Intelligence Group and Honorary Departmental Fellow at Aberystwyth University. In 2005 he received the degree of Honorary D.Litt from Nottingham University. He is a leading British intelligence scholar and author of *Intelligence Power in Peace and War* (Cambridge, 2001).

Frederick P. Hitz is Lecturer (Diplomat in Residence) in Public and International Affairs, Woodrow Wilson School, Princeton University.

Max M. Holland is the author of *The Kennedy Assassination Tapes* (Knopf, 2004).

Arthur S. Hulnick is Associate Professor of International Relations at Boston University. He is a veteran of thirty-five years of intelligence service, including seven years in Air Force Intelligence and twenty-eight years in the CIA. He is author of *Fixing the Spy Machine* (Praeger, 1999) and *Keeping Us Safe* (Praeger, 2004).

Rhodri Jeffreys-Jones is Professor of American History at the University of Edinburgh. The author of several books on intelligence history, he is currently completing a study of the FBI.

Ephraim Kahana is Professor of Political Science and faculty member in the Western Galilee College, Acre, Israel. He teaches courses on international relations, national security and intelligence, and foreign policy in the National Security Program in the University of Haifa. Kahana has written numerous papers on intelligence and foreign policy. His most recent book is the *Historical Dictionary of Israeli Intelligence* (2006).

Patrick Radden Keefe is a graduate of the School of Law at Yale University and is presently a Fellow with the Century Foundation in New York City. He is the author of *Chatter: Uncovering the Echelon Surveillance Network and the Secret World of Global Eavesdropping* (Random House, 2006), and has published essays in *The New York Review of Books*, *The New York Times Magazine*, the *New York Times*, the *Boston Globe*, the *Yale Journal of International Law*, *Legal Affairs*, *Slate*, and *Wired*. He has been a Marshall Scholar and a 2003 fellow at the Dorothy and Lewis B. Cullman Center for Scholars and Writers at the New York Public Library.

Jennifer D. Kibbe is Assistant Professor of Government at Franklin and Marshall College. Between 2002 and 2004, she was a postdoctoral fellow at the Brookings Institution. Her research interests include U.S. foreign policy, intelligence and covert action, presidential decision making, and political psychology. She has published work on U.S. policy in Iraq and the Middle East, and the military's involvement in covert actions.

Katharina von Knop is a doctoral candidate in Political Science at Leopold-Franzens University in Innsbruck, Austria, specializing in counter- and antiterrorism, and coeditor with Heinrich Neisser and Martin van Creveld of *Countering Modern Terrorism: History, Current Issues, and Future Threats* (2005).

Lawrence J. Lamanna is a doctoral candidate in the School of Public and International Affairs at the University of Georgia. He holds an M.A. from Yale University and a B.A. from the University of Notre Dame.

Ian Leigh is Professor of Law and Codirector of the Human Rights Centre at the University of Durham. He lives in Durham, England.

Kristin M. Lord is Associate Dean at George Washington University's Elliott School of International Affairs. In 2005–2006, she was a Council on Foreign Relations International Affairs Fellow and Special Adviser to the Under Secretary of State for Democracy and Global Affairs. Lord is the author of *The Perils and Promise of Global Transparency: Why the Information Revolution May Not Lead to Security Democracy or Peace* (SUNY Press, 2006); coeditor, with Bernard I. Finel, of *Power and Conflict in the Age of Transparency* (Palgrave Macmillan, 2000); and the author of numerous book chapters, articles, and papers on international politics and security. Lord received her doctorate in government from Georgetown University.

Minh A. Luong is Assistant Director of International Security Studies at Yale University, where he teaches in the Department of History. He also serves as adjunct Assistant Professor of Public Policy at the Taubman Center at Brown University.

Cynthia M. Nolan earned a doctorate at American University in the School of International Service, researching intelligence oversight. She is a former officer in the Directorate of Operations in the CIA and has published in the *International Journal of Intelligence and Counterintelligence*.

Kevin A. O'Brien is a former research associate with the Canadian Institute of Strategic Studies and is currently a senior analyst for RAND Europe.

Mark Phythian is Professor of International Security and Director of the History and Governance Research Institute at the University of Wolverhampton, United Kingdom. He is the author of *Intelligence in an Insecure World* (2006, with Peter Gill), *The Politics of British Arms Sales Since 1964* (2000), and *Arming Iraq* (1997), as well as numerous journal articles on intelligence and security issues.

Harry Howe Ransom is Professor Emeritus of Political Science at Vanderbilt University. He has a B.A. from Vanderbilt and an M.A. and Ph.D. from Princeton University. He was a Congressional Fellow of the American Political Science Association and a Fellow of the Woodrow Wilson International Center for Scholars. He taught at Princeton, Vassar College, Michigan State University, Harvard University, and the University of Leeds. His books include *Central Intelligence and National Security* (1958), *Can American Democracy Survive Cold War?* (1963), and *The Intelligence Establishment* (1970).

Jeffrey T. Richelson is Senior Fellow with the National Security Archive in Washington, DC, and author of *The Wizards of Langley*, *The U.S. Intelligence Community*, *A Century of Spies*, and *America's Eyes in Space*, as well as numerous articles on intelligence activities. He received his doctorate in political science from the University of Rochester and has taught at the University of Texas, Austin, and the American University, Washington, DC. He lives in Los Angeles.

Jerel A. Rosati is Professor of Political Science and International Studies at the University of South Carolina since 1982. His area of specialization is the theory and practice of foreign policy, focusing on the U.S. policy-making process, decision-making theory, and the political psychological study of human cognition. He is the author and editor of five books and over forty articles and chapters. He has received numerous outstanding teaching awards. He has been Visiting Professor at Somalia National University in Mogadishu and Visiting Scholar at China's Foreign Affairs College in Beijing. He also has been a Research Associate in the Foreign Affairs and National Defense Division of the Library of Congress's Congressional Research Service, President of the International

Studies Association's Foreign Policy Analysis Section, and President of the Southern region of the International Studies Association.

Richard L. Russell is Professor of national security studies at the National Defense University. He is also an adjunct associate professor in the Security Studies Program and research associate in the Institute for the Study of Diplomacy at Georgetown University. He previously served as a CIA political-military analyst. Russell is the author of *Weapons Proliferation and War in the Greater Middle East: Strategic Contest* (2005).

Frederick A. O. Schwarz Jr. received an A.B. from Harvard University and J.D. from Harvard Law School, where he was an editor of the *Law Review*. After a year's clerkship with Hon. J. Edward Lumbard, U.S. Court of Appeals for the Second Circuit, he worked one year for the Nigerian government as Assistant Commissioner for Law Revision under a Ford Foundation grant. He joined the New York City law firm of Cravath, Swaine and Moore in 1963 and was elected a partner in 1969. From 1975 through mid-1976, he served as Chief Counsel to the Senate Select Committee to Study Government Operations with Respect to Intelligence Activities (the Church Committee); from 1982–89, he served as Corporation Counsel and head of the Law Department of the City of New York. In 1989, he chaired the New York City Charter Revision Commission.

James M. Scott is Professor and Chair of the Department of Political Science at Oklahoma State University. His areas of specialization include foreign policy analysis and international relations, with particular emphasis on U.S. foreign policy making and the domestic sources of foreign policy. He is author or editor of four books, over forty articles, book chapters, review essays, and other publications. He has been President of the Foreign Policy Analysis section and President of the Midwest region of the International Studies Association, where he has also served as conference organizer for both sections and has been a two-time winner of the Klingberg Award for Outstanding Faculty Paper at the ISA Midwest Annual Meeting. Since 1996, he has received over two dozen awards from students and peers for his outstanding teaching and research, including his institution's highest awards for scholarship in 2000 and 2001. Since 2005, he has been Director of the Democracy and World Politics Summer Research Program, a National Science Foundation Research Experience for Undergraduates.

Len Scott is Professor of International Politics at the University of Wales, Aberystwyth, where he is Director of the Centre for Intelligence and International Security Studies. Among his recent publications are *Understanding Intelligence in the Twenty-First Century: Journeys in Shadows* (2004, coedited with Peter Jackson) and *Planning Armageddon: Britain, the United States and the Command of Nuclear Forces, 1943–1964* (2000, coedited with Stephen Twigge).

Katherine A. S. Sibley is Professor and Chair of the History Department at St. Joseph's University. She is currently working on a biography of Florence Kling

Harding, titled *America's First Feminist First Lady*. Sibley's work will revise the typical portrait of Mrs. Harding as manipulative, unhappy wife, casting new light on her public and private life. In 2004, Sibley published *Red Spies in America: Stolen Secrets and the Dawn of the Cold War* with the University Press of Kansas. She is also the author of *The Cold War* (1998) and *Loans and Legitimacy: The Evolution of Soviet-American Relations, 1919–1933* (1996). Her work has appeared in journals including *American Communist History, Peace and Change*, and *Diplomatic History*, and she also serves as book review editor for *Intelligence and National Security*. She is a three-term Commonwealth Speaker for the Pennsylvania Humanities Council.

Jennifer Sims is Director of Intelligence Studies and Visiting Professor in the Security Studies Program at Georgetown University's Edmund A. Walsh School of Foreign Service. She also consults for the U.S. government and private sector on homeland security and intelligence related matters. Prior to this, Sims was Research Professor at Johns Hopkins University's Nitze School of Advanced International Studies in Washington, DC (Fall 2001–Summer 2003). She has served as defense and foreign policy adviser to Senator John Danforth (1990–94), a professional staff member of the Senate Select Committee on Intelligence (1991–94), Deputy Assistant Secretary of State for Intelligence Coordination (1994–98), and as the Department of State's first Coordinator for Intelligence Resources and Planning in the office of the Under Secretary for Management. In 1998 Sims was awarded the U.S. Intelligence Community's Distinguished Service Medal. She received her B.A. degree from Oberlin College and her M.A. and Ph.D. in national security studies from Johns Hopkins University in 1978 and 1985, respectively. She is the author of a number of books and articles on intelligence and arms control. The most recent of these include "Foreign Intelligence Liaison: Devils, Deals and Details," *International Journal of Intelligence and Counterintelligence Affairs* (Summer 2006); *Transforming US Intelligence,* coedited with Burton Gerber (Georgetown University Press, 2005); "Transforming U.S. Espionage: A Contrarian's Approach," *Georgetown Journal of International Affairs* (Winter/Spring 2005); "Domestic Factors in Arms Control: The U.S. Case," in Jeffrey A Larson (ed.), *Arms Control: Cooperative Security in a Changing Environment* (Lynne Rienner, 2002); "What Is Intelligence? Information for Decision-Makers," in Roy Godson, Ernest R. May, and Gary Schmitt, *U.S. Intelligence at the Crossroads* (Brassey's, 1995); "The Cambridge Approach Reconsidered," *Daedalus* 120 (Winter 1991); and *Icarus Restrained: An Intellectual History of American Arms Control* (Westview Press, 1990).

Robert David Steele is CEO of OSS.Net, an international open source intelligence provider. As the son of an oilman, a Marine Corps infantry officer, and a clandestine intelligence case officer for the CIA, he has spent over twenty years abroad in Asia and Central and South America. As a civilian intelligence officer he spent three back-to-back tours overseas, including one tour as one of the first officers assigned full-time to terrorism, and three headquarters tours in offensive counterintelligence, advanced information technology, and satellite program management. He resigned from the CIA in 1988 to be the senior civilian founder of the Marine Corps Intelligence Command. He resigned from the Marines in 1993. He is the author of three works on intelligence, as well as the editor of a book on peacekeeping intelligence. He has earned graduate degrees in international relations and public administration, is a graduate of the Naval War College, and has a certificate in Intelligence Policy. He is also a graduate of the Marine Corps Command and Staff Course and of the CIA's Mid-Career Course 101.

John D. Stempel is Senior Professor of International Relations at the University of Kentucky's Patterson School of Diplomacy and International Commerce, where he was Associate Director (1988–93) and Director (1993–2003). He came to the University of Kentucky following a 24-year career in the U.S. Foreign Service. There he focused on political and economic affairs, with overseas assignments in Africa (Guinea, Burundi, Zambia), Iran, and India, concluding with three years as U.S. Consul General in Madras. His Middle East service (1975–79) in Tehran provided the material for his book *Inside the Iranian Revolution*. His subsequent academic writings have focused on religion and diplomacy, intelligence and diplomacy, and American views of negotiation. His Washington assignments featured duty for both the State and Defense Departments, including a two-year tour as Director of the State Department's Crisis Center. He has taught at George Washington and American Universities, plus two years as Diplomat in Residence at the U.S. Naval Academy, Annapolis. Stemple is a member of the New York Council on Foreign Relations and is listed in *Who's Who in the World* and *Who's Who in America*. He holds an A.B. degree from Princeton University and M.A. and Ph.D. degrees from the University of California at Berkeley.

Stan A. Taylor is an Emeritus Professor of Political Science at Brigham Young University in Provo, Utah. He has taught in England, Wales, and New Zealand and in 2006 was a visiting professor at the University of Otago in Dunedin, New Zealand. He is founder of the David M. Kennedy Center for International Studies at Brigham Young University. He writes frequently on intelligence, national security, and U.S. foreign policy.

Athan Theoharis is Professor of History at Marquette University whose research has focused on government secrecy, Cold War politics, and the history of the FBI. He is the author, coauthor, and editor of eighteen books, including *The FBI and American Democracy* (2004), *Chasing Spies* (2002), *A Culture of Secrecy* (1998), and *The FBI: A Comprehensive Reference Guide* (1998). He has received numerous awards, including the American Bar Association's Gavel Award and selection as a fellow by the Wisconsin Academy of Arts, Sciences, and Letters.

Gregory F. Treverton is senior analyst at the RAND Corporation. Earlier, he directed RAND's Intelligence Policy Center and its International Security and Defense Policy Center, and he is Associate Dean of the Pardee RAND Graduate School. His recent work has examined at terrorism, intelligence, and law enforcement, with a special interest in new forms of public-private partnership. He has served in government for the first Senate Select Committee on Intelligence, handling Europe for the National Security Council, and most recently as vice chair of the National Intelligence Council, overseeing the writing of America's National Intelligence Estimates. He holds an A.B. *summa cum laude* from Princeton University, a master's in public policy, and Ph.D. in economics and politics from Harvard University. His latest books are *Reshaping National Intelligence for an Age of Information* (Cambridge University Press, 2001), and *New Challenges, New Tools for Defense Decisionmaking* (edited, RAND, 2003).

Michael A. Turner is a political scientist who has taught international relations and national security matters in San Diego, California, for the past twelve years. Before that, he spent over fifteen years in various positions within the CIA. Turner is the author of *Why Secret Intelligence Fails* (2005; 2006) and the *Historical Dictionary of United States Intelligence* (2006).

Michael Warner serves as Historian for the Office of the Director of National Intelligence.

Nigel West is a military historian specializing in security and intelligence topics. He is the European editor of the *World Intelligence Review* and is on the faculty at the Center for Counterintelligence and Security Studies in Washington, DC. He is the author of more than two dozen works of nonfiction and recently edited *Guy Liddell Diaries*.

Reg Whitaker is Distinguished Research Professor Emeritus, York University, and Adjunct Professor of Political Science, University of Victoria, Canada. He has written extensively on Canadian and international security and intelligence issues.

James J. Wirtz is Professor in the Department of National Security Affairs at the Naval Postgraduate School, Monterey, California. He is Section Chair of the Intelligence Studies Section of the International Studies Association and President of the International Security and Arms Control Section of the American Political Science Association. Wirtz is the series editor for *Initiatives in Strategic Studies: Issues and Policies*, published by Palgrave Macmillan.

Amy B. Zegart is Associate Professor of Public Policy at the University of California, Los Angeles. A specialist on national and homeland security, she has served on the National Security Council staff, as a foreign policy advisor to the Bush-Cheney 2000 presidential campaign, and as a consultant to California state and local homeland security agencies. She has published articles in leading academic journals, including *International Security* and *Political Science Quarterly*, and is the author of *Flawed by Design: The Origins of the CIA, JCS, and NSC* (Stanford, 1999). She received her Ph.D. in political science from Stanford, where she studied under Condoleezza Rice, and an A.B. in East Asian Studies from Harvard University.